THE IMPEACHMENT AND TRIAL
OF
PRESIDENT ANDREW JOHNSON

THE IMPEACHMENT AND TRIAL OF ANDREW JOHNSON

SEVENTEENTH PRESIDENT OF THE UNITED STATES

A HISTORY

BY

DAVID MILLER DEWITT

NEW YORK / RUSSELL & RUSSELL

FIRST PUBLISHED IN 1903
REISSUED, 1967, BY RUSSELL & RUSSELL
A DIVISION OF ATHENEUM HOUSE, INC.
L. C. CATALOG CARD NO.: 66-24686

PRINTED IN THE UNITED STATES OF AMERICA

PREFATORY NOTE

The author, by permission of Martha J. Patterson, a daughter of Andrew Johnson, since deceased, has had the benefit of examining, among the other private papers of the ex-President, a series of scrap-books compiled by Col. William G. Moore, one of the private secretaries of President Johnson, from documents, periodicals and newspapers of the day; and, for the few statements made, and papers, letters and telegrams cited or referred to, in the following work, not otherwise authenticated, these books are the authority.

D. M. D.

December 1, 1902.

CONTENTS.

INTRODUCTION.

1865–6.

THE IMPEACHMENT AND TRIAL

OF

PRESIDENT JOHNSON

INTRODUCTION

SECTION I

The Problem of Reconstruction

The impeachment of President Johnson was the culmination of a struggle between the executive and legislative branches of the government of the United States over the problem of what came to be called Reconstruction—a struggle which, ante-dating Johnson's own administration, troubled the administration of his lamented predecessor. At an early period of the civil war, in portions of certain insurgent states, which were swept clear of the enemy and contained an appreciable number of adherents to the cause of the Union, frameworks of government were set up, and were recognized as such by the authorities at Washington. The refusal of western Virginia to abide by the ordinance of secession necessitated the evocation of a phantom legislature for old Virginia (sneered at by Sumner after its work was done as "the common council of Alexandria"),* to give the consent required by the Constitution to her dismemberment; and, in consequence, the old Dominion was represented in 1863 by four senators in the Senate of the United States as well as by two in the Senate of the Confederate States. Tennessee, likewise, was represented in both Houses of Congress; in the Senate by Andrew Johnson until he was appointed her military governor in March, 1862; in the House until March, 1863; and Louisiana sent two representatives from recovered districts, who were admitted to seats in February, 1863.

But, notwithstanding these precedents set with virtual unanimity, when President Lincoln sent to the Congress his annual message of December, 1863, outlining the plan of reconstruction he purposed to follow, together with his proclamation of amnesty putting the plan into actual operation, the radical wing of the dominant party inaugurated an opposition so extensive and so fierce as, at one time, to put in jeopardy his re-election, if not his renomination. The plan had two features: first, amnesty to all insurgents (with a few specified exceptions) who would take an oath to support the Constitution, the Union and the acts of Congress and proclamations of the President concerning slavery; second, recognition by the Executive Department of the United States of any republican form of government which might be established in any of the eleven seceded states by insurgents who should have taken the amnesty oath and were qualified voters

* *Globe*, 2d Sess. 38th Cong., p. 846.

in 1860: provided they were not less in number than one-tenth of the votes cast in the state that year. The opposition, passing by the amnesty as beyond their reach, fastened upon the other feature of the plan, seeing that, without the co-operation of the legislative department in admitting senators and representatives, it was impossible of being carried out. Indeed, they declared that the whole matter of reconstruction rested exclusively within the jurisdiction of the legislative branch, and that it was not much better than usurpation on the part of the executive to initiate, or meddle in any way with, the process. Lincoln, however, persisted in pushing his plan, and governments were established in the states of Arkansas and Louisiana, whose delegates were admitted by the National Convention which renominated Lincoln and, for Vice-President, nominated Andrew Johnson of Tennessee despite the vehement protest of Thaddeus Stevens that he was an alien. In the last hours of the session, the Congress sent to the President a reconstruction measure which the majority had concocted with difficulty because of dissensions in its ranks, but the President, withholding his consent, adopted the extraordinary expedient of submitting the congressional plan to the insurgent states not yet reorganized, for them to accept if they preferred it to his own. Lincoln's triumph in the election was followed by the reappearance of senators and representatives from Arkansas and Louisiana and the rapid reorganization of civil government in Tennessee; and nothing prevented the readmission of the two former states, to be silently followed by the readmission of the latter, but the filibustering tactics of Sumner, Wilson and Wade, with three other radical senators, aided by an adroit move of Sherman that prevented a vote at the close of the short session.*

The sudden collapse of the rebellion so soon after the second inauguration and the dispersion of the Congress, left Lincoln, for the moment, absolute master of the whole field; and, during the few weeks he had yet to live, he made no uncertain record of what he meant to do. On the eleventh of April, 1865, in his last speech to the people of Washington he suspended his congratulations on the surrender of Lee to commend his Louisiana experiment, announce the unanimity of his Cabinet on his reconstruction policy and express a modest hope that suffrage might be granted to the intelligent, and the Union soldiers, among the negroes. Once more, on the fourteenth, at the last meeting of his Cabinet, he directed the extension of his plan so as to take in the recovered state of North Carolina, and, with words of charity even for the chiefs of the overthrown Confederacy on his lips, he went forth unwittingly to his death.

The cessation of the war and the disbandment of the armies of the Confederacy widened the scope of the problem from portions comparatively small of four of the insurgent states containing minorities comparatively feeble, to the area of the whole eleven with their entire population. The struggle, in consequence, became much more formidable and vital under Johnson, and the problem, ceasing to be speculative or experi-

* *Globe*, 2d Sess. 38th Cong., pp. 1107–11, 1129.

mental in any degree, demanded an immediate and practicable solution. It is highly improbable that even Lincoln, with all the prestige with which his re-election and the suppression of the rebellion had crowned him, could have extended his plan over the entire subjugated section without causing a dangerous if not fatal schism in his party. And Andrew Johnson was not Abraham Lincoln. Lincoln had been a Republican from the origin of that party and twice chosen its leader. Johnson had been a life-long Democrat and slave-holder. Nothing but his gallant stand in the Senate, when solitary and alone he faced his colleagues from the South in denouncing secession as treason, could have redeemed such a record in the eyes of Republicans, and it was only his subsequent phenomenal course in armed opposition to the rebellion that brought about his nomination for the Vice-Presidency as a shrewd stroke to secure the support of the War Democrats of the North and the Union men of his state and section. He came to the presidency under the red cloud of the assassination—a crime that exasperated the Northern people to a vindictiveness reaching the point of frenzy. By the secessionists he was hated as an apostate from his own party, a traitor to his own section and an oppressor of his own state. The leaders of the party of his adoption he had disgusted by a scandalous exhibition of himself at his inauguration as Vice-President. Lincoln, the radical wing of his party had been most reluctant to assail, and the majority appeared content to follow his lead. Not so with Johnson. At first, indeed, because of his fierce denunciations of treason and traitors, many influential radicals were inclined to rejoice at his accession. The day after Lincoln's death, the committee on the conduct of the war waited upon him and amid their congratulations, senator Wade was heard to exclaim: "Johnson, we have faith in you. By the gods, there will be no more trouble in running the government."* But such a burst of feeling, by its very nature, could not but be transitory. No threats to make treason odious would avail to condone an independent policy on the far more vital question of reconstruction; and it needed no inspired prophet to foretell that, if Johnson followed Lincoln's plan, the dominant party in the Congress would open a fight upon him compared with which the preceding struggle was but a skirmish.

The pressing question was: How shall the work of the soldier be completed by the restoration of the Union for which he fought? To this question there were two answers logically coherent. One—which we may call the constitutional solution—had for its basis the proposition that, as long as the Constitution itself endures, every one of the United States is indestructible either by the acts of its people or by the power of the federal government; that the territory known by the historical name of a particular state—*e. g.*, South Carolina or Virginia—having a definite geographical boundary, must ever be known by that name and described by that boundary (unless under an express provision of the Federal Constitution the state consent to its own dismemberment); that the sover-

* Julian's Political Recollections, p. 257.

eignty of every single state over its own affairs is immovably resident in its people and cannot be forfeited to the other states or to the general government (whatever may be the case with a foreign power) by any act of its people; that the general government has the power to enforce upon the citizens of any state only that supremacy delegated to it by the states, and when that is done the power is exhausted; and that no resistance of the people of a state—much less of a portion of them—can give the federal government any right to go beyond such enforcement and invade those functions of sovereignty resident in the state or the people, which neither has ever delegated or can ever forfeit. Granting these premises it followed, that, as soon as the insurrection of the inhabitants of any state was suppressed or was abandoned and the federal government had replaced its officers, retaken its property and set in motion the enforcement of its laws; its task was accomplished. The rehabilitation of the state itself, if rehabilitation can be said to be necessary at all, was the exclusive work of the people of the state; they were to bring back the state into its constitutional orbit from which the illegitimate attraction of secession, for the moment, caused it to swerve. This solution was the only one in the mind of the Northern people at the outbreak of the war. It inspired the letters of Seward to our ministers abroad. It underlay the pledge the two Houses of Congress made after the disaster at Bull Run. It was the ideal of Lincoln before the Emancipation Proclamation, and after with the single modification made necessary by that paper. General Sherman took it for granted when he stipulated with General Johnston that the "Executive of the United States" should "recognize" "the several State Governments" on their officers and legislators "taking the oath to the U. S. Constitution."

The other strictly logical solution—which may be called the extra-constitutional—was based upon the proposition that as soon as the insurrection of the Southern people assumed proportions of sufficient magnitude to entitle its participants to the rights of belligerents, the contest became a civil war between two *de facto* governments; and the Southern states, being subjugated by the power of the federal government, became conquered lands and people, with no right to name, boundaries, territory, much less statehood. That, therefore, the United States government might rule over these overthrown states as one wide waste or as eleven distinct territories, as the government might choose, and, at any future period, might admit them to the Union as states, with name, boundaries and constitutions such as the conqueror might prescribe; or the government might hold them by the naked power of the sword until, having been carved into the shape the federal authority deemed safe and desirable, they might be dragged back into the Union, like bound and mutilated captives by the heels. This was the theory of Thaddeus Stevens, enunciated by him as far back as 1862, and to which he had clung through every vicissitude of the war.

Another and companion theory to this of Stevens was thought by some to combine the advantage of steering clear of the offensive dogma of state suicide and still accomplishing the same result. This was the Sumner theory, which the statesman of that name had advocated from the outset of the war. It rested for its sole basis on the alleged political equality of the freedman with the white man. The inevitable result of the appeal to arms (so it was reasoned out) must be the emancipation of the slave; and the inevitable result of emancipation must be the elevation of the blacks to the same level of civil and political rights as that occupied by the whites. Therefore, no state government could be republican in form whose constitution denied the freedmen the right of suffrage simply on account of color or race; and, under the provision of the Federal Constitution obligating the United States to guarantee to every state a republican form of government, the United States were bound to see to it that no state should resume its relations with the Union with a constitution imposing any restrictions of suffrage upon negroes which did not apply equally to white men.

Now, no reasonable being could have expected Andrew Johnson with his well-known antecedents to look upon either the Stevens or the Sumner solution with favor. In fact, his position on both had been already publicly defined. As long before as November, 1863, in a letter or telegram to Montgomery Blair, then Postmaster-General,* he had warned President Lincoln against "the proposition of states relapsing into territories and held as such," and he had, again and again,

* McPherson's Hist. of Reconstruction, p. 199.

while expressing a hope that the suffrage might ultimately be granted to the literate and taxpayers among the freedmen, declared that the regulation of the matter was confided exclusively to every state for itself. Besides, the Stevens theory had been pointedly condemned by the convention that nominated him for Vice-President and by the people who elected him to that office; and, at the period when he was called upon to act on the problem, there can be no doubt that the majority of the Republican party was opposed to negro suffrage qualified or unqualified. On the other hand, the precedents established under Lincoln's administration in setting up Union state governments in Virginia, Tennessee, Arkansas and Louisiana over against the old state governments gone over to secession, rendered the constitutional solution impossible of complete application. The assumption that the old state authorities had incapacitated themselves by treason from participating in the work of restoration was universal. Lincoln may have had a lingering idea that these were the most natural and logical starting points for the re-establishment of relations between the states and the Union, when immediately after the capture of Richmond he permitted the reassembling of the legislature of Virginia; but the rough repudiation of this movement by Stanton caused him to beat a hasty retreat. And this appears to have been the only departure, if departure it was, from the general belief that secession had shattered the governments of the seceding states and vacated all their offices. This assumption, made without reflection, was founded on error. Forfeiture of office did not follow from the mere notoriety of the offence in the case of the authorities of a commonwealth, any more than forfeiture of life and property in the case of an individual. Conviction of treason must first take place in the one case as in the other, and, as was subsequently shown, conviction was impossible. But, erroneous though it was, after the precedents made by Lincoln during the war when a rival government was the only recourse, the assumption was inevitable and constituted a fundamental flaw in the plan of the President which his adversaries were not slow to take advantage of. What is the material difference, they asked, between the suicide of a state and the suicide of a state government? "It matters little," said Stevens, whether they are "conquered territories" or are "only dead as to all national and political action, . . . whether they are not out of the Union but only dead carcasses lying within the Union."* And, said others, if the federal government had the right to interfere to regulate the suffrage in the case of delegates to a convention to make a new constitution for a state that has forfeited the old, why not interfere to some purpose and dictate the franchise provision?

At the Cabinet meeting held by President Lincoln on Friday, the last day of his life, Stanton brought forward a written project for the military government of both Virginia and North Carolina as one district until such time as elections for delegates to frame constitutions for the respective states and the adoption of those constitutions should have taken place. His

* *Globe*, 1st Sess. 39th Cong., p. 72.

avowed object in thus presenting his views at so early a date was to satisfy the President that there was no necessity to employ the old state structures as nuclei of restoration. More than one member of the Cabinet objected to the joining together of the two states in one district, on the ground that such union ignored the existing Pierpont government of Virginia. The President, yielding to the force of this objection, directed the Secretary of War to divide his project and submit at a future meeting separate plans for the two states —the one for Virginia to recognize the Pierpont government.* Johnson made no change of Cabinet officers, acquiescing even in the appointment of James Harlan in the place of Usher, which was not to take effect until the fifteenth of May, and, especially as there was no alternative, he cannot be blamed for following in the footsteps of his illustrious predecessor. As early as the day succeeding Lincoln's death—Sunday, April 16th—at the first meeting of the Cabinet under the new administration, the Secretary of War stated that, in accordance with the directions of the late President, he had divided his project of government submitted the Friday before, but copies were not yet ready; and on this ground the matter was postponed.† In the meantime the governors of some of the lately insurgent states, *e. g.*, McGrath of South Carolina, Brown of Georgia, Clark of Mississippi, had called

* "Lincoln and Johnson," art. in *Galaxy* of April, 1872, by Gideon Welles, pp. 526–7; *cf.* Stanton's testimony in Impeachment Investigation (1867), p. 401 *et seq.*

† Welles, *ut sup.*

their respective legislatures together to resume the normal relation of their states to the Union as a consequence of their submission to the event of the war. Instead of welcoming these overtures, as under other circumstances and influenced by other considerations might have been done, the Secretary of War ordered the major generals in command in their respective localities to disperse the legislatures and to drive the governors out of office.

At length, on the fifth day of May, the President directed Stanton to send copies of his divided project to every member of the Cabinet, preparatory to a special meeting called for Monday, the eighth, expressly for its consideration; and, accordingly, on that date Stanton's plan for the reconstruction of Virginia alone was laid before the President and the Cabinet. In compliance with the directions of the late President, the Secretary recognized Francis Pierpont as governor; but only to "request him to take measures for the re-establishment of the state government and the election of state officers"—in other words to accomplish the overthrow of his own government—and that too under the direction and control of the Department of War. In respect to both these features, the project was entirely altered by the action of the Cabinet. It was put into the shape of an Executive Order of nine sections. The first forbade any recognition of the Confederate or old state government within the limits of Virginia; the following seven provided for the resumption of the federal authority, offices and property within the state; and the last contained a full recognition of the government of Pierpont and pledged the aid of the United States in all lawful measures he might take for the extension and administration of the state government throughout the geographical limits of such state; and in this shape the Executive Order was promulgated next day.

So far no difficulty and little dissension had been encountered. The case was one where, before the close of hostilities, the loyal population had attempted with more or less success to reconstruct the state. The cases of Arkansas, Louisiana and Tennessee were very similar and in such cases the present administration had merely to follow precedents. An equivocal suggestion had been made on two occasions, one under the late, and one under the present, administration; but its author on both occasions had given it but feeble support and on both occasions it had been unanimously rejected. But on the ninth was taken up the project for the reconstruction of the state of North Carolina; an entirely new case in the important respect that no loyal government had been set up while the war was in progress, and, consequently, either the old state government must be recognized or the work of reconstruction begun from the bottom. Consequently, it was considered a measure of cardinal importance, to be followed as a model in the reconstruction of the remaining insurrectionary states. The draft submitted provided, first, for the appointment of a military governor to preserve order and to aid the inhabitants of the state in holding an election of delegates to a convention to frame a constitution. It then followed the Virginia order in directing the several departments of the federal executive to proceed in the enforcement of the federal authority throughout the state. Then came a provision, on its face unobjectionable, that "loyal citizens of the United States residing within the State of North Carolina," on a day named, "may elect members of a state convention." The Cabinet, after substituting the word "provisional" for the word "military" in the title of the governor, proceeded to the consideration of this apparently harmless clause. Welles, the Secretary of the Navy, asked what was meant by the phrase "loyal citizens," and, Stanton admitting that the intent was to include blacks as well as whites, at once the whole subject of negro suffrage was thrust upon the board. It appears that as early as the evening of Sunday, the sixteenth of April, a private consultation was held by Stanton with such advanced spirits of the Republican party as Sumner, Dawes and Colfax, of which Welles happened to be an unwilling witness for a part of the time, and at this meeting, in face of the fact that under the foregoing administration it had been decided both by the Executive and the Congress that suffrage was a matter exclusively of state regulation, Stanton had allowed Sumner and Colfax to interpolate into his project of government the clause in question, possibly in the hope that the ambiguous phrase might pass muster, leaving its construction to himself, or, it may be, to test his colleagues and the President on the subject it embraced. However, when its true intent was thus disclosed Stanton deprecated any preliminary discussion and suggested that each member should say whether the negro should vote in North Carolina. A vote was then taken, all the members of the Cabinet being present but Seward, who was still disabled from his wounds and illness. In favor of retaining the provision were the Secretary of War (Stanton), the Postmaster-General (Dennison), and the Attorney-General (Speed). Against, on the ground that the federal government had no power over the question, were the Secretaries of the Treasury (McCulloch), of the Navy (Welles) and of the Interior (Usher)—an equal division. The President, expressing no opinion, took the paper and the meeting was over.*

When the subject was again brought before the Cabinet (May 24th), Seward was able to attend and Harlan had taken the place of Usher. The President laid before them his own plan of reconstruction, which followed step by step that of Lincoln, differing only in unimportant details. First, there was a proclamation of general amnesty to all insurgents who should take the oath prescribed in the paper, with the exception of certain high officers in the army and navy of the late Confederacy and high civil officials in the Confederate and state governments and of all persons who had voluntarily participated in the rebellion, the value of whose property exceeded $20,000—an exception not in Lincoln's proclamation and owing its insertion to Johnson's belief that secession was the special work of the men of wealth in the South. Second, a

* Welles, *ut sup.*, and second paper in *Galaxy* for May, 1872, at p. 666.

proclamation having particular reference only to the state of North Carolina but designed to be a formal, public, explanatory *pronunciamento* of the plan to be followed as to all the other states in a similar condition. This paper appointed William W. Holden Provisional Governor of the state and declared his duty to be to prescribe rules for the assembling of a convention "composed of delegates to be chosen by that portion of the people of the state who are loyal to the United States, and no others, for the purpose of altering or amending the constitution thereof"; endowing him with authority to enable such loyal people to restore the state to its constitutional relation with the federal government and to present such a republican form of government as will entitle the state to the guarantee of the United States therefor. Then came the decisive proviso—viz: that in choosing delegates no person shall be qualified as an elector, or eligible as a delegate, unless (1) he shall have taken the oath prescribed by the Amnesty Proclamation, and (2) has the qualifications prescribed by the constitution and laws of North Carolina at the date of her secession. The convention, however, or the legislature thereafter assembled "will prescribe the qualifications of electors and the eligibility of persons to office"—"a power the people of the several states composing the Federal Union have rightfully exercised from the origin of the government to the present time."*

To this plan the Cabinet, so far as it appears, made no objection. The Amnesty, the exceptions in which

* McPherson's Reconstruction, pp. 9, 11.

were more sweeping than Lincoln's, no doubt, was unanimously approved. Those members who on the ninth seemed to favor the introduction of negro suffrage in some shape or form, though they were now reinforced by Harlan, made no remonstrance. Stanton, having done his duty to his secret friends, thought he had gone far enough in putting forward their ticklish proposal and submitted without a word. He subsequently testified before the Impeachment committee: "The objection of the President to throwing the franchise open to the colored people appeared to be fixed, and I think every member of the Cabinet assented to the arrangement as it was specified in the proclamation relating to North Carolina."*

The proclamation in her case was followed at short intervals by similar measures in the case of every one of the six Southern states in the same situation, viz: Mississippi on the 13th, Georgia and Texas on the 17th, Alabama on the 21st, and South Carolina on the 30th of June, and Florida on the 13th of July.† So that, in less than two months, proceedings had been initiated by the new administration for the complete restoration of every seceding state to the Union; in the cases of Virginia, Arkansas, Louisiana and Tennessee, by recognizing the state governments raised up in the midst of war and supported by Lincoln; in the cases of the remaining seven by setting forth the process by which their people returning to loyalty might raise up governments for themselves. During the fall, under the

* Impeachment Investigation (1867), p. 401.

† McPherson's Reconstruction, p. 12.

guidance of provisional governors—Union men, more or less of the type of Andrew Johnson—the citizens of North Carolina, South Carolina, Georgia, Alabama and Mississippi (five of the seven states unreconstructed under Lincoln), having taken the oath with hopeful unanimity, held conventions, annulled the ordinances of secession; then selected governors, members of the legislature and representatives in Congress; inaugurated the new state governments; by their new legislatures appointed senators of the United States, and, with the exception of Mississippi, ratified the thirteenth amendment to the federal Constitution abolishing slavery. Irritating embarrassments, it is true, were encountered by the administration. In one or two states a reluctance was manifested to repudiate the debt incurred in the support of the insurrection. Acts were passed for the purpose of guarding the whites against apprehended pauperism or savage outbreaks of the blacks, which imperiled the newly-won freedom and civil rights of the latter. There was a natural disposition to lament the lost cause and to glorify its leaders. Petitions were circulated for the repeal of the test oath which stood in the way of those leaders being admitted to seats in Congress, and, in some instances, men were sent to the Senate or to the House known to be incapacitated to serve. The broad scope of the exceptions to the Amnesty frequently hindered the process of reorganization, and, in some cases, brought proceedings to a standstill. Special pardons from Washington fell thick and fast. In short, it was demonstrated now for the first time, as it continued to be demonstrated years after this period, that it was practicably impossible to carry on any kind of respectable government in these states without the help of men who had been the leaders of their people in the war. To William M. Sharkey, the provisional governor of Mississippi whose convention was the earliest held—meeting on the fourteenth of August—President Johnson sent a telegram the next day, making a suggestion which shows how fully awake he was to the designs of the radical element of the party:

> "If you could extend the elective franchise to all persons of color who can read the Constitution of the United States in English and write their names, and to all persons of color who own real estate valued at not less than two hundred and fifty dollars and pay taxes thereon, you would completely disarm the adversary and set an example the other States will follow.
>
> "This you can do with perfect safety, and you thus place the Southern States, in reference to free persons of color, upon the same basis with the free States. I hope and trust your convention will do this, and, as a consequence, the radicals, who are wild upon negro franchise, will be completely foiled in their attempt to keep the Southern States from their relations to the Union by not accepting their senators and representatives."*

If this shrewd suggestion had been adopted by the Mississippi convention and followed, as in likelihood it would have been, by the conventions of the other states, the battle of reconstruction either would never have been joined or victory would have perched

* McPherson's *id.*, p. 19.

on the banner of the Administration. It was identical with the suggestion of Lincoln in his letter to Hahn, the governor of Louisiana,* and with the hope he expressed in his last speech to the citizens of Washington. And there can be no doubt that on the issue presented by this overture the President represented the bulk of the Republican party. But the convention rejected the proposition. The blacks in the state exceeded the whites in numbers by about 80,000. The sense of their inferiority and of their utter unfitness to participate in the government was too universal, the dread of anarchy and bloodshed too pervading among the members to permit of its acceptance. The other conventions did nothing to revive it, and it was heard of no more until a bitterer alternative waked it to life. Notwithstanding these drawbacks, however, the great task of the restoration of the eleven lately insurgent states in constitutional subordination to the general government may be said to have been accomplished, so far as the executive department could accomplish it, when the thirty-ninth Congress met in its first session: four, Virginia, Louisiana, Arkansas and Tennessee, under Lincoln, the remaining seven under Johnson; Florida and Texas not quite ready, but sure to follow. It remained for the legislative department to do its part, and the Union for which the armies of the North had fought would become once more an actuality.

* *Id.*, note to p. 20.

SECTION II

The Meeting of the Thirty-Ninth Congress

The Republican members of Congress gathered together at Washington at the opening of the session, in December, 1865, under the universal impression that the supremacy of their party in the councils of the nation was at stake. Of the fifty senators from the twenty-five non-seceding states, thirty-nine were classed as Republicans and but eleven as Democrats; and of the one hundred and eighty-four representatives in the House, one hundred and forty-one were classed as Republicans and but forty-three as Democrats. Should the twenty-two senators and fifty-eight representatives from the eleven reconstructed states be allowed to take their seats, the nominal majority of the party in power in the Senate would be reduced from twenty-eight to but six, and the nominal majority in the House from ninety-eight to forty; provided all the recruits sided with the Democrats. And that was precisely what it was foreseen they would be bound to do with but very few exceptions. All those not barred from taking their seats by inability to take the iron-clad oath (as it was called) were Union men of the Andrew Johnson type, sure to gravitate to their old-time party, while those who were so barred would return to their constituents to be soon replaced by others exempt from the disability but no fonder of the Republican party. Besides, the nominal majority was by no means stable. Four senators heretofore classed as Republicans, Dixon, Cowan, Doolittle and Norton, were avowed supporters of the President's policy and others were suspected of leaning that way, while there was a growing contingent in the House whose orthodoxy was more or less in doubt. In a word, the dominating motive of the opposition to the Lincoln-Johnson plan of reconstruction was the conviction that its success would wreck the Republican party, restore the Democrats to power and bring back the days of Southern supremacy and Northern vassalage. As Thad. Stevens with his customary frankness said in his first speech at this session: "With the basis unchanged, the eighty-three southern members, with the Democrats that will in the best times be elected from the North, will always give them a majority in Congress and in the Electoral College. They will at the very first election take possession of the White House and the halls of Congress."* And the most exasperating feature of the whole perplexing situation was that this catastrophe (to the minds of the entire majority the most sweeping they could contemplate) was being brought about by an Executive of their party's own choice. The President with his Cabinet appeared to be pressing on with headlong eagerness a restoration of the Union which could not but prove fatal to the ascendency of the party which had borne the heat and burden of administration during the war, a result which the President, supported

* *Globe*, 1st Sess. 39th Cong., p. 74.

by his old-time party associates, seemed to regard with the utmost equanimity.

Under these trying circumstances, the Republican members of the House met in caucus on the Saturday evening before the meeting of Congress to formulate a plan of opposition, and, in the absence of Henry Winter Davis, who had not been re-elected, Thaddeus Stevens, by tacit consent, at once assumed the leadership. This man was probably the most remarkable of the time. In his seventy-fourth year, his once stalwart form was enfeebled not only by age but by disease. His cadaverous countenance was surmounted by a brown wig, and from under beetling brows flashed eyes whose fire the flight of years seemed to have made only the more intense. A cripple from birth, one of his legs terminating in a mere bunch of flesh, his deformity, it is likely, had embittered his spirit. Migrating in the dawn of manhood from Vermont to Pennsylvania, he had spent the greater part of his life on the southern border, and, being a lawyer of eminence, he had been often brought in contact with the slave flying for freedom from the adjoining state. His was a soul easily set on fire by any instance of cruelty and oppression coming within his observation, and he learned early to pity the slave with a consuming pity and to hate his master with a consuming hate. Having been an abolitionist of the most uncompromising type before there was an abolition party at all, he hailed the advent of the war as the death-knell of what he branded as the Satanic Institution. The representative of the congressional district of James Buchanan since 1858, he had never swerved for a moment from his view of the contest. In the dark hour of the Bull Run defeat, he refused to join in the congressional pledge that the war was not a war of abolition or subjugation, and his career from that hour to the present had been one incessant effort to wring from his party a repudiation of this unanimous but, as he denounced it, craven resolve. He was for universal, uncompensated emancipation long before Lincoln was forced to concede it, and no pleading of his party associates could restrain him from showering the coarsest vituperation on the tenderness with which the President approached this institution of his deepest abhorrence. He was the open advocate of wholesale and indiscriminate confiscation of the lands of the insurgents and their distribution among the neighboring freedmen. Though kindly to individuals with whom he came in personal association and by nature not a man of blood, he was the very soul of vindictiveness toward classes who embodied principles or customs he detested, and he would not have hesitated to wade through seas of blood to redress the wrongs of the poor and down-trodden. His lifelong and ingrained hostility to negro slavery colored all his thoughts and quickened his every emotion, unsettling his judgment and unfitting him for the intricate problems of statesmanship. He was never troubled with any reverence for the limitary provisions of the Constitution. He stigmatized that instrument as spotted with the weakness of its framers and their times and he welcomed the victory of the North as an opportunity to make it what he thought it ought to be. He had no love for the Union as long as it was a Union with slaveholding states, and the destruction of his private property in the raids of Lee across the border served only to make the more lurid his chronic rage against the slave-hunters of the Southern section. Like Marat, he shocked the cautious party leaders by the outspokenness with which he hurled his scorching anathemas against the Southern aristocrats. Like Marten, he was not ashamed to shout out the secret purpose which lurked hidden in the heart of hearts of his associates but which they would have blushed openly to avow. He had the courage—nay, the audacity—of his convictions; and, while he poured out on his opponents invectives that withered to the innermost fibre and sarcasms that burnt to the bone, to the wavering, the calculating, the time-serving amongst his own ranks, he was the very incarnation of scorn. Since the first year of the war he had dominated the House, though far in advance of the majority in the extreme radicalism of his opinions. He had an ever-ready, biting wit and a sardonic humor. He was short and sententious in speech, and, at times, eloquent from the very concentrated bitterness of his diction. He knew what he wanted, and was restrained by no sense of propriety from saying what he wanted, both for himself and his party. The popular watchword that this was a white man's government drove him into paroxysms of anger, and, in face of the shafts of lightning he shot around him on all sides when laboring under such a seizure, the boldest of his adversaries shunned a close encounter, and the more conservative of his own party sank into silence and dismay. The chief weapons of his rule were the remorselessness with which he pushed the party on from the premises agreed upon to their full logical conclusion, and the vigour with which he laid on the lash. Conventionalities he despised and respectabilities he ridiculed. He had but little regard for the opinion of his fellows, good or bad. He would have scorned to play the demagogue, even if a wirepuller could have been found foolhardy enough to suggest such a course. He chose his line at the behest of his deepest passion, and he kept it to the end, regardless of friends, enemies, party policy, the entreaties of the cautious and the whimperings of the sly. According to his creed, the insurgent states were conquered provinces to be shaped into a paradise for the freedman and a hell for the rebel. His eye shot over the blackened Southern land. He saw the carnage, the desolation, the starvation and the shame; and, like a battered old-warhorse, he flung up his frontlet, snuffed the tainted breeze and snorted Ha! Ha!

The very fact that he was so far in advance of the bulk of the party contributed more than anything else to his choice as leader in so perilous a crisis. The plan of the President, being destructive of the party, must be blocked at all hazards, and here was the man to block it, as he had shown in the days of Lincoln. Holding in abeyance for the moment his theory of state suicide, he laid before the caucus the following programme: First, to claim the whole subject-matter of reconstruction as the exclusive business of the Congress. Second, to regard all that had been done hitherto in the re-edification of the eleven states, as well those reorganized under Lincoln as those under Johnson, either in effect as not done at all, or as merely experimental, provisional, subject to the approval or disapproval, revision or reversal, ratification or nullification of the Congress. Third, that, each House declining to exercise its function of judging of the election and qualifications of its members in case of persons from the eleven states claiming to be senators or representatives, both unite in refusing to acknowledge the right of representation of these states until Congress pronounce the reconstructed local governments valid and satisfactory. These propositions being accepted without objection, a committee was appointed which, in ten minutes, made a report directing the clerk of the House to leave off the roll the names of every person claiming to be a representative of any of the eleven states, and presenting a joint resolution for the appointment of a joint-committee of fifteen—nine from the House and six from the Senate—"to inquire into the condition of the States which formed the so-called Confederate States of America and report whether they or any of them are entitled to be represented in either House of Congress," and providing that "until such report be made and finally acted upon by Congress no member from such States be received into either House." This programme was carried out to the letter when the House met on Monday, despite the protest of Maynard from the President's own state, and without deigning to wait for the President's message.*

* *Globe, supra,* pp. 3, 5.

That document came the next day, and, in contrast to the unpleasant reiteration of phrases and occasional incoherency of thought which characterized Andrew Johnson's speeches, surprised the Houses and the country by the smoothness of its diction and the power of its argumentation. He dealt with the Stevens theory as follows:

> "States, with proper limitations of power, are essential to the existence of the Constitution of the United States.
>
> "The perpetuity of the Constitution brings with it the perpetuity of the States; their mutual relations make us what we are, and in our political system this connection is indissoluble. The whole cannot exist without the parts nor the parts without the whole. So long as the Constitution of the United States endures, the States will endure; the destruction of the one is the destruction of the other; the preservation of the one is the preservation of the other.
>
> "The true theory is that all pretended acts of secession were, from the beginning, null and void. The States cannot commit treason, nor screen the individual citizens who may have committed treason, any more than they can make valid treaties, or engage in lawful commerce with any foreign Power. The States attempting to secede placed themselves in a condition where their vitality was impaired, but not extinguished—their functions suspended but not destroyed."

After reciting the first steps of his plan the President continues: "The next step" in the process of restoration was "the invitation to the States to participate in the high office of amending the Constitution." A ratification of the amendment forever abolishing slavery had been exacted in the interests of future harmony and as "a pledge of perpetual loyalty and peace."

> "The amendment to the Constitution being adopted it would remain for the States, whose powers have been so long in abeyance, to resume their places in the two branches of the national Legislature, and thereby complete the work of restoration. Here, it is for you, fellow citizens of the Senate, and for you, fellow citizens of the House of Representatives, to judge, each of you for yourselves, of the elections, returns, and qualifications of your own members."

He treats the absorbing topic of suffrage for the freedmen as follows:

> "On the propriety of making freedmen electors by proclamation of the Executive, I took for my counsel the Constitution itself, the interpretations of that instrument by its authors and their contemporaries, and the recent legislation of Congress." He found them all unitedly inculcating the doctrine that the regulation of the suffrage was a power exclusively for the states. "So fixed was this reservation of power in the habits of the people, and so unquestioned has been the interpretation of the Constitution, that during the civil war the late President never harbored the purpose—certainly never avowed the purpose—of disregarding it; and in acts of Congress nothing can be found to sanction any departure by the Executive from a policy which has so uniformly obtained."

He expressed the opinion that the settlement of the question was much better left to the several states. "They can each for itself decide on the measure and whether it is to be adopted at once and absolutely or introduced gradually and with conditions." He avows the belief that after the tumult of emotions has subsided the freedmen "will receive the kindliest usage from some of those on whom they have heretofore most closely depended," and "if they show patience and manly virtues" "will sooner obtain participation in the elective franchise through the states than through the general government even if it had the power to intervene." He affirms that good faith requires their security in their liberty, their property, their right to labor and to claim a just return for their labor.*

The message was received with approval on all sides; by the Republican majority except the extreme Radicals, by the Democratic minority and by the country at large. Senator Dixon, three months later, could ask with confidence: "Was ever a message submitted to a more approving Congress? Was there ever a message read by a more admiring public?"† The majority were reluctant as yet to come to an open breach and thus create a dangerous schism in their party, especially as long as, by the President's own admission, they held the key of the situation in the power to refuse to complete the President's plan by the admission of the senators and representatives sent by his reconstructed states. The resolution of the House was passed by the Senate so far as it provided for the appointment of a joint committee, but the Senate refused to enter into a joint pledge of non-action and a joint relinquishment of the privilege to

* Message in McPherson, p. 64.

† Dixon's remark: *Globe,* 1st Sess. 39th Cong., p. 1046.

admit members until such time as a report was made; and the House was compelled to content itself with renewing both pledge and relinquishment for itself.

To the committee of fifteen all matters relating to the eleven states were referred, all credentials of members from those states were sent there by the House and laid on the table by the Senate. Until this committee should see fit to make its will known, the work of reconstruction was necessarily at a stand-still. The President might fret, especially over the exclusion of his own state. He could do nothing for which the majority could fasten a quarrel upon him. Even Stevens refrained from personal attack. Seizing upon the admission in the message that the late rebel states had lost their constitutional relations to the Union and were incapable of representation in Congress, he asserted triumphantly that this admission settled the whole question, and with transparent irony claimed the President as his own. "As there are no symptoms that the people of these provinces will be prepared to participate in constitutional government for some years, I know of no arrangement so proper for them as territorial governments. There they can learn the principles of freedom and eat the fruit of foul rebellion. Under such governments while electing members to the Territorial Legislature they will necessarily mingle with those to whom Congress shall extend the rights of suffrage."*

But Charles Sumner, no scheme of party policy could restrain. Of that type of men who never feel the need

* *Globe, id.*, p. 74.

of a revision of their judgments, he had never looked up to a living man as greater than himself nor felt himself impelled to follow any leader. From the very outset of his career his course was unalterably fixed. His first goal was the emancipation of the negro, and he never deviated an inch from the straight line which led to that end. That goal being reached or sure of being reached, he staked down another—suffrage for the freedmen—and then dedicated to its attainment the same unwearied energies. Like a law of nature, he bent neither to the right nor to the left, crushing without pity, because without appreciation of its presence, every obstacle in his path, and deaf alike to solicitations to compromise, to appeals for respite or pleas for charity. Like Robespierre, though blood was hateful to his sight and offensive to his nostrils, though war had no place in his scheme of things and by hypothesis ought not to exist at all, yet, in pursuit of his purpose, he could look with indifference on the cutting down of legions of men because by some unaccountable fatality they managed to throw themselves in his way. Renowned throughout the world as one of the great humanitarians of his day, nevertheless the good old phrase would best express him—he was without bowels. Unemotional in a marked degree, he loved without passion, and hated without warmth. A philanthropist, if that could be called love of his fellows which was wholly intellectual. An implacable antagonist, his bosom was too frigid to swell with a gust of righteous wrath and his blood too sluggish to carry him away in the heat of temper. The creed he believed in, the course he followed, the theories he advanced, the principles by which he was distinguished assumed somehow in his hands a factitious, unreal aspect. His anti-slavery crusade he nursed and coddled and then rode as a hobby. His presupposition that the Declaration of Independence had the force of organic law was fantastic. The argumentation by which he sought to prove that the slaveholding framers of the Constitution believed that no government could be republican in form which disfranchised a portion of its people on account of such a permanent natural mark as race or colour, was ingenious but had no footing on the solid earth. With painstaking elaboration he arranged his speeches in blocks, each headed by some *ad captandum* label to arrest the attention of the reader and the gaze of posterity. Even his invective was artificial—made up without the excuse of passion, in the silence and solitude of the closet, and read from manuscript, without fervour, on the floor of the Senate. As he did not himself feel the venom of his speech, he had no appreciation of its legitimate effects. With the cool neutrality of a scientist, he sprinkled upon the skin of his opponent drop after drop of double-distilled aqua-fortis; and when the victim waxed vociferous under the sting, he was shocked at the vulgarity of his violence. He informed a brother senator in scholarly phrase that he was a liar, a hypocrite, a thief, a whoremonger, a trafficker in his own flesh and blood, a traitor to his country and a blasphemer of his God; and, then, was astonished that the object of his candor did not receive the charge as a friendly admonition. He used habitually epithets which only the hottest anger could excuse, without feeling the slightest warmth in his veins, and he delivered blow after blow such as men deal about them in a paroxysm of rage, without the stiffening of a muscle or a quickening of the pulse. Human rights, in the abstract, were the object of his intellectual worship. The individuals to whom human rights appertained, and the manifold compromises of the social union necessary to the security of human rights in the workaday world never disturbed the complacency of his contemplation. The slave-power, the slave-holder, the slave-hunter—as a generalized universal—was the object of his most elaborate malediction. The concrete specimens that crossed his path inspired at most a feeble dislike and provoked only a transient growl. His nature lacked spontaneity. He never laughed a full-throated, heartfelt laugh in his life. His smile, when he did smile, was sardonic. He never shed a tear over a defeat, no matter how humiliating. He never let himself out in a shout of exultation over a triumph, no matter how complete and soul-satisfying. Sumner was tall in stature and appeared stalwart in form. He dressed with the unstudied neatness and intuitive taste of a gentleman. He had an Apollo-like head whose hyacinthine locks, tinged with grey and thinned by years, hid a retreating brow. His eye was small and insignificant, his features commonplace, his voice harsh, loud and tuneless. He possessed none of the graces of the orator, except the felicity of his diction. He had a multitude of acquaintances, many admirers, a few intimates, but hardly one own familiar friend.

With so self-sufficient and independent a character, it was at all times difficult to co-operate in schemes of party management, and the most carefully laid devices of the politicians were liable to be broken into by so mechanical a strider after ideals. For Lincoln while he lived, Sumner never cherished a lively admiration, and that such an illiterate plebeian as Johnson should be President of the United States filled him with disgust. In September he declared to a Republican convention in Massachusetts over which he presided that no one could say that "a generation must not elapse before the rebel communities have been so far changed as to become safe associates in a common government. . . . Time, therefore, we must have. Through time all other guarantees may be obtained; but time itself is a guarantee."* And he was now watching his opportunity to denounce the President for his disregard of this important factor. Even on so inappropriate an occasion as the obsequies of the deceased senator Collamer† he did not refrain from praising that statesman's course in opposition to the policy of Lincoln, "who," as he said, "undertook in disregard of Congress and solely by executive power to institute civil governments throughout that region where civil governments had been overthrown, imitating in the agencies he employed the Cromwellian system of ruling by 'major-generals.' . . . The eggs

* Speech on "The national security and the national faith"—quoted by Dixon in *Globe ut supra*, p. 1046.

† *Globe, id.*, p. 56.

of crocodiles can produce only crocodiles, and it is not easy to see how the eggs laid by military power can be hatched into an American State.'' But his opportunity came on the nineteenth day of December when the President sent in a special message setting forth the bright prospects of the Southern states, accompanied by a report by General Grant of the same optimistic tenor. General Grant stated: ''I am satisfied that the mass of thinking men of the South accept the present situation of affairs in good faith''; slavery and the right of secession ''they regard as having been settled forever by the highest tribunal, arms, that man can resort to''; that they considered ''this decision a fortunate one for the whole country.'' He continued: ''My observations lead me to the conclusion that the citizens of the Southern States are anxious to return to self-government within the Union as soon as possible: that while reconstructing they want and require protection from the Government; that they are in earnest in wishing to do what they think is required by the Government, not humiliating to them as citizens, and that, if such course was pointed out, they would pursue it in good faith.''*

Sumner characterized the message of the President as similar to ''the whitewashing message of Franklin Pierce with regard to the enormities in Kansas. That is its parallel.''† And the next day, in support of a sweeping measure of his colleague, which nullified at a stroke all laws of the states lately in rebellion

* Report in McPherson, p. 67.

† *Globe, id.*, p. 79.

recognizing inequality in civil rights on account of colour and prohibiting the enactment of any such in the future, he delivered one of his elaborately constructed addresses, in which, after recurring to his doctrine that it was the duty of Congress to enforce negro suffrage in the eleven states under the guarantee clause of the Constitution, by a favorite device of his, viz: reading from letters of correspondents whose names were frequently withheld to shield, as he said, the writers from the anger of the communities they assailed, he unrolled a hopeless picture of the Southern land, "the sickening and heart-rending outrages" which the President attempted "to white wash," "to throw the mantle of official approval" over "the sacrifice of Human Rights" and to give a "new letter of license" to "rebel Barbarism."*

Cowan of Pennsylvania, in reply, made a spirited defence of the President and his policy, and Stewart of Nevada created a great sensation by coming out squarely on the side of the administration, opposing any plan "to govern eleven states as conquered provinces," opposing universal negro suffrage, and winding up with the painful interrogatory: "Are we willing to prolong the restoration of the Union and risk the experiment of taxation without representation for fear that the application of the rule that the voice of the majority is law, shall drive us from power?"† The bias of Cowan and Doolittle and Dixon in favor of the President was well known, but this defection of the

* *Id.*, 91.

† *Globe, id.*, pp. 109–11.

young senator from the youngest state shocked the motherly soul of Wilson. Henry Wilson, like Andrew Johnson, sprang from a low grade of the social scale—the one having been a cobbler as the other had been a tailor. But as the two men grew up under the influences of their respective surroundings, while the Tennessean's nature hardened into the fixity of cast-iron, the New Englander's softened so as to run over with every breath of feeling. To his well-born, high-cultured colleague he presented a strong contrast;—not in physical form, for he was dignified in appearence, a sleek-looking, clerical figure, with smooth-brushed dingy-white hair; not so much in manner of speech, although he was fluent, given to extemporaneous utterance, powerful on the stump and rolled along with the heave and swell of the practiced exhorter—but in mind and heart. If Sumner was all intellect inaccessible to emotion, Wilson was all emotion unrestrainable by intellect. His whole heart was dissolved into a fountain of tears over the wrongs of the black man, and he became the champion of negroes in the concrete as his colleague became the champion of Human Rights as embodied in the negro in the abstract.

He now burst forth into a lamentation over the inhuman incredulity of the senator from Nevada as to "the atrocities and cruelties perpetrated" on the poor, dumb, toiling freedmen; and then, with apprehension depicted upon his countenance, protested that he had no apprehensions. There had been "a studied and systematic attempt to separate the President from the great party that elected him"; but he had no fears of the President;

the President "had labored according to his sense of public duty, to prepare the rebel States for restoration." "He had made no issue with Congress and Congress had made no issue with him." "I do not believe any issue will be made by the President." The senator had undoubting faith that "needful legislation" would "receive the sanction and approval of the Executive." "The committee we have appointed . . . will report proper measures; Congress will pass them; the President will sign them; these vacant seats will be filled with loyal men"; and every thing will turn out as the party and Providence have unitedly decreed.*

The House on the same day listened to the first speech in that body of a member whose career hitherto had aroused great expectations. Henry J. Raymond was an influential party-man and a lifelong supporter of William H. Seward; but what gave him peculiar prominence was he was the founder and editor of the New York *Times,* one of the leading newspapers in the country. That paper had given to the President's course during the past summer a judicious support, apparently without being aware that it was doing anything less than its duty to the party; and its editor was now expected to echo with power the opinions of his organ on the floor of the House. His speech, (generally considered a disappointment) consisted mainly of an argument against the theory of Stevens, and its effect was greatly impaired by the incessant interruptions with which he was pestered and which

* *Globe, id.,* pp. 111–2.

he too good-naturedly allowed. The radicals made a concerted attack upon this deserter who threatened to become too influential. One after another, they baited him, until at last Bingham of Ohio advanced to give the finishing blow. Plying Raymond with self-confident questions, he suddenly landed himself in apparent antagonism to the President; and when the victim of his persecution by an adroit turn of the debate took advantage of this mistake, he retreated amid a cloud of expostulations: "I am sorry to see the gentleman assume that he alone represents the President." "I make no issue with the President." "I respectfully deny the gentleman's assertion that I seek to make an issue with the President"; and the member from New York was allowed to finish his argument in peace.* And so, with protests of harmony in both Houses, Congress adjourned over the holidays.

* *Globe, id.*, pp. 120–124.

SECTION III

THE FIRST VETO

THUS far, it may be said, peace prevailed between the Capitol and "the other end of the Avenue." The more conservative Republicans of both Houses, anxious that peace should be kept, were casting about for some course of action on which Executive and Congress might unite and thus heal the incipient schism in the party. On the one hand, to satisfy the more impatient friends of the negro, measures should be passed according full and lasting protection to the freedmen in all their civil rights. On the other, to placate the President, his own state should be immediately readmitted as the happy prologue to the speedy readmission of all in the same category. Accordingly, on the reassembling of Congress (January 5, 1866), Trumbull, the chairman of the Judiciary Committee of the Senate, introduced two bills: one enlarging the powers of the Freedmen's Bureau, the other protecting the civil rights of the negro.

From the start, however, the progress of this movement was obstructed by the negro-suffragists, whose chief exponents were Sumner in the Senate and George S. Boutwell in the House. As an earnest of what they meant to demand before any of the excluded states should be readmitted, they pressed forward the bill conferring unqualified suffrage on the colored men of the District of Columbia, which, after a debate mainly between the partisans of simple manhood suffrage and the partisans of qualified suffrage disclosing serious breaks in the ranks of the majority, passed the House; Mr. Boutwell ending the discussion with the expression of his belief "that any restoration of either of the eleven states lately engaged in the rebellion to political power in the Government of this country, which is not coupled with, or preceded by, the condition that the negroes of the South are to vote, opened the way to the destruction of this Government from which there is no escape."* In the Senate, however, the conservatives succeeded in laying the bill upon the shelf and going on with the two measures of Trumbull, the former of which passed the Senate on the twenty-fifth of January, and the latter on the second of February (with a sweeping amendment, added after its introduction, making all negroes citizens of the United States); such prominent supporters of the President among the Republicans as Dixon, Doolittle, Lane of Kansas and Stewart being numbered with the majority.

But what finally wrecked this promising scheme was the immovability of the Committee of Fifteen and the temper of the House. The leading members of the former body had no sympathy with the senators seeking a compromise with the President. Stevens had been hostile to Johnson from the beginning and Stevens at present ruled the committee. What exasperated

* *Globe, id.*, pp. 309–311.

the President more than any other one thing was the treatment accorded his own state. As early as last June he had proclaimed Tennessee, alone as yet of her insurrectionary sisters, free from insurrection. He had watched the election of her senators and representatives with solicitude and congratulated himself that every man of them was competent to take the iron-clad test oath. And yet the state was treated like an alien, although one of her citizens was President of the United States. Pressure was brought to get out of the committee a special resolution admitting the members from Tennessee by themselves. "Parson" Brownlow—the fiery governor of the state—wrote a letter to the Speaker of the House (January 15th) stating:

> "I am decidedly in favor of admitting the Tennessee delegation. . . . The Tennessee delegates, as a whole, are loyal, can take the required oath, and would, if in their seats, add to the strength of the Union party. . . . Finally, they ought to be admitted as a means of preventing a rupture between Congress and the President, which for the sake of the country ought to be avoided. The President ought to be satisfied with the admission of the Tennessee delegates to their seats, and I have no doubt would be."*

But it was all to no purpose. What the committee did was to report a fourteenth amendment to the Constitution reducing representation in states withholding suffrage from male citizens on account of race or colour, which, after a long and hard struggle, passed the House by the necessary two-thirds, on January the

* For letter see *Globe, id.*, p. 1017.

thirty-first. Until this amendment, after having been adopted in like manner by the Senate, was ratified by the legislatures of three-fourths of the states, it seemed to be the determination of the omnipotent committee to keep the lately insurgent states out of the Union, including Tennessee. Having apparently committed itself to this view the House took up the Freedmen's Bureau bill which, after a dispute with the Senate over amendments, was finally (February 9) sent to the Executive. Although it was known even before the bill reached the President that he was dissatisfied with some of its features, yet the preponderance of expectation was in favor of his signing it. Symptoms were not wanting of growing dissensions. While the debate was going on in the House on the proposed fourteenth amendment, in a published interview with senator Dixon (January 28), the President expressed doubts of the propriety of making any further amendments to the Constitution, and stated that "the agitation of the question of negro suffrage in the District of Columbia as an entering wedge to the agitation of that question throughout the country was ill-timed, uncalled-for and calculated to do great harm."* On the seventh of February, to a delegation of colored men come to press the granting of suffrage to their race, he declared emphatically he would not adopt a policy that he believed would end in a conflict between the races and the extermination of one or the other.† On the tenth, he told a committee of the legislature of

* McPh. Recon., p. 51.

† *Id.*, p. 53.

reconstructed Virginia that he was in favor of the immediate restoration of these states, that he had fought against the doctrine that a state could go out of the Union and could never be brought to acknowledge it: that from the beginning and before the rebellion there were "extreme men North." "The Government has taken hold of one extreme and with the strong arm of physical power has put down the rebellion. Now, as we swing round the circle of the Union . . . if we find the counterpart or duplicate of the same spirit . . . this other extreme, which stands in the way, must get out of it."* On the other side, the fourteenth amendment, despite the eccentric opposition of Sumner who, in a two-days' carefully prepared speech, belabored the measure in his most classic style as "introducing discord and defilement in the Constitution," "polluting the text hitherto kept blameless" by the verbal recognition of "race and color," was finding support from those conservatives of the Senate who were the authors of the plan of compromise, although its adoption would render it practically impossible for them to furnish the stipulated equivalent for any concession on the part of the President. Nevertheless, as the ten days allowed for deliberation were passing by, the majority kept hoping that all would go well. Representatives even of the radical sort expressed "unfaltering confidence" in the President. Some stated that to their personal knowledge the President endorsed the substance of the bill; Cullom of Illinois going so far as

* *Id.*, pp. 56–8.

to say "the bill has become a law, as I take it for granted the Executive will sign it."* The Committee of Fifteen (so it was stated after the event), was on the point of recommending the immediate admission of Tennessee. A veto of this, the first bill sent to the Executive bearing upon the South, was dreaded by all sections of the party, and all the more because a veto in this case carried with it the veto of the civil-rights bill, a far more important measure, already passed the Senate and sure to pass the House. Yet on Monday, the nineteenth, when suddenly it was whispered that a message from the President was on the way, the Senate galleries were instantly surcharged with an excited throng aware that a message could only mean a veto.

The President objected to the bill as unnecessary, the existing act not having expired and its powers ample; as prolonging military measures from a state of war where they were proper into times of peace where they were incongruous; as unconstitutional in creating tribunals for the summary trial of offenders without jury and without the right of appeal; as making a grant of such unlimited powers a part of the permanent legislation of the country, and clothing the President with powers "such as in time of peace certainly ought never to be trusted to any one man."

The last and "very grave" objection, upon which the President dwelt longer than any other, was the one that carried the sting:

"The Constitution imperatively declares, in connection with taxation, that each State shall have at least

* *Globe, id.*, pp. 908, 911.

one Representative and fixes the rule for the number to which in future times each State shall be entitled. It also provides that the Senate of the United States shall be composed of two Senators from each State, and adds with peculiar force, 'that no State, without its consent, shall be deprived of its equal suffrage in the Senate.' " While the original Freedmen's Bureau Bill passed in the absence of the states chiefly to be affected, this was necessarily the case because "their people were then contumaciously engaged in the rebellion." "Now the case is changed and some at least of those States are attending Congress by loyal representatives soliciting the allowance of the constitutional right of representation." When this bill was passed there was "no senator or representative from the eleven States which are mainly to be affected by its provisions." "There should be no taxation without representation." The right of Congress to judge of the qualifications of its members "can not be construed as including a right to shut out, in time of peace, any State from the representation to which it is entitled by the Constitution." "At present, all the people of the eleven states are excluded—those who were most faithful during the war not less than others. The State of Tennessee for instance"—and the President's soreness over the treatment administered to his own state can be discerned beneath the calm words with which her heroic resistance, her present loyalty and her unforced adoption of the abolition amendment are sketched. The reading closed amidst applause and hisses from the galleries which were instantly ordered cleared. The majority in the first flush of its anger was for forcing a vote without consideration, but, after remonstrance from two Republican senators, calmer feelings prevailed and the matter was allowed to go over until the morrow.* The next day, accordingly, the question was put whether the bill should pass notwithstanding the objections of the President, and uncertainty as to the result added to the intensity of the excitement. The bill was originally passed by yeas 37 to nays 10—more than two-thirds, and therefore enough to override a veto. The roll-call had not proceeded far, however, before ominous changes appeared. Cowan (who was absent on the first vote), as might have been expected, voted in the negative. Dixon and Doolittle who voted for the bill now went with Cowan; Stewart, also, and the two West Virginia senators; while, to the consternation of the majority, Morgan of New York joined the nays; in all, five changes direct from affirmative to negative, besides three former absentees (Cowan, Nesmith and Willey) added to the nays. Lane of Kansas, a staunch friend of the President, and Henderson still voted for the bill. The total stood: Yeas 30 and Nays 18. The President pro-tem. (Foster) arose and announced to the chagrined majority: "Two-thirds of the members present not having voted for the bill, it is not a law." The galleries applauded, hissed, and were cleared again. The thing was done. War had broken out and the first victory was with the President.

* *Globe, id.*, pp. 915, 917.

The House manifested its ill-temper by passing a concurrent resolution reiterating the caucus decree of the beginning of the session that no senator or representative of any of the eleven states shall be admitted until Congress shall have declared such state entitled to representation. Stevens, after stating that "until yesterday there was an earnest investigation into the condition of Tennessee to see whether we could admit the State," declared that "since yesterday there has arisen a state of things which the committee deem puts it out of their power to proceed further . . . without surrendering the rights of this body to the usurpation of another body."*

Thursday, the birthday of Washington, was commemorated by the two Houses assembling in the Hall of Representatives with solemn pomp and ceremony (which, it was thought, parodied the pomp and ceremony with which the obsequies of the revered Lincoln had been celebrated only ten days before) to honor the memory of Henry Winter Davis, the master spirit of the opposition to Lincoln's policy of reconstruction. On the other hand, the 22d was a great day for the supporters of the President. They were bestirring themselves everywhere throughout the country, holding public meetings, firing guns over his victory, telegraphing him words of cheer. In the evening there was a large gathering of Union men in the city of New York, addressed by Secretaries Seward and Dennison; and another in Washington, which at the close of the pro-

* *Globe, id.*, pp. 943–4.

ceedings marched to the White House to greet the President; a multitude of people joining it on the way. In response to the shouts of the crowd, Johnson appeared on the portico and made a speech.

There had been two extremes (we give but a part of his remarks), one who were willing to break up the government to save slavery; the other to break up the government to destroy slavery. He had been against both. He was for the government slavery or no slavery. The attempt of the one extreme had been frustrated and they now acknowledge its futility and ask to be restored. He was in favor of opening the door of the Union. Still maintaining that "the conscious, intelligent traitors" should be punished, he believed in amnesty to the multitude. But "the other extreme are now attempting to concentrate all power in the hands of a few at the federal head and thereby bring about a consolidation of the republic which is equally objectionable to its dissolution." "An irresponsible central directory has assumed all the powers of Congress and taken from the Senate and the House their separate power to judge of the qualification of their members," thus admitting a State to be out of the Union, which was the very thing we all had been fighting against—insisting that this a State could not do. "I have opposed the Davises, the Toombses, the Slidells—but when I perceive on the other hand men"—so far had he proceeded when there were loud cries for names—"Call them traitors." "We know them." "Give us the names."

"Well," he hesitated, "I suppose I could give them. I look upon them as being as much opposed to the fundamental principles of this government and believe they are as much laboring to prevent and destroy them as were the men who fought against us."

"What are their names?" interrupted a voice. On this the President, amid the most vociferous shouting, burst out: "I say Thaddeus Stevens of Pennsylvania—I say Charles Sumner—I say Wendell Phillips and others of the same stripe." Another voice here cried out: "Give it to Forney!" (the secretary of the Senate and editor of two papers "both daily" and both filled with abuse of the President). And the President replied, "I do not waste my ammunition on dead ducks." He continued: "I do not intend to be bullied by my enemies; what usurpation has Andrew Johnson been guilty of that, as a gentleman (Stevens) had said, ought to cost me my head?" The same man had said also that we were in the midst of an earthquake. "Yes there is an earthquake coming—the ground swell of popular judgment." In allusion to his own career, he was saying: "Beginning from alderman and running through all branches of the Legislature," when he was interrupted by a voice, "from tailor up"—"Yes," he said, "and when I was a tailor I always was punctual and did good work—no patchwork, but a whole suit." Passing by this "little facetiousness," as he termed it, he came back to the charge of usurpation:

"They may talk about beheading and usurpation, but when I am beheaded I want the American people to witness." "I do not want by innuendoes, by indirect remarks in high places, to see the man who has assassination in his bosom exclaim 'This presidential obstacle must be gotten out of the way.' I make use of very strong language when I say that I have no doubt the intention was to incite assassination and so get out of the way the obstacle from place and power."

"I know they are willing to wound but they are afraid to strike." "I tell the opponents of the government—I care not from what quarter they come—whether from the East, West, North or South—you who are engaged in the work of breaking up the government by amendments to the Constitution—they may seem to succeed for a time, but their attempts will be futile.

"They may think now it can be done by a concurrent resolution; but when it is submitted to the popular judgment and to the popular will, they will find that they might as well undertake to introduce a resolution to repeal the law of gravity as to keep this Union from being restored."

With this allusion to the latest move of his opponents and an exhortation to the people to stand by the Constitution and the principles of the fathers, the President retired amidst the acclamation of his hearers.*

Though his speech may have weakened the effect of the veto message on the country, none the less did its audacity astound the Radicals. They awoke to the certitude that the President meant to fight for his policy with all the resources of his great office, and that to gain his end he would not scruple to rend their party in twain and make an alliance with its rival. If the calm logical tone of the message drove them from their propriety, the rugged defiance of the speech brought them to a realization of the true nature of the conflict. The twenty-second day of February, 1866, began a new epoch in their calendar. On that day, the chief of political apostates flung his glove into the face of the party of freedom and returned to the horrors of his old creed. From that day, he became

* McPh., Recon., p. 58; *cf.* newspapers of the day.

an outlaw undeserving of quarter. From that day, they began to plot the purging of the Senate and his impeachment and removal. The part of the speech they more particularly resented was the imputation cast upon them of a design to assassinate the man they designated as "the acting President," and, in retaliation for so baseless a charge, they went so far as to insinuate that the man who made it had himself conspired with assassins the death of his predecessor. The day after the speech the Senate took up the concurrent resolution, which the House in a fit of spleen had rushed through the day after the veto, but it was not until the second day of March that it was brought to a vote. The week's debate was chiefly remarkable by reason of a speech by John Sherman, which may be called an elaborate apology for the course of the President. He protested that Congress and the President ought to agree on some plan of reconstruction. If they did not in a reasonable time, either House can and will exercise its undoubted power to admit senators and representatives. We have failed in our constitutional duty and have no right to arraign Andrew Johnson for trying to do his by following the foot-steps of his lamented predecessor. The senator declared the course of the President on the subject of negro suffrage was not a subject for censure. With the President's antecedents he could not have done otherwise. "Up to and including the recent veto message . . . there had been no act of Andrew Johnson which in my judgment was inconsistent with the high obligations he owed to the great Union party." While he regretted the speech of the twenty-second and condemned some passages in it as reported, he could not refrain from palliation. The President, he reminded the Senate, "is thoroughly combative in his disposition; he has been fighting all the days of his life; the very courage with which he resists opponents whenever they present themselves, we commended five years ago as the highest virtue of Andrew Johnson's life"; "Wendell Phillips has arraigned and abused the President in a shameless manner"—classing him with Arnold and Burr, saying "that he had taken Jeff. Davis's place as a leader of the confederacy," and threatening "impeachment"; Sumner had let drop "an expression about 'whitewashing' which greatly wounded and irritated the mind of the President"; and "Mr. Stevens proclaimed Andrew Johnson to be an alien enemy, a citizen of a foreign State, in the convention that nominated him as Vice-President, and therefore not now legally President"; "in a recent debate he made use of an expression that would irritate any man, especially when coming from a leader in the House of Representatives"—quoting the remark of Stevens that if a British King had so violated the privileges of Parliament it would have cost him his head. "Regarding the President as he is, a man who never turned his back upon a foe, personal or political, a man whose great virtue has been his combative propensity; as a man who repelled insults here on the very spot where I now stand, when they came from traitors arming themselves for the fight; can you ask him, because he is President, to submit to insult? Every sentiment of manhood, every dictate of nature would induce a man when he heard these words uttered, in the heat of passion to thrust them back." He exhorted the Senate to "cast over the remarks the mantle of charity," and pronounced what was left of the speech, the "ideas" in it, deserving the grave "consideration of the Senate." He sympathized very much with the feelings of the President in regard to the long-delayed admission of his own state. Tennessee "was reconstructed . . . before the death of President Lincoln, under his guiding hand, with Andrew Johnson as his main agent." "Its government was reorganized before President Johnson came here. It was organized by his own personal friends who shared his fortunes. The men who are sent here to represent Tennessee are as true and loyal as either of you Senators, without exception." "I think it is the common feeling and desire of the people of the United States, whom we represent, the mass of the Union people, that she should be admitted as soon as possible." There were but two things which he could not forgive. The President "is bound as a principle of honor to select as the agents of the Government those who shared with him the political feelings which gave rise to his election." "If he seeks fellowship, counsel, aid or association from or with those who either took up arms in the recent contest, or who, regarding the war as a failure, would have passively yielded to the rebels, he commits an offense from which no man occupying his high position can or will recover."

"This is no time to quarrel with the Chief Magistrate unless we are compelled to do so by his base betrayal of the obligations he imposed upon himself when he became our candidate.''*

Near the close of this debate Garrett Davis of Kentucky enunciated a startling proposition:

> ''The President has the right to ascertain and decide what body of men is the Senate and what the House of Representatives, when there are two bodies claiming to be such. He is to communicate with the two Houses of Congress. Before he can communicate he must ascertain what men constitute the Senate and what men constitute the House. It is his right to do so, and the people of America will sustain him. . . . It ought to have been done at the beginning of the session. . . .
>
> ''Whenever Andrew Johnson chooses to say to the Southern Senators, 'Get together with the Democrats and the Conservatives of the Senate, and if you constitute a majority I will recognize you as the Senate of the United States,' what then will become of you gentlemen? You will quietly come in and form a part of the Senate.''†

Here was treason most foul uttered in the Senate-house! The radicals could not get over it. Howard denounced it as ''revolutionary, unconstitutional, and treasonable''; Wilson, in a speech of a half hour's length, deified the Republican party—''embracing,'' as he said, ''in its ranks more of moral and intellectual worth than was ever embodied in any political organization in any age or in any land''; ''created by no man or set of men, but brought into being by Almighty God

* For Sherman's speech, see *Globe*, *id.*, Appendix, p. 124.

† *Id.*, App., pp. 300–4.

Himself''; and endowed by the Creator with all political power and every office under Heaven.*

The concurrent resolution then passed the Senate by a vote of 29 to 18; Lane of Kansas, Morgan and Stewart still with the President.

This was the counter-stroke to the veto. The Executive might bar the passage of measures which the Congress desired to enact. But ''the Central Directory'' (as Senator Cowan said) ''carried on its girdle the keys of the Union,'' and unless it unlocked the door, the ''wayward sisters'' could not get in.

* *Globe*, App., pp. 140, 142.

SECTION IV

The Struggle for the Two-Thirds

But a deadlock on so vital a question, instead of proving fatal to the President, was the one thing more than likely to prove fatal to the party of the Congress. By the masses of the Northern people no plea in excuse for the non-restoration of the constitutional Union for which their soldiers had fought would be admitted —not negro suffrage, not punishment of treason, not salvation of a particular party. The President had a plan which seemed to point directly to the attainment of this supreme object of the popular desire. The leaders of the Congress party had none. Besides, to all appearances the administration was a unit as yet, and moved as a unit. Seward, deaf to the appeals of the radicals who were enraged by the President's speech, stood only the closer to his chief. Stanton, whatever he may have been doing in private, in public betrayed no signs of disaffection. The residence of Secretary Harlan was pointed out as the place where the more belligerent radicals did congregate. But, with this doubtful exception, the Cabinet seemed firm in the support of the President. On the other hand, among the Congressional majority there were everywhere signs of division and disintegration. The one remedy proposed by the Joint Committee, indefinite and dilatory as it was, was killed in the Senate by the radicals. Sumner read a second studied speech against it, from which Fessenden in his reply culled the following "flowers of rhetoric" with which the senator from Massachusetts assailed a constitutional amendment which two-thirds of his political associates in the House had approved: "Compromise of human rights;" "violating the national faith;" "dishonoring the name of the Republic;" "bad mutton;" "muscipular abortion;" "new anathema maranatha;" "abomination;" "paragon and master-piece of ingratitude;" "abortive of all good;" "shocking to moral sense;" "the very Koh-i-noor of blackness;" "essential uncleanliness;" "disgusting ordure;" "loathsome stench;" the men who support it "Harpies;" "Pontius Pilate with Judas on his back." "You are now hurrying to drop into the text" (of the Constitution) "a political obscenity." "Here is nothing less than a mighty House of ill-fame, which it is proposed to license constitutionally for a political consideration."

The amendment received but twenty-five votes, not near the necessary two-thirds. Nine Democrats, eight Johnson-Republicans and four ultra radicals made up the twenty-two noes.*

The Civil Rights bill, which passed the Senate on the heels of the Freedmen's Bureau bill, provoked in the House dissensions of a different character. Many Republican members entertained doubts of the constitutionality of the first section making negroes citizens. Many feared its provisions would furnish a pretext for

* Fessenden in *Globe*, 1st sess. 39th Cong., p. 1278. Sumner's speech, *id.*, p. 1224.

forcing negro suffrage on the Northern states—a policy their constituents would not stand as yet. It was not until the thirteenth of March, after postponement and amendment after amendment, that the majority made up its mind and passed the bill.

Under such stringent circumstances, the leaders were not slow in recognizing the imperative necessity of action. Go back they would not. They dared not stand still. Move forward they must. A majority in both Houses they had; but, with only a majority, they could neither do even so much as propose a constitutional amendment, nor, in the face of a disapproving executive, make a single law. They must pull themselves together, formulate a coherent and complete plan of reconstruction which would command the united support of the party; and, as an essential preliminary, they must capture the machinery by which their plan, once formulated and backed by disciplined unanimity, could be made the law of the land. In a word, a steady reliable two-thirds majority in each House—this was the need of needs, without which all else was useless and their eventual overthrow certain.

With the House, there would be little difficulty, the normal majority there being much more than two-thirds, and, though somewhat fluctuating on such tender questions as negro suffrage and the admission of Tennessee, safe enough for any measure the party could unite upon in caucus. In consequence of the veto and the speech of the 22d, all minor divisions were forgotten in bitter animosity to Andrew Johnson, and the majority was content to follow Stevens to any length in abusing the President. It was at this period that the habit, persisted in to the last, of studied disrespect and open insult to the Chief Magistrate of the nation was contracted: *e. g.*, putting his messages aside without deigning to read them, jeering at every mention of his name, insisting that he was but a Vice-President acting as President because of the assassination of the rightful owner of the title; and allowing any ribaldry the press might heap upon him to be read from the clerk's desk amid the mocking laughter and applause of both floor and galleries. On a Saturday (March 10th) when the House met for debate only, "Old Thad," as Stevens was affectionately called, being interrupted in an ironical eulogy of the President's "integrity, patriotism, courage and good intentions," by an inquiry whether it was possible he was the Thaddeus Stevens mentioned in the President's speech, informed the laughing House as a confidential communication that that speech never was delivered; it was a myth, one of the grandest hoaxes ever perpetrated, more successful than the moon hoax. "I am glad to have at this time the opportunity (although I do not wish the matter to go before the public, for they might misunderstand my motives) to exonerate the President from ever having made that speech. It is a part of the cunning contrivance of the copperhead party, who have been persecuting our President since the 4th of March last. Why, sir, taking advantage of an unfortunate incident which happened on that occasion, they have been constantly denouncing him as addicted to low and degrading vices." Sending it to the clerk's desk, he had read an extract from the *New York World* of March 7, 1865, in which Andrew Johnson is described as "an insolent drunken brute, in comparison with whom even Caligula's horse was respectable"; and then denounced the report as "a vile slander" got up by "the copperheads";—the Republicans never believed it, but "if these slanderers can make the people believe the President ever made that speech then they have made out their case."*

So much to show the temper of the House. But it was otherwise in the Senate. In that body lay the real nodus of the situation. It was the Senate that shelved the bill granting suffrage to the freedmen of the District of Columbia. It was the Senate that killed the amendment which the Joint Committee elaborated and two-thirds of the House adopted. It was in the Senate that the presence of a minority of more than one-third made the veto of the Freedmen's Bureau bill final. Of the fifty senators, eleven were Democrats, four (Cowan, Dixon, Doolittle and Norton) were out-and-out supporters of the President, three (Lane of Kansas, Stewart and Morgan) were more or less inclined to favor the administration, while the two West Virginia senators could be relied on by neither side; making a total of twenty and leaving but thirty steady Republicans—four short of two-thirds. As it happened one senator from each side was absent at this crisis. Foot of Vermont—the father of the Senate —had not been in his seat since the sixteenth of February, and was lying hopelessly ill at his residence in the

* *Globe, id.*, pp. 1307–8.

capital. Wright of New Jersey had gone to his home in that state as long ago as February the eighth, as announced by his colleague, "exceedingly ill." So that the senators present numbered forty-eight—one-third being sixteen, two-thirds thirty-two. Two certain votes were absolutely indispensable; three would be felicitous to guard against the possibility of the return of Wright before the lingering death of Foot gave the legislature of Vermont the opportunity for which it sat ready to send on a reliable successor; four would make everything safe and sound.

Two methods of recruiting the majority in the Senate were available; one by the admission of new states, the other by turning out minority senators to make place for others more agreeable. The first method was inconvenient because it required the passage of a law; and the passage of a law required the assent of the President or the presence of the two-thirds to obtain which was the final cause of the manœuvre. The second method was encumbered with no such troublesome formality, requiring only the presence of a majority sufficiently unscrupulous and unflinching. Despite the greater facility of the latter, the party managers in the first instance resorted to the more difficult method, for one of two reasons; either they had not yet been able to ferret out what they considered a sufficiently plausible case for the application of the turning-out process, or—which is the more probable reason—they felt that on the question of the admission of a petitioning territory of the West they could rely on the support of western senators hitherto favorable to the President. As a matter of fact, two territories at the moment were applying for admission—Colorado and Nebraska. In the case of Colorado, her people in the summer of the year 1864 rejected the constitution framed and submitted in pursuance of her enabling act by a majority of three to one out of a total vote of 6,192. A portion of her inhabitants, however, without obtaining any additional authority from Congress, held a convention of their own in the summer of the following year, adopted a constitution, submitted it to the people and secured its ratification by a majority of 155 out of a vote of 5,895. A legislature, having been chosen, sent two senators to Washington at the beginning of the present session, but the President declined to proclaim the territory a state and submitted the whole matter to the Congress. A bill was pending before the Senate for her admission introduced by Stewart and advocated by him and Lane of Kansas, but hitherto it had been set aside for more important measures. Discerning the advantage given them by the committal of these two erring senators, the leaders in the movement now brought the bill to the front. Once again, however, the opposition of Sumner, aroused by the presence of the word "white" in the constitution of the proposed state, spoiled his party's scheme. He laid bare every weak point in the case—the illegality of the second convention and the second election; the paucity of the population, not exceeding 25,000, whereas the existing ratio for a representative was 127,000; and although, as was anticipated,

Stewart and Lane voted for the bill, it got but fourteen votes in its favour.*

Dropping for the present their abortive experiment to recruit the Senate by the first method, the managers, turning to the second, lit upon a rare chance of depleting still further the already scant forces of their adversaries. At the opening of the session the credentials of John P. Stockton as senator from New Jersey were presented by his colleague and he was sworn in. No question was made as to his right to his seat; but senator Cowan, by request, presented a protest of several members of the legislature of New Jersey, which, without being read, was laid on the table whence it found its way to the judiciary committee. Apparently no importance whatever was attached to the protest and it attracted no public notice. On the thirtieth of January, Trumbull laid before the Senate a report of the committee recommending the adoption of a resolution declaring Stockton entitled to his seat. The report carried the signature of every member of the committee except Clark who manifested his dissent in no other way. The resolution was read but not acted on, and the matter passed off without comment. Nothing more was heard of it until the failure to pass the Freedmen's Bureau bill over the veto, when Clark began to press his political associates on the committee to bring up the resolution. Accordingly, after the House amendments to the Civil Rights bill had been concurred in and that measure sent to meet an inevitable veto, on

* Sumner, *Globe, id.*, p. 1327 *et seq.* Population, *id.*, 1353.

Thursday (March 22), the report and protest were read at length, and, thereupon, Clark moved to substitute for the resolution reported another declaring that Stockton was not entitled to his seat; and upon this negative proposition opened the debate.

By great good fortune, the facts lying at the bottom of the almost incredible piece of injustice about to be narrated are matters of record and down to the minutest detail never for a moment the subject of dispute.*

On the fifteenth day of February, 1865, the legislature of the State of New Jersey, as by the law it was required to do, met in joint-meeting to elect a successor to John C. TenEyck, whose term as senator of the United States expired on the ensuing fourth day of March. The constitution of the state in the clauses empowering the legislature to appoint certain state officers designated the two branches when meeting together for such purposes, "The Legislature in Joint-meeting"; and from time immemorial "the Legislature in Joint-meeting" had prescribed rules for the government of its proceedings. The legislature was composed of a senate of twenty-one and an assembly of sixty members numbering on joint ballot eighty-one. There being a vacancy caused by death, the joint-meeting of the fifteenth of February, after changing a rule as hereafter stated, adjourned to the first of March, and then to the fifteenth, by which day, the vacancy having been filled, its numbers were complete. In the Senate

* For facts in Stockton case, see *Globe*, *id.*, p. 1564 *et seq.* Journal of N. J. Leg., *id.*, p. 1669. Vote, *id.*, p. 1677–9.

were thirteen Democrats and eight Republicans; in the Assembly there was a tie: 30 to 30; so that on a joint ballot the legislature was Democratic by five. There would have been no hitch in the election of a Democrat had it not been for the fact that nine Democratic members, having refused to go into the caucus which chose John P. Stockton as the party's candidate, refused to vote for him after he was so chosen. At its first session —February 15—probably because of the closeness of the contest, the joint-meeting changed the existing rule which required only a majority of the votes cast to elect, to the more stringent rule requiring a majority of all the members elected to the legislature; and, under this change, it became impossible for any candidate to be elected as long as the bolting Democrats held out and scattered their votes. Stockton could muster, apparently, but thirty-four out of the forty-three Democrats. TenEyck, the choice of the Republicans, could get but thirty-eight if he got the full Republican strength. The certainty of the dead-lock being perceived, the first business of the adjourned session of the fifteenth of March was a motion to rescind the rule adopted at the first meeting requiring a majority of all the members elected, and to adopt in its stead an entirely new rule: "That any candidate receiving a plurality of the votes of the members present should be declared duly elected." This movement, if not indeed initiated, was supported by the Republican members who anticipated that the proposed change would result in the election of their own candidate—he apparently being sure of a larger number of votes than his strongest competitor could get. When, however, they saw six of the bolting Democrats voting in the affirmative, the eight or ten Republicans who had already voted hastened to change their votes to the negative—all but one, who remained steadfast. The new rule, consequently, was adopted by a majority of one of all the members elected—eleven senators and thirty assemblymen in the affirmative, ten senators and thirty assemblymen in the negative, three Democrats voting against it and one Republican for it—the Republican, therefore, casting the decisive vote. The joint-meeting thereupon proceeded to ballot for United States senator; and upon the first ballot John P. Stockton received forty votes, James W. Wall one, Peter D. Vroom one, and Henry S. Little one—making up the forty-three Democratic members; John C. Ten-Eyck received thirty-seven and F. T. Frelinghuysen one—making up the thirty-eight Republicans. And, in pursuance of the rule just adopted by a majority of the legislature in joint-meeting, the presiding officer rising in his place declared the Hon. John P. Stockton duly elected United States senator for the term of six years from the fourth of March instant, with the unanimous acquiescence of the assemblage—not a single protest, objection or even a dissenting murmur being heard. And, then, after appointing several state officers, the legislature in joint-meeting adjourned without day. The legislature sitting in senate and assembly continued in session for fifteen days longer and no note of dissatisfaction was sounded. The protest, therefore, must have been an after-thought. The document itself was nominally dated as early as the twentieth of March, it is true, and bore the signature of every Republican member of the legislature, including even his whose single vote carried the plurality rule; but it was not presented to the legislature, Stockton heard nothing of it until months afterwards, and some, at least, of the signatures were not put to it until within a month of the meeting of Congress, and by that time it was known that the next legislature would be Republican on joint ballot.

The report of the judiciary committee upon the facts as above stated reached the conclusion: "That in the absence of any law either of Congress or the State on the subject, a joint-meeting of the two Houses of a Legislature, duly assembled and vested with authority to elect a United States Senator, has a right to prescribe that a plurality may elect; on the principle that the adoption of such a rule by a majority vote in the first instance makes the act subsequently done in pursuance of such majority vote its own."

Clark, in opening the debate, maintained that, in the absence of a statute, by what he called parliamentary law, a majority was necessary to a valid election, and that the joint-meeting of the legislature had no power by a mere rule to abrogate the parliamentary law; that, to accomplish such a modification, an act passed by both Houses acting separately and signed by the governor was indispensable. The whole contention of the impugners of Stockton's title rested upon the validity of this one argument, which Hendricks went far towards demolishing by quoting from

Cushing's "Law and Practice of Legislative Assemblies" the following:

> "The law of the majority is universally admitted in all legislative assemblies, unless . . . a different rule is prescribed by some paramount authority, or is agreed upon beforehand by the assembly itself, by which a smaller number is permitted . . . to do a particular act. But even in these cases it is the will of the majority that governs, because it is by the major vote, in the first instance, that the rule itself is established."

He cited also the cases of elections of Speaker of the House, where, after a vain struggle for a choice by majority, that body first adopted a plurality rule and then elected under it, as in the cases of Howell Cobb and Nathaniel P. Banks. Hendricks also laid great stress upon one consideration:

> "The joint-meeting agreed to elect by a plurality. They did so elect. The presiding officer announced the result, and there was no objection to it. The convention proceeded to other business on the result being announced, and by silence acquiesced. I say that is conclusive upon the question."

And so it seems to us.

Sumner urged if the case was doubtful the doubt should be given—not, it seemed, to fairness or justice—but to "the law of the majority." "If there ever was an occasion where every doubt was to be counted against the assumption of power, it is the present. I know very little of cards, but I remember a rule of Hoyle: 'If you are in doubt take the trick' "—a quotation, the accuracy of which senator McDougall instantly questioned, insisting that the proper reading was, "When you are in doubt play trumps," a direction which, whether in Hoyle or not, the radicals, in this instance, were predetermined to follow. When a vote came to be taken at the close of Friday (23d of March) there were forty-four senators present; the absentees being Dixon, who had fallen ill and had not paired, Foot dying at his residence in the capital, Howard, paired with VanWinkle, Doolittle and Williams paired with each other, and Wright, who before going home had been careful to secure a pair with Morrill of Maine upon this particular question, so vital to his colleague and his state. The Senate had been thoroughly canvassed and great pressure brought upon Morrill to terminate his agreement, so much so that on the evening of the preceding Wednesday he had yielded so far as to write a note to Stockton stating that "the question was not expected to run on . . . so long," and "upon reflection he thought it not unreasonable so to regard it," and "to avoid embarrassment" he suggested this "so that he (Stockton) might advise his colleague." The next morning (Thursday), the first day of the debate, Stockton having prepared a telegram informing his colleague that, "after allowing you (him) a reasonable time to get to Washington," Morrill would "consider himself at liberty to vote in my (Stockton's) case"; he read it over to Morrill, obtained his approval of its contents, and sent it to Newark, New Jersey. On this Friday, a telegram from Wright was received by his colleague to the effect that he was still confined to his room and could not be in Washington until the middle of the next week; that he was uncertain whether the telegram of yesterday meant that the pair was off; that he had heard nothing direct from Morrill and trusted he would adhere to his agreement; and this telegram was immediately communicated to the senator from Maine.

Such was the condition of the opposing forces when the secretary began to call the names of senators on Clark's amendment. The intensest excitement prevailed, as though all were conscious that the issue of the battle between the President and the Congress hung on the decision of the moment. The vote, as announced, stood yeas 19, nays 21; VanWinkle, Morrill, Stockton and Wilson were present but did not vote, VanWinkle being paired with Howard, Morrill still true to his pair with Wright, Stockton for an obvious reason, and Wilson. Among the nays were every Republican member of the judiciary committee except Clark (*i. e.*, Trumbull, Harris, Poland and Stewart), and such Republican senators as Anthony, Foster, Henderson and Morgan. The Clark resolution being lost by a majority of two, the question recurred on the adoption of the resolution, reported by the committee, affirming Stockton's right to his seat. The white-heat still continued. The matter evidently was not yet considered closed. Some new development was evidently at hand. When the roll-call ceased, the vote stood yeas 21, nays 20—the only change being that Wilson, who did not vote before, now voted with the radicals where he belonged. Then took place a scene brief but deeply disgraceful to the American Senate. A dead set was made upon Morrill, senator after senator calling out to him to vote. Even his stately colleague urged him to vote. The boisterous Nye rudely pressed him to vote. High above all, the hoarse voice of Sumner was heard ejaculating, Vote! Vote! Vote! The distressed senator, driven hither and thither by conflicting claims, came at length to a decision. Addressing the secretary, he said: "Call my name." The secretary called "Mr. Morrill," and Mr. Morrill voted nay. There was a tie, and the resolution was, at least, not carried. But Stockton is upon his feet. He tells of the pair with his colleague, of the telegram of the day before, of the telegram of that day, and states that his colleague still holds the senator from Maine to his agreement without which he would not have gone home at all. He then directs the secretary to call his own name and votes in the affirmative. The result is announced, Yeas 22, Nays 21. The New Jersey senator is safe. With blank faces and in ominous silence the contrivers of the scheme look on while the Senate adjourns over Sunday.

But the struggle was not yet abandoned. The more thorough-going partisans of the House joined those of the Senate in holding conclaves during Saturday and Sunday, so that by Monday a programme had been mapped out by which it was hoped to retrieve the situation. To Charles Sumner was confided the task of redeeming what with unconscious irony he called "The Honor of the American Senate." At the opening of Monday's session, he moved to strike out Stockton's vote as "null and void," first, because "according to the principles of natural law, or in other words, the principles of universal law," "no man can be a judge in his own case" and, second, because "according to the principles of parliamentary law" (embodied in a rule in the House but not in the Senate) "no member shall vote on anything in the event of which he is immediately interested." The right of a senator to vote in defence of his own seat was ably expounded by the minority. Stockton detailed the circumstances connected with the broken pair, reading a letter from a son of his sick colleague in which it was stated that, "not a single word" had the senator from Maine communicated to the writer's father of his intention to disregard his pledge. Fessenden and Sumner both admitted that they had urged the paired senator to vote, justifying their action by the twofold plea (1) "that a pair for so long a period was not originally contemplated by the parties," and (2) that a man even so ill as Wright had ample time to arrive between the receipt of Thursday's telegram and Friday's vote. On this delicate and rather unpleasant subject, it will suffice to quote Hendricks' answer on the first point, which seems conclusive—the second needing no answer.

> "There is force in that suggestion where there is a general pair. If I pair with the Senator from Maine upon questions of a class, for instance upon all questions in relation to the rebel States, . . . of course if I remain absent for a protracted time, he has the right to terminate the pair. . . .

"But if I pair with him in regard to any particular question, what difference does it make to him whether the vote upon that question is taken to-morrow or a month hence? If the seat of his colleague is to be contested and I am to be absent, . . . and he and I agree to pair off, not generally upon a class of subjects, but upon that particular question, how is it of interest to him whether that particular vote comes up to-morrow or next month?"

It being ascertained, however, that Trumbull and his Republican colleagues on the judiciary committee were a unit against his right to vote, Stockton, in deference to the opinion of these friends of his title, expressed his willingness to withdraw his vote; and in consequence of this offer, the Senate reconsidered the resolution carried on Friday, and, on Sumner's motion, declared that on the pending question Stockton's vote should not be received. An effort made by the minority to postpone the matter until Thursday was vehemently opposed by Sumner, Clark and Nye. Because Friday's vote was presumed to have settled the question, Wright's coming had been thought unnecessary; and, since Friday, Morgan by an extraordinary fatality had been added to the sick list. The managers of the plot, therefore, had good reasons to object to any delay. They meant to make the most of the time before the recovery of Morgan and the possible arrival of Wright. And this motive was blurted out by Nye:

"We have reached a point in the consideration of this case where the Senate should act promptly upon it. It is due to the State of New Jersey. It is a thing perfectly well known that the Legislature of the State of New Jersey are holding on now for no other purpose than, if the vote in this body is such as to relieve Mr. Stockton from further duty here, that they may elect a man in his place. . . . They are now adjourning from day to day for no other purpose."

The Senate adjourned until the morrow with the understanding that the subject should come up immediately in the morning. The next day—Tuesday, March 27th—the Senate Chamber was crowded. It was whispered that a veto of the Civil Rights bill was on the way. Every senator was at his post except Dixon, Foot and Wright, Morgan having convalesced. A telegram was read from Wright begging the Senate, if it had not already done so, to defer the case until Thursday, when he either would be present or ask no further delay. In answer to Clark's objection that there was not a shadow of reason why the absent senator, if able to be there on Thursday, could not have been there to-day, another telegram was read stating that his physician had warned him not to start last night or this morning, nor before to-morrow, when the journey might be risked. But the radicals were inexorable. The reception of the veto at this moment made them doubly so; they would not grant even a day's delay. Sumner solemnly reminded his associates: "There is a Reaper whose name is Death; he, too, may come among us. Disease has made a pair between the absent Senator from New Jersey and the absent Senator from Vermont. Let that pair continue"—losing sight of the absent senator from Connecticut. He and his followers sneered at the possibility of Wright's coming

—the man was sick unto death and would never come, and they scouted the suggestion that this grave question should be put off for a single day on such a chance. On the heels of this cruel decision, Clark moved to amend the pending resolution affirming Stockton's title by inserting the word "not"; and in this form the test vote was taken. Stockton, knowing he was about to be sacrificed, made a last speech, recounting the whole history of his election, reading the journal of "the Joint-meeting of the Legislature" of his state, so as to preserve for the eyes of an impartial posterity the full extent of the approaching iniquity. Then, after further ineffectual efforts to amend and to postpone until the next day, the roll-call began.

The veto of the Civil Rights bill lay on the secretary's desk as he rose to call. Morrill, as if he found it unendurable to face dishonour a second time, had arranged another pair with Foster and fled the chamber. Stewart, present in the morning, had suddenly disappeared. Every other senator was present except the three disabled by illness (Dixon, Foot and Wright). Every senator voting voted the same way as on Friday, and every senator present voted, but two—Stockton, denied the right to vote, and Foster paired with Morrill. The yeas were 22, the nays 21. The resolution as amended was immediately adopted by the same vote, except that senator Riddle went with the majority so as to move a reconsideration and thus keep the matter alive until Wright should arrive. This last effort was defeated by Clark, who, forestalling Riddle, moved a reconsideration himself and called upon his forces to make "the trial now." At this critical juncture, a messenger arrived from Newark, with the intelligence that every arrangement was made to convey Wright to Washington in time to vote to-morrow. But the plot was too near accomplishment to run any risk of failure now. The day's delay was denied without compunction, and Clark's motion to reconsider lost by the same vote as before—Stewart still in hiding. The struggle was at an end. The senator from New Jersey was ejected by a majority of one. Without Morrill's broken pair the outrage could not have been consummated; and Morrill's broken pair would not have sufficed had it not been for Stewart's defection.

It must not escape notice, however, that by a most humorous twist of Fortune's finger this hard-won but shameful victory was rendered half-barren for the moment. Stockton had gone, but his successor did not come. The legislature of New Jersey, holding on from day to day, patiently awaiting the triumph of what was called "loyalty" in the United States Senate, was not permitted to complete the great work after all. One James M. Scovel chanced this year to hold the casting vote in the upper House over which he presided, and having been won over by the Johnsonites with the bait of the federal patronage of the state, he stubbornly refused to allow the senate to go into joint-meeting. In vain did "Old Thad" belabour him from Washington with telegram after telegram. He would not budge. And, so, after many days of arrested mobility, the two houses were at last forced to adjourn, leaving Stockton's chair still standing vacant, a silent reminder of what Charles Sumner called, "The Honor of the American Senate."*

Immediately after the ejection of Stockton, came the reading of the veto of the Civil Rights bill. Brief, calm, courteous and dignified in its tone, cogent in its logic and invulnerable in the points it made—in these particulars the message furnished a refreshing contrast to the unseemly struggle which had just ended in the Senate, as well as to the indecorous exhibition in the House seventeen days before. The unconstitutionality of the main provision—so plain that even the strictest radicals could not blind themselves to it—was expounded with a master's stroke. The death of the venerable and much-loved senator from Vermont, occurring the next day, prevented consideration of the veto until April the fourth. Just before the debate opened Stewart made an attempt to smooth over his defection by airing his own particular project of reconstruction. But this was his last effort to retrieve his independence, and he soon sank into the ranks of those steady supporters of party measures upon whom the leaders count as a matter of course. The second day of the debate was signalized by the appearance of George F. Edmunds, appointed to the vacancy occasioned by the death of Foot; the celerity of the governor of Vermont giving poignant emphasis to the paralyzed condition of the legislature of New Jersey. The presence of the new recruit sharpened the impatience of the majority to dispose of the veto. In the evening the minority proposed that a time should be fixed for

* Scovel's testimony, Imp. Inv., p. 619 *et seq.*

taking the vote on the morrow so that the two senators who were ill in the capital might attend. It was known that Dixon had suffered a relapse, and, if brought to the Senate at all, could remain but a short time, and that Wright had arrived in the care of his son, but in a like feeble condition. At this moment the suspense was so heavy that business was interrupted—senators gathering in buzzing groups or moving to and fro with hurried mien. The value of the ill-gotten gain of the struggle for the two-thirds was about to be tested, and the uncertainty was too great for comfort. The accession of Edmunds was a cheering stroke of good fortune. But the unexpected return of Wright, the probable presence of Dixon, the doubtful attitude of Willey and Morgan, once again, put the result in jeopardy. Wade sprang to his feet and burst forth into a thundering protest against any further delay:

> "I will not yield to these appeals to comity on a question like this; but I will tell the President and everybody else, that if God Almighty has stricken one member so that he cannot be here to uphold the dictation of a despot, I thank Him for His interposition and I will take advantage of it if I can."

Nothing but the prospect of an all-night's session forced the majority to consent to an adjournment.

The next day (April 6) at the opening hour, every chair was filled but two. Dixon was kept away by the rain which was falling, but it was whispered that should his presence at any moment become necessary he would be carried into the chamber. Stockton's chair stood conspicuous by its emptiness; but, like the stool of the murdered Banquo, Wright's was "full." When, near the close of the day, the debate had run itself out and the question was about to be put, the excitement of the critical moments of the Stockton episode was renewed in an intensified form. Failure to override the veto meant nothing less than progressive disintegration ending in final defeat of the party, or submission to Andrew Johnson. Tremendous must have been the pressure brought to bear on Morgan whose fidelity to Seward had hitherto held him to the President's side. As the names of the senators were called in alphabetical order, the first change noticed was the prompt response of the recruit from Vermont. When the name of Morgan was pronounced there was a painful pause for a moment; but when his yea was heard, the galleries broke loose in an uproar and the leaders on the floor heaved a great sigh of relief. There was a last moment of suspense when Willey's name was reached, but his separation from his colleague who had just voted nay settled the question beyond a peradventure. The death-stricken senator from New Jersey was the last but one to vote. He could not save the veto as he might have done had he been permitted to save his colleague. What compunctious visitings troubled the radicals as they gazed at his pale face and reclining form, it were idle to conjecture. But his presence served to bring to shame the prophecies that death would not let him come, which, in excuse for their refusal of even a day's delay, they had so heartlessly thrown about the Senate. The yeas were thirty-three, the nays fifteen, absent one (Dixon). Two-thirds having voted in the affirmative, the bill was passed, the objections of the President to the contrary notwithstanding.*

It was a cardinal triumph—but missing defeat only by a hair. The majority could not have spared a single vote. Had either Morgan or Willey or even Stewart stood firm, Dixon lay ready to be carried into the chamber and the veto would have been sustained. Moreover, close as it was, the victory was soiled by a breach of plighted faith. Had not Stockton been turned out, the defection of Stewart and Willey and Morgan would not have averted defeat, and Stockton could not have been turned out had not Morrill broken his word. On the following Monday, the House of Representatives, which during the ordeal in the Senate had been attending strictly to non-political legislation, took up the Civil Rights bill, and choking off all debate, passed it over the veto with a rush. At the conclusion of the roll-call, the speaker, although the result could be in no way affected by his vote, ostentatiously directed the clerk to call his name and responded in the affirmative with great gusto and to the delight of the majority. His exultant declaration, made, as he said, by authority vested in him by the Constitution, that the bill "has become a law," was hailed with shouts and with clapping of hands and stamping of feet, both on the floor and in the galleries; the scene of disorder, which no attempt was made to check, continuing for several minutes.†

* *Globe, id.*, 1809.

† *Id.*, 1861.

The Congressional majority might well rejoice; for this was the pivotal point of the contest. The failure to override the veto of the Freedmen's Bureau bill showed that the President still held the initiative. The passage of the Civil Rights bill over the veto showed that the scale had shifted, and the initiative was now in the hands of the Congress. Viewed from another and higher standpoint, the enactment of the Civil Rights law marks an epoch in our constitutional history. Since the foundation of the federal government, the veto power had been exercised with relative frequency, and, up to the present time, its exercise had been effectual, except in two minor instances which serve only to emphasize the rule. From the inauguration of Washington, for fifty-six years every bill vetoed by a President failed to become a law. In the last days of the administration of Tyler a bill was passed over the veto of the President for the first time in our history; but it was a bill simply forbidding payment for certain vessels the President had ordered built, and was of no national significance whatever. Beside this single instance, during the first session of the thirty-fourth Congress a series of special bills was passed over the vetoes of President Pierce; but they were ordinary appropriations for river and harbor improvements, involved no important principle, and provoked but little comment. Never until now had a public measure of importance been made a law in defiance of the objections of the President.* Furthermore,

* Schouler's Hist. of U. S., Vol. IV, p. 491; Vol. V, p. 364.

every previous exercise of the veto power on measures of importance had been grounded on the objection, sometimes accompanied by others, that the measure was unconstitutional. And every one of these vetoes had stopped the passage of the proposed enactment and so far preserved the Constitution from what in the judgment of the executive was a violation of its provisions. But, in the present instance, for the first time in the history of the country, a measure of wide-reaching scope and primary significance had been made into a law notwithstanding the disapproval of the executive not only, but also in the face of the protest of the President that the Constitution contained no grant of power to pass it and that many of its provisions violated the constitutional rights of the states and the people. Such an exigency being without precedent gave birth to startling questions. What would the executive do with an act which in his judgment contravened the Constitution and was, therefore, void? Jackson laid down the rule that the interpretation put upon the Constitution by one department was not binding on any other, that every department of the government had the right to construe the Constitution for itself; and, to this doctrine, since the Dred Scott decision, the Republican party, in practice if not in theory, had subscribed. An act of Congress in accordance with that decision, passed over a veto, would have had scant respect from that party, and a refusal by the President to execute such a law would have been hailed with acclamation by its leaders. And these leaders appear now to have anticipated, and perhaps hoped, that President

Johnson would refuse, or at least neglect, to enforce a measure he had denounced as unconstitutional, though passed over his objections. So that the question had arisen: What was to be done in case their carefully contrived legislation should become a dead letter in the hostile hand that penned the veto? When the country came to comprehend the drift of such considerations as these, suspicion began to filter into the minds of the masses that the struggle for the two-thirds carried a deeper significance than the taking off a senator or two so as to pass a law. All at once it was recalled that, though a majority of the House of Representatives might impeach the President, the Constitution required two-thirds of the Senate to effect his conviction and removal from office. This popular suspicion, there can be no doubt, embodied an element of truth. The impeachment and removal from office of their indomitable adversary already hovered in the minds of the most active and zealous among the leaders of the party. For so revolutionary a movement, however, the margin they had won in the Senate was too narrow and unstable. Something further remained to be done.

SECTION V

Colorado, Fourteenth Amendment and Tennessee

It is not likely that the victors in the recent engagement indulged in any expectation that the menace of impeachment and of packing the court to pass judgment would cow Andrew Johnson. In 1861, when he was made the target of all sorts of threats on account of his solitary stand against secession in the Senate, he quietly let fall this characteristic utterance: "I want to say, not boastingly, with no anger in my bosom, that these two eyes of mine never looked upon anything in the shape of mortal man that this heart feared."* His one idea of a fight was to return with arithmetical precision blow for blow. On the Monday succeeding the turning out of Stockton (April 2), he issued a proclamation of peace throughout all the late insurgent states, except Texas, formally withdrawing the proclamations of war of his predecessor and declaring the restoration of civil rights and the cessation of martial law.† On the eighteenth of the same month, to a delegation of soldiers and sailors he announced his unalterable determination "to stick to his position," and against his traducers he blew a blast of defiance: "Men who, when he was battling in the Senate and in his own State for the Union, were lolling in ease and

* *Globe*, 2d Sess. 36th Cong., p. 1350.

† McPh. Recon., p. 15.

comfort''; he heeded them not. ''The whole pack, Tray, Blanche and Sweetheart, little dogs and all coming along snapping at my heels.'' And he did not stop with proclamations and speeches. He began to act on the offensive, to make reprisals. A harvest of spoils such as the politicians of the Jackson epoch never dreamed of was being reaped by the dominant party and constituted one of the chief elements of its strength. The dispensation of a multitude of offices had come to be, through immemorial custom, almost exclusively an executive function. This function, it now appeared, Johnson meant to exercise with the purpose of rewarding the supporters of his policy, whether Republicans or Democrats, and thus to build up a party of his own; or, failing that, to reinvigorate the party of his youth and earlier manhood. This was the one course of conduct which even the apologists of the President still left among the Republican leaders, such as John Sherman, declared they could not forgive. Difference of opinion on such capital questions of state as negro suffrage, rebel disfranchisement, reconstruction, they could tolerate for the time being. But the offices were consecrated to the party. Any interference with their enjoyment by ''loyal'' party men, especially in the interest of an unholy alliance with the Northern Democrats, would be looked upon as treachery so perfidious as to banish any lingering scruples over the character of the means by which it might be forestalled.

Upon no prominent politician could this threatening aspect of affairs have had a more powerful influence than upon Henry Wilson, who, at the time of the defeat of the bill for the admission of Colorado, had entered a motion to reconsider.* At that date, the admission of a territory, the population of which did not equal one-fourth of the number required by law for one representative in Congress, the voters of which had rejected the constitution submitted to them at the only election held under the enabling act and, according to the best attainable evidence, were averse to state-hood; for no other purpose than to increase the majority on the floor of the Senate, was an enormity too scandalous for even the men who turned out Stockton to perpetrate. The bill got but fourteen votes, Wilson himself voting against it. But, in view of the increasing aggressiveness of the President, the project grew more and more tempting, and, on the seventeenth of April, Wilson revived his motion. In the present emergency, he said in effect, he would waive his hostility to the word "white" in the constitution of the proposed state; we need her two votes in the Senate. But he counted without his colleague who would abate no jot of his former opposition. On the contrary, Sumner, in addition to his former arguments, now showed that the population, being a mining population, was diminishing instead of increasing, impugned the credibility of one of the senators-elect, and denounced the second election as illegal, fraudulent and marked with violence against the negro. In short, he stripped the measure of every semblance of merit. At the close of his remarks, he startled the Senate from its propriety by exclaiming:

* *Globe*, 1st Sess. 39th Cong., p. 1386. See Section IV, *supra*, p. 65.

"It is whispered that we need two more votes on this floor. Sir, there is something that you need more than two votes." Again: "Tell me not it is expedient to create two more votes in this Chamber." This time, however, his opposition was unsuccessful. The bill passed the Senate by the vote of 19 yeas and 13 nays; not voting 17, all but five of whom were paired. Nine Republican senators, who either voted against the bill before or were absent or did not vote at all, now voted for it, and one was paired in its favor. Of the Republicans who opposed the measure before, Foster, Fessenden, Grimes, Harris, Morgan, Poland and Sumner stood firm. Edmunds voted nay from antipathy to the word "white." The real division of the Senate was 25 yeas and 19 nays.*

The bill did not pass the House without a struggle over the obnoxious word, and, then (May 3d), by a vote of but 81 yeas to 57 nays. An atmosphere of distrust hung around the senators-elect. Both sides seemed to count upon their support. The suspicions concerning their attitude, entertained by certain radical senators, which there is reason to believe seriously contributed to the first defeat of the bill, must by some means have been allayed; yet their unconditional committal against the President's policy could not have been publicly known, for close friends of Johnson continued to favor the admission of the state:—among them Edward Cooper, one of the representatives-in-Congress-elect from Tennessee, who, in the interval he was denied his seat, acted as the private secretary of

* *Globe, id.*, pp. 1982, 2135–44, 2180.

the President. To him in that capacity, as late as Saturday, the twelfth of May, the Colorado senators addressed a joint letter in which they pronounced the prevailing rumor that "they had sold out to the radicals" "entirely untrue," and protested that they had "pledged themselves to support no man or measures." On the evening of Monday, the tenth day after the passage of the bill, they had an interview first with Cooper and afterwards with the President. Cooper wanted them to strengthen his own arguments with his chief, by avowing their adherence to the policy of the immediate admission of all the unrepresented states whose members could take the test oath; and there is reason to believe that they did make an avowal of this kind, more or less unequivocal. The interview with the President was inconclusive, except that Johnson let his visitors know that he did not think it in consonance with the future welfare of the Union to admit two more men into the Senate to carry out the schemes of the radicals.* The veto message must have been written at this very moment, as it was sent in that evening. The message was laid upon the table as in view of the vote on the passage of the bill there was no hope of overcoming the veto. The second trial of this indefensible scheme, like the first, had ended in failure. A third was still to come.

But all other subjects of legislation were swept aside by the plan of reconstruction reported by the joint-committee on the thirtieth day of April and taken up by the House on the eighth of May. The plan was in two

* Testimony of Cooper, "Impeachment Investigation," pp. 23–7.

parts: (I.) A proposed amendment to the Constitution. (II.) Two bills supplementary to the amendment. The amendment, unlike the one first reported and killed in the Senate, contained five sections instead of one. The first section was a repetition of the main provision of the civil rights law. The second was the single section of the amendment first reported (modified as to its phraseology to suit Sumner's fastidious philanthropy) basing representation on population and providing proportionate reduction on account of the denial (or abridgment) of the elective franchise to male adult citizens for any cause except for participation in rebellion or other crime. The third section excluded from the right to vote for representatives in Congress and presidential electors until the 4th day of July, 1870, all persons who had voluntarily adhered to the late insurrection. The fourth inhibited the payment of the rebel debt and the fifth simply gave Congress the power to enforce the foregoing four. Of the accompanying bills, the first provided that when the proposed amendment shall have become part of the Constitution, and any state lately in insurrection shall have ratified the same, the senators and representatives from such state, if found duly elected and qualified, may, after having taken the "iron-clad" oath, be admitted to Congress; the second rendered ineligible to office under the United States five classes of the late Confederates.*

The plan bore evidence on its face that it was a compromise of conflicting views among the members of the

* McPh. Recon., pp. 103–4.

committee. Radicals of the Stevens type were dissatisfied because the state governments organized under the President's plan were recognized. Radicals of the Sumner type were dissatisfied because negro suffrage was not made a condition precedent to admission. But radicals of all types, for the most part, dissembled their dissatisfaction because they perceived that, by incorporating into the proposed amendment a section disfranchising the leaders of the late Confederacy and then exacting the ratification of the amendment as a whole, the plan was rendered impracticable; and they had but to bide their time. As senator Dixon pointed out, the project, instead of being "a practical scheme for hastening the reëstablishment of all the states in their full constitutional relations," will inevitably postpone this desired end. "It is hardly worth while to discuss the merits of measures which to be valid must be accepted by communities sure to reject them."*

The country had not long to wait to learn the attitude of the Executive Department towards this counterplan of the Congress. The day after its submission there was a meeting of the Cabinet, and an apparently authoritative statement of the opinion of the President and his confidential advisers came out in the press. As might have been anticipated, the President was "against all conditions precedent to the admission of loyal representatives from the Southern states, in the shape of amendments to the Constitution or the passage of laws"; and, according to the report, in this position he was sustained by secretaries Seward, Mc-

* *Globe*, 1st Sess. 39th Cong., p. 2332.

Culloch, Stanton and Welles; Dennison, the Postmaster-General, expressing some doubts as to the precise time representatives should be admitted, Harlan being reticent, and Speed, the Attorney-General, absent.* The administration presented the same external appearance of harmony as did the joint committee; but it was known that internal dissensions were beginning to disturb the peace of the one, as they had all along disturbed the peace of the other.

The debate continued in the House for two days, the chief contention being over the disfranchising section which was allowed to remain by a majority of but five, and then the amendment was passed by more than the necessary two-thirds. It encountered stormy weather in the Senate. The debate opened on the twenty-third, when the third section was virtually thrown overboard as of no practical benefit and another suggested similar to the one finally inserted. After another day's discussion, there was an interval of some days during which a caucus was held and a series of modifications agreed to, so that when the subject was resumed on the twenty-ninth there was but little difficulty in carving the amendment into the shape it now bears as the Fourteenth Amendment of the Constitution. Instead of disfranchising the leaders of the late Confederacy until July 4, 1870, as the third section originally provided, the substitute inserted by the Senate provided for the ineligibility to office—state as well as federal—of any person who, having held any office requiring the

* Quoted from *National Intelligencer* of May 2, 1866, by senator Grimes, *Globe*, *id.*, p. 2333.

taking of the constitutional oath before the war, should have engaged in insurrection or rebellion against the United States; Congress being given power by a two-thirds vote to remove the disability:—the clause embracing, as Reverdy Johnson said, "perhaps nine-tenths of the gentlemen of the South."* On Monday, June fourth, the discussion was resumed and lasted until Friday night, when the whole measure having been subjected to a minute revision was adopted by the necessary two-thirds. Before the vote was taken, a proposition was made by the minority to submit to the states the several sections as so many separate articles, any one or more of which might be ratified or rejected; an expedient adopted by the first Congress in submitting the first twelve amendments, only ten of which were ratified; but, although several Republicans during the course of the debate avowed the belief that the Southern people would accept the penal section as well as the rest, the proposition found no favour.† Indeed, that the radicals not only did not expect, but, also, did not desire, the South to ratify this amendment is shown by the fate of the first of the two supplementary bills reported by the joint committee. The second bill was rendered useless by the alteration which the third section of the amendment underwent in the Senate. But the first was a constituent part of the proposed plan of reconstruction, if that plan was to be reconstructive in anything more than a contingent sense; providing as it did for the restoration of the

* *Globe, id.*, p. 2898.

† *Id.*, pp. 3040–2.

Southern states on the ratification of the amendment. That Sumner meant that this bill should never become a law is shown by an amendment he introduced adding, as a further condition to the readmission of any state, that she should have stripped her constitution of every trace of negro disfranchisement.* But the bill itself never reappeared in the Senate. It was taken up and considered in a desultory manner while the House was waiting for the close of the long debate in the Senate on the amendment; the radicals making it plain that they did not mean to admit any of the eleven states without the establishment of "an equal and just system of suffrage for all male citizens," and the conservatives giving the measure but a lagging and grumbling support. Debate on it was renewed from time to time but no serious effort was made to bring it to a vote. The passage of a second Freedmen's Bureau bill prolonging that institution two years furnishes one more piece of evidence that there was no expectation on the part of the majority of the acceptance by the South of their mutilated plan. One section of this last bill embodying the provisions of the Civil Rights act gave the President in his veto message the opportunity to set at rest all apprehensions of a refusal to enforce a measure that he had condemned as unconstitutional and at the same time to blight the anticipations of the advocates of impeachment in this direction: "'the civil rights bill,'" he said, "now the law of the land," "will be faithfully executed as long as it shall remain unrepealed

* *Id.*, p. 2869.

and may not be declared unconstitutional by courts of competent jurisdiction."*

In the meantime the Fourteenth Article as it came from the Senate having been concurred in by the House (June 13), sped on its way north, south, east and west. Connecticut ratified on the twenty-ninth day of June, New Hampshire followed on the sixth of July. But these instances had little significance. All eyes were turned on Tennessee. Her remodeled government, on the whole, was the most acceptable to the Republicans of the Congress of all those of the reconstructed states. The franchise was not as yet granted to the negroes but her constitution gave the legislature power to grant it at any time. She had disfranchised every white man in the state who had participated to any extent in the insurrection. The election of Andrew Johnson Vice-President had given place to another leader of the whites of East Tennessee who now ruled the state. William G. Brownlow, called the "Fighting Parson," prided himself on having been a rival of Johnson's in the affections of the people. His life had been a running fight with the power of slavery, and the fiery passions burning constantly in his heart and finding voice in a reckless tongue and a still more reckless and remorseless pen, combined, with untold suffering undergone in the course of the long combat, to fasten upon his attenuated frame a palsy which shook him in every limb. But no disease however terrible could shake his untamable soul. He was elected governor on the same day that Andrew Johnson

* McPh. Recon., pp. 147–8.

congratulated the Senate upon that event in his famous speech on his own inauguration as Vice-President. From the moment Johnson's accession to the presidency removed him from the field of state politics, the Parson-Governor let loose the animosity which no doubt had long been slumbering in his bosom against his too successful competitor. The breach between the President and the Congress gave him his opportunity and he threw himself into the embrace of the radicals, prepared to follow them to any length short of negro suffrage.

On the twenty-eighth day of May the legislature of the state, after passing an act disqualifying for office all persons who had held conspicuous positions in the Confederacy, adjourned until the next fall. No sooner, however, had the joint resolution proposing the Fourteenth Amendment passed both Houses of Congress, than Brownlow made haste to call the legislature back so that the President's own state might be, if possible, the first to ratify a constitutional amendment which the President opposed. But the governor might call, yet in the unsettled condition of the state the legislators would not come. There seems to have been no difficulty with the Senate. But, to make a quorum of the House, fifty-six members or two-thirds of the whole number must be got together, and fifty-six would not or did not come. Some sent in their resignations; the governor refused to accept them; others refused to attend at all until the proposed amendment was submitted to their constituents. Others attended but at the critical moment absented themselves and broke the quorum. The governor applied to General Thomas, who commanded the United States troops still in the state, for military assistance, which under instructions from Washington Thomas refused. The fighting parson thus driven to the wall proved equal to the emergency. On the nineteenth day of July, he managed to get together fifty-four members—two short of a quorum. Two more were in the capital but being friendly to the President they persisted in absenting themselves from the House. They were taken into custody by the sergeant-at-arms, dragged into the room of that officer adjoining the Hall of the House, held there by main force while the voting was going on, and counted as present by the Speaker. The amendment was declared ratified by the House by a vote of forty-three yeas to eleven nays—not voting two.

During these days the majority in Congress were differing among themselves over a mode of adjourning so as still to keep a check upon the President's power of removal and his general disposition to thwart their measures. The weather was hot. The members wanted to go home. But they were afraid to leave the President alone. A call for a convention of Union men without distinction of party to meet in Philadelphia, the public adhesion of prominent members of the Cabinet to the movement, the resignation of the Postmaster-General on the eleventh of July and of the Attorney-General on the sixteenth and the appointment of Alexander W. Randall and Henry Stanbery as their respective successors, an address to the country by the Democratic members of Congress:—all added to the solicitudes of the hour. Into this arena buzzing with party anxieties, party perplexities, party passions and suppressed party quarrels, the tidings of Parson Brownlow's latest achievement dropped like a spell. On the day of its date, the secretary of the Senate read to the grave and reverend signiors gathered around his desk the following telegram sent him by the jubilating governor of Tennessee:

"NASHVILLE, July 19, 1866.

HON. J. W. FORNEY,

Secretary United States Senate, Washington.

We have fought the battle and won it. We have ratified the constitutional amendment in the House—43 voting for it, 11 against it, two of Andrew Johnson's tools not voting. Give my respects to the dead dog of the White House.

W. G. BROWNLOW."

As was remarked next day by senator Cowan: "This is the first time in the history of the Senate, unquestionably, that such a dropping as this has fallen from so foul a bird into this chamber, and it is the first time, I think, in the history of this chamber, where members of this body would sit patiently by and not vindicate themselves from the charges of being accessories to such vituperation. And this is published with joyful acclaim by an officer of this body, published in the very sanctuary of American decency."*

The immediate consequence of the news conveyed by this scurrilous missive was the passage by the House of a joint-resolution declaring that Tennessee was "restored to her proper practical relations to the

* *Globe, id.*, p. 3957.

Union and again entitled to be represented by senators and representatives in Congress, duly elected and qualified, upon their taking the oath of office''; though not without a struggle by the radicals, headed by Stevens, to postpone the matter, and a protest and speech by Mr. Boutwell against it. When reported to the Senate the resolution had undergone a metamorphosis which gave rise to a lengthy debate highly illustrative of the diversity of opinion among the majority. From a simple declaration of the admission of Tennessee it had become an elaborate document. The preamble might be described as a synopsis of the history of the state during her insurrection and reconstruction, made up to exhibit the exceptional circumstances which justified her admission, together with the assertion of the doctrine that none of the seceding states can ''be restored to its former political relations in the Union without the consent of the law-making power of the United States.'' The resolution proper was also entirely remodeled so as to declare ''that the United States do hereby recognize the government of the state of Tennessee . . . as the legitimate government of said State, entitled to all the rights of a State government under the Constitution of the United States,'' and there end. The Senate preamble, after being once stricken out, was finally adopted after being amended to placate Sumner and Brown (to no purpose), but the House form of the resolution prevailed over that of the Senate. In this shape the joint resolution passed both Houses, protests being made in the course of the debate by many members that the proceeding should not be considered a pledge or precedent for the admission of the other excluded states. The affirmation of the Congressional dogma of reconstruction, explicit in the preamble and implicit in the resolution, it was thought, would place the President in a most embarrassing position. Either he must veto the resolution and thus defeat one of his most cherished objects, viz: the admission of his state, or he must approve a doctrine he was known by frequent utterances wholly to condemn. He met the occasion like a statesman. The resolution reached him in the evening. He did not keep it ten days. He did not veto it. He signed it the very next morning; and he accompanied his signature with a message to the House expressing his dissent on matters of form, of which this is the opening paragraph:

> "The preamble simply consists of statements, some of which are assumed, while the resolution is merely a declaration of opinion. It comprises no legislation nor does it confer any power which is binding upon the respective Houses, the Executive, or the States. It does not admit to their seats in Congress the Senators and Representatives from the State of Tennessee; for, notwithstanding the passage of the resolution, each House, in the exercise of the constitutional right to judge for itself of the election, returns and qualifications of its members, may, in its discretion, admit them or continue to exclude them. If a joint resolution of this kind were necessary and binding as a condition-precedent to the admission of members of Congress, it would happen, in the event of a veto by the Executive, that senators and representatives could only be admitted to the halls of legislation by a two-thirds vote of the two Houses."

"Notwithstanding the anomalous character of this proceeding," the President approved the resolution, with the proviso, however, that such approval was not to be considered "as an acknowledgment of the right of Congress to pass laws preliminary to the admission of the duly qualified representatives from any of the States"; nor as committing him to all the statements in the preamble, some of which, he remarks, are contrary to fact, especially the assertion that the state of Tennessee has ratified the proposed constitutional amendment, no official information of which has been filed in the Department of State; on the contrary, "unofficial information from the most reliable sources induces the belief that the amendment has not yet been constitutionally sanctioned by the Legislature."* After the reading of the message, the eight representatives elected as long ago as August, 1865—four Johnson and four radical Republicans—were declared entitled to their seats, and those present were sworn in. In the Senate matters did not move so smoothly. Joseph S. Fowler, one of the senators-elect, whose opinions on the burning issues were well known, was sworn and took his seat without a word; but when the credentials of his colleague were presented, there was trouble. The fidelity of David T. Patterson to the Union had been shown, not at a distance and in safety, but in the very midst of the battle. He had suffered arrests and imprisonments, had been driven into the woods and banished from his home. But he was a son-in-law of

* For admission of Tennessee see *Globe, id.*, pp. 3987, 4008, Sen.; Pres. Mess. 4102; p. 4056, House.

Andrew Johnson and known as a supporter of his policy. It was gall and wormwood to those of the leaders who had turned out Stockton, to witness the reinforcement of the scanty ranks of the minority by so close an ally of the President. Scanning his record with hostile eye they discovered one weak spot. A judge of the Circuit Court of his state since 1854, he was reëlected by his Unionist neighbors over an open secessionist in 1862 by four thousand majority; but that section of the state being overrun after this time by Confederate soldiers he could not serve unless he took the oath to the Confederate States. He yielded to the entreaties of the struggling Union men who had elected him, and was sworn in; at the same time declaring that he owed no allegiance to the Confederate States and did not consider that part of the oath binding. He held a few terms of court where he could find grand juries of Union men until September, 1863, when the federal troops reaching Knoxville he succeeded in escaping, not to return to his own district until the close of the war. Upon this one delinquency in an otherwise heroic career, Sumner laid his cold finger and moved a reference of the credentials. The senator-elect stood ready to take the test oath, not doubting in his heart and conscience that he could lawfully and honorably do so; but such senators as Sumner thought they had the right to judge for him in this respect; and by his own solicitation the reference was conceded so that he might give a full explanation to the committee.

During the interval that elapsed before the committee's report, Wade, as if to countervail this imminent accession to the ranks of the minority, called up a bill for the admission of the territory of Nebraska as a state, which he had introduced a few days before. Why he took this course, instead of bringing up for consideration his bill for the admission of Colorado which lay on the table under a veto, it is difficult to explain. If he could not override the veto of the one, how could he expect to override the veto of the other? The same obnoxious word "white" disfigured the constitution of Nebraska; and, although the number of negroes in the territory was but fifty, that word was certain in the one case as in the other to arouse the antagonism of Sumner. In fact, upon that senator the effect would have been the same were there no negroes in the territory at all. If Wade cherished any expectations of placating the Massachusetts senator he was cruelly awakened. Sumner went at him with his favorite argument that the constitution was not republican in form, to the height of which he wished that his friend "could lift himself." Wade deserved his punishment. On the merits the Nebraska case was no better than the case of Colorado. The territory was a vast wilderness inhabited by a scattered population of not more than forty thousand—or less than one-third of the number required under the ratio for one representative. At an election held, not under the enabling act of Congress but under an act of the territorial legislature, to ratify the constitution of the future state, less than eight thousand votes were cast and the majority in favor of the constitution was only one hundred, though many frauds and much intimidation were charged. But, notwithstanding the opposition of Sumner, the Ohio senator did succeed in getting his bill through the Senate, but by the disheartening vote of 24 to 18. The House passed it the same day. The President failing to sign it, the adjournment of Congress prevented it from becoming a law.*

In the middle of the contest over this territory, the committee made its report on the case of the senator from Tennessee. After giving the facts as we have given them already, it presented a resolution declaring that David T. Patterson was duly qualified and entitled to his seat; stating also "that in accepting the office of judge and taking the official oath he did not intend to acknowledge any allegiance to or any friendship for the Confederate government," but acted throughout "with a sincere desire to benefit and preserve the Union." Even so ultra a radical as Clark confessed: "That there was not a shadow of doubt in the mind of any person who heard him (Patterson) before the committee that he had been throughout a Union man; and not only a Union man but such a Union man as would put some of us to shame that we should be admitted into the Senate because we were Union men and he should be put out." After an effort to solve the question by modifying the test-oath to suit the particular case, to which the House with much heat refused its consent, the Senate in the last hours of the session adopted the resolution declaring the senator entitled to his seat by a vote of twenty-one yeas to eleven nays. After a brief interval,

* For Nebraska see *Globe, id.*, pp. 4204–4213, 4219–4222, 4276.

Reverdy Johnson moved that he be permitted to qualify. There was no dissent. Amid an impressive silence, David T. Patterson advanced to the desk and, without the slightest hesitation or a single apparent tremour, took the full ''iron-clad'' oath, which so many of his colleagues, now looking on, affected to believe he could not take without manifest perjury.*

The closing scene of the absorbing drama of the session placed the rebel-judge, as he was called, upon the bench of the High Court of Impeachment.

* For Patterson, *Globe, id.*, pp. 4162–4169, 4213–4219, 4293.

SECTION VI

The Appeal to the Country

The contest was now transferred to the country. Another House of Representatives was to be chosen, and, if the administration by a coalition of its Republican supporters with the Democrats could manage to capture more than one-third, the veto would become once more effective to guard the reconstruction plan of the President while it grew in favor with disinterested lovers of the Union. A political revolution in the North could hardly be expected, but the states of Connecticut, New York, New Jersey, Pennsylvania, Ohio and Indiana, as shown by recent local elections, furnished fair fighting-grounds. The dispersal of the Congress left the President with a free hand to weed out the opponents of his policy from the crowded ranks of office-holders, and the President was now resolved to use his power. Twelve hundred and eighty-three postmasters, for example, were removed during the campaign, and the same process went on in the Treasury Department with its custom-houses and internal revenue districts. The Cabinet was reconstructed; such doubtful or lukewarm supporters as Dennison, Speed and Harlan giving place to such staunch followers as Randall, Stanbery and Orville H. Browning, once a bosom friend of Lincoln's. The real choice before the people, it should be borne in mind, was not between the reconstruction plan of the President and the reconstruction plan of the Congress, because the Congress proffered no plan. A constitutional amendment was before the legislatures of the several states for ratification or rejection, but the bill which opened the door of the Union to the excluded states as a reward for ratification had failed to become a law. The admission of Tennessee, as we have seen, was due to exceptional circumstances and accompanied with loud protests that it was to be no pledge or precedent. The real issue of the campaign, as made by the attitude and course of action of the Congressional majority, was: Shall the excluded states be admitted into the Union with constitutions denying suffrage to the freedmen? There can be no doubt that at this period the most influential leaders of the Republican party had come to the conclusion that any restoration of the Union unaccompanied by some measure of white disfranchisement, on the one hand, and of negro enfranchisement, on the other, would be fatal to the continued supremacy of that party in the councils of the nation. The powerful radical wing openly avowed its determination to permit no restoration of the Union without negro suffrage; and, judging from its success in the Congress in striking the keynote of the opposition to the President, it was bound to drive the party for the sake of its self-preservation if for nothing else into the embrace of its creed. The majority in the northern states, however, was not ready yet for negro suffrage either at home or in the South; and the bold presentation of the real issue might eventuate in the overthrow of the party. That issue, therefore, the politicians set to work to obscure or falsify. They insisted that the only question was whether the states reconstructed under the President's plan should be admitted into the Union without ratification of the proposed amendment, or, as in the case of Tennessee, after its ratification. Knowing that the amendment had been carefully constructed so as to make it certain of rejection by the South, they promised the people of the North an immediate restoration of the Union if only the people of the still excluded states, by adopting an amendment of the federal Constitution, would make such fair and moderate concessions as the reduction of their representation because of the multitude of freedmen they would not permit to vote, the guarantee of the Union, and repudiation of the rebel, debt. And, under this false issue, the campaign was fought and won.

Two days after the adjournment of Congress, an event occurred which, by rekindling the exasperation of northern Republicans against the Southern people, struck a serious blow against the cause of the President at the very opening of the battle. A massacre was perpetrated in New Orleans over an unlawful attempt to revive and pack the convention of 1864, which framed the constitution under which the present government of Louisiana was acting, for the purpose of grafting upon the constitution a provision granting suffrage to the negroes; notwithstanding that the convention had been extinct two years and the constitution ratified by the people. The police made an attack upon the hall where the members of the convention and a crowd of colored people were gathered together, and numbers of them were shot down or stabbed, and mutilated after they were down and appealing for mercy. After the slaughter was over, the United States troops reached the scene and that same night the city was placed under martial law. The President was assailed in one breath for not having protected the convention, and in the next for not having instructed the commander of the troops what to do, although a telegram from the commanding officer to the Secretary of War asking instructions was not communicated to the President, and was suffered to remain unanswered by Stanton. Prominent members of Congress were in complicity with the convention-plot, and the President on his side openly charged that the riot was "substantially planned by the radical Congress."*

On the fourteenth of August, 1866, the convention of the National Unionists met in Philadelphia. Extra effort had been put forth by the Republican supporters of the administration to make it a success significant of the strength of their peculiar position. The President and every member of the Cabinet but the silent Secretary of War had been conspicuously active in the promotion of the same object. A notice had gone forth to all the office-holders that they were expected by the administration to support the movement by their presence at the convention if convenient, but at all events by their open advocacy of the principles

* Report of Board of Investigation, Imp. Inv., p. 1075. St. Louis Speech, *id.*, 531.

the convention was called to advance. The assemblage was called to order by Randall, the War-Governor of Wisconsin and now Postmaster-General. General John A. Dix was temporary president. Major-General Couch, the head of the delegation from Massachusetts, walked up the aisle arm-in-arm with James L. Orr, the head of the delegation from South Carolina. Every one of the thirty-six states was represented by a delegation of respectable, intelligent, well-known and influential citizens. Officers of renown in the armies so recently victorious shook hands under the old flag with officers of renown in the armies so recently vanquished. Doolittle was made permanent chairman, Cowan reported the resolutions, Henry J. Raymond read the address to the people. The friends of the convention thought it a great success, while, to the leading politicians of the dominant party, the presence of the statesmen and heroes of the councils and battlefields of secession, which alone gave the gathering any historical significance, furnished a cry which served to keep their following in line, and, in the end, rendered the movement detrimental to the cause of the administration. They denounced it as a hobnobbing with "redhanded rebels." They ridiculed it under the name of the "Arm-in-arm Convention." A committee of two members from every state was appointed to present to the President a copy of the proceedings, and, on Saturday, the eighteenth, this body of over seventy men gathered in the east room of the White House, where Reverdy Johnson, the chairman, in a courtly speech discharged the duty of the committee. The President, with General Grant standing at his right hand, in a quiet conversational tone uttered these sentences, little dreaming that he was committing what the House of Representatives by and by was to pronounce "a high misdemeanor in office."

> "We have witnessed in one department of the government every endeavor to prevent the restoration of peace, harmony and union. We have seen hanging upon the verge of the government, as it were, a body called, or which assumes to be the Congress of the United States, while, in fact, it is a Congress of only a part of the states. We have seen this Congress pretend to be for the Union, when its very step and act tended to perpetuate disunion and make a disruption of the states inevitable. . . . We have seen Congress gradually encroach step by step, upon constitutional rights, and violate, day after day and month after month, fundamental principles of the government. We have seen a Congress that seemed to forget that there was a limit to the sphere and scope of legislation. We have seen a Congress in a minority assume to exercise power which, allowed to be consummated, would result in despotism or monarchy itself."*

Having sounded this note of defiance, the President made his preparations for a tour through the North. The cornerstone of a monument to the memory of Stephen A. Douglas was to be laid in Chicago on the sixth of September, and the President, having been invited to be present at the ceremony, purposed to avail himself of the opportunity to visit the principal cities

* Version used in Article X. For whole speech see Pres. Trial, Vol. 1, p. 301.

along his route and address himself in person directly to the people. He had an unbounded faith in their sense of justice and their collective wisdom, and a confidence no less unbounded in the efficacy of his homely methods of appealing to the masses face to face. On the twenty-eighth of August he started on this unlucky journey. In his remarks to the Virginia delegation the February before, he made use of the expression, "As we swing round the circle of the Union";* and the present progress was called by all the wits "a swinging round the circle." He was accompanied by Welles and Randall of his Cabinet (Seward joining the party in New York), by General Grant and Admiral Farragut. The municipal authorities of Philadelphia, in fear of committing themselves to the side of the administration, scattered to the surrounding summer resorts at the approach of the distinguished party and there was no official welcome; but the citizens headed by General Meade turned out in goodly numbers. New York, the next day, by an ovation, both official and spontaneous, made up for the coldness of the Quaker City. The crowds were uproarious for "Andy," for Grant and for Farragut, as these three were driven in procession to the City Hall. There, in the historic Governor's Room, they were welcomed by Mayor John T. Hoffman. While Johnson, in a low conversational tone, barely audible throughout the Chamber, was addressing the mayor who stood directly in front of him, Seward sat almost immediately beneath his own portrait as governor of the state that hung on the

* McPh. Recon., p. 58.

wall. The contrast was striking and in some respects mournful. The picture was a full-length representation of a tall, slender, agile, clean-looking figure, in the prime of manhood, which seemed about to spring out of the canvas. The figure below, huddled together in its seat, wrinkled, untidy, the face swollen and red, the cheek and drooping jaw deformed by a jagged scar, looked like the broken relic of the young Apollo that stared at it from the frame. That night, at a gorgeous banquet, the President made one of his characteristic speeches which the radical press misprinted and made fun of the next day. Up the Hudson the presidential cortege went to the capital, where Governor Fenton accorded the President a reception so chilling as to draw subsequently from the Secretary of State a severe animadversion. Thence across the state, stopping one night at Auburn, the home of Seward, they were welcomed at Buffalo by Ex-President Fillmore in a speech remarkable for its unqualified condemnation of the Republican party's present course. Thence to Cleveland, where they arrived on the evening of the third of September. Going out on the balcony of the hotel where he stopped, the President was formally welcomed by the mayor, and, then, in obedience to the clamours of a large crowd in the streets, he was introduced. Greeted by repeated calls for Grant, he excused the general's failure to appear by the plea of illness. In the course of his remarks, alluding to the saying that he was an alien and could not be President, he said: "All that is necessary, therefore, is to declare the office vacant or on the pretext to prefer articles of impeachment'' and drive him from power; when a reference to his being on the same ticket with Lincoln was met by the exclamation: ''Unfortunate,'' uttered by some one in the audience. Johnson retorted: ''Yes, I know there are some who say 'unfortunate.' Yes, unfortunate for some that God rules on high and deals in justice. Yes, unfortunate. The ways of providence are mysterious and incomprehensible, controlling all those who exclaim 'unfortunate.' If my predecessor had lived, the vials of wrath from a mendacious press and subsidized gang of hirelings would have been poured out upon him, as upon me.'' Another cried: ''Hang Jeff Davis.'' His answer was ready: ''Why don't you hang him? Haven't you got the Court? Haven't you got the Attorney General? Who is your Chief Justice who refused to sit on his trial? I am not the Attorney General. I am no jury.'' ''I called upon your Congress that is trying to break up the government.'' ''Did your Congress order any of them to be tried?'' Another shouted: ''Traitor, traitor.'' He inquired for the man who could place his finger upon one pledge Andrew Johnson had violated: ''Who is he? What language does he speak? What religion does he profess? Traitor! my countrymen: Will you hear me? . . . If I were disposed to play the orator and deal in declamation . . . I would take Mr. Seward and bring him before you and point to the hacks and scars upon his person. I would ask you when he turned traitor?'' A voice shouting ''Hang Thad. Stevens and Wendell Phillips,'' he burst out: ''Why not hang them? I have been fighting traitors South. They have been whipped and crushed and acknowledge their defeat and now as I go round the circle I am prepared to fight them at the North." "I understand the discordant notes in this crowd to-night." "Some of you talk about traitors in the South who have not the courage to go away from your homes and fight them." The brave men were in the field "while you remained cowardly at home," "speculating and committing frauds on the government." Some protesting: "Is this dignified?" —he exclaimed: "I understand you. You may talk about the dignity of the President. I have been upon the battlefields of this country." "I care not for my dignity. There is a certain portion of our countrymen who will respect a citizen whenever he is entitled to respect. There is another class who have no respect for themselves, and consequently they cannot respect any one else. I know a man and a gentleman whenever I see him. I have only to look in his face; and (pointing at one of the noisiest in the crowd) if I were to see yours by the light of day I do not doubt but that I should see cowardice upon it. Come out here where I can see you. If ever you shoot a man you will do it in the dark, and pull the trigger when no one is by." Having silenced his would-be tormentors at last, he proceeded to commit without rebuke his second "high misdemeanor in office" (according to the subsequent charge of the House):

"In bidding you farewell I would ask you, with all the pains this Congress has taken to poison the minds of their constituents against me—what has this Congress done? Have they done anything to restore the Union of these States? No; on the contrary, they have done everything to prevent it; and because I stand now where I did when the rebellion commenced, I have been denounced as a traitor. Who has suffered more, who has run greater risks than I? But this factious domineering party in Congress has undertaken to poison the minds of the American people."

He closed quite triumphantly; replying to one or two belated cries about "New Orleans," "Louisiana." "You let the negroes vote in Ohio before you talk about negroes voting in Louisiana. Take the beam out of your own eye before you see the mote that is in your neighbor's. You are very much disturbed about New Orleans but you won't let the negro go to the ballot box in Ohio. We understand these questions."*

The next morning, the presidential party sped on across the states of Ohio and Indiana to Chicago. The exercises there were conducted with comparative decorum, and the illustrious visitors then started for St. Louis, reaching that city on the eighth. In the evening the President attended a banquet at the Southern Hotel. A great crowd assembled outside and clamoured for a speech. The President, at last but with manifest reluctance, yielded to repeated calls and came out on the balcony, intending to make a short address of thanks. Hardly had he uttered a word, however, when interruptions, evidently preconcerted, began. The New Orleans riot being now thrown in his teeth he

* McPh. Recon., pp. 134 *et seq.*, and Trial, Vol. 1, p. 328 *et seq.*

was provoked to commit a third "high misdemeanor in office," as defined by the House of Representatives:

"Perhaps if you had a word or two on the subject of New Orleans you might understand more about it than you do. . . . If you will take up the riot at New Orleans and trace it back to the radical Congress, you will find that the riot at New Orleans was substantially planned. If you will take up their proceedings in their caucuses you will understand that they knew that a Convention was to be called which was extinct by its power having expired; that it was said that the intention was that a new government was to be organized and on the organization of that government the intention was to enfranchise one portion of the population, called the colored population, who had just been emancipated, and at the same time to disfranchise white men. When you design to talk about New Orleans you ought to understand what you are talking about. When you read the speeches that were made and take up the facts on the Friday and Saturday before that Convention sat, you will there find that speeches were there made incendiary in their character, exciting that portion of the population, the black population, to arm themselves and prepare for the shedding of blood. You will also find that that Convention did assemble in violation of the law, and the intention of that Convention was to supersede the reorganized authorities of the state government of Louisiana, which had been reorganized by the government of the United States; and every man engaged in that Convention with the intention of superseding and upturning the civil government which had been recognized by the Government of the United States, I say, that he was a traitor to the Constitution of the United States, and hence you find that another rebellion was commenced having its origin in the radical Congress. . . . So much for the New Orleans riot. And there was the cause and origin of the blood that was shed; and every drop of blood that was shed is upon their skirts and they are responsible for it."

After this he appears to have cut loose from all restraint:

"I have been traduced, I have been slandered, I have been maligned, I have been called Judas Iscariot and all that. Now, my countrymen, here, to-night, it is very easy to indulge in epithets, it is easy to call a man Judas, and cry out traitor; but when he is called upon to give arguments and facts he is very often wanting. Judas Iscariot! Judas! There was a Judas and he was one of the twelve apostles. Oh, yes the twelve apostles had a Christ. (A voice "And a Moses too"; laughter.) The twelve apostles had a Christ and he never could have had a Judas unless he had had twelve apostles. If I have played the Judas who has been my Christ that I have played the Judas with? Was it Thad. Stevens? Was it Wendell Phillips? Was it Charles Sumner? These are the men that stop and compare themselves with the Saviour; and everybody that differs with them in opinion and try to stay and arrest their diabolical and nefarious policy, is to be denounced as a Judas."

Again:

"But a short time since I heard some one say in the crowd that we had a Moses. Yes, there is a Moses; and I know sometimes it has been said that I would be the Moses of the colored man. . . . I have tried to do as much and have done as much—and when they talk about Moses, and the colored man being led into the promised land, where is the land which this clan proposes to lead them into? . . .

Why, it is to give us a Freedmen's Bureau. . . . The Freedmen's Bureau was a simple proposition to transfer four millions of slaves in the United States from their original to a new set of taskmasters. I have been laboring for years to emancipate them; and then I was opposed to seeing them transferred to a new set of taskmasters to be worked with more rigor than they had been worked before. Yes, under this new system they would work the slaves, and call on the government to bear all the expenses and if there were any profits left why they would pocket them. Thus, you the people must pay the expenses of running the machine out of your own pockets while they get the profits of it."

Again:

"Because the President chose to exercise the veto power, he committed a high offense and therefore ought to be impeached. Yes, yes, they are ready to impeach him. And if they were satisfied they had the next Congress by a decided majority as this, upon some pretext or other—violating the Constitution, neglect of duty, or omitting to enforce some act of law—upon some pretext or other, they would vacate the executive department of the United States."

With reference to the pardoning power he said:

"I reckon I have pardoned more men, turned more men loose, and set them at liberty that were imprisoned, I imagine, than any other living man on God's habitable globe. I turned forty-seven thousand of our men loose who were engaged in the struggle, with the arms we captured with them, and who were then in prison. I turned them loose. Large numbers have applied for pardon and I have granted them pardon; yet there are some who condemn and hold me responsible for doing wrong. Yes, there are some who staid at home, who didn't go into the field, that can talk about others being traitorous and being treacherous. There are some who can talk about blood and vengeance and crime and everything to make treason odious, and all that, who never smelt gunpowder on either side. Yes, they can condemn others, and recommend hanging and torture and all that. If I have erred, I have erred on the side of mercy. Some of these croakers have dared to assume that they are better than the Saviour of men himself—a kind of over-religious—better than anybody else; and all wanting to do Deity's work, thinking He cannot do it as well as they can."

As to office-holders he said:

"Don't you see, my countrymen, it is a question of power; and being in power, as they are, their object is to perpetuate their power, since, when you talk about turning them out, oh, they talk about bread and butter. Yes, these men are the most perfect and complete bread and butter party that has ever appeared in this Government. When you make an effort or struggle to take the nipple out of their mouths, how they clamor. They have stayed at home here five or six years, held the offices, grown fat, and enjoyed all the emoluments of position; and now, when you talk of turning one of them out, oh, it is proscription; hence they come forward and propose, in Congress, to do what? To pass laws to prevent the Executive from turning anybody out. . . . How are these men to be got out? (Voice, "Kick'em out") —unless your executive can put them out, unless you can touch them through the President? Congress says he shall not turn them out, and they are trying to pass laws to prevent it being done. Well, let me say to you if you will stand by me in this action, if you will stand by me in trying to give the people a fair chance—soldiers and citizens—to participate in these offices, God being willing, I will kick them out. I will kick them out just as fast as I can. Let me say to you, in concluding, that what I have said I intended to say. I was provoked into this, and I care not for their menaces, the taunts and the jeers. I care not for threats. I do not intend to be bullied by my enemies nor overawed by my friends. But, God willing, with your help, I will veto their measures whenever any of them come to me."*

Turning homeward from St. Louis, the President, on reaching Indianapolis and attempting to address the citizens, was silenced by the mob. They yelled at him: "No; no; we want nothing to do with traitors." "Shut up." "We want to hear from Grant." The President held on, repeatedly requesting the privilege of being heard. But the crowd waxed more and more infuriated. They absolutely refused to hear a word. Guns were flourished. The President retired discomfited for once. A fight ensued in the streets. Pistol shots were fired and two men were wounded.

Thus ended the "swing around the circle." When Johnson reentered the White House, he was followed by a storm of hisses, hootings, guffaws and jeers from the hosts of Republican party partisans throughout the whole North. Had this been all, he might have bidden defiance to their rage and their ridicule. But his want of dignity, as he was made to appear, his insensibility to the decorum due to his high office, his

* McPh. Recon., pp. 136–140.

eagerness to exchange repartee with any opponent no matter how low, his slovenly modes of speech and his offences against good taste, unfairly blazoned as they were before the country, disgusted many persons who were half-inclined to his policy; made many of the judicious among his supporters hesitate and grow lukewarm; forced his warmest supporters to hang their heads for lack of apology; scattered abroad the ugliest scandals about his personal habits and irretrievably hurt his cause. Even the Democrats, while they had no alternative but to support his policy, came to recognize that he was not the man to lead their party, and the Southern whites, while they regarded with wonder their unexpected champion, gradually lost the fond hopes that his championship would mitigate their woes. Indeed, perhaps it is not too much to say, that if Andrew Johnson had kept himself within the doors of the Executive Mansion during this critical campaign, the result of the elections would have been the beginning of the triumph of his policy, General Grant would not have turned to the radicals, and he himself would have been elected President in 1868. And yet there was no small amount of injustice involved in this fatality. In the first place, as we have already intimated, the scenes, so derogatory to the personal dignity of the chief magistrate of the republic, were made to appear much grosser than they really were. There was always something imposing in the mere presence of Johnson which to some extent counter-balanced the undue familiarity, the lapses from good taste and decorum disfiguring his interviews with the populace. And his encounters with the multitude cannot correctly be called speeches; they were essentially colloquies, mere talks, conversations in undress. Nevertheless, they were mercilessly exposed in the columns of a hostile press with all their deformities intensified, as monstrous travesties of the stately, measured addresses of the great statesmen of the past; the strong, quiet, resolute personality of the speaker being transformed in the imagination of the reader into a loud, blaring, wildly-gesticulating figure of some frenzied, illiterate demagogue. Now, whatever may have been the faults of Johnson as a speaker, he was never noisy and gesticulated but seldom. Even that supreme threat so awful to the office-seeking population, that he would "kick the radicals out," was uttered, doubtless, in a low voice with no violent gesture. In the next place, these unlucky utterances, whatever else they show, show the sincerity of the man—his devotion to his cause and his indomitable determination to stand by it to the last. There seems to be something mean in sniffing about the want of dignity, the lack of drawing-room manners, even the grammar of a leader in a just cause. Andrew Johnson at Cleveland and St. Louis was the same man he was in Tennessee, where he won in old times many a triumph by just such colloquies with the crowd; the same man he was when, assailed by the Southern senators for his faithfulness to the Union, he gained such universal glorification in the North by modes of retort essentially of the same kind. If he had swung round the circle in the company of Jack Hamilton of Texas and "Parson" Brownlow, preaching the orthodox radical doctrine, his lack of dignity would have been attributed to his absorption in a great mission, his slips into bad taste to the refreshing earnestness of a primitive nature, and his want of grammar to a quaint American mode of speech. He might even have dropped into drink, as he was falsely accused of doing, and escaped censure, had his availability as a candidate been sufficiently conspicuous.

The truth of this remark could find no clearer illustration than in the convention of the "loyal Unionists" of the South:—otherwise called "The Jack Hamilton Convention"—which met at Philadelphia on the third of September in the historic hall that witnessed the signing of the Declaration of Independence. The municipal functionaries, who fled the approach of the President the week before, were now on hand with smiles of welcome. "Parson" Brownlow was the hero of the hour, and was received by the city with a perfect ovation. The border states—Missouri, Kentucky, Maryland, Delaware—together with West Virginia and the newly admitted Tennessee, were represented by delegations comparatively respectable and all opposed to negro suffrage. In these states the rebel whites, as they were called, were disfranchised, and as the men in power did not need the negro vote to maintain their supremacy, their instinctive antipathy to the race held full sway. On the other hand, the representatives from the excluded states, if representatives in any sense they can be called, whose constituents, outside of a small number of colored men capable of understanding the crisis, were really in the North, composed a motley band. Renegades from their states, their section, and their race; sojourners from the North; attaches of the army; petty federal office-holders expecting removal—mitigated here and there by a full-blown over-earnest fanatic and a few honest colored men kept in the background—their very existence as a party rested entirely on the hope of a grant of suffrage to the negro and of its withdrawal from the vast majority of the whites. Many of the most prominent and influential men of the Republican party attended as delegates from the North, but they took the singular course of separating themselves at the outset from the Southern delegates, so, as they said, to leave them "perfectly free in their proceedings," and held a convention by themselves. The Southern wing, presided over by Speed and guided by Hamilton and Brownlow, adopted a series of resolutions that stopped short of negro suffrage and thereby necessitated a third convention, held after the adjournment of the other two by the delegates of the excluded states, which appealed to Congress for the only boon that could keep them politically alive.

This September month was signalized by two more conventions. On the seventeenth there met at Cleveland a convention of soldiers and sailors who had served in the army and navy in the late War and were in favor of the resolutions adopted by the National Philadelphia Convention of the fourteenth of August, endorsing the administration. The call was signed by a formidable array of illustrious names—forty-eight major generals and fifty-six brigadier generals, it was counted, officers of renown such as Custer, McCook, Ewing, Dix, Steedman, Blair, Slocum, Sickles, Granger, McClernand, Couch, Averill, Franklin, Crittenden and Patrick. In addition to these, the administration organs openly claimed that the movement was approved by Grant, Sherman and Sheridan, without eliciting a denial from any of these heroes. Henry Ward Beecher wrote a strong letter in its favor. This convention of soldiers and sailors on the one side provoked the calling of a convention of soldiers and sailors on the other consisting mainly of men who had served as privates or non-commissioned officers, which met on the twenty-sixth. It was to be a demonstration that the rank and file were not represented in the officers' convention. Its leading spirit was the man who had originated the movement—Benjamin F. Butler. He called out the privates, marshalled them in caucuses, guided them in the selection of representatives, welcomed them at the place of meeting, wrote, reported and read their resolutions, and sent them home with his benediction. His present purpose, in which his whole nature was absorbed for the time being, was the impeachment and removal of the President, and, accordingly, the resolutions of his convention exhibited the utmost hostility to the whole course of the administration.

Even while these rival conventions were being held, the result of the campaign was distinctly foreshadowed by the elections in Vermont and Maine; and, in October, Pennsylvania, Ohio and Indiana settled the verdict beforehand.

In the interval between these state elections and the presidential, an incident took place of no great importance in itself and bearing a most innocent aspect, but subsequently magnified into sinister proportions. On the seventeenth of October, the President sent for General Grant and told him that, at the President's own suggestion, in order to give prestige to the mission to Mexico, the Cabinet had decided that the General of the army should accompany the United States minister, Lewis D. Campbell, about to depart in a war vessel to the country to which he was accredited. The situation there was a critical one. According to an arrangement entered into by the Emperor of the French with the United States in May, the French troops were to evacuate Mexico in three instalments—the first in November, 1866—leaving the Mexicans themselves to decide between the government of Maximilian and the government of Juarez. Our own government naturally sympathized with the Juarez Republic, to which in fact our minister was accredited, but it was feared that on the departure of the French troops serious disturbances would break out, necessitating the utmost caution and tact on the part of the envoys of the United States, and rendering it highly desirable that our government should assume as imposing an attitude as possible. Grant, though at first (so at least it seemed to the President) evincing satisfaction with the proposed arrangement, a few days afterwards declined peremptorily to receive the instructions the Secretary of State had drafted for his guidance, and with great urgency excused himself to the President from accepting a duty he claimed was "entirely out of his sphere," "for which he was not fitted," and "one, too, which can be much better performed by others." When the President found that the General was unalterable in his determination, he quietly acquiesced and appointed General Sherman on that officer's own suggestion. The mission amounted to little on account of the fact that the French troops, in partial breach of the Emperor's promise, did not depart until the spring; minister Campbell not being able to find Juarez at all. On this slight foundation was built up the story that the President conspired with the Secretary of State to banish Grant from the country and then to supersede him by the appointment of Sherman in his place or as Secretary of War in place of Stanton. At the date of this incident, as subsequent events clearly showed, the President had no more reason to distrust Grant than to distrust Sherman.*

Connected with this imaginary conspiracy was the affair of the Baltimore police commissioners—with which the President had but little to do and that little of the simplest and most inoffensive character. Un-

* Diary of William G. Moore, private secretary of President Johnson, among the papers of Andrew Johnson left with his daughter, Martha Patterson, recently deceased; extracts concerning the Mexico mission printed in *The Memphis Daily Appeal* of November 1, 1885. Gen. Grant's letter in McPh. Recon., p. 296. Gen. Sherman's Memoirs (4th ed., two vols. in one), Vol. 2, pp. 414 *et seq.* Sherman is "sure this whole movement was got up for the purpose of getting Grant away from Washington . . . because he was looming up as a candidate for President, and nobody understood the animus and purpose better than did Mr. Stanton." *Cf.* Mr. Boutwell's Article in *North Amer. Rev.* of December, 1885.

der the constitution of Maryland, adopted in 1864, disfranchising all citizens who participated in the rebellion, the political complexion of the registrars or inspectors at the polls in the city of Baltimore had a most decisive influence on the result of the election in both city and state—those officers having the power to determine what constituted participation in the rebellion, and what evidence established such participation. The police commissioners, who superintended the elections and possessed the power of selecting the election officers and binding them by instructions—at this period strong radicals—issued instructions to the election officers on the interpretation to be put on the proscriptive clauses of the constitution; and certain citizens preferred charges against them of misconduct in office, for which the law provided they could be removed by the legislature, or by the governor when the legislature was not in session. Governor Swann (the legislature not being in session) heard the defendants on the point of his want of power to act in this case (the only point they consented to present), and shortly before the election decreed their removal and appointed their successors. The incumbents refusing to surrender and the newly appointed officers calling upon the sheriff to put them in possession, these latter were arrested on the charge of conspiracy in pursuance of a warrant of a United States judge. On the first of November the President directed the Secretary of War to take measures for the protection of the capital and to call General Grant's attention to the state of affairs in Baltimore. Recruits under way from New York to Texas were detained at

Fort McHenry; and this is all that appears to have been done in the premises. The election passed off quietly under the auspices of the radical inspectors. The action of Governor Swann was afterwards sustained by the courts and the militant commissioners were ejected without trouble. This small tempest, also, was subsequently magnified into an attempt of the President to usurp control of the capital in the absence of the General of the army.*

At the November elections the regular Republicans carried every Northern state by largely increased majorities over the year before. The majority in the House of Representatives, however, remained nearly the same—the Republicans numbering one hundred and forty-three to the Democrats forty-nine in a House of one hundred and ninety-two members. The result in the Southern states wore a different aspect. Those border states in which the whites were not disfranchised —Delaware and Kentucky—were Democratic by large majorities, while the result in Maryland clearly foreshadowed what must happen in West Virginia and Missouri—states like Maryland where the so-called rebels were not allowed to vote—as soon as the normal condition of the constituencies was restored. In those of the still excluded Southern states where elections were held at all—North Carolina, Arkansas and Texas—the majorities for the President's policy were overwhelming.

* Col. Moore's Diary, extract in *Memphis Appeal* as in last note. McPh. Recon., p. 297. See letter of Grant to H. R. on removal of Stanton, pub. as Ex. Doc., No. 57, 40th Cong., 2d Sess., at p. 63 *et seq.* Grant's Testimony, Imp. Inv., p. 838 *et seq.*

And this was the very quarter of the political horizon where the Republican pilots descried portents of peril. No matter how thorough the victory in the North, an irrepressible and most formidable minority would still remain. Once allow the incorrigible white men of the South to swing their states at one and the same instant into the Union and into the Democratic party, and the defeat of a political organization having no substantial following in the South could not be far off.

THE IMPEACHMENT AND TRIAL

OF

PRESIDENT JOHNSON

CHAPTER I

Preparations for Impeachment

The Congressional majority came back to their seats for the short session flushed with triumph and bent on vengeance. They meant to strip the President of the prerogatives and functions of his office, as far as they could do so by statute, and, if he struggled against the process of emasculation, as they had every reason to believe he would, to impeach and remove him out of the way. No other department of the government should be suffered to interfere with the execution of the plan of reconstructing the South with the negro on top and the white man on the bottom, which the legislative had at length determined to adopt. Should the judicial stand in the way, as it seemed it might do from the decisions just handed down by the Supreme Court in the Milligan, Cummings and Garland cases, then so much the worse for the judicial department. They would block up the path to its sanctuary by denying to all parties aggrieved the right of appeal.

They would minimize, if not altogether destroy, its tutelary function over the Constitution by exacting a two-third vote or even unanimity of the judges in every decision involving the validity of an act of Congress.* Should the President, disregarding the recent popular rebuke, persist in his obstructive course, they would admit the territories of Colorado and Nebraska, add four judges to the High Court of Impeachment, and proceed to his official decapitation.

The first bill passed by the House on the first day of the session repealed a section of the act of 1862 which authorized the President to proclaim amnesty to persons who had participated in the rebellion; with the avowed object of trenching upon the prerogative of pardon and the unavowed intent of depriving the President of a plausible answer to one of the grounds of impeachment; his abuse of the pardoning power. The bill became a law without the signature of the President, who entirely ignored it when he issued his proclamation of universal amnesty. Indeed, Andrew Johnson's extraordinary clemency, in view of his threatenings at the time of his accession; his failure to make treason odious, as he promised so often to do, by the punishment of even a single traitor; had caused a growing dissatisfaction among the more bloodthirsty radicals for a year past, filling their minds with all sorts of sinister suspicions; and was now at last denounced as a crime. There was Jefferson Davis, captured as far

* For exacting unanimity, see *Globe*, 2d Sess. 39th Cong., p. 616. Debate, *Globe*, 2d Sess. 40th Cong., p. 478 *et seq.* Bill requiring two-thirds passed House, p. 489.

back as May eleventh, 1865, and imprisoned in Fort Monroe. He was under indictment for treason. Why was he not tried? He was charged with complicity in the assassination of Lincoln, and $100,000 reward had been offered and paid for his capture on that charge. The military commission that condemned the accused assassins actually before it, found him guilty as a co-conspirator, in his absence. Why was he not hung? As to the indictment, the real causes of delay were the refusal of the Chief Justice to hold court in Virginia while the military held even partial control of the state, mistrust of a Virginia jury, and the desire to avoid the opening of embarrassing constitutional questions which the defendant's counsel were sure to raise on the trial. The President was in no way responsible for the tardiness of the prosecution; on the contrary, he, probably, was the only member of the administration having no misgivings as to its success. As to the charge of complicity, the real cause of delay in pressing it was that the testimony on which it was based—taken in secret before the military commission—in its subject-matter was of the most flimsy and inconclusive character, was incompetent under the most elementary rules of evidence and came from the mouths of professional witnesses testifying under pay.* But these reasons were unknown or unsatisfactory to those radicals who were careless how or on what charge Davis was tried or by what testimony he was proved guilty, so long as he was convicted; and chief among these was George

* Testimony in Imp. Inv., Seward, pp. 379, 380, 381; Stanton, 397; Speed, 798–802.

S. Boutwell of Massachusetts. At the last session (April 9, 1866) he it was who offered (and the House adopted) a resolution instructing the judiciary committee of which he was a member, to inquire whether there was probable cause to believe in the guilt of the persons charged in the proclamation with inciting the murder of Lincoln and the attempted assassination of Seward; and, during the remainder of the session, from time to time he, with one or two kindred spirits on the committee, employed himself in examining the captured rebel archives and the records of the Bureau of Military Justice and in listening to the stories of the professional witnesses of the military commission and others of the like kidney, in the hope to connect the distinguished prisoner of war by some semblance of a link with the murder of his great antagonist. Joseph Holt—the Judge-Advocate-General of the army—the employer and patron of Sanford Conover, that head-centre of professional witnesses—was his main reliance in this work. He furnished the committee, first, with the copy of his spy's testimony given before the military commission, and, second, the depositions of seven persons brought by Conover to Holt's office in the fall of 1865 and sworn to statements involving the complicity of Davis, Thompson, Clay and others in the assassination; among the rest two men calling themselves Campbell and Snevel who testified that they were present, with John H. Surratt, at an interview with Davis and Benjamin, in the early spring of 1865, at Richmond, when the plot to assassinate Lincoln was discussed and approved. The committee despatched an officer to New York to find Conover and his affiants, who succeeded in seeing Conover, Campbell and Snevel and in bringing Campbell back with him. He reported to the committee that Campbell confessed to him that his deposition was fabricated by Conover, and the committee thereupon telegraphed for Conover to come to Washington. Conover suspecting nothing came; and on the eighth day of May, 1866, the master and his tool were confronted with each other in the rooms of the committee. Campbell was sworn and testified that his deposition was false in every particular; that his real name was Joseph A. Hoare; that the deposition was written out for him by Conover and he committed it to memory; and that the other deponents had given false names and were likewise the creatures of Conover. In his turn, Conover swore that Campbell's present testimony was false and that he himself had no reason to doubt the truth of the depositions. He was allowed to go to New York with the sergeant-at-arms to find the other witnesses, but on his arrival in that city he escaped from the custody of the officer and vanished. Snevel was found and, appearing before the committee (May 24), testified that his real name was Roberts and that, like Campbell's, his deposition also was fabricated by Conover. These self-confessed scoundrels were both paid by the Bureau of Military Justice—Campbell receiving $625, and Snevel $475.

Even such astounding revelations as these failed to convince Mr. Boutwell of the hopelessness of his quest; and, a rumour circulating about this time that Jefferson Davis was to be admitted to bail, he hurried a resolution through the House (June 11) to the effect that Davis, being notoriously guilty of treason and also charged with complicity in the assassination of Abraham Lincoln, should be held in custody until tried; and, in consequence, Davis was still kept in prison. On the eighteenth of June, Holt reappeared before the committee affecting great astonishment at the break-down of his witnesses. He gave a full account of his intercourse with Conover and protested his implicit trust in the latter's statements. He remarked of the witnesses that he "conferred freely with them before and while examining them; that they appeared to possess ordinary intelligence and certainly assumed perfect self-possession and frankness of manner and seemed to be, so far as I could judge, under no improper influence; and there was nothing either in the testimony they gave . . . or in their manner while deposing calculated in any degree to excite doubt as to their truthfulness." Nevertheless, the Judge-Advocate condescended to confess that the retractions of Campbell and Snevel, followed by Conover's escape, disappearance and subsequent non-communication with Holt himself, "left on my (Holt's) mind a strong impression that Conover had been guilty of a most atrocious crime, committed under what promptings I am wholly unable to determine." At this stage of the proceedings, the committee, having accumulated a voluminous mass of documents on which after all it could come to no conclusion, turned all the papers over to Mr. Boutwell for him to prepare a report, which, on the last day but one of the session, he presented to the House, together with two resolutions which were adopted; the first declaring that there was "no defect or insufficiency in the law to prevent or interfere with the trial of Jefferson Davis for the crime of treason or any other crime"; the second, "that it is the duty of the executive department of the Government to proceed with the investigation of the facts connected with the assassination of the late President, Abraham Lincoln, without unnecessary delay, that Jefferson Davis and others named in the proclamation of President Johnson of May 2, 1865, may be put upon trial and properly punished, if guilty, or relieved from the charges against them if found to be innocent."

The evidence chiefly relied on by the report to sustain the charge of complicity with Booth consisted of certain wild projects to blow up the capitol at Washington and to dispose of leading officers of the United States, sent at various times to the President of the Confederacy and referred by him in the usual course of business to the appropriate department; together with testimony of inhumanity to prisoners and of expeditions sent against the North of a character forbidden by the laws of war; this evidence, wholly irrelevant on its face, being adduced, as the report states, to "bar the plea, which otherwise, perhaps, might with force and reason be tendered, that Davis and his associates named were incapable of the great crime of assassination." The depositions, furnishing as they did the only direct evidence of the crime under investigation yet so fatally discredited, Mr. Boutwell still clung to with desperate clutch. Speaking of the two villains who swore before the committee that their depositions were fabricated, he writes: "They failed, however, to state to the committee any inducement or consideration which seemed a reasonable explanation for the course they had pursued. And the committee are not at this time able to say . . . whether the original statements of these witnesses are true or false." The report was printed, as well as one by the minority of the committee (A. J. Rogers); and the publicity thus given to the investigation, besides calling out Judge Holt in a "Vindication" with exculpatory letters from Mr. Boutwell and Stanton, had one beneficial result. On an affidavit of Hoare, *alias* Campbell, a warrant was issued for Conover, and in November, he was arrested and brought to Washington, confessing on the way to the officer that he had suborned the witnesses produced before the bureau and the committee, actuated solely by "a desire to avenge himself on Jeff. Davis by whose order he had been confined in Castle Thunder" and who had "also insulted his wife." In the following February (1867), he was tried for perjury committed in his testimony contradicting Campbell, was convicted and, in April, sentenced to imprisonment in the Albany Penitentiary for ten years. For the present we leave him in the jail of the District of Columbia awaiting transportation to that institution.*

Still, though the committee could come to no conclusion on the complicity of Davis, Mr. Boutwell found

* Boutwell's and Roger's Reports (No. 104, 39th Cong., 1st Sess.), Imp. Inv., Greeley's testimony, p. 779. Holt's "Vindication" in public prints.

enough to feed a suspicion of the complicity of Johnson. Among the discoveries he made was the unaccountable neglect of the proper authorities to procure the arrest and extradition of John H. Surratt, the son of the woman who was condemned to death by the military commission that tried the alleged assassins of Lincoln. The young man was an associate of Booth's, and it was the still prevalent belief that he was present in Washington on the night of the tragedy, had taken some active though as yet unidentified part in the conspiracy and had escaped in the early morning by a train moving North. Detectives sent on the instant tracked him through St. Albans in Vermont to Canada, where they lost trace. Nothing was heard from the fugitive until the October following (1865) when tidings came from the American consul at Liverpool that Surratt, having crossed the ocean in a steamer from Quebec, was at that moment in Liverpool;—tidings shortly after corroborated by the American consul in Canada. From both these quarters came the written statement of the man who had betrayed the fugitive that Surratt had confessed to him that he was implicated in the assassination. The only notice taken by the administration of these communications was (October 13) to notify the consul at Liverpool that upon consultation with the Secretary of War and Judge-Advocate-General it was thought advisable that no action be taken in regard to the arrest; to request the Attorney-General (November 13) to procure an indictment against Surratt with a view to his surrender; and the issuance of an order from the War Department (November 24) revoking the reward of $50,000 offered (April 20, 1865) for his arrest. Meanwhile, Surratt traveled unmolested from Liverpool to London, and from London to Paris, and from Paris to Rome, reaching this last city some time in November; and, although the Secretary of State was informed by the authorities that announced his presence in Liverpool that it was to Rome he was bound, no notice was sent to our minister there to look out for him. It was not until the latter part of the following April (1866) that the apparent apathy of the heads of the administration on this delicate matter was disturbed by another communication from abroad. An old acquaintance of Surratt's betrayed the latter's presence as a soldier in the Papal Zouaves at a place about fifty miles from Rome, to Rufus King, the American minister at the capital; accompanying the information, in this instance also, with the statement that the confiding murderer had acknowledged his own guilt, and, going still further this time, had declared the guilt of his own mother and the complicity of Jefferson Davis. King made haste to send this startling news to the State Department at Washington; and, here again, appeared the same indifference—the only result being the expression of an ardent desire on the part of Judge-Advocate Holt to secure from King's informant a full, verified statement of the particulars of Surratt's confession. This was at last obtained, but, although the man was very anxious to return home and affected to be in fear of his life because of his revelations, the verified statement turned out to be vague and indefinite at the most critical points.

Such was the situation of affairs at the end of the session. Mr. Boutwell went home to Massachusetts troubled with dark surmisings—perplexed, however, that the evidence, in so far as it made against the President, should implicate the victim of Payne and the masterful Secretary of War. He kept a watchful eye on the mystery; and, before the beginning of the next session, his vigilance was rewarded. Cardinal Antonelli, the prime minister of the Pope, signified to minister King on the seventh of August, that, on a request from the United States in so extraordinary a case, he had no doubt Surratt would be delivered up; and this intimation was instantly despatched to Seward. Yet nothing was done—Seward was away "swinging round the circle" with the President and, on the return of the discomfited train, fell ill. The sole advantage taken of the cardinal's friendly overture was to send a photograph of Surratt to Italy, which, as Mr. Boutwell discovered, was one taken years before and, so far from leading to identification, more likely to contribute to the discharge of the accused. Finally, just before the meeting of Congress, the news came that the Papal government, in its zeal to oblige the United States not even waiting for the long-delayed request, had ordered the arrest of Surratt (November 8); then, that Surratt had broken from his captors, plunged down a precipitous declivity, effected his escape into the territory of Naples and thence taken ship to Alexandria by way of Malta.

Such culpable negligence on the part of the executive, followed by so unlucky a slip in the diligent efforts of others upon whom no such imperious obligation rested, filled the cup of Mr. Boutwell's indignation to the brim; at the Saturday-night caucus preceding the opening of the second session, he gave vent to his suspicions; and, on the Monday following, submitted a resolution to the House calling for the correspondence, which was adopted. News arriving at the War Department (Sunday night) that Surratt had been caught after all at Alexandria and would be forwarded to the United States in a government vessel, the President was able to send to the House the news of the capture of the fugitive. On the twenty-first of December, Surratt was lodged on board the "Swatara," well-loaded with irons. The vessel bore her burden across the ocean and in February the administration had a white elephant on its hands. Mr. Boutwell, apparently not at all disconcerted, pursued his investigations: summoned the Secretary of State, the Secretary of War and the Judge-Advocate-General before the judiciary committee, and, in the last hours of the session, made a report coming to the rather feeble conclusion: That the testimony of these distinguished officials did not "excuse the great delay in even attempting to arrest a person charged with complicity in the assassination of the late President; and, while the Committee do not charge improper motives upon the officers of the government, they are constrained to report that, in their opinion, due diligence in the arrest of Surratt was not exercised by the executive department of the government."*

* Boutwell's Report with testimony and correspondence, Cong. Docs. *Globe*, 2d Sess. 39th Cong., pp. 5, 12, 1753-4.

The object of this investigation lies on the surface. Obviously, the movement could not have been directed against either Seward or Stanton. Andrew Johnson was the man aimed at, and the inference that it was designed should be drawn from the negligence of the executive department was, that Johnson not only did not desire but actually feared the arrest of Surratt; because in some mysterious way Surratt was an accomplice of Johnson as well as of Booth. Such a suspicion seems too monstrous for any sane man to entertain. The military commission found as a fact that Vice-President Johnson was an intended victim of the wide-branched plot, and condemned a poor wretch for lying in wait to murder him. Nevertheless, General Butler convinced himself, or allowed others to believe that he was convinced, that Johnson was privy to the assassination of Lincoln. Ashley, at this very time, openly proclaimed his belief in the truth of the incredible accusation. And Mr. Boutwell, brooding over trunks-full of rebel archives, wild stories of double spies, cipher correspondences, traitors' pardons, revocations of rewards, winkings at escapes, Jefferson Davis's long impunity, even if he did not entertain the suspicion himself, furnished the material which clothed the shapeless spectre in flesh and blood. And the curious part of the matter is that in the first steps he took he was on the right track. The truth was that the President was *not* anxious for Surratt's apprehension; not anxious for the same intelligible reason that Seward and Stanton were not—Stanton least of all. The days of military commissions were over, at least in the capital; and, with the evidence that sufficed to condemn the mother before such a tribunal, they shrank from facing a jury on the trial of the son.

The foregoing recital derives its historical interest only from the fact that the investigation was designed as a make-weight to the projected impeachment. Indeed, it is manifest that the early proceedings of both Houses were regulated and marshalled with an eye to this ultimate remedy. The annual message showed no sign of yielding to what the majority thought the logic of events nor the slightest indication that the President, however much disappointed, felt the result of the elections as a condemnation of his policy or a personal rebuke. He wrote:

> "If the admission of loyal members to seats in the respective Houses of Congress was wise and expedient a year ago, it is no less wise and expedient now. If this anomalous condition is right now—if, in the exact condition of these States at the present time, it is lawful to exclude them from representation, I do not see that the question will be changed by the efflux of time. Ten years hence, if these States remain as they are, the right of representation will be no stronger, the right of exclusion will be no weaker. . . .
>
> "I know of no measure more imperatively demanded by every consideration of national interest, sound policy and equal justice, than the admission of loyal members from the now unrepresented States. This would consummate the work of restoration, and exert a most salutary influence in the re-establishment of peace, harmony and fraternal feeling. . . . "*

* Message in McPherson, p. 143.

These words, although they may be considered words of wisdom at the present day, fell upon deaf ears; serving only to sharpen the animosity felt by the leaders of the Congress against the President and to strengthen their determination to get rid of him. Probably, a majority of the Republican members of the House at this date were in favor of his impeachment. They thought the cup of his offences already full and running over. The bill fixing the meeting of every Congress immediately at the close of the preceding one, passed by the House as early as the tenth of December and by the Senate a month later, shows that it was thought necessary to have the impeaching body always on the watch. Schenck of Ohio advocated its passage on the ground that had it been the law on the fourth day of March, 1865, there would have been no difficulty over reconstruction; the South would have accepted gladly any terms Congress might have offered them; adding: "Nay, if one were permitted to speculate upon the possibilities of the past, it is not at all certain but the then Vice President, . . . considering the exhibition made by him on the fourth of March, would have been so dealt with by Congress, after its assembling, that we would not have been troubled with any consideration of the questions now before us."*

The veto of the bill granting manhood suffrage to the negroes of the District of Columbia added fuel to the flame. This measure—regarded by the radicals as the forerunner of the establishment of negro suffrage throughout the country—passed the House at the last

* *Globe*, 39th Cong., 2d Sess., p. 31.

session, but "went over" in the Senate in view of the coming election, as Wilson confessed "by the assent of its most earnest friends in the full conviction that . . . the growth of public sentiment . . . would enable us to carry a clean bill early in this session." It was now revived and passed both Houses before the holiday recess. Sumner, in closing the debate in the Senate, said:

"If it were regarded simply in its bearings on the District it would be difficult to exaggerate its value; but when it is regarded as an example to the whole country under the sanction of Congress its value is infinite. It is in the latter character that it becomes a pillar of fire to illumine the footsteps of millions. Now, to my mind nothing is clearer than the absolute necessity of the suffrage for all colored persons in the disorganized States. It will not be enough if you give it to those who read and write: you will not in this way acquire the voting force which you need there for the protection of Unionists, whether white or black. You will not secure the new allies which are essential to the national cause. As you once needed the muskets of the colored men, so now you need their votes; and you must act now with little reference to theory. You are bound by the necessity of the case."*

To veto such a measure was regarded by the advocates of negro suffrage as hardly less than an act of sacrilege; and one or two statements in the message were not calculated to soothe their resentment.

"It may also be urged," the President significantly wrote, "that the dominant party in each House may, by the expul-

* *Globe*, 2d Sess. 39th Cong., p. 107.

sion of a sufficient number of members, or by exclusion from representation of a requisite number of States, reduce the minority to less than one-third. Congress, by these means, might be enabled to pass a law, the objections of the President to the contrary notwithstanding, which would render impotent the other two departments of the Government, and make inoperative the wholesome and restraining power which it was intended by the framers of the Constitution should be exerted by them. This would be a practical concentration of all power in the Congress of the United States—this, in the language of the author of the Declaration of Independence, would be precisely the definition of despotic Government."

The closing paragraph follows:

"After full deliberation upon this measure, I cannot bring myself to approve it, even upon local considerations, nor yet as the beginning of an experiment on a higher scale. I yield to no one in attachment to that rule of general suffrage which distinguishes our policy as a nation. But there is a limit, wisely observed hitherto, which makes the ballot a privilege and a trust, and which requires of some classes a time suitable for probation and preparation. To give it indiscriminately to a new class, wholly unprepared by previous habits and opportunities to perform the trust which it demands, is to degrade it and finally destroy its power; for it may be safely assumed that no political truth is better established than that such indiscriminate and all-embracing extension of popular suffrage must end at last in its destruction."*

* Message in McPherson, pp. 154, 158–9.

The Senate listened, at least, to the reading of the message, and, after a short debate in tone respectful to the President, passed the bill over the veto. The House, for its part, did not wait to hear it; it was enough that they knew it was coming. Indeed, every veto was regarded by the majority of the House as a defiant insult flung in their faces; as an act of the rankest usurpation; and many of them actually came to consider a veto an impeachable offence of itself. Their antics over these blows from the tenant of the White House recall the Jacobins of the French Revolution breathing out curses against Monsieur Veto. Before the message reached the House, Loan, a bitter radical from Missouri, submitted a resolution declaring it "the imperative duty of the Thirty-Ninth Congress to take without delay such action as will accomplish the following objects:

"1. The impeachment of the officer now exercising the functions pertaining to the office of President of the United States and his removal from said office upon conviction of the high crimes and misdemeanors of which he is manifestly and notoriously guilty.

"2. To provide for the faithful and efficient administration of the executive department."

A point of order carried this resolution to the joint committee, and then Ashley of Ohio knew that his hour had come. Rising, as he solemnly said, "to perform a painful but, nevertheless, to me an imperative duty," he impeached "Andrew Johnson, Vice President and acting President of the United States, of high crimes and misdemeanors."

> "I charge him with a usurpation of power and violation of law;
>
> "In that he has corruptly used the appointing power;
>
> "In that he has corruptly used the pardoning power;
>
> "In that he has corruptly used the veto power;
>
> "In that he has corruptly disposed of public property of the United States;
>
> "In that he has corruptly interfered in elections, and committed acts which, in contemplation of the Constitution, are high crimes and misdemeanors."

And, therefore, he submitted a resolution authorizing the committee on the judiciary "to inquire into the official conduct of Andrew Johnson, Vice President of the United States, discharging the powers and duties of the office of President of the United States," and report whether he "has been guilty of acts which are designed or calculated to overthrow, subvert or corrupt the Government of the United States or any department or office thereof." This resolution was adopted, and the next day the House passed the District Suffrage bill over the veto without a word.*

In order to show the character of the man who now posed as the Atlas of the Impeachment, we are compelled to touch once again the notorious Conover whom we left in the jail of the district, lying under a conviction of perjury.† Both before and after his trial he set about obtaining a pardon on the extraordinary ground that in committing his perjuries and subornations of perjury he was but the tool of high-placed government

* *Globe,* 2d Sess. 39th Cong., pp. 319–321.

† *Supra,* p. 142.

officials, who, being threatened with public exposure, to save themselves threw him over, set on foot his prosecution and procured his conviction. Andrew J. Rogers, the Democratic member of the committee investigating Jefferson Davis's complicity, became convinced that this was the true view of the case, and, believing, as he said, Conover "less guilty than others, or at least one other" (no doubt Holt), wrote a letter to the President recommending his pardon, in which four leading Democratic representatives, on the faith of Rogers's minority report and his statement in the letter, concurred. At the very time he was burrowing his way to executive clemency by betraying his employers and posing as their castaway accomplice, Conover was opening up another channel of approach by preparing a bait for their rabid appetite for testimony against the executive whose clemency he was invoking. He managed by means of his wife—he was now passing under the name of Charles A. Dunham—to spread abroad a rumour that he could furnish damnatory evidence against Andrew Johnson. Such a rumour was enough of itself to set the enemies of the President wild and to secure the detention of the convict in a place where he was easily within reach. Distinguished visitors crowded his receptions in the jail, among whom was Ashley, the self-appointed scavenger to the judiciary committee searching high and low for material to feed the delusion under which he was labouring. Dunham and his wife assured this pioneer of the Impeachment that they could lay their hands on certain letters written by Andrew Johnson to Jefferson Davis and to J. Wilkes Booth implicating the President beyond peradventure in the assassination of his predecessor. Notwithstanding the notoriety of the criminal with whom he was dealing, Ashley showed no hesitation in taking his word; and we shall soon find him actively employed with Holt in attempting, from their side of the line, to filch from the President a pardon of the perjured witness they meant to use to prove him an accomplice of assassins. In the meantime, and until Conover could obtain his pardon, Ashley fell back upon LaFayette C. Baker, the late chief of the Detective Bureau, whom the President dismissed from office for his insolence in the case of Mrs. Cobb—a pardon-broker who haunted the precincts of the White House in the fall of 1865. He, too, was eager to rekindle his declining notoriety, and Ashley bore him in triumph to the committee, there to unfold his wondrous tale, as follows: In the fall of 1865, a man from Nashville by the name of Adamson, who was prowling around Washington in search of an office or a job, showed him a letter written by Andrew Johnson, while Military Governor of Tennessee, to Jefferson Davis—which letter a colored servant of a son of Parson Brownlow had purloined from Johnson's desk before it was sent. Baker had carried the letter to the White House and, showing the signature only to the President's private secretary, ascertained its genuineness, and afterwards returned the letter to Adamson who, as Baker with the most engaging candour admitted, wanted to sell it to the best advantage. This letter Baker read several times, and he now gave to the committee from memory a vague version of its contents. It was a reply to a letter from the Confederate President or some one high in authority, and after disclosing the position of the Federal forces in Tennessee, suggested a certain line of policy, on the adoption of which by the Confederacy, the writer "would turn the whole power he possessed in Tennessee over to the rebel cause"—"he was going with them." Other persons had seen this letter—three members of Congress, for instance, and one Matchett; and Baker was confident, if employed for that purpose, he could produce it as well as other letters which Adamson said he had also. The committee, after listening to Baker's version of the Cobb case, in which he besmirched the President to his heart's content, dismissed him to hunt up the letters in the existence of which Ashley for one professed to believe.* Beside this star-witness, the labours of the committee consisted in hearing one or two subordinates of the State Department describe the practice there in making appointments and removals; in hearing a witness tell of a Tennessee railroad which, having been taken possession of and partly built by Governor Johnson, was turned over to the corporation that owned it before the war by order of President Johnson; and in hearing the provisional governors of Alabama and Mississippi reveal the qualifications of the test-oaths they took, the restoration of captured cotton in their states and the opposition of the President to the fourteenth amendment. Up to the admission of Nebraska, an event to the narration of which we are about to

* Imp. Inv., Testimony of Baker, pp. 2 *et seq.*

turn, the investigation seemed to lag. After that date, the proceedings became somewhat brisker, but the testimony was fragmentary and taken in the most desultory way. We come upon bits of evidence concerning New York Custom House frauds, negotiations with the senators-elect of Colorado; campaign intrigues; removals from office for political reasons; the New Orleans riot; even a transaction by which it was sought to prove the military governor of Tennessee contrived to make ten thousand dollars; but as yet these were mere hints and led to nothing definite.* Nevertheless, the majority of the committee did not scruple to report in the last hours of the Congress "that sufficient testimony had been brought to its notice to justify and demand the further prosecution of the investigation." The solitary Democrat on the committee, in a minority report, found that "there is not one particle of evidence to sustain any of the charges"; "that the case is wholly without a particle of evidence upon which impeachment could be founded"; "the case is entirely void of proof"; statements in which any candid reader of the testimony will now concur. The majority in the House, however, were determined to keep the proceeding on foot; and, although disappointment was expressed by the more fiery spirits that the removal of the usurper could not have been accomplished during the current session, yet, in view of the great work done in the enactment of measures of pressing importance, the leaders were content to pass the "crowning labor" over to a Congress coming fresh from the people,

* Imp. Inv., testimony *passim*.

whose members, they had taken care to provide, would appear on the instant their predecessors dispersed.*

While the House was thus engaged in holding the grand inquest, the Senate was engaged in making ready for the trial. Some of the men who were to be judges of the High Court resorted again to the same methods of reinforcing the majority which came to naught at the last session. Early in December, Wade reintroduced the bill for the admission of Nebraska which failed before to become a law owing to the adjournment of Congress and the withholding of his signature by the President, and, instead of calling up the Colorado bill now lying on the table under a veto, introduced a fresh bill for her admission. There was the less excuse for the adoption of this transparent device to add four senators to the majority, because the Republicans were stronger than ever in the Senate. Scovel, that interesting rover who at a critical moment held back the New Jersey senate from joining in the election of a successor to the evicted Stockton, having been reconverted, as he himself pretended, by the New Orleans riot, the legislature (called together by the governor) elected a sound Republican to fill Stockton's place, Alexander G. Cattell. Wright died on the first day of November, 1866, and the governor immediately appointed another sound Republican, Frederick T. Frelinghuysen, to fill the vacancy; so that, at the opening of the session of Congress, New Jersey having regained her equal suffrage, the twenty-six states allowed to put in an appearance were represented by

* *Globe*, 2d Sess. 39th Cong., pp. 1754–5.

thirty-eight senators of the dominant party and by only fourteen supporters of the administration, of whom but nine were Democrats proper. With three to spare over the necessary two-thirds, it would seem these honourable men might have shown the meagre forces of their opponents a slight glimpse of magnanimity. But such radicals as Wade who had charge of these measures could put no trust in that cautious type of statesmen who cherished an old-fashioned regard for the superior sanctity of constitutional limitations as against the passionate desires of the current reformer. They could not forget how such eminent Republican senators as Fessenden and Trumbull and Grimes had failed them before, and they feared that in the last desperate wrench they might fail them again. On the fourteenth of December, when Wade moved his new Nebraska bill, Hendricks inquired why the Colorado bill which had passed both Houses and been vetoed by the President was not first taken up and disposed of. Wade explained that at the last session he did not think he had the numbers to pass it over the veto; but, at this session, he did not intend "to take up the veto message at all because new light has come before our eyes showing the propriety of the admission of Colorado, so that the President on the presentation of a new bill will be glad to let it pass without his veto. I have no doubt of it."* This strange and, viewed in the light of subsequent events, incredible statement was accepted in silence; but the hardy senator from Ohio had more trouble with Sumner

* *Globe*, 2d Sess. 39th Cong., pp. 122, 124.

who prided himself on the minute precision of his consistency. It is to his tireless hostility to the word "white" in the franchise provision of the constitutions of the proposed states that we owe the exposure of the utter lack of merits of both measures from the lips of one of the radicals themselves; and he now renewed his antagonism with redoubled vigour. Wade, who was as anxious for negro suffrage as the senator from Massachusetts, was greatly annoyed, and pointed to Sumner's vote in favour of the fourteenth amendment and the admission of Tennessee, "that now has her representation on the floor equally divided between rebellion and loyalty" (as the senator expressed it, with little regard for the feelings of Patterson). He wanted Nebraska in for a certain purpose, and he regarded an objection that the Constitution denied suffrage to the fifty negroes of the population as trivial and captious. "I hope," he said, "that we shall not on this mere technicality coldly turn away a territory comprised of patriotic men. . . . These men, let me tell gentlemen around me, believe just as you do; they are ready to aid and assist you in carrying out your great principles. . . . On their admission they will add power to your arm to enforce them."* But the appeal was useless. Sumner, after showing by the journal of the Senate that he voted not for but against the admission of Tennessee, loftily exclaimed: "In other days we all united in saying 'No more slave States!' I now insist upon another cry: 'No more States with the word white in their constitutions!' "† Brown of Mis-

* *Globe*, 2d Sess. 39th Cong., 127.

† *Id.*, p. 124.

souri—a radical of the Sumner type—offered a proviso that the act should not take effect except upon the fundamental condition that there should be no denial of the elective franchise on account of race or colour; a condition to which the people of the territory should declare their assent at an election. An identical proviso offered by Sumner last July got but five votes, and, offered again by him in the case of Tennessee, got but four (including, however, Wade's own); so insuperable was the objection then thought to be that Congress could not make a constitution for the people of a state. But Wade cared for nothing now but to avoid delay. He not only wanted the senators in but he wanted them in instantly. As he said:

> "The respectable, truth-loving gentlemen who have been sent here to represent that Territory as Senators on this floor . . . announce the fact that this Territory is up to the high-water mark on the subject of human rights. I want them here because I want this body strengthened immensely by the reinforcement that these gentlemen will bring to bear upon every question you can get up; and you stand cavilling here over a mere technicality."*

For some reason he was in great haste. He begrudged the time spent in eulogies upon the deceased senator, Wright. He tried to rescind the resolution providing for the usual holiday recess. Wilson proposed that the assent to the fundamental condition should be given by the legislature instead of the people, thus cutting off much of the delay so dreaded by Wade; and, in doing so, he gave notice that, although he had voted for both the

* *Globe*, 2d Sess. 39th Cong., pp. 147–163.

Nebraska and Colorado bills last session, he must now revert to the central principle he had violated to meet an emergency.

> "But, sir," he said, "by the course of events our power in the Senate is now assured, and after the fourth of March next will be quite as strong as it is now. I need not state, for we all know how our members have increased until now we have a clear, undoubted two-thirds vote here upon all the leading questions that may arise. . . . Satisfied to admit Colorado and Nebraska, always excepting that word 'white' that stained their constitutions, I gave voice and vote to their admission to secure for the holy cause for which we were struggling the control of the Senate. That control has been otherwise secured. The commanding necessity under which I then acted exists no longer. Then the admission of these young States in spite of the word 'white' seemed to me to be demanded by the needs of the periled country; now their admission with the word 'white,' it seems to me, is not demanded by the needs of the country."*

Wade tried to force a vote but Sumner, for the first time since he defeated the admission of Louisiana in Lincoln's time, resorted to filibustering, and the measure went over until after the holidays, when, Wilson's suggestion being rejected, the debate centred on the Brown proviso which Wade implored the Senate to vote down for the reason that it would kill the bill.

> "Now, Mr. President, why is it that I stand here the advocate of the admission of this State . . . when I have . . . been generally the advocate of equal rights, . . . ?

* *Globe,* 2d Sess. 39th Cong., p. 191.

It is because, when I consider the condition in which the country is, and when I look to the terrible struggle which is right ahead of us, I feel disposed to arm myself and be equipped with all the forces that are legitimately within my power. The Senator from Wisconsin said yesterday that he once voted for the admission of this State because he thought we wanted to be reinforced. . . . Sir, it was a good idea. Now, he says, however, that the clouds have passed by and all is fair weather, and there will be in the future no necessity for reinforcements."

Howe—"I said that we had got votes enough now."

Wade continuing:

"But how he could come to the conclusion that we shall not want any reinforcements I am unable to say. When he gave the vote to which he referred, had the Supreme Court of the United States made a decision which lets loose upon all the Union men of the South the bloodhounds of those rebellious unrestricted States, and denies the right of the military power to protect them? Did he know then that two of the departments of the Government . . . had turned in with the adversary and were ready now to abet his course?

"Suppose . . . there are enough in numbers; but yet you are in default. I want to reinforce you with some that will make no default; I want to bring you soldiers who will not shirk from any responsibility; and such are knocking at your door to-day. They are not of the limping sort who will leave your friends in peril. . . .

"Although I believe that, by a bold, determined performance of our duty, we have the remedy in our hands still; I want to make sure that, if the remedy must be here, we shall have force enough to look down all opposition. . . .

I will leave nothing to doubt that I can make certain in the emergency.''

''I will not sacrifice this republic to the ghost of a technicality.''*

This, certainly, was explicit enough in regard to the ''true inwardness'' of the measure. Nobody could doubt, after this, the exact position on the question of impeachment of the senator from Ohio. In the midst of his perplexities, Edmunds furnished him a way out. The senator from Vermont contended that the assent of the people of the coming state was not necessary to give validity to any fundamental condition Congress might exact, and the amendment he offered simply appended to the act of admission a ''fundamental and perpetual condition that there shall be no denial of suffrage by reason of race or color in the state of Nebraska''; involving, therefore, no delay in the seating of the two senators, while preserving intact the consistency of the negro-suffragists. It was true that many of the best lawyers in the Senate were of the opinion that the section amounted to nothing more than the expression of the wish of Congress and had not the binding force of a law. Wade undoubtedly thought so; but, seeing that without some such *placebo* the bill could not pass, at least over a veto, he snatched at the timely aid, and the amendment being adopted the bill passed by a vote of twenty-four yeas to fifteen nays. Instantly on its passage, Wade moved the consideration of his fresh Colorado bill. Edmunds moved the application of his specific, the motion was agreed to and the Senate passed

* *Globe*, 2d Sess. 39th Cong., pp. 335–6.

the bill by virtually the same vote. For neither bill did Fessenden or Trumbull vote, and among the nays in both cases were such Republicans as Foster, Grimes and Morgan. What in the case of any other man would have provoked great surprise, Sumner voted for both bills. If any single senator had demonstrated the gross practical demerits of these measures it was, as we have seen, the senator from Massachusetts. But these objections upon which he had rung the changes both in the last and the present session, it now appeared, were mere ciphers, employed only to increase the value of the one fixed aversion absorbing the senator's mind. The word "white" once nullified; this "ghost of a technicality," as Wade truly called it, once laid; such objections as the glaring insufficiency of the population, the rejection of the constitution at the regular election, and the violence, fraud and illegality of the second election, became immaterial, and Sumner could welcome the four votes from Nebraska and Colorado with all the alacrity of Wade.

At the close of the debate Doolittle remarked:

"The Senator from Ohio in the beginning of the discussion, and before the political necessities had pressed upon him as they have been pressing upon him of late, in an argument which he has not answered and which has not been and cannot be answered, showed conclusively that this Territory of Colorado was in no condition to be admitted as a State into the Union. But, sir, there are other reasons, pressing reasons, reasons of political necessity, he would have us understand. It is necessary to reinforce a majority of three-fourths in this body by the admission of new members from the new State of Colorado, and that is the reason why this is to be pressed."*

But what must have been Wade's mortification when the House refused to adopt the Edmunds specific! And what the sardonic astonishment of Sumner, when the body that had once approved the constitution which he denounced as not republican in form, turned upon him and denounced the condition, which induced him to vote for the bills, as a loophole through which all the excluded states might creep back into the Union with the word "white" still defiling their constitutions! Garfield sounded the alarm: "Suppose a bill offered to-morrow to let South Carolina in on the same condition!"† Dawes wanted to know whether a violation of the "condition-subsequent" would make Nebraska no longer a state.‡ Washburne sought to lay the bill on the table, remarking: "I want to kill it and to kill all such bills." Blaine struck the "condition" a fatal blow:

> "If gentlemen wish to admit Nebraska here without any condition at all, just as States have been admitted heretofore, leaving the question of suffrage to be settled by that State in its own legislature or constitutional convention, I can understand it. That is a fair, square and manly proposition. If, on the other hand, you mean to say that Nebraska shall be admitted on this condition, only, I can understand it. But to dodge between the two propositions, to say, upon one side, that this position effects the object, and then turn round and say to the other side that it does

* *Globe*, 2d Sess. 39th Cong., p. 362.

† *Id.*, p. 399.

‡ *Id.*

no harm because it is a mere *placebo* to certain prejudices here, I confess I think it disgraceful legislation."*

The truth is, a reaction had begun in the House against impeachment; and the high-handed proceedings of Wade, rendering it clear that he was packing the Senate for the trial, disgusted many members not lost to a saving sense of public decorum. These men seized the advantage which the ineffectuality of the Edmunds proviso gave them to out-Sumner Sumner in sedulity for the negro and so "kill the bills." But the tactics of the impeachers were too skillful. As a harmonizer of all differences between them and the negro-suffragists, Mr. Boutwell proposed to add "the further fundamental condition that the Legislature of said State, by a solemn public act, shall declare the assent of said State to said fundamental condition"; on receipt of a copy of which, the President shall forthwith announce the fact; "whereupon said fundamental condition shall be held as a part of the organic law of the State": and "the admission of the said State into the Union shall be considered as complete": the state legislature to be convened within thirty days. This proposition was accepted, the amendment was made, the bill was passed, and the same process was applied to the Colorado case.† The opponents of impeachment among the Republicans in the House were forced to content themselves with the trivial advantage of having postponed the admission of the senators until the next Congress. It should be noted that not a single Republican member took any thought, apparently,

* *Globe*, 2d Sess. 39th Cong., p. 449.

† *Id.*, pp. 480–2.

of the practical demerits of these two measures, flagrant on their face. Raymond alone called attention "to the many other questions entering into the decision beside the question of suffrage."

> "There is a great question, a question of paramount interest to me and to the State I in part represent, which I cannot help considering; the question whether it is just, and wise, and politic to allow the great States of the Union, such as New York, Pennsylvania and Ohio, the old, populous and powerful States, to be overborne, year after year, in one branch of the Legislature by States whose population is not sufficient to entitle them to a single member on this floor."*

And he likened "the creation of new States" to the English expedient of creating more peers. Even as it was, the two bills came near shipwreck in the Senate. Edmunds opposed concurrence with the House amendment in an argument unanswerable:

> "Either Congress has the power in setting up this Territory into a State to declare what shall be the practical exercise of equal rights there, or else it must be left to the people in the act of forming their constitution to decide. There is no middle ground. We might as well leave it to the common council of the city of Washington to decide how that shall be in the Territory of Nebraska, as to the Legislature."

The Brown proviso submitting the question to the people came within three votes of being adopted; when

* *Globe*, 2d Sess. 39th Cong., p. 478.

Wade and his more immediate allies by a united effort succeeded in obtaining a concurrence with the House.*

It will have been noticed that, of these twin measures, the Nebraska bill, at this session, was given the right of way, the debate centred exclusively upon it, and, after it was disposed of, Colorado followed in silence and very much as a matter of course. But the President, with the tact of an expert combatant, in sending both vetoes to the Senate, put the Colorado case, with its more flagrant vices, in the front; and, when his short but unanswerable message was read, "new light" had come, not indeed "showing the propriety of the admission of Colorado," but of sufficient power to discover the cause of Wade's mysterious timidity over this particular measure, though not to penetrate the secret recess where lurked his more mysterious hope of Presidential approval.

After alluding to his former veto still awaiting the consideration of the Senate, and remarking that he was "unable to perceive any reason for changing his opinion already communicated," the President declared that, on the contrary, he found many objections of which he had been before unaware, and that "while several of those he then assigned had gained in strength, yet others have been created by the altered character of the measure now submitted." These new objections he now proceeded to enumerate:

1. "The constitution under which this State government is proposed to be formed very properly contains a provision that all laws in force at the time of its adop-

* *Globe*, 2d Sess. 39tn Cong., pp. 484, 487.

tion and of the admission of the State into the Union shall continue as if the constitution had not been adopted. Among those laws is one absolutely prohibiting negroes and mulattoes from voting. . . . Yet in the bill now before me, by which it is proposed to admit the Territory as a State, it is provided that 'there shall be no denial of the elective franchise or any rights to any person by reason of race or color, excepting Indians not taxed.'"

2. The President incorporated in his message a copy of the protest of the House of Representatives of the territory against the passage of the law admitting the state, "without first having the question submitted to a vote of the people"; made, as it set forth, for the reasons: "first, that we have a right to a voice in the selection of the character of our government; second, that we have not a sufficient population to support the expenses of a State government."

3. A census of the population of the territory was being taken, and the returns already received from fifteen out of eighteen counties, showed a population of 24,909; which, with the three remaining counties estimated to contain 3,000, would make the total population 27,909: or not one fourth of the number required for a single congressional district in the states (127,000).

4. The fourth objection brought to the attention of the Congress a most suspicious variation in the wording of the "further fundamental condition" affixed to the Colorado bill from the wording of the corresponding condition affixed to the Nebraska bill. As proposed by Mr. Boutwell and added to the Nebraska bill, this condi-

tion required that the assent of the state to the guarantee of negro suffrage should be given by "the Legislature of said State," and directed "said State Legislature" to be convened by "the Territorial Governor" within "thirty days." In passing the Colorado bill, which followed immediately, the House and the Senate afterwards evidently presumed that the condition added in the one case was identical with that in the other. But it now appeared that the condition affixed to the Colorado bill had been surreptitiously altered, so that the assent of the state must be given by "the Legislature elected under said State Constitution," "the said State Legislature" to be convened within "sixty" days by the "Governor-elect." The President, speaking solely with reference to the text of the bill before him without comparing it with the text of the Nebraska bill, pointed out that these very alterations rendered the execution of the bill "almost impossible." The "governor-elect," to whom was given authority to convene the legislature, had "no more authority than a private citizen" until after the admission of the state, which could not take place until after the session of the legislature it was attempted to authorize him to call together. Furthermore, what constituted "the Legislature elected under said State Constitution," as contradistinguished from "the Legislature of said State"—the phrase used in the Nebraska bill? Was it the legislature elected at the time the constitution was claimed to have been adopted, or was it the new legislature to be elected? If the former, the terms of all the members of the lower House, and of one half of the members of the upper House, had already expired; and that body was in no condition to give the assent of the state to any fundamental condition. If the latter, sixty days was a time entirely inadequate, considering the unsettled and isolated condition of large portions of the territory especially from November to May, to hold an election and then convene the representatives of the people.*

Before such an array of objections well might even the lion-hearted Wade quail. He called for an immediate vote; but it was evident he had lost heart. Hendricks badgered him for an explanation of the variation in the phraseology of the proviso:

"The fact is communicated to the Senate by the veto message that one branch of the Legislature of Colorado has expressed views . . . hostile to this proceeding. I want to know if the vote upon this question is taken away from that Legislature because . . . it is hostile to this particular measure; and I think the Senator when the subject was up before should have called the attention of the Senate to the difference in the two bills. I know that when we voted I supposed the third section of each bill was in precisely the same language. Now, I ask the Senator from Ohio . . . to explain the difference and to give the Senate to understand why there is a difference in the two bills in this section."

Wade sat silent. He simply would not explain. After a pause Hendricks continued:

"As the Senator from Ohio declines to make any explanation we have a right to assume that there was some purpose in the matter, . . . that if this were submitted to the Legis-

*Message in *Globe*, 2d Sess. 39th Cong., p. 818. McPh. Recon., p. 160.

lature of Colorado in the same terms in which it was submitted to the Legislature of Nebraska it would probably be rejected. Then we have the spectacle before Congress of one bill submitted to one Legislature to secure a particular result and a similar bill under exactly the same circumstances submitted to another and a different Legislature in another Territory, for the purpose of securing a result which could not be secured if the submission was in the same language as in the other bill. I do not think, that being properly understood, the Senate of the United States would be a party to business of this sort."

The exposure of the trick was complete; and the reconsideration of the bill was quietly dropped.*

The veto message on the Nebraska bill was not taken up until the next morning. Wade did not want it read at all. "I do not know that anybody wants it to be read," he grumbled. "It takes up time and nobody listens to it." After it was read, he did not press its consideration. His hurry to push the matter appeared to be gone. For more than a week of the rapidly flying session, nothing was heard of it.† On the seventh of February, 1867, a telegram, read by Fowler announcing that "the battle was won" in Tennessee—the bill granting negro suffrage having passed the day before—seemed to arouse him from his apathy; for, at the close of the next day's session, by an arrangement with the minority he was able to crowd the bill through over the veto. He then made a tentative effort to call up the Colorado bill, but, on the Democrats protesting that such a move was not in the bond, he acquiesced without a

* *Globe*, 2d Sess. 39th Cong., p. 820.

† *Id.*, pp. 851-2.

word, and Colorado once more receded into the background.* It is hardly necessary to add that, the next day, the Nebraska bill passed the House over the veto amid applause from the floor and galleries, the Speaker ostentatiously directing the clerk to call his name; and, in less than the thirty days allowed by the statute for the assembling of the legislature, the full design of the act was accomplished; Nebraska ratified the fundamental condition; Nebraska was admitted into the Union; and, on the first day of the next Congress, the two senators from Nebraska—John M. Thayer and Thomas W. Tipton—men of approved and superabundant loyalty—were numbered among the already overwhelming majority;—thenceforth, *ex officio,* judges of the Court for the trial of Impeachments—sure to find the President guilty upon any charge the House might present.

Another move in anticipation of the impeachment, made at this juncture, deserves a passing notice. LaFayette S. Foster, the President *pro tempore* of the Senate, would cease to be a member of that body on the fourth day of the coming March. An excellent presiding officer and a man of conservative instincts, on certain critical occasions he had not come up to the standard of party loyalty, recoiling for instance from such barefaced maneuvres as the turning out of Stockton and the dragging in of Nebraska. His occupation of the place next in the line of succession was a source of uneasiness to those radicals who, looking forward to the removal of the President as a stern necessity, felt that a man of Foster's mildness and regard for the proprieties would

* *Globe,* 2d Sess. 39th Cong., p. 1096.

be no match for Johnson defending the crown of his ambition; and who were resolved that, once they accomplished a revolution in the palace, no second apostate should arise to balk their aims. From the beginning of the session, the question: Who was to be the next President of the Senate? had been agitating the minds of the Republican members of both Houses. Those radicals who favoured impeachment, as time went on and they witnessed his bold and unscrupulous conduct of the measures to reinforce the Senate, gradually united upon Benjamin F. Wade as the man for the crisis. Probably, no man less fitted for the duties of a presiding officer could be found in the Senate. He himself confessed: "You all know I am no parliamentarian."* But he was chosen for a purpose in comparison with which such duties were trivial. He was known to be brave and unflinching; and, if Andrew Johnson whom in the stubbornness of his pugnacity he resembled, should resist removal by force, they wanted a leader of undaunted mettle. Yet it was because of the very traits which endeared him to the revolutionist—his reckless boldness, his predisposition to violent methods, his tendency to dash headlong to his object over every impediment—that his accession to the chief magistracy was dreaded by the conservative statesmen and politicians of the party. Men of such temperament and troubled by such apprehensions turned to William Pitt Fessenden. The senator from Maine was a statesman rather than a politician. He was called a perfectly safe man. Dignified in bearing, cautious in judgment, experienced in public

* *Globe*, 2d Sess. 39th Cong., p. 2003.

affairs, familiar with the finances, he was a figure that would cut no grotesque capers in the seat of Lincoln. A strict party man, ready to go great lengths with his political associates; yet, as he had repeatedly shown, there were limits he would not transgress. He would not knowingly put by the restraints of the Constitution, no matter how obstructive they were to the success of some favourite party project. If the emergency of the removal from office of the President proved unavoidable, then the succession of so fair-minded a man and so safe a statesman would reduce the inevitable shock to the whole framework of the government to a minimum. But these timid friends of order and law were now to learn that summary methods of reaching party ends, short-cuts across the open instead of plodding along the beaten roads of administrative government—remedies cutting asunder at one stroke the knot, in fumbling to untie which formal statesmanship lets the supreme hour go by—were to be the order of the day. To Stevens and Boutwell and Howard, the presence of the punctilious Fessenden on the joint committee on reconstruction during the last session had been a source of constant irritation. His conservatism, they believed, leavened the whole body and tainted the constitutional amendment. Sumner thought he was not sound on the negro suffrage question, because he favoured an educational qualification. He even insisted on treating the President with respect. If the foundations of the executive department were to be broken up, at all risks no such martinet should emerge as the futile birth of the cataclysm; but a leader rejoicing in the hurricane and at home in the storm. As the end of the session drew near it becoming evident that none but a radical of the ultra type could succeed, the friends of Fessenden abandoned the field; and at the senatorial caucus Wade was selected without opposition.

Bearing this state of affairs in mind, the reader will be prepared to appreciate to what lengths this chosen champion of the impeachers was now ready to venture. The fourth of March of this year came on Monday; and the last week of the session was unusually crowded with business. The two Houses were waiting for the vetoes of the Tenure-of-office and Reconstruction bills, and employed the anxious interval in bringing up the arrears of indispensable legislation which the importance of these two measures had forced them to neglect. At a little before midnight, on Thursday the twenty-eighth of February, the Senate being engaged by express arrangement on the Internal Revenue bill—Wade, suddenly and without a word of previous notice, moved to postpone all other business and take up the Colorado bill with the veto message. Fessenden protested on account of the pressing nature of the bill under discussion. Hendricks suggested that Wade's object must be merely to set a future day for a vote. But Wade bluntly informed him he expected to get a vote that night. "I do not know that I can succeed; but I shall try it." Hendricks proposed that, without debate, a vote be taken at half past twelve to-morrow; senator Riddle was ill with rheumatism, he said, and could not come out at night; senator Grimes was ill also. But Wade refused to assent; and when asked why? responded:

"It is because I think I am better prepared to-night than I shall be to-morrow to decide this question. I want to be frank and plain about it. I think that that is the case."

The fact was a caucus had been held on this measure* and it was ascertained that Fessenden, Harris and Morgan would not submit, and, therefore, in a full Senate, Wade despaired of overriding the veto. Now, at midnight, was his final opportunity. With Grimes and Harris and Riddle absent, he might succeed. He meant to take full advantage, as he said on another occasion, of the dispensations of Almighty God. But, at this point, Doolittle arose and uttered a few words of expostulation:

"Mr. President. I think the proposition which has been made . . . is a proposition which has never before been declined in the Senate of the United States, never. . . . Now, here, at half past eleven o'clock—almost midnight—right in the midst of the business of the Senate upon an important measure, . . . to have pressed upon us by surprise a motion to postpone a bill like this, and take up Colorado for a vote to-night, is beyond anything I could ever have anticipated. Sir, we are not without being observed. The world stands looking on. The people of the United States know what is transpiring in this body; and there are peculiar reasons which connect themselves with the Senator from Ohio, which will draw some attention to him, and to the course he is pursuing on this occasion. We all know, time and again, that Senator, in pressing this matter of Colorado, has said over and over that his purpose was to reinforce a majority in this body, already more than two thirds. And for what, sir?"

*** See *Globe,* 1st Sess. 40th Cong., p. 497.**

Wade hastily interrupted, remarking that "many of his friends here" did not agree with him, but thought the proposition of the other side reasonable and he therefore acquiesced. He had thrown his last die and lost. The next morning (March first), the question was put whether this bill shall pass, the objections of the President notwithstanding. There were yeas 29, nays 19, not voting 4; Edmunds, Fessenden, Foster, Grimes, Harris and Morgan, all strict Republicans, voting no.* The two-thirds majority was broken. The bill was lost. The high-water mark of impeachment had been reached. At half past ten o'clock on the morning of Monday, March the fourth, 1867, Foster arose and bade farewell to the Senate; and Wade was thereupon elected President *pro tem.* It is a bitter commentary on the vaunted disinterestedness of the advanced patriots of this period, that, had they had their way; had their own selected leader succeeded in forcing a vote at that midnight hour, letting in the two senators from Colorado, as he had let in the two senators from Nebraska;—then in all human probability, Andrew Johnson would have been convicted and removed from office, and Benjamin F. Wade made President in his stead.

* *Globe,* 2d Sess. 39th Cong., pp. 1922, 1928.

CHAPTER II

The Tenure-of-Office and Reconstruction Acts

While these preparations for impeachment were going on, the two-fold task the majority had imposed upon themselves at the beginning of the session—the stripping the executive of its prerogatives and the subjugation of the South to the Republican party—was not lost sight of. The Tenure-of-office bill and the Reconstruction bill—the two main measures necessary to its accomplishment—proceeded steadily step by step and side by side. About nothing were the Republicans so sensitive as the security of their office-holders. The host of offices that had sprung up during the war were considered the inalienable assets of the party, to disturb the tenure of which was nothing less than a violation of vested rights. Of all the sins of the President, none was so unpardonable as his removal from office of tried Republican politicians to give place to supporters of his policy. What exasperated the radicals more than anything else in the late campaign was the increasing frequency of such removals; and the threat of Johnson on his western tour "to kick them out" rankled in their breasts more deeply than all his other utterances. At the last session, an amendment to the Post Office appropriation bill cutting off the pay of appointees not eventually confirmed by the Senate was agreed to, then reconsidered and disagreed to. The amendment was directed against what was a real abuse, the practice of holding back appointments to the last moment and, after adjournment, reappointing officers not confirmed, or even rejected, by the Senate. At the stage of the combat we have now reached, such timid methods were worse than useless. The attack must be made in front and along the whole line. Upon other questions—impeachment, reconstruction, negro suffrage—there may have been at times a lack of unanimity, but upon the rigourous necessity of depriving the President of the power to turn their partisans out of office the Republicans were a unit.

That the powers of appointment and removal belong to the executive department of a government maintaining the three-fold division is clear enough as a theoretical proposition. But the Constitution of the United States does, in fact, expressly qualify the power of appointment by requiring the advice and consent of the Senate to the filling of the higher offices, and, also, by granting to the Congress the power to vest by law the power of appointment to the inferior offices in the heads of the departments and the courts of law as well as in the President alone. These provisions may be regarded as infringements on the theoretical scope of the power by itself, but they leave the power of removal wholly intact. No word is expressed tending to curtail this branch of the prerogative; and the only point on which to hang an argument is that, the power of removal being correlative with the power of appointment, the restrictions expressly put upon the one must by implication be put upon the other. And, in fact, it was this argument that constituted the entire stock of the advocates of the Tenure-of-office bill. Formidable embarrassments, it is true, hung about its employment. The precise question arose in the very first Congress, was thoroughly discussed, and was decided adversely to the views of the assailants of the prerogative; and that decision had been recognized by the judicial department of the government as an authoritative construction of the constitutional provisions involved, and, although sometimes questioned, had been followed by every President of the United States. Indeed, the power of removal by the President alone for no other reason than difference of political opinion was asserted by President Lincoln by a more sweeping change in the persons of office-holders than had ever taken place before in the history of the country. Embarrassments such as these, however, could not check the leaders of the dominant party, believing as they did that its very existence was involved in overcoming them.

As Williams of Pennsylvania put it in the House:

"If you would impeach successfully, you must strip him of his power over the fortunes of the citizen. No glittering bauble must be allowed to dazzle the vision, or tempt the cupidity of or ambition of either the prosecutor or the judge. No army of stipendiaries must be allowed to surround his person and depend upon his will. Invested with all these imperial prerogatives and backed by the power of the sword, another President, with more discretion and wiser counselors, may threaten the public peace, and threaten it more successfully, by flinging himself into the arena, with an array more formidable than either the

Household Swiss or the incipient Prætorian guard who lately mustered on the royal summons, and disputing with you the mastery of the empire."*

The joint committee on retrenchment, having been directed at the last session to inquire into the whole matter, in December of the present session reported a bill, the first section of which required the consent of the Senate to the removal of all officers to whose appointment the Constitution required the consent of the Senate, excepting officers of the Cabinet. This exception, it is worth while to notice, was sustained by the House at this early date (by a slim vote, however) and a substitute that Cabinet officers should hold "for and during the term of the President appointing them" unless sooner removed with the consent of the Senate, was defeated by the close vote of yeas 77 to nays 81; showing that the leaders of the House had not yet united upon the necessity of protecting any particular member of the present Cabinet.† The second section gave the President power during the recess of the Senate to suspend any civil officer within the purview of the first section for misconduct or because of disqualification or incapacity, and to designate some person to perform the duties of the office; but, within twenty days after the meeting of the Senate, the President must report such suspension and the reasons therefor to the Senate; if the Senate concur, the President may remove such officer and with the consent of the Senate appoint another; if the Senate refuse to concur, the suspended officer shall

* *Globe*, 2d Sess. 39th Cong., p. 22.

† *Id.*, pp. 73, 94.

forthwith resume his office. The third section provided that the President may fill vacancies happening during the recess "by reason of death, resignation, expiration of term or other lawful cause" by granting commissions to expire at the end of the next session; if no complete appointment was made by the end of the session then the office shall remain in abeyance.

This bill was not taken up for consideration by the Senate until the tenth day of January, 1867; when, the reason why Cabinet officers were excepted from the operation of the first section being demanded, Edmunds, who had charge of the bill, answered:

> "It did seem to the Committee, after a great deal of consultation and reflection, that it was right and just that the Chief Executive of the nation" should have "persons personally agreeable to him" as his "confidential advisers"; "in whom he could place entire confidence and reliance"; "and that whenever it should seem to him that the state of relations between him and any of them had become so as to render this relation of confidence and trust and personal esteem inharmonious," "he should in such case be allowed to dispense with the services of that officer."

This explanation was unsatisfactory to Howe of Wisconsin, who went so far as to deny that the heads of the departments were the confidential advisers of the President. "The Cabinet was not the President's Cabinet; it is the Cabinet of the people," he said. Disagreement with the President on political questions, this future member of the Cabinet of President Arthur thought a virtue in a cabinet-minister and a reason why he should be kept in office. The senator was profuse in asseverations that he had "not the slightest reference to the person of the present incumbent" of the Presidential office; that this measure was no piece of occasional legislation but for all time. Not a senator came forward to sustain him, and his motion to strike out the exception was negatived without a division.*

In considering the third section, the practice of making appointments during recess to fill vacancies created by removals and, then, either not sending the name of the appointees to the Senate at all, or, if sent and the appointees not confirmed, reappointing the same men after the close of the session, was condemned on all sides, and, though supported by the examples of successive Presidents and the opinions of successive Attorney-Generals, acknowledged to be at war with the spirit of the Constitution. But the opposition senators claimed that the section in providing that where an appointment during recess was not made complete by confirmation during the session, the office must remain unfilled, went too far and trenched upon the power of the President to fill "all vacancies that may happen during the recess." The advocates of the bill replied that the "vacancies" mentioned in this clause of the Constitution were only those *happening* in that sense of the word "implying contingency, chance, uncertainty," and not brought about by the arbitrary act of the President; further, in no sense could a vacancy be said to "happen" during recess which already existed during the previous session. Their opponents, however, showed

* *Globe*, 2d Sess. 39th Cong., pp. 382–9.

that this construction was contrary to the uniform usage of the government; the clause having been held by the law officers to mean "happen to exist" and not "happen to occur."

The contest over the constitutionality of the provision of the first section requiring the concurrence of the Senate to removals by the President was not begun until the fourteenth, when Williams of Oregon assumed the burden of the affirmative. That a legislative construction adverse to the bill was put upon the Constitution in this respect by the first Congress, he did not dispute but strove to belittle its effect. He cited from the Federalist the opinion of Hamilton: "The consent of that body (the Senate) would be necessary to displace as well as to appoint"; and, not denying that Madison was the sponsor of the contrary opinion, he asserted that Madison was by no means infallible—instancing the Virginia Resolutions of 1798 and the United States Bank. He claimed, also, that while the Supreme Court had made no direct decision, still its deliverances so far as they went tended to sustain the provision; citing the case of *Ex parte Hennen* (13 Peters), the celebrated case of *Marbury vs. Madison,* and the opinion of Justice McLean in *U. S. vs. Guthrie* (17 How.). It was a dangerous experiment, however, to cite authorities loosely when Reverdy Johnson was to reply. The senator from Maryland proved that Hamilton, too, was not infallible by showing that, after having been Secretary of the Treasury, he changed the opinion expressed in the Federalist. He showed that *Marbury vs. Madison* had no reference to the higher offices of the government, but to "inferior" offices over which Congress was given control and had exercised it. He showed that in both *Ex parte Hennen* and *U. S. vs. Guthrie,* the opinions cited not only did not bear out Williams's contention, but really militated against it; in the former case, Justice Thompson saying: "It was very early adopted as the practical construction of the Constitution that this power was vested in the President alone," and in the latter, Justice McLean saying: "this power of removal has been perhaps too long established to be now questioned."

But the most logical and exhaustive argument was delivered by Buckalew of Pennsylvania. He began by laying down the following fundamental proposition:

> "There are but two possible locations in this Government for the power of removal under the Constitution of the United States. . . . It must be vested in the President . . . alone who is the head of the executive department and charged with the execution of the laws, or it must be vested in the President by and with the advice and consent of the Senate upon the ground of implication from the Senate's association in the appointing power. . . . If the power be not vested in the President alone or in the President and Senate, it is located nowhere; it exists nowhere; and the argument in favor of the enactment of a law proposing to vest it anywhere else must be upon the ground that it is an ideal or latent power which may be created or called into active existence by virtue of those general powers of legislation which are vested in the Congress of the United States. But inasmuch as this is a government of granted and vested powers and inasmuch as the grants to Congress are specific, upon the very statement of the point itself the conclusion must be against it."

If the power of removal be in the President and Senate jointly neither can exercise it alone; and the bill is condemned in that "it proposes to allow the President a power of suspension to be exercised alone, and a separate power of removal of the officers of the Cabinet."

The senator gives a detailed history of the debate of the first Congress, with copious citations showing that the precise question involved in the present bill was thoroughly ventilated in every respect; and that the question was decided at the most auspicious moment in the life of the government, when no private or party questions could by any possibility have been affected. Mr. Madison is quoted as saying in the debate:

"In another point of view it is proper that this interpretation should now take place rather than at a time when the exigency of the case may require the exercise of the power of removal. At present the disposition of every gentleman is to seek the truth and abide by its guidance when it is discovered. I have reason to believe the same disposition prevails in the Senate. But will this be the case when some individual officer of high rank draws into question the capacity of the President, without the Senate, to effect his removal? If we leave the Constitution to take this course it can never be expounded until the President shall think it expedient to exercise the right of removal, if he supposes he has it; then the Senate may be induced to set up their pretensions. And will they decide so calmly as at this time, when no important officer in any of the great departments is appointed to influence their judgment? The imagination of no member here or of the Senate or of the President himself is heated or disturbed by faction. If ever a proper moment for decision should offer, it must be like the present." (Annals of Congress, vol. 1, p. 547.)

"These words of wisdom," remarked Buckalew, "exhibit in contrast the superior competency and fitness of the Congress of 1789, before parties were formed and personal interests in the tenure of office had come into existence, over the present Congress filled with heated partisans and subject to the influence of thousands of officers deeply interested in the subject of our debates." The senator read extracts from letters of Madison, written at the time the question was again agitated under Jackson, wherein Madison reiterated his old opinions. In one to John M. Patton (March, 1834), he said, with prophetic vision: "If the right of the Senate be, or be made, a constitutional one, it will enable that branch of the government to force on the executive department a continuance in office even of the Cabinet officers, notwithstanding a change from a personal and political harmony with the President, to a state of open hostility toward him."*

For some reason the debate languished. The advocates of the bill were greatly overmatched in argument by its opponents. The ablest debaters among the Republicans were silent. Sumner enlivened the discussion by offering an additional section providing that all officers now appointed by the President or by the head of any Department, whose compensation exceeds $1,000 per annum, shall be appointed by the President and the Senate; and that the terms of all officers appointed by the President or the heads of departments since July, 1866, shall expire on the last day of February, 1867. This was, indeed, what Edmunds called it, "a sweeping

* For debates see *Globe, id.*, pp. 407 *et seq.*, 438–40, 461–3.

proposition''; bringing under the protecting wing of the Senate a host of office-holders, not only, but retroacting on deserters from the party by snatching away the rewards of their treachery. Edmunds, nevertheless, opposed it, with great earnestness, as ''loading an important bill meant to settle a high principle with a mere matter of detail,'' and ''subjecting the friends of the measure to the imputation of their opponents that the purpose of the bill was merely temporary, directed against Andrew Johnson,'' ''to undo something the President had done.'' Treating the protests of Edmunds as though unuttered or uttered only in a diplomatic sense, Sumner out with the naked truth: This ''is a proposition which grows out of the exigency of the hour. The bill, on a larger scale, is just such a proposition; it grows out of the exigency of the hour; and that is its strength and merit. We shall pass it . . . in order to meet a crisis. We all feel its necessity. . . .''

''The President, for the time being at least, ought to be deprived of the extraordinary function which he has exercised. He has announced openly in a speech that he meant to 'kick out of office' the present incumbents.'' Therefore we owe them our protection. ''It belongs to the duty of the hour.''* The day but one after, he recurred to the subject: ''This, Sir, is the duty of the hour. . . . There was no such duty on our fathers; there was no such duty on our recent predecessors . . . ; because there was no President of the United States who had become an enemy to his country.''† Being called to

* *Globe*, 2d Sess. 39th Cong., pp. 468–9.

† *Id.*, p. 525.

order, he was sustained by the Chair and on appeal the Chair was sustained by the Senate. The next day, in vindication of freedom of speech in the Senate, he said:

> "Andrew Johnson . . . has become the successor of Jefferson Davis in the spirit by which he is governed and in the mischief he is inflicting on his country. . . . "
>
> "In holding up Andrew Johnson to judgment, I do not dwell on his open exposure of himself in a condition of beastly intoxication while he was taking his oath of office; nor do I dwell on the maudlin speeches by which he has degraded the country as it was never degraded before; nor do I hearken to any reports of pardons sold, or of personal corruption. . . . Those things are bad; very bad; but they might not, in the opinion of some senators, justify us on the present occasion."
>
> But "the President has usurped the powers of Congress on a colossal scale, and he has employed these usurped powers in fomenting the rebel spirit and awakening anew the dying fires of rebellion." "He has become a terror to the good and a support to the wicked." "This is his great and unpardonable offense. . . . He is an usurper, who, promising to be a Moses, has become a Pharaoh."
>
> "I shall not be led aside to consider the full remedy for this usurpation."

Reverdy Johnson gravely rebuked the indulgence in such epithets against the President by a senator at that particular juncture, when impeachment proceedings were pending in the House. "What sort of a trial, as far as that particular senator is concerned, would the President of the United States have should he be impeached for being an enemy to his country, for being a usurper . . . ? Suppose we all went on following the authority of the honorable member from Massachusetts, and expressed the same opinion; what would the world say?'"*

Sumner's section being voted down, Howe renewed his motion to strike out the exception of Cabinet officers; and he supported it by a consideration now for the first time openly broached. Quoting from the New York *Herald* a rumour that senator Cowan, to whom the President had tendered the appointment of minister to Austria, had been offered the portfolio of Secretary of War, he said: "If my amendment be adopted, then this portfolio will not operate at all to dissuade the gentleman alluded to from going to Austria." "I should prefer to see the present incumbent retained in the custody of that portfolio; and therefore I am not willing to leave the power in the hands of the President to take it from him without the consent of the Senate." Cowan denied the report with emphasis, and Conness of California, on behalf of the Secretary of War, rather resented the idea conveyed by Howe that that distinguished citizen needed any protection which might be afforded by the amendment. "I take it," he said, "that it is scarcely necessary to be said here, or necessary to be said anywhere, to those who know him or know his character, that he would be the last man to seek or wish protection to himself in that or in any other place." Howe, protesting that the Secretary of War "had no idea the amendment was to be offered," added: "I should think the Congress of the United States assumed a grave responsibility if, knowing that there was a probability of his being re-

* *Globe*, 2d Sess. 39th Cong., pp. 542–4.

moved, they allowed it to be done when they could prevent it.''* When the Senate came to a vote upon Howe's motion Stanton was left to the tender mercies of the President by a vote of yeas 13 (all regular Republicans) to nays 27 (of whom 16 were regular Republicans). During the course of the debate there had been added certain penal sections—making appointments and removals in violation of the act, the acceptance of any such appointments, and the disbursement of any money from the treasury to any person so appointed, ''high misdemeanors'' punishable by a fine not exceeding $10,000 or imprisonment not exceeding five years or both: evidently with an eye to the impeachment clause of the Constitution. With this addition, the bill now passed the Senate substantially in the shape it came from the committee.†

The House labouring at this time desperately over the reconstruction measures, the Senate bill could not be taken up until the first of February. By that day a change had come over the minds of many of the majority leaders upon the question of the tenure of Cabinet officers. Since the twelfth of December, when the proposition to make his confidential advisers independent of the President was defeated in the House, many things had happened. The negro suffrage bill for the District had been vetoed. Rumours were abroad that since that veto trouble had arisen in the Cabinet where Stanton at last was showing his hand. Military rule over the unreconstructed South was seen to be coming and the great

* *Globe*, 2d Sess. 39th Cong., pp. 547–8.

† *Id.*, pp. 405, 550.

War-Minister must be fixed in his place. Accordingly, a motion was made to strike out the questionable exception, and a member who had voted against the motion before now openly supported it on the floor. On the first trial, indeed, the motion was lost by almost the same vote (76 to 78); but the leading Republicans were all now in the affirmative. The next day the motion was reconsidered, the exception was stricken out by a vote of 82 to 63; and with this single amendment the bill was passed.*

The new stand taken by the House forced a renewal of the contest in the Senate, where Edmunds moved to disagree and request a conference. Howe came forward as the champion of the House amendment, contending that the power of removal was not vested in the President at all but in the Court of Impeachment; and arraigning the first Congress for passing what he did not hesitate to call "a dishonest statute," "a cowardly and skulking statute." Reverdy Johnson predicted that, if the amendment passed, the first Congress after the next presidential election, if it contain a majority in each branch friendly to the President elected, will repeal it—a prophecy substantially fulfilled. But Sherman it was who opposed the amendment with the greatest vigour:

> "It is a question with me," he said, "not of constitutional law but a question of propriety." "Suppose that some Cabinet minister under the old Administration should hang on to his office. It is hardly a probable supposition, I admit, because I do not see how any gentleman could do it, or how any man could hold an office of that kind against

* *Globe*, 2d Sess. 39th Cong., pp. 937, 943–4, 970.

the will of his chief; yet if we adopt the amendment . . . we compel the President to retain in office . . . any man who has not courtesy enough to retire."

"I would as soon think of imposing upon the President a Private Secretary with whom he had no kindly relations, personal and political, as to impose upon him a Cabinet minister with whom his relations were not kind."

"Any gentleman fit to be a Cabinet minister, who receives an intimation from his chief that his longer continuance in that office is unpleasant to him, would necessarily resign. If he did not resign it would show he was unfit to be there. I cannot imagine a case where a Cabinet officer would hold on to his place in defiance and against the wishes of his chief; and if such a case should occur I certainly would not by any extraordinary or ordinary legislation protect him in that office."*

The Senate remained firm, refusing to concur by a vote of yeas 17, nays 28. The House, insisting upon its amendment, appointed its committee of conference (Schenck, Williams and Wilson): to which the Senate responded by the appointment of Williams, Sherman and Buckalew. On the evening of the eighteenth a report was made, signed by Williams and Sherman on the part of the Senate and all the conferees on the part of the House, by which the exception was stricken out, and a proviso substituted that Cabinet officers "shall hold their offices respectively for and during the term of the President by whom they may have been appointed, and for one month thereafter, subject to removal by and with the advice and consent of the Senate." The majority of the House in adopting the report evidently

* *Globe*, 2d Sess. 39th Cong., pp. 1039-40. 1043, 1046.

considered that they had gained a victory and congratulated themselves that their favourite minister was safe. Schenck, after stating the terms of the proviso, explained: "It is, in fact, an acceptance by the Senate of the position taken by the House."* Its language was scanned with no particular scrutiny and its precise significance passed unperceived. It was not so in the Senate. When first read, the report was considered an abandonment of the position of the Senate by its conferees whose concurrence aroused much indignation. Their explanation, however, cleared up the matter. Williams stated that the proviso left an incoming President free to select his own Cabinet and gave him a month to do it in, adding that he thought the question immaterial, for:

> "I have no doubt that any Cabinet minister who has a particle of self respect—and we can hardly suppose that any man would occupy so responsible a position without having that feeling—would decline to remain in the Cabinet after the President had signified to him that his presence was no longer needed. As a matter of course, the effect of the provision will amount to very little one way or the other; for I presume that whenever the President sees proper to rid himself of an offensive or disagreeable Cabinet minister, he will only have to signify that desire and the minister will retire."

Hendricks, on the other hand, took a different view:

> "A mean man getting into the Cabinet would say, if the President desired him to leave, 'Congress has said I may stay; therefore I will stay.' The very person who ought to be turned out is the very person who will stay in. A gentleman, of course, would not."

* *Globe*, 2d Sess. 39th Cong., p. 1340 House, p. 1514 Sen.

Sherman's remarks are especially noteworthy. He apologized to the Senate for agreeing to the report, saying that he had done so "with a good deal of reluctance," but, he plead, the House conferees were "very tenacious" and "the general purpose of the bill is so very important" that he thought "it ought not to be endangered by a dispute on a collateral question." He proceeded: "I think that no gentleman, no man with any sense of honor, would hold a position of Cabinet officer after his chief desired his removal, and therefore the slightest intimation on the part of the President would always secure the resignation of a Cabinet officer."

Doolittle struck the heart of the matter:

> "I desire to look into this most marvelous production of this committee of conference, which has utterly failed to accomplish the very thing which they design by the terms of the bill and the language which they use. I suppose it is aimed at the present head of the Executive Department, to bind him to keep certain members of his Cabinet, for it was openly avowed in the discussion of this bill when it was up before that it would be intolerable to allow the present Executive Magistrate to have the power of removal over certain members of the Cabinet mentioned by name. Now, this project does not reach those members at all."

He then read the proviso, and continued:

> "Now, let us look at the facts. The Secretary of War was appointed by Mr. Lincoln during his first term; he never has been appointed since. . . . Mr. Lincoln gave him no appointment during his second term, and he held over. Mr. Johnson has given him no appointment, but he has

held over. So of the Secretary of the Navy, and so of the Secretary of State. The Secretary of the Interior, to be sure, and the Postmaster-General and the Attorney-General have been appointed by Mr. Johnson since the presidential office devolved on him; and by the terms of this law the Secretary of the Interior, the Postmaster-General and the Attorney-General must remain during Mr. Johnson's term; but the Secretary of State, the Secretary of War, and the Secretary of the Navy, according to the terms of this provision, may be removed by him to-morrow."

Not a single senator questioned the correctness of this construction. Sherman denied with much heat that the conference committee had any such purpose as that attributed to it by Doolittle:

"I say that the Senate have not legislated with a view to any persons or to any President, and therefore he (Doolittle) commences by saying what is not true. We do not legislate in order to keep in the Secretary of War, the Secretary of the Navy or the Secretary of State."

Doolittle here interrupted, saying he heard in the debate "that it was not to be tolerated that the present Chief Magistrate should have the power to remove the Secretary of War, by name."

Sherman thereupon admitted that "some Senator may have had that purpose." But, he continued:

"That the Senate had no such purpose is shown by its vote twice to make the exception. That this provision does not apply to the present case is shown by the fact that its language is so framed as not to apply to the present President. The Senator shows that himself, and argues truly that it would not prevent the present President from removing the Secretary of War, the Secretary of the Navy and the Secretary of State. And if I supposed that either of these gentlemen was so wanting in manhood, in honor, as to hold his place after the politest intimation by the President of the United States that his services were no longer needed, I certainly, as a Senator, would consent to his removal at any time, and so would we all."

With this construction so unanimously put upon the proviso, the conference report was adopted (Monday, February 18), and the bill sent to the President.*

Two days afterwards followed in the same direction the other of the two main measures thought necessary, as we have said, to the accomplishment of the task undertaken by the majority. Not so intimately connected with the subject of this work as the Tenure-of-office act, the Reconstruction act, its provisions and the history of its passage call for but a brief exposition. On the sixth of February, the joint committee reported a bill which, after wiping out "the pretended state governments" of the ten still excluded states, divided these "so-called states" into five military districts—Virginia, the first; North and South Carolina, the second; Georgia, Alabama and Florida, the third; Mississippi and Arkansas, the fourth; and Louisiana and Texas, the fifth—each to be commanded by an officer of the Army, not below the rank of brigadier-general, with unlimited powers, and each to be assigned by the General of the Army. This bill, but not without a serious struggle, passed the House on the thirteenth. A substitute was adopted by the Senate differing from the original in these respects: I. The

* *Globe*, 2d Sess. 39th Cong., 1515–18.

governments of the ten states were styled "not legal" instead of "pretended." II. The President was to designate the military commanders, not the General of the Army. III. A section was added enumerating the successive steps required to be taken before any of the ten states could escape the yoke of military rule and regain their place in the Union, as follows: 1. The fourteenth amendment must have become a part of the Constitution of the United States. 2. A constitution for the state must be framed by a convention of delegates chosen by all the adult male citizens without distinction of colour, excepting those disfranchised for rebellion or felony; and this constitution must guarantee manhood suffrage to the negro but might disfranchise the white man for participation in rebellion. 3. The constitution must be submitted to the same class of voters for ratification. 4. If ratified by a majority it must be submitted to Congress for examination. 5. If approved by Congress, the state must then assent to the fourteenth amendment, with its section, in effect, making ineligible to all offices, state or federal, the leaders of the Southern people. 6. The senators and representatives from these states must be competent to take the "iron-clad" oath.

The majority being in favor of military rule, pure and simple, and opposed to pointing out as yet to "the pretended states" any way of escape, the House refused to concur; the Senate insisted upon its substitute and declined a conference. The whole measure being put in jeopardy by this disagreement, the House reluctantly accepted the mitigating section, adding two amendments, however, that made its conditions still more stringent, viz: 1. A proviso that "no person excluded from the privilege of holding office by the proposed fourteenth amendment shall be eligible as a member of the convention to frame a constitution for any of the rebel States, nor shall any such person vote for members of such convention." 2. An amendment declaring that any civil governments existing in the ten states until they are admitted into the Congress are provisional only, and liable to abolition, supersession or revision at any moment by the United States; but that, in the meantime, in all elections carried on under these governments no person should vote and no person should hold office except as provided in the present bill. The Senate finally agreed to the House amendments, thereby passing the bill.*

The House might not have concurred in the Senate amendment giving the President, instead of the General of the Army, power to designate the military commanders, had not that body incorporated into the army appropriation bill a section fixing the headquarters of the General of the Army at Washington and providing that all orders issued by the President relating to military operations must be issued through that officer; further, that "the General of the Army shall not be removed, suspended or relieved from command or assigned to duty elsewhere, without the previous approval of the Senate"; all orders contrary to this section were made void, the officer issuing them declared guilty of a misdemeanour, and any officer of the army transmitting them made subject to imprisonment. A more palpable viola-

* *Globe*, 2d Sess. 39th Cong., pp. 1037, 1215, 1459, 1469, 1340, 1570, 1399–1400, 1645.

tion of the Constitution could not be imagined. It was an attempt to make a subordinate independent of his superior officer, to circumscribe the powers of the officer expressly made commander-in-chief of the army by the Constitution, and actually to associate the Senate with that officer in the command of the army. And yet the section received the vote of every Republican senator present, Henderson excepted. The bill containing this attack on his prerogative reached the President at so late a date that he might have prevented its becoming a law by withholding his signature. But, rather than defeat the appropriations for the pay of the soldiers, he felt constrained to sign it, accompanying his signature, however, with a protest against the section "as depriving the President of his constitutional functions as Commander-in-Chief of the Army," and "out of place in an appropriation bill."*

When the Tenure-of-office bill reached the President, he laid it before his Cabinet, every member of which pronounced it unconstitutional; and none with more emphasis than the Secretary of War. The point being mooted, it was taken for granted, without dissent, that neither Stanton, nor any other member appointed by Lincoln, was within the bill. The President was so much struck by the full mastery of the constitutional

* Mr. Boutwell takes pride in claiming the honour of having drafted this section under the dictation of Stanton, as far back as the first of December, 1866, to circumvent some black design of the President which was troubling their patriotic imaginations. Art. by Boutwell in *North Amer. Rev.*, December, 1885; repeated in art. in *McClure's Mag.*, December, 1899. For history of section see *Globe*, 2d Sess. 39th Cong., pp. 1013, 1351–2, 1353–6, 1404 *House*, pp. 1851–5 *Senate*. Message in McPh. Recon., p. 178.

question displayed by Stanton that he requested the Secretary of War to prepare the veto message. That officer, pleading physical disability, declined to undergo the labour of writing, but declared his readiness to aid in the preparation of the paper. The message was in fact composed by Seward with the assistance of Stanton. It was a calm and thorough review of the proceedings and decision of the first Congress and of the series of precedents in all the departments of the government following that decision ever since; but it did not delay for a moment the passage of the bill over the veto.*

The Reconstruction bill, the President might have defeated by simply putting it in his pocket, but, contrary to the expectations of his enemies, he took no advantage of the opportunity, but sent his veto to the House at the same time he sent his veto of the Tenure bill to the Senate. On hearing the message read the House was in no humour to appreciate this magnanimous forbearance of its author. To the majority, in premises, in argument, in conclusion and in tone, it was nothing less than an impeachable offence. Every paragraph constituted a high misdemeanour. We owe to the Impeachment Trial the information that the veto message on the Tenure bill was written by Seward aided by Stanton. We owe to the Impeachment committee that extorted the item from the lips of the writer, the information that the veto message on the Reconstruction bill was first written by Jeremiah S. Black and then thoroughly revised by Andrew Johnson. Black was one of the profoundest

* President's Message to Senate on Stanton's suspension in Trial, Vol. 1, pp. 148, 150--1. Offer of testimony, *id.*, p. 676.

and at the same time one of the acutest lawyers of his generation; and, besides, he was one of the most brilliant advocates—brilliant before a jury and brilliant before the full bench. He had been a great judge as well as a great lawyer, and at a perilous crisis he showed his mettle as a statesman when Attorney-General and Secretary of State under President Buchanan. But, great as he was as a lawyer, judge and statesman, as a controversial writer he was greatest. In this field, his habit of driving home a proposition, ill-conceived and half-comprehended by the average man, by a seeming audacity in its statement became of marvellous service. The ease with which the clear-cut sentences grow out of each other and, finally, with an epigrammatic clinch culminate in what one rejoices over as an absolutely demonstrated truth, has the effect of humour. The completeness of his refutation of an opposing argument by a single wave of his pen has the effect of wit. Compassion over the decapitation of an adversary is swallowed up in admiration at the deftness of the stroke. His epithets are photographic. His sarcasms are syllogistic. His invectives carry with them the force of the intuitive reason. His logic is so severely perfect that it becomes rhetoric raised to the highest power. The Reconstruction bill, which could not but be regarded by Black as a double-headed monstrosity holding the unsheathed sword over the prostrate South with one hand and offering her the two-fold curse of negro enfranchisement and white disfranchisement with the other, was an object well-fitted to call out to the utmost the power of his unrivaled pen. But, as he testified before the committee, if the President had signed what he wrote, the message "would have been a much more objectionable document to the majority in Congress than it is"; "it is all toned down from much stronger expressions in the same direction into something considerably tamer."* So that we have not before us the pure product of that "most miraculous organ." We confess we should like to have seen the document before the toning down process began.

But the actual message is not what the reader would call tame. Here are one or two specimens:

> "The power thus given to the commanding officer over all the people of each district is that of an absolute monarch. His mere will is to take the place of law. . . . " "Being bound by no State law, and there being no other law to regulate the subject, he may make a criminal code of his own; he can make it as bloody as any recorded in History, or he can reserve the privilege of acting upon the impulse of his private passions in each case that arises. He is bound by no rules of evidence; there is indeed no provision by which he is authorized or required to take any evidence at all. Everything is a crime which he chooses to call so, and all persons are condemned whom he pronounces to be guilty. He is not bound to keep any record or make any report of his proceedings. He may arrest his victims wherever he finds them, without warrant, accusation, or proof of probable cause. If he gives them a trial before he inflicts the punishment, he gives it of his grace and mercy, not because he is commanded so to do."
>
> "Such a power has not been wielded by any monarch in England for more than five hundred years. In all that

* Imp. Inv., p. 271.

time no people who speak the English language have borne such servitude. It reduces the whole population of the ten States—all persons of every color, sex, and condition, and every stranger within their limits—to the most abject and degrading slavery. No master ever had a control so absolute over his slave as this bill gives to the military officers over both white and colored persons." "The head of a great empire has sometimes governed it with a mild and paternal sway; but the kindness of an irresponsible deputy never yields what the law does not extort from him. Between such a master and the people subjected to his domination there can be nothing but enmity; he punishes them if they resist his authority; and if they submit to it he hates them for their servility."

"Here is a bill of attainder against nine millions people at once. It is based upon an accusation so vague as to be scarcely intelligible, and found to be true upon no credible evidence. Not one of the nine millions was heard in his own defence. The representatives of the doomed parties were excluded from all participation in the trial. The conviction is to be followed by the most ignominious punishment ever inflicted on large masses of men. It disfranchises them by hundreds of thousands, and degrades them all—even those who are admitted to be guiltless—from the rank of freemen to the condition of slaves."

"The bill says to them, take martial law first, then deliberate. And when they have done all that this measure requires them to do, other conditions and contingencies, over which they have no control, yet remain to be fulfilled before they can be relieved from martial law. Another Congress must first approve the constitutions made in conformity with the will of this Congress, and must declare these States entitled to representation in both Houses. The whole question thus remains open and unsettled, and must again occupy the attention of Congress, and in the meantime the agitation which now prevails will continue to disturb all portions of the people."*

The House lost not a moment in passing the bill over the veto, and the Senate followed its example.

With the passage of this act the work of the Thirty-ninth Congress was done. Yet it seemed loth to die. It kept its eye on the President up to the moment when the eye of its successor took in the object of its watch. Its hand relaxed not from the reins until another hand caught them up. As minute by minute it faded from view, minute by minute the Fortieth Congress more and more distinctly appeared. The stroke of the gavel knelling the expiration of the one was echoed by the stroke of the gavel calling the other to order.

"The King is dead! Long live the King!"

Every change in the personnel of the new Congress was favourable to the radical wing. In the Senate, Cowan gave place to Cameron, thereby reducing the Johnson Republicans to four; the Democrats lost two senators (McDougall and Nesmith) reducing their number to seven, of whom but two came from states north of Mason's and Dixon's line (Buckalew and Hendricks). As for the regular Republicans, Conkling displaced the too cautious Harris; Ferry, the too conservative Foster; Drake, one of Missouri's fiercest radicals, Brown; Har-

* Message in McPh. Recon., p. 166 *et seq.*

lan, late of the Cabinet, came back; Morrill (of Vermont), who was in the last House, changed places with Poland, and Oliver P. Morton of Indiana succeeded Lane. The two senators of the new state of Nebraska—"men of the right sort" as Wade certified them to be—swelled the numbers of the majority to forty-two; there being one vacancy caused by the retirement of Cresswell of Maryland, this figure exceeded three-fourths of the present membership. In the House the changes were not so conspicuous. The same Republican leaders were there, but the Johnson *tertium quid* was about eliminated. One new face there was—a face, once seen, not to be forgotten. The broad forehead shelving up to the top of the bald crown, the fringe of thin hair encircling the lower head, the eyes asquint and half-hidden by pointed lids, the sharp nose with its nervous sniff, the spasmodic puffing out of the cheeks, the turned-down collar exposing the wide throat, and the right hand uplifted in the attitude of affirming without book;—these striking peculiarities betokened the presence of Benjamin F. Butler. His appearance on the floor meant business. Advocate, party-leader, warrior, apostle of an idea, representative; whatever part he essayed, he was at all times and above all the politician; and, though resembling the Mansfeldts of the Thirty Years' War in the number and suddenness of his changes of flag, for the time being he was the most devoted of partisans. Nothing gave him pause. He was radical by nature, in the etymological sense of the term. Radical in his Democracy, he supported Jefferson Davis rather than Douglas. Radical as a military commander, he solved the fugitive-slave problem by the word "contraband." Radical in his new-born Republicanism, he demanded the summary impeachment of Andrew Johnson, his suspension during trial and his speedy removal. For this cause alone, it may be said, he had joined the impeaching body; and, in the earnestness with which he pushed forward the prosecution, he was to contest the palm of leadership with Stevens, to oust Ashley from his self-chosen perch, and in the culminating scene become the protagonist of the drama. The people at large were growing sick of this threatened removal of their chief magistrate so long hanging over them. The finances of the country were being seriously affected; industry was partially paralyzed; there was a constant uneasiness in commercial circles as though revolution were imminent. The lame conclusion to which the committee of the last House had come strengthened the spreading belief that the whole movement was fatuous as well as futile. This state of feeling more or less influenced the new House, and many a member of the majority would have secretly rejoiced to hear that the wild scheme beginning to play havoc with the party had been dropped. Such men, however, were silent, for the most part, while the leaders of the movement were loud in their assertion of the necessity of getting rid of the renegade of the White House.

On the third day of the session, a resolution was introduced to continue the investigation during the session and the recess. Ashley, feeling the growing luke-warmness towards his cherished hobby, in his speech in support of the motion, more than insinuated that Johnson was privy to the assassination of his predecessor. "He came into the Presidency through the door of assassination," he said. He alluded to "the dark suspicion which crept over the minds of men as to his complicity in the assassination plot," and "the mysterious connection between death and treachery which this case presents." He called upon the people "to declare that no man hereafter elected President or Vice President shall present himself at his inauguration drunk; that no President shall be permitted to turn the White House into a den of thieves and pardon-brokers; nor shall he be permitted to address in vulgar, seditious language a drunken, howling mob from the steps of the Executive Mansion"; to protest against "another drunken electioneering tour, such as last year." "The Nation cried out in its agony to Congress to deliver them from the shame and disgrace the acting President has brought upon them. They demand that the loathing* incubus which has blotted our country's history with the foulest blot shall be removed." And he concluded by giving public notice to "citizens and foreigners" having any "documents or facts tending to show technically the guilt of this man" to bring them to the committee, warning such persons that by withholding their testimony they became "an accessory in the crime of this man," and "a co-partner in his guilt." He transcended the bounds of propriety so far as to elicit rebukes from his political associates on the floor and, finally, from the Speaker himself. So disgusted was one of his Republican colleagues that he denounced "the whole scheme of impeachment as one of consummate folly," asserting

* *Sic.*

that "not one act amounting to a crime or misdemeanor has as yet been proved against the Executive" and challenging any one to "reply to that averment." He said more. He charged that "it was not expected by some that proof will be obtained"; it is enough that the President is an "obstruction" and it is the duty of the party to remove him from office. This challenge, Butler instantly accepted, declaring that "an absolute majority of the whole House," when the final report is made, "will be in favor of the impeachment of Andrew Johnson"; that "common fame," "common report of misconduct," was sufficient proof in cases of impeachment; that "if any man stands in the way of the great march of this country to honor, glory, peace, unity, happiness, liberty and law," it was enough, "he must be taken out of the way." On a test vote to lay the resolution on the table, every Republican member voted in the negative but five, and they did not vote at all. And so the investigation was continued.*

The first session of the fortieth Congress lasted until the thirtieth of March, and its chief business was to supply an omission in that section of the reconstruction act which prescribed the process by which the excluded states could escape from military rule and regain their places in the Union. The process was prescribed, but how the process should be set in motion was nowhere indicated. Delegates to a constitutional convention were to be chosen by certain constituencies, but, as to what authority should call the convention and conduct the election, the section was silent. This omission, there is

* *Globe*, 1st Sess. 40th Cong., pp. 18–25.

no doubt, was intentional. It was the design of the framers of the section that the process outlined by its terms should not be forced on unwilling communities but held out to them as a boon to be accepted or not as they chose, and, in the absence of any statutory direction, the presumption would prevail that the machinery provided was to be started by the existing state authorities rather than by the military commanders. Moreover, many radicals in the last Congress, anticipating that the South would prefer even martial law to white disfranchisement and negro enfranchisement, favoured the omission because they were not yet ready for reconstruction on any basis. With Sumner, they wanted time. The majority in the new Congress, however, were resolved that something must be done towards the restoration of the Union without delay; and the greater part of the session was spent in concocting a supplementary bill directing the military commanders, before the first of September, 1867, to cause a registration to be made in each county of the states of their respective districts of persons qualified to vote under the act; after registration, to fix a day for the election of delegates to a constitutional convention; to appoint inspectors of election competent to take the test oath; and, after the constitution was framed, to hold an election for its ratification; and, if ratified, to send it to the Congress. The bill was passed (Tuesday, March 19) with a proviso that occasioned more discussion than the bill itself and was to the effect that, notwithstanding a majority of the votes cast were in favour of holding a convention, no convention should be held unless the majority of the registered voters voted at the election, either for or against; and that no constitution should be deemed ratified unless at least one-half of all the registered voters should have voted on the question.*

The interval of waiting for the inevitable veto was enlivened by an episode which has a distinct bearing on the impeachment proceedings. The House was in debate over a bill to aid destitute persons in the South without regard to their loyalty or disloyalty, which John A. Bingham was supporting with his customary enthusiasm; and, in so doing, inadvertently wandered over to the Democratic side of the Chamber, when Butler, who was opposed to the bill, made the remark that the gentleman from Ohio had "got over on the other side not only in body but in spirit." This pardonable hit stung Bingham (who, it should be borne in mind, had distinguished himself as the special assistant judge-advocate on the trial of the alleged assassins of President Lincoln) to the quick, and he charged rough-shod upon the General who, it will be remembered, had not taken Fort Fisher:

> "I desire to say that it does not become a gentleman who recorded his vote fifty times for Jefferson Davis, the arch-traitor in this rebellion, as his candidate for President of the United States, to undertake to damage this cause by attempting to cast an imputation either upon my integrity or my honor. I repel with scorn and contempt any utterance of that sort from any man, whether he be the hero of Fort Fisher not taken or of Fort Fisher taken."

* McPh. Recon., p. 192.

Butler's retort was admirable in tone and crushing in effect:

"I have never concealed, Mr. Speaker, the fact which is now so offensively put forward, that before the war, I, in the convention of my party, voted fifty-seven times for Jefferson Davis for President. I thought him the representative man of the South, and I hoped by his nomination to prevent threatened disunion. I was foiled and disunion came. The difference between me and the honorable gentleman from Ohio is this: while Jefferson Davis was in the Union, a Senator of the United States, and claiming to be a friend of the Union, I supported him; but he now supports him when he is a traitor. I left him as soon as he left the Union."

"The gentleman has had the bad taste to attack me for the reason that I could not do any more injury to the enemies of my country. I agree to that. I did all I could, the best I could. Other men of more ability could do more; and no man is more ready to give them the highest plaudits for valor and discretion and conduct than I. And because I could not do more I feel exceedingly chagrined; but if during the war the gentleman from Ohio did as much as I did in that direction I shall be glad to recognize that much done. But the only victim of that gentleman's prowess that I know of was an innocent woman hung upon the scaffold, one Mrs. Surratt. And I can sustain the memory of Fort Fisher if he and his present associates can sustain him in shedding the blood of a woman tried by a military commission and convicted without sufficient evidence in my judgment."

The suddenness of this blow stunned Bingham for a moment. He lost his self-possession; his habitual fluency deserted him so far that he found it necessary afterwards to revise his remarks for the record; an indulgence which gave Butler the opportunity, a few days later, to dilate upon the grounds of his charge. The diary written by Booth during the days of his flight, which the judge-advocates kept out of sight before the military commission and which had lain concealed ever since, the judiciary committee in conducting the impeachment investigation had at length unearthed. Several leaves, the remains of which bore evidence that the missing pages had been written on, were cut out;—giving rise to the suspicion that the same hand that suppressed the book might have mutilated it in fear of the full disclosure of its contents. Butler now urged that this diary, being moral if not legal evidence, ought to have been produced on the trial for two reasons: 1. It proved that there had been a plot to abduct the President, changed only at the last moment to a plot to murder; and "if Mrs. Surratt did not know of the change of purpose, there is no evidence that she knew in any way of the assassination." 2. The country was entitled to every particle of evidence throwing light on the great crime, in order to be able "to find who were all the accomplices of Booth; to find who it was that changed Booth's purpose from capture to assassination; who it was that could profit by assassination who could not profit by capture and abduction of the President; who it was expected by Booth would succeed to Lincoln if the knife made a vacancy." "Who spoliated that book?" he demanded with pointed significance. "Who suppressed that evidence? Who caused an innocent woman to be hung when he had in his pocket the diary that states at least what was the idea and purpose of the main conspirator in the case?" Quoting what he called "this most remarkable sentence written apparently but a few hours before Booth died," "I have endeavored to cross the Potomac five times and failed. I propose to return to Washington and give myself up, and clear myself from this great crime"; he continued: "How clear himself? By disclosing his accomplices? Who were they? Who spoliated this book after it got into the hands of the Government, if it was not spoliated before?"* These questions Butler would have answered by charging that the book was mutilated to shield Andrew Johnson, whom he believed to have been an accomplice of Booth's. "Such a charge," said Bingham, employing a contemptuous remark General Grant was reported to have applied to General Butler, "is only fit to come from a man who lives in a bottle and is fed with a spoon."

The President did not keep the Houses waiting long. Four days after the passage of the supplementary bill the veto arrived. One extract from the message will suffice:

> "When I contemplate the millions of our fellow citizens of the South, with no alternative left but to impose upon themselves this fearful and untried experiment of complete negro enfranchisement and white disfranchisement, it may be, almost as complete, or submit indefinitely to the rigor of martial law, without a single attribute of freemen, deprived of all the sacred guarantees of our Federal Con-

* *Globe,* 1st Sess. 40th Cong., pp. 262–3, 363, 364.

stitution, and threatened with even worse wrongs, if any worse are possible, it seems to me their condition is the most deplorable to which any people can be reduced."*

Senator Nye pronounced this "one of the strangest messages ever written."† The two Houses paid no attention to it and passed the bill over the veto without remark.

The business of the session being concluded, an angry quarrel broke out among the majority over the question of adjournment. It began in the House, when Blaine offered a resolution to adjourn on Tuesday the twenty-sixth, to meet again on Monday, November the eleventh. Butler objected that "the Thirty-ninth Congress by ordering this special session said . . . that Andrew Johnson was a bad man, and that this House and the Senate should sit here to take care of his acts"; and that, above all, the question of the impeachment should not be put off for eight months longer, but should be settled at once one way or the other. Blaine replied that there was no popular demand for impeachment and that in the public mind of the country the question was already settled. Stevens reproached him for the "growing inclination in some quarters" on this subject, since the election of the president of the Senate, repeating a declaration he remembered to have heard Blaine make in the House that "there will be no impeachment by this Congress; we would rather have the President than the shallywags of Ben Wade." Hot words were exchanged between the two members, Blaine insisting that his re-

* McPh. Recon., pp. 178, 180.

† *Globe*, *id.*, p. 353.

mark was made in private conversation and only to the effect that Fessenden was the safer man for President of the United States, and conveyed no slur upon Wade; and Stevens reiterating, with acerbity, that the name of Fessenden was not mentioned, that the declaration was in the very words he had used, was made after the election of the president *pro tempore,* and addressed generally to the members of the House.*

The fight was just as bitter in the Senate. Trumbull offered the customary resolution to adjourn the next Tuesday to the first Monday in December—the time fixed by the Constitution. Drake moved to amend by making the day of meeting Tuesday, the fifteenth of October, and was voted down. Sumner, then, moved that the President of the Senate and the Speaker of the House, on Thursday next, adjourn their respective Houses until the first Monday in June, "and on that day, unless it is otherwise ordered, they further adjourn their respective Houses until the first Monday of December"; and got but fourteen votes for his motion. Yates was most bitter against a long adjournment. It was the duty of Congress to watch the President. "He is not to be trusted. He is opposed to our laws." "Whoever that man be," he declared, "whether President of the United States or any other person, who stands in the path of this country for union, to honor and to glory, should be taken out of the way. I am not saying how." Nye warned the Senate that the Supreme Court of the United States might, next month, decide the reconstruction measures unconstitutional, and where would the

* *Globe, id.,* pp. 315–7.

Congress be then, unable to assemble until December? Williams shrewdly remarked that Congress could not control the President by remaining in session. "We know by experience that the President will do as he sees proper whether Congress is or is not in session." But, in this high contention, it was Sumner who bore away the palm. With cool candour and with judicial precision, he arrayed his arguments against adjournment. There were "two controlling facts staring him in the face." First. "Our President is a bad man"—"the author of incalculable woe to his country." "Search history," this future judge of the President went on,

> "and I am sure that you will find no ruler, who during the same short space of time has done so much mischief to his country. He stands alone in bad eminence. Nobody in ancient or modern times can be his parallel. Alone in the evil he has done, he is also alone in the maudlin and frantic manner which he has adopted."
>
> " . . . And now I ask can Congress quietly vote to go home and leave this bad man without hindrance of any kind?"

Second. The other "fact" he illustrated by an engraving in *Harper's Weekly* where, as he described it:

> "President Johnson is represented as a Roman emperor presiding in the amphitheater with imperatorial pomp, and surrounded by his trusty counselors, among whom it is easy to distinguish the Secretary of State and the Secretary of the Navy, all of whom look with complacency at the butchery below. The victims are black, and their sacrifice, as gladiators, makes a 'Roman holiday.' Beneath this

picture is written '*Amphitheatrum Johnsonianum,* Massacre of the Innocents at New Orleans, July, 1866.' This inscription tells a terrible story. The massacre proceeds under the patronage of the President. His presidential rod is the law. At his will blood spirts and men bite the dust. . . . This whole country is an *Amphitheatrum Johnsonianum.*"

But Sumner, notwithstanding his renown as an orator and as one of the great men of his generation, had very little influence over the Senate; and Trumbull's resolution passed by a vote of 29 to 16.*

This was not the end of the matter, however. Wilson moved a reconsideration and, the House having adopted a resolution "to assemble again on the first Wednesdays of May, June, September and November unless the President of the Senate and the Speaker of the House shall by joint proclamation issued ten days before the time fixed declare there is no occasion for a meeting," the judiciary committee was instructed to inquire whether Congress had the right to vest such a power in the presiding officers; but the committee shirked the constitutional question, reporting a simple resolution to adjourn without day. Two amendments were offered—one by Howe to adjourn until June and then unless otherwise ordered until December, one by Drake to adjourn until June and then if no quorum be present until September and then there being no quorum until December; but both were rejected. Sumner offered a proviso that the President of the Senate and the Speaker of the House at any time before December might by

* *Globe*, *id.*, pp. 303–8.

proclamation convene the two Houses, and it received but fifteen votes. Once again, the resolution adjourning *sine die* was adopted by the Senate. The House sent it back amended so as to provide for two intermediate meetings unless the presiding officers proclaim there is no occasion. Sherman was of the opinion that Congress could delegate to the presiding officers "the right to designate the time when we shall meet." But Buckalew in a few words demonstrated that the power was exclusive in the President, and Edmunds did so likewise, in an argument so neat as to convince every senator except Sumner whose forensic habit was silently to ignore an unanswerable argument and restate the disproved proposition with increased emphasis. At length, on Friday, the two Houses came to an agreement to adjourn until the first Wednesday in July "when the roll shall be called and the presiding officer of each House shall inform the presiding officer of the other whether or not a quorum is present, and if a quorum of the two Houses shall not have appeared, they shall adjourn the two Houses without day."*

During this long struggle, the subject of the impeachment was continually obtruding itself, the members who favoured the movement, opposing, the members, who opposed, favouring, adjournment without day. The investigation was dragging along, an occasional witness appearing before the judiciary committee during the session. The President's bank account was overhauled; newspaper men were examined about interviews with the President; the New Orleans riot was touched on;

* *Id.*, pp. 352–60, 401–2–8, 438–41.

and General Butler exulted in the discovery of what he believed to be a damning offence in the pardoning of about two hundred deserters in order to render them available as voters for the President's policy. But it was becoming daily more and more manifest that the selection of Wade as the heir-apparent had given impeachment its death-blow. Unless some event occurred to rekindle the fire, it must eventually die out. Butler's startling interrogations about Booth's diary revived for a moment the dwindling excitement. The committee called Stanton and Holt before it to explain the mutilation of the leaves.* It was rumoured that some of its members sought the cell where John H. Surratt was confined to ascertain whether the prisoner might be induced to implicate the President. But these spasmodic efforts availed but little. It was true, as Blaine said, the conservative element among the Republicans preferred to bear the ills they had with Andrew Johnson than fly to others that they knew not of with Wade. The day before the adjournment a final effort was made to show that the movement had some life in it still. Clarke of Kansas submitted to the House a long preamble reciting what had been done by the committee and declaring it dangerous for Congress to adjourn with the impeachment of the President hanging over the people, and a resolution that Congress adjourn until the first Monday in June for the purpose of acting upon the report of the committee on the charges against the President. A member of the committee stated that it had resolved to separate until the first of May when it purposed to con-

* Imp. Inv., *passim; id.*, pp. 285, 408.

tinue its labours. Butler made the most of his newly-discovered pardoned deserters. Stevens made the staggering remark:

> "For the last three or four months I have been satisfied that the Committee are making but a mere pretence of prosecuting impeachment by way of throwing it out of doors. I do not believe they ever intended it, and I do not believe they intend it now."

The House substituted the Edmunds resolution for Clarke's and laid the preamble on the table.*

Sumner, who opposed all adjournments, had predicted that there would be a July session and a session for "business"; and his prediction was fulfilled. The President, with a promptness which disappointed his enemies, named the military commanders under the main reconstruction act as early as the eleventh day of March; General Schofield remained in the first district; General Sickles in the second; General Thomas was assigned to the third but declined and General Pope was substituted; General Ord took charge of the fourth; and General Sheridan was continued in command of Louisiana and Texas, these two states, Florida being transferred to the third, now constituting the fifth. Serious questions arose concerning the power of the military commanders, in connection with the civil governments still allowed to exist, and the duties of the registrars, both under the main and the supplementary acts; and they came pouring in upon the President and by him were referred to the Attorney-General. In the latter

* *Globe, id.*, pp. 446–50.

part of May, that officer wrote an opinion holding that, under the supplementary act, the boards of registration had no right to examine an applicant and investigate the question of his competency, provided he was ready to take the oath required by law; an interpretation characterized by Sheridan in a letter to Grant as "opening a broad macadamized road for perjury and fraud to travel on." On the twelfth of June, the Attorney-General delivered another opinion on a more far-reaching and important question. His general conclusion was that, until the process of reconstruction was complete, the two acts contemplated the coexistence of two forms of government; one, the civil governments of the states included in the district, which were to be regarded, as heretofore, the ordinary organs of the sovereign authority; the other, the military governments, which were to be auxiliary, suppletory to the others upon adequate occasion. As corollaries of this main conclusion the Attorney-General held: 1. That, in the absence of any express grant in the acts in question, the military commanders had no power to remove or suspend any civil officer of the governments of these states, much less to appoint civilians in their place, and that all attempts to exercise such power were null and void. 2. That the military commanders possessed no powers of legislation whatever—*i. e.,* to promulgate decrees and give them the force of laws. The President having embodied the substance of both opinions in a series of instructions which were sent to the military commanders, the cry went forth over the North that the reconstruction plan so carefully contrived by the Congress was being emasculated by a perfidious President and his wily Attorney-General. Messengers darted forth east, west, north and south to summon the members; and in the blazing days of July they came flocking to the capital to make the presence of a quorum in each House certain. It took them just one week to reverse the Attorney-General by passing a second supplementary act declaring the true intent and meaning of the other two acts to be that the civil governments allowed to exist provisionally in the ten states were subordinate in all respects to the military commanders; granting the military commanders power to suspend or remove every officer of these states, from governor or legislator down to a justice of the peace or an alderman and to appoint some person in his place; and making valid acts of this character already done. It further provided that the oath of the applicant for registration was not conclusive on the board, and that the board was not bound to register unless satisfied the applicant possessed the qualifications of an elector under the acts of Congress; and that these boards had the right to revise the lists, and to strike off or add any names they might determine were, on the one hand, not rightfully there, or, on the other, ought to be there; and that the military commanders and the boards of registration should pay no regard to the opinions of any civil officer of the United States.*

The veto message on this measure stirred up an angry agitation. In the many previous messages of this character, while the objections of the President were set forth with firmness, there was nothing like a declaration of

* McPh. Recon., p. 335.

resistance to the ultimate action of the Congress. But, now, when the triumph of the reconstruction policy of that body appeared to be assured and the President's power of restraint at its lowest ebb, Johnson for the first time struck a clear note of defiance, giving notice that there was a limit to the submission of the executive.

"Within a period less than a year," so ran the message, "the legislation of Congress has attempted to strip the executive department of the Government of some of its essential powers. The Constitution and the oath provided in it devolve upon the President the power and duty to see that the laws are faithfully executed. The Constitution, in order to carry out this power, gives him the choice of the agents, and makes them subject to his control and supervision. But, in the execution of these laws the constitutional obligation upon the President remains, but the power to exercise that constitutional duty is effectually taken away.

"The military commander is, as to the power of appointment, made to take the place of the President, and the General of the Army the place of the Senate; and any attempt on the part of the President to assert his own constitutional power may, under pretense of law, be met by official insubordination. It is to be feared that these military officers, looking to the authority given by these laws rather than to the letter of the Constitution, will recognize no authority but the commander of the district and the General of the Army.

"If there were no other objection than this to this proposed legislation it would be sufficient. While I hold the chief executive authority of the United States, while the obligation rests upon me to see that all the laws are faithfully executed, I can never willingly surrender that trust or the powers given for its execution. I can never give my assent to be made responsible for the faithful execution of laws and at the same time surrender that trust and the powers which accompany it to any other executive officer, high or low, or to any number of executive officers. If this executive trust, vested by the Constitution in the President, is to be taken from him and vested in a subordinate officer, the responsibility will be with Congress in clothing the subordinate with unconstitutional power and with the officer who assumes its exercise.''*

Stevens contemptuously recommended that the House better pass the bill and then go home ''so that the committee so diligently engaged in providing for the impeachment of the President may complete their work in the shortest possible time''; but Mr. Boutwell could not allow such treasonable declarations to go to the country without a word:

''The language of this document convinces me of that of which indeed I had but little doubt before, that from the oppression which through the instrumentality of this man, has rested upon twelve millions of people, and which has only been temporarily removed by the measures against which the President in this document vainly protests, there is no relief except in the assertion of that great power which resides in this House alone, and for the neglect to exercise that power the people of the country will hold us to a strict account. Posterity, not intimidated by the fears which seem to control us, will render its stern verdict against us if we hesitate to arraign the President for the

* Message in *Globe, id.*, pp. 741–3.

crimes and misdemeanors of which he is guilty before the country and the world."

Randall rose to tell "the Massachusetts Impeacher" that he had no faith in the bluster about impeachment. "You do not mean impeachment, gentlemen, for you do not dare do it." Butler admitted the charge: "We dare not do our duty in this respect. With shame and confusion of face I for one confess the truth and justice of that accusation to the country." Williams, a member of the committee, exclaimed: "There is a time when timid counsels, which betray like treason, must cease to govern the Legislative Assembly of this nation. I think that this time has now arrived. For the first time in our history the Chief Executive Magistrate of this nation strides into its great council chamber and flings his mace, in the way of defiance, at our very feet." Schenck joined in the chorus: "There is spread upon the public journals of this country in shape of documents to which the name of the President is attached, enough of history to satisfy me that he has assumed a position of hostility to a coördinate branch of the Government and to the proper rule in this country, which amounts to a great political crime, for which he might be, and if we are true to our duty ought to be degraded from the office he holds." Stevens, in his original way, put an end to the furor: "I agree with my amiable colleague (Randall) that you cannot impeach the President of the United States. . . . There are unseen agencies at work, invisible powers operating everywhere in this country which when called upon can and will protect a man of that kind from all danger. I have taken some pains to look into the position of this House and of the Senate and am quite sure that there is power enough, first to prevent the voting of impeachment here, and secondly, if impeachment were voted to prevent conviction elsewhere." The House then overrode the veto by the usual overwhelming majority.*

The reading of the message in the Senate provoked no such explosion; but, when the question of adjournment was taken up, the pent-up bitterness of certain senators broke loose. The House having sent to the Senate a resolution fixing the thirteenth of November as the day to which Congress should adjourn, Sherman moved to amend it by providing for an adjournment without day; and upon this motion Sumner opened the fight:

> "How Congress, after listening to the message of to-day, . . . can quietly vote to go home and leave this post of duty until next winter, passes my understanding. . . . The message from the beginning to end was of defiance. . . . As I listened to this appeal, which was calculated to revive the dying rebellion, I felt that one of two things must be done; its author must be removed from the executive chair, or Congress must continue in permanent session to watch and counteract him. Such is the alternative. One failing, the other must be done. . . . Unquestionably it belongs to the other House to initiate the proceedings which shall set the President at your bar. But until then it is the right and the duty of every senator to express himself freely with regard to his conduct; nor can there be any limit to this latitude. It is as broad as human thought. No future

* *Globe, id.*, pp. 743-7.

duty can be a straight-jacket now. Because the President may be impeached the Senate is not obliged to be silent with regard to him. Our Constitution is guilty of no such absurdity. . . . If I had powers of persuasion I would use them all to induce you to remain as a guard to the Constitution and a constabulary force for the rebel States. . . . Sitting in your seats here, you are a mighty police, at the call of general or citizen, and you are also a terror to that evil-doer, the President.''

Sherman failed to appreciate this distinction between the denouncing senator and the impartial judge embodied in the same man. ''It does seem to me,'' he said, ''a very strange thing that a judge by whose vote alone the President can be removed should declare he must be removed. . . . Shall we, the judges . . . decide beforehand that the President ought to be removed?'' Buckalew's rebuke was more direct: ''In my opinion the Senator from Massachusetts forgets his audience and forgets the place where he speaks, in the remarks which he now submits to us, . . . and that out of respect to our political institutions and the Constitution of the country under which we assemble, and to the reasonable and just opinions of the American people, we should withhold ourselves from the expression of judgment upon a question which is not here and which cannot come here unless it be brought here by the House of Representatives, over whose action we have no control.'' To such an admonition the senator from Massachusetts was absolutely impervious. He replied: ''The Senator says the question is not here; in other words, that this is not the time to discuss the President. . . . If he is

President, we must remain at our posts, precisely as Grant remained before Richmond. . . . Because we have the successor of Jefferson Davis in the presidential chair therefore Congress must stay. That is my argument in a nutshell.''*

The two Houses having come to an agreement by conference committees to adjourn until the twenty-first day of November, this second meeting closed on the twentieth day of July.

* *Globe, id.*, pp. 732–4.

CHAPTER III

Edwin M. Stanton

On the thirteenth day of May, 1867, Jefferson Davis sat in the United States court-room at Richmond accompanied by his counsel, Charles O'Conor and George Shea. After two years' captivity as a prisoner of war, he had been brought from Fort Monroe in obedience to a writ of *habeas corpus* and surrendered to the civil authorities for trial on an indictment for treason. The United States district judge (Underwood) was on the bench, but Chief Justice Chase, not being able to leave Washington until the following week, was absent. The radicals, for the most part, would have given the illustrious captive short shrift. Mr. Boutwell would have had him condemned to death by a military commission as the chief instigator of the assassination of Lincoln. Stevens, as he declared, "would have organized a military tribunal and . . . have put him and all the members of his Cabinet on trial for the murders of Andersonville and of Salisbury." Logan said in the House: "Had I captured Jefferson Davis and his disposal had been committed to my hands I would have organized an able court-martial and have given him a fair trial, a just sentence and prompt execution." Nye said in the Senate: "If I had my way I would have hung Jeff. Davis, no matter how I tried him. When the two great armies, that of General Sherman and the army of the Potomac, were mustered out in this city, I would have had them formed in a hollow square and hung him there, and the world would have said amen.'"* But not a whisper of these horrid charges or of these blood-thirsty methods is heard in the court. O'Conor announces that the defendant is ready for trial on the indictment, William M. Evarts announces that the United States are not. A postponement until November is agreed to. The amount of bail is fixed at $100,000. Gerritt Smith, Horace Greeley, Horace F. Clark, the son-in-law of Cornelius Vanderbilt, step forward and sign the bond, and the late president of the Confederate states steps out into the streets of the city that was so recently their capital a free man.

This incident served to quicken the flagging movement for impeachment. The committee were in session, having reassembled on the sixth of May, and were groping along in the dark to find food for the suspicion that Andrew Johnson was somehow a co-conspirator of Jefferson Davis, when this discharge of the arch-traitor with the consent of the government flashed a sudden light upon the track they were following. Members of the Cabinet were summoned—Seward, Stanton and Stanbery; and, afterwards, Chief Justice Chase, Evarts, Judge Underwood and the district attorney, and Horace Greeley. But their testimony was a grievous disappointment. So far from implicating the President particularly, it appeared, rather, that he was the only offi-

* *Globe*, 1st Sess. 40th Cong., p. 546. *Id.*, App., p. 16. *Id.*, 1st Sess. 39th Cong., p. 2527.

cial anxious to prosecute; the postponement and bailing having been managed without his interposition. Seward, whose scars were visible proof that he at least was free from plotting the assassination, told the committee that the infamy into which such professional witnesses as Conover had fallen rendered impossible the prosecution of Davis as an accomplice of Booth and Payne. Stanton, the author of the proclamation offering $100,000 reward for the capture of Davis as such accomplice, testified that he himself advised the return to the writ of *habeas corpus*. Stanbery swore that there was no evidence in his department to warrant any charge but that of treason; and that, in his opinion, after the suppression of the rebellion, prosecutions for treason ought to stop.* Ashley came to the committee's relief with his champion witness, LaFayette C. Baker, who, since his last appearance on the stand, had been searching for the man Adamson—the pretended possessor of Andrew Johnson's letters to Jefferson Davis. He cheered the committee with the information that, though he had not been able to find Adamson, he had lit upon one Mrs. Harris, who knew about the letters and whom he thought the committee might induce to appear for a valuable consideration. He testified also that when Booth's diary was delivered up to the Secretary of War, no leaves were missing, there were no stubs; the book was intact.† He was sent on his rollicking way in search of his Mrs. Harris who eventually proved to be as mythical a personage as the corresponding familiar of Mrs. Gamp.

* Imp. Inv., pp. 644 *et seq.*, 554 *et seq.*, 397, 371, 544, 578, 778.
† *Id.*, pp. 449 *et seq.*, 458.

The committee, also, examined the agent of the associated press in Washington, who followed the President as he "swung round the circle" and reported his speeches; and, while its members listened to the rehearsal of his flings at the Congress and his threats against faithful office-holders, they heard with less gratification that the President was "not drunk" or "excited with liquor" on that memorable tour.*

On Saturday, the first of June, the committee ceased to take testimony, and on Monday came to a vote. It was decided by a majority of one "that from the testimony before them it did not appear that the President of the United States was guilty of such high crimes and misdemeanors as called for the exercise of the impeaching power of the House." The five in the affirmative were Wilson (the chairman), Woodbridge and Churchill, Republicans, and Marshall and Eldridge, Democrats. The four in the negative were Boutwell, Thomas, Williams and Lawrence; all Republicans.† The members then separated, but the sudden summons to the July session brought them together in a hurry to prepare their report to be laid before the House. The minority of the committee, exasperated more than ever against the President because of his recent interference with reconstruction and more thoroughly convinced than ever of the necessity for his removal, protested against reporting a conclusion favourable to the enemy at the moment of a fresh onset, and demanded a reopening of the case;—

* Imp. Inv., pp. 525–28.

† Rep. Minority report on Imp. See also *Globe*, 1st Sess. 40th Cong., p. 811.

which was conceded. The first of the additional witnesses they called was Anna Surratt, the daughter who once begged on her knees for access to the President to implore a respite of a few hours for her condemned mother, and begged in vain. In the city where the committee sat, her brother was undergoing trial on the charge of complicity with his mother in the assassination, and, at the very hour the daughter was testifying before the committee, the government witness, Weichman, was trying his best in the court-room to do for the son what he had been so successful in doing for the mother. The papers of Mrs. Surratt, seized by the government at the time of her arrest, had been delivered to the daughter, and Mr. Boutwell asked her whether there were any letters of Booth's amongst them; thus revealing the motive of the return of the papers which to his prepossessed understanding looked highly suspicious. The papers turned out to be purely of a business character. The witness testified she never saw a letter written by J. Wilkes Booth; she never went to the President to apply for the papers—never went to the President's house but once, she said with pathetic significance. She never saw the President to have any conversation with him. "I do not want to see him either," she added.*

The persevering minority went on calling witnesses until the beginning of the July session, and from time to time during its progress. On the first of July a piece of evidence came out which, to Mr. Boutwell's mind at least, filled up the measure of Johnson's wickedness. Stanley Matthews (afterwards a senator of the United

* Imp. Inv., pp. 777–8. *Cf.* Trial of Surratt, Vol. 1, p. 391.

States and an associate justice of the Supreme Court of the United States) testified that, as long ago as February, 1865, at Cincinnati, Andrew Johnson, then Vice President-elect, on his way to his inauguration, made this prophecy: "I will tell you what it is, if the country is ever to be saved, it is to be done through the old Democratic party."* James Speed was summoned from his retirement in the expectation that he might implicate the chief from whom he had parted; but, from aught that appeared, he too had invariably sustained the President. The committee found the actor, to whom Booth handed his vindicatory letter on the afternoon before the assassination, but who in his terror destroyed it that night. The oral version he gave of its contents made no mention of Andrew Johnson, and impliedly exculpated the Surratts.† Notwithstanding the ill-success attending the committee's efforts in this direction, Butler introduced in the House, on the eighth of July, resolutions providing for a special committee to investigate "all the facts and circumstances connected with the assassination of the late lamented President," and recommending an act of grace and amnesty to all persons giving evidence throwing light on the great conspiracy. The House suspended the rules to adopt the resolutions and directed that the testimony taken by the judiciary committee germane to this subject be turned over to this select body, fitly called "the Assassination Committee." Butler, who was appointed chairman, kept his creature alive for some time. It was heard of now and then wan-

* Imp. Inv., pp. 780–1.

† *Id.*, pp. 782–8.

dering about the corridors of the capitol, but it never made a report and the Impeachment Trial blew it out of existence.* Among the last witnesses sworn before the judiciary committee was General Grant, summoned, it would seem, by the Democratic members. He testified to the harmonious action of the President, his Cabinet and himself on the question of reconstruction. Mr. Boutwell attempted to elicit from the witness some evidence that the President, plotting the recognition of a Congress made up of members-elect from the South and Northern Democrats, had made overtures to him to use the army to effect this object; but he failed of his purpose.†

When the members dispersed for the summer, the entire course and every act of the President had been gone over with Argus-eyes that allowed not the slightest peccadillo to escape. Nothing remained to be done but to print the testimony and report the conclusion. One small gap, it is true, remained. LaFayette C. Baker failed at the last moment to appear either with or without his Mrs. Harris. The chairman of the committee

* *Globe,* 1st Sess. 40th Cong., pp. 515–7, 522.

† Imp. Inv., pp. 825–836. Mr. Boutwell in his article in the *North American Review* of December, 1885, gives a statement which he says President Grant made to him, that "in the summer or early autumn of 1866 Johnson said to him (Grant), 'If I should have trouble with Congress, which side would you support?' to which Grant said, 'that would depend upon which side the law was.'"

In view of this statement, it is interesting to note that on July 18, 1867, Mr. Boutwell put the following question to General Grant on the witness-stand: "Did you at any time hear him (Johnson) make any remark looking to any controversy between Congress and the Executive?" and that Grant answered: "I think not." *Id.*, p. 834.

obtained a warrant from the House for his apprehension. A messenger, who had been sent to Nashville in search of Adamson and returned with the information that he could find no trace of such a man, was despatched after Mrs. Harris, whose personal appearance had been minutely described to him by Baker. He returned disgusted, believing himself duped, and bluntly swore to his impression that "she is a myth and there is no such woman." With this gap to be filled up when Baker was caught, the investigation which began with such loud-sounding menace may be said to have ended.*

Considering how pugnacious and unyielding Andrew Johnson was, it is remarkable with what wariness and tact he had hitherto steered his difficult course so as to lend no handle to his numerous adversaries, all on the alert to unhorse him. The bills he pronounced unconstitutional with such vigour and pertinacity, when once passed over his veto, he put into execution, notwithstanding the Congress blocked the way to the Supreme Court to which tribunal he was anxious to submit all the matters in dispute. One point there was, however, as he intimated in his recent message, at which submission would cease. On no account whatever would he suffer the duty "to see that the laws were faithfully executed" to be snatched away from him by legislative violence and confided to some officer inferior to himself. The constitution expressly made him commander-in-chief of

* Imp. Inv., pp. 858-9. *Globe, id.*, p. 757.

the army, and commander-in-chief, as long as he held on to his office, he was determined to be. By three consecutive acts, the Congress had made it certain that the ten Southern states were to be placed under the absolute control of the army. On behalf of the civil governments of those states, the President had made one effort to mitigate the infliction, and the Congress, in retaliation, only riveted the bonds of military rule the tighter. Since, then, absolute government by the army was inevitable, he now resolved that that government should be by the army with him as its commander-in-chief. If his official oath bound him to execute three odious acts and, in executing them, to preside over the inauguration of a military domination he abhorred; then that domination, at all hazards, should be tempered as much as possible in practice by instructions emanating from its constitutional head, to be interfered with by no inferior authority and to be carried out in letter and spirit by every subordinate officer. The enforcement of this momentous determination involved, in the first place, the alternative of the cessation of disobedience on the part of the military commanders of the five districts or the transportation of the protesting, recalcitrant, or insubordinate commander to another sphere of labour, and the assignment of a more docile officer in his stead. It involved, in the second place, something of much more far-reaching importance. It meant the assumption, at length, by the President, in fact, of that which belonged to him in law; the full control of the department of war.

At the head of that department was a personage whose protracted presence in the Cabinet was an enigma alike to his friends and his foes. Indeed, the character and career of Edwin M. Stanton are so enveloped in enigma that we are compelled to pause in our narrative, where for the future he is to play so prominent a part, to gain, if possible, some adequate conception of the man. To do this is made exceedingly difficult because of the curious phenomenon that, alternately appearing and disappearing before the eye of the inquirer, now blending, now separating, there are two Stantons—one the direct contradictory of the other. Listening to the chorus of his panegyrists, we see a war-minister greater than the elder Pitt; an organizer of victory more skilful than Carnot; a life-long abhorrer of African slavery; a pioneer-advocate of negro suffrage; an orthodox champion continuing to sit in the secret councils of the schismatics that he may, with secret thwartings at first, and with open defiance at last, bring to naught the machinations of the Arch-Apostate; until in the end he sinks beneath the weight of his unparalleled labours—a self-sacrifice to his country and a martyr to his party. Listening to the voice of his detractors, we see an indefatigable, bustling secretary, making up for the timidity of his conceptions by the ruffianism of his demeanour and the tyranny of his rule; a life-long dissembler, taking on the colour of the political atmosphere he happens for the time being to be breathing; a recipient of the prizes of one party while maligning its policy to the other, currying favour in the meanwhile with the leaders of both by fulsome professions of gratitude on the one hand and pretended revelations of valuable secrets on the other; a Cabinet officer obsequious to his superiors or his equals in authority to the point of servility, and insolent and overbearing to his inferiors to the point of outrage; governed by no loftier motive than the lust for office and the power that office gives; an official parasite battening upon the life-blood of his chief and letting go his hold only with the breaking of his last claw; until, at length, his early friends having discarded the discovered renegade and his new friends having no further use for the detected spy, he is flung up on a barren shore, and left to die of infinite disappointment and, it may be, by his own hand.

If we wipe out both these portraits as the creations of disordered fancy or a diseased optic nerve, and resort to the rigid historical point of view, a similar double image still affects the sight. Up to the date we have now reached, there appear in the history of the time two different Stantons, likewise—the exoteric Stanton or the Stanton of the public records, and the esoteric Stanton or the Stanton of the private coterie. The attitudes he assumes before the world, his open political associates, the various official positions he holds, proclaim one Stanton, the disciple of one political creed, the supporter of one political policy. The unanimous voice of a sect of extremists, with whom he seems to have worshipped in secret, proclaim another Stanton, wholly one of themselves. And, what renders a choice between these two images still more difficult, there is not upon record, prior to the breach with President Johnson, a single authentic public utterance of the man himself incompatible with his ostensible position or corroboratory of the claim of his cryptic brethren; while there do survive, here and there, sentences inconsistent with any such secret confabulation. Indeed, the fact of the communion of Stanton with the extreme radicals receives support from no authentic testimony coming from himself at first hand, but, apart from external circumstances, rests entirely upon the testimony of the extreme radicals themselves. With these formidable hindrances to any summary portraiture of the man, we can better fulfil our purpose and avoid the censure of the friends of his memory by letting the witnesses on the one side and on the other speak for themselves, the man himself speak for himself, and the reader draw his own conclusion.

Edwin M. Stanton first rose into national notoriety on account of the bellicose demeanour and aggressive eloquence with which, as the associate of those eminent criminal lawyers, James T. Brady and John Graham who were the warm personal friends of the prisoner, he defended Daniel E. Sickles on his trial for the murder of Philip Barton Key. The homicide was committed in the streets of the capital of the nation; the victim was the district attorney of the District of Columbia; the perpetrator was a conspicuous member of the House of Representatives, having been secretary of the legation when James Buchanan, now President of the United States, was the American minister at London; the provocation was the seduction of the slayer's wife. The trial, which owing to these circumstances attracted the attention of the whole country, began on the fourth day of April, 1859, and ended on the twenty-sixth of the same month with the acquittal of the accused. Stanton is depicted in the newspapers of the day, rushing in the heat of his argument from the prisoner's dock towards the bench like a maddened lion. In one of his addresses to the court it was that, in explanation of a previous remark of his which the opposite counsel construed as reprehensive of the institution of slavery, he judged it prudent to proclaim: "He had the blood of slave-holding parents in his veins; his father had been a North Carolinian and his mother a Virginian." At this date, he was a practicing lawyer in Washington, having removed thither from Pittsburg two years before with his patron and friend, Jeremiah S. Black, who resigned a seat upon the bench of the Supreme Court of Pennsylvania to become Attorney-General in the Cabinet of President Buchanan. Black gave him important and lucrative employment in defending the government against the exorbitant claims of the California miners, and he passed the winter of 1857–58 in that state engaged on behalf of the government in what were designated as the California land cases. According to the testimony of his distinguished friend and employer, at this time, "he made himself appear a Democrat of the most ultra class." "In all the conflicts of the Buchanan Administration with the abolitionists and their allies he was an open-mouthed opponent of the latter. He was always sound on the Kansas question, and faithful among the faithless on the Lecompton Constitution." "To Mr. Buchanan himself, and to the members of his Cabinet, he paid the most assiduous court, and showed his devotion in ways which sometimes went rather too close to the verge of obsequiousness." Again: "We were close and intimate friends and I thought I knew him as well as one man could be known to another. . . . I advanced him in his profession and thereby improved his fortune, but he got nothing in that way for which he did not render equivalent services." In the month before the Sickles trial, the Postmaster-General, Aaron V. Brown, died, and Black "recommended him pressingly" for the vacant place, which was filled, however, by Joseph Holt.

Such was the Stanton of the years 1857–59 when he emerged into the public eye, in the prime of his life and in the fullness of his powers. For this short period, the testimony is concordant. Respecting his previous career, the testimony is discordant to a most wonderful degree. Born on the nineteenth day of December, 1814, at Steubenville, on the right bank of the Ohio just below where the river bends round the apex of that wedge of territory, called "The Pan Handle," which Virginia interposes between Ohio and Pennsylvania, Stanton was destined to reap benefits from every one of the three contiguous states. Ohio gave him office; Virginia the Wheeling Bridge case; Pennsylvania employment which raised him to eminence in his profession. The first sinister bit of information we have concerns his early youth. Henry Wilson and that veteran abolitionist, Samuel May, relate that he told them in after days, as a reminiscence of his childhood, that Benjamin Lundy, the early pioneer of abolitionism, the forerunner of Garrison, was a frequent visitor at his father's house and held long talks with the former North Carolinian while the boy sat upon Lundy's knee and drank in his inspired words. The impression produced by these early teachings must have worn away with time, for, according to the testimony of another veteran abolitionist, Theodore D. Weld, when he came to Steubenville "in the early spring of 1835" to give "a course of lectures on slavery," he was told that "a young lawyer was to reply" to him. The young lawyer attended the first and second lectures and took notes, but, although at the close of each lecture objections were called for, he failed to respond. The third morning found the young champion of the dominant party of the town seeking the veteran missionary at his lodgings, confessing that "he meant to fight" but that "his guns were spiked," and acknowledging himself a convert. In the words of Weld written thirty-five years after: "a conversation of half an hour followed, during which he greatly impressed me with his hearty frankness, independence, moral insight and keen mental force." So ignominious a defection may have had something to do with the young man's removal in the following year to Cadiz in the adjoining county; but his conversion to the abolitionists must have remained a profound secret, as the next year he was elected by the Democrats prosecuting attorney of Harrison County; and after serving a term of two years in that office he returned to his native place. His open adhesion to the Democratic party was still maintained in the year 1842, when the legislature "by a strict party vote" elected him to the post of law reporter, in which he served three years; yet Chief Justice Chase testifies that, on the eve of his election, when Chase was actively engaged in the organization of the "Liberty party," "Mr. Stanton accosted him in the streets'' of Columbus "and said that he was in entire accord with the anti-slavery sentiments he had just put forth,'' "and hoped he should soon be able to take his place by his side.'' "Though he never did so,'' as Henry Wilson says, "and continued to act with the Democratic party,'' "yet he always maintained his intimacy with Mr. Chase.'' After his term of service as law reporter, he became engaged in the celebrated Wheeling Bridge case, on behalf of the state of Pennsylvania then under Democratic control; and this advance necessitated his admission as an attorney of the Supreme Court of the United States, which took place in 1849 and was followed by his removal to Pittsburg and his frequent appearance at Washington before the highest tribunal in the land. Now began his close intimacy with Judge Black, whose ardent admirer, faithful follower and able coadjutor he became, and with whom, as we have said, he finally removed to Washington. Speaking of him during this second period, Judge Black says:

> "Among us, his political principles were thought to be as well known as his name and occupation. He never allowed his fidelity to be doubted for a moment. . . . His condemnation of the abolitionists was unsparing for their hypocrisy, their corruption, their enmity to the Constitution, and their lawless disregard for the rights of States and individuals. Thus he won the confidence of the Democrats. On the faith of such professions we promoted him in his business, and gave him office, honor, and fortune.'' He "seemed to be a sound and sincere friend, political and personal, of the men who showered their favors on his head.''

On the other hand, Charles Sumner testifies that in the year 1851 he was introduced to Mr. Stanton by Mr. Chase as a friend of the latter who would be glad to know him; that, though they met but seldom, "whenever they met, it was as friends"; that in June, 1854, Stanton became "excited" over the set made upon Sumner "by the slave-masters of the Senate" in the debate over the surrender of Burns, the fugitive slave, and "afterwards spoke of the incident with much sympathy"; and at the same evening was present at a gathering at the house of the veteran abolitionist, Dr. Gamaliel Bailey, the editor of the anti-slavery organ called *The National Era* at the capital, "when he dwelt on the conduct of certain senators," and where, as Wilson records, he was a frequent visitor, and "often met and associated with anti-slavery men."

We now advance to a crisis in public affairs when, it would seem, the political principles of every public man could not be a matter of doubt. The presidential election of 1860 was at hand. The Republican party was united and triumphant throughout the whole North. The Democratic party was split in twain and despondent. The Union was visibly in danger. Stanton, through 1859 and 1860, was constantly associated with Attorney-General Black in the conduct of cases before the Supreme Court. According to that officer, "he was out and out for Breckenridge in 1860, and regarded the salvation of the country as hanging on the forlorn hope of his election." After the campaign was over (on the twentieth of November) the Attorney-General furnished to President Buchanan the opinion that, while the government of the United States had the right to enforce the federal laws against individuals everywhere and in every state, to hold or retake federal property and to collect the revenue, it had no right to make war on a state to coerce it to remain in the Union—an opinion concurred in by every member of the Cabinet and the substance of which was incorporated in the message of the President which aroused such widespread animadversion throughout the North. The author of the opinion says that Mr. Stanton indorsed it "with extravagant and undeserved laudation; he gave his adhesion to the annual message in many ways; and the special message of the eighth of January, 1861, which expressed the same principles with added emphasis, was carefully read over to him before it was sent to Congress, and it received his unqualified assent." He adds that the evidence of this is "direct as well as circumstantial, oral as well as documentary, and some of it is in the handwriting of Mr. Stanton himself." And yet, Henry L. Dawes writes that Stanton, after becoming Secretary of War under Lincoln, told him and Mr. Washburne that President Buchanan, before writing his annual message, sent for him "to answer the question 'Can a State be coerced?' that for two hours he battled, and finally scattered for the time being the heresies with which secession had filled the head of that old broken-down man"; furthermore, at the President's request he prepared an argument in support of the power to be inserted in the forthcoming message; that it was so inserted, but that in his absence "two days before the meeting of Congress" "the traitors frightened" the President into expunging it and "to insert in its place the contrary doctrine." It is hardly necessary to say that of such a paper or of the draft of a message with such an argument in it, Black, then Attorney-General, according to his own statement, never heard, and he scouts the idea of any such occurrence as absolutely incredible, considering the personal character and official habits of the President and under the known circumstances of the time. "In all the discussions on the subject," he says, Stanton "did not once intimate that there was, or ever had been, the slightest difference between him and the members of the Administration."

Congress met on the third day of December, and the next day the annual message was sent in. On the eighth, Howell Cobb of Georgia, the Secretary of the Treasury, resigned and Philip F. Thomas of Maryland was appointed in his place. On the fifteenth Lewis Cass, the Secretary of State (by a letter dated on the twelfth), resigned, not on account of the doctrine of the message, but because the President and the rest of the Cabinet did not concur with him in the expediency of sending immediate reinforcements to the forts in Charleston harbour. Attorney-General Black was thereupon promoted to his place, and, on the twentieth, the very day South Carolina adopted her ordinance of secession, Edwin M. Stanton was appointed Attorney-General. Respecting this appointment Judge Black says:

> "I strove long, and at last successfully, to remove the prejudices of Mr. Buchanan and others against him, because I thought them unjust, and because it was inconvenient for me that the President should not trust a man in whom I had

unlimited confidence. . . . I caused him to be appointed Attorney General because I knew (or thought I knew) that he and I were in perfect accord on all questions, and because I was sure that he could handle them not only with fidelity but with consummate skill. But though he was not in my debt, the apparent warmth of his nature impelled him to express his gratitude in most exaggerated language. . . . He sometimes overwhelmed me with hyperbolical demonstrations of thankfulness and friendship."

Buchanan, in a private letter to his niece under date of January 16, 1862, *apropos* of Stanton's appointment as Secretary of War by President Lincoln, writes:

"I appointed him Attorney General when Judge Black was raised to the State Department because his professional business and that of the Judge's, especially in California cases, were so intimately connected that he could proceed in the Supreme Court without delay. He is a sound, clear-headed, persevering and practical lawyer, and is quite eminent, especially in patent cases. He is not well-versed in public, commercial or constitutional law, because his professional duties as a country lawyer never led him to make these his study. I believe him to be a perfectly honest man, and in that respect he differs from ———. He never took much part in Cabinet councils because his office did not require it. He was always on my side, and flattered me *ad nauseam.*"*

The new Attorney-General was hardly warm in his seat before Major Anderson's transfer of his forces from Fort Moultrie to Fort Sumter furnished Floyd, the Secretary of War, a pretext for handing in a resigna-

* Curtis' Life of Buchanan, Vol. 2, p. 522.

tion which had already been demanded by the President on other grounds; and Joseph Holt, Postmaster-General, was promoted to his place. Thompson, the Secretary of the Interior, followed on the eighth of January, whose place was not filled; and Thomas, on the eleventh, who was succeeded by John A. Dix. So that, for the greater part of the period up to the fourth of March, during which Stanton was a member of the Cabinet of Buchanan, his associates were Black, Dix, Holt, Toucey and Horatio King, the assistant Postmaster-General, acting in Holt's place; all of them citizens of adhering states, and every one of whom has borne witness to the masterful firmness, impressive dignity, wise caution, enlightened statesmanship, and fervent patriotism of his chief. Black speaks of his *protégé's* relations with the President and the members of the Cabinet as follows:

> "Mr. Stanton was in perfect accord with the Administration, before and after be became a part of it, on every question of fundamental principle. He had unlimited confidence in the men with whom he was acting, and they confided in him. For his chief and some of his colleagues he professed an attachment literally boundless; for all of them who stayed during the term, and for Thompson who did not stay, he was warm in his friendship." "Stanton was no stormer in the presence of such men as he then had to deal with. His language was habitually deferential, his whole bearing decent, and his behavior at the council-board was entirely free from insolence." "He maintained unbroken his fraternal relations with his colleagues."

Again, speaking of Stanton's entrance into the Cabinet, he says:

"His language glowed with gratitude, his words spoke all the fervor of personal devotion to his chief and his colleagues; he gave his thorough approval to the measures they thought necessary to preserve the unity of the nation in the bonds of peace.

"To Mr. Toucey's face Mr. Stanton breathed no syllable of censure upon his official conduct as head of the Navy Department. To the President or Cabinet he expressed no doubt of his wisdom, much less of his honesty. He met him every day with a face of smiling friendship."

What ought to be conclusive to every man assuming to be a judge of the matter, he expressed to Mr. Seward, as Seward himself states, "entire confidence in the loyalty of the President and of the heads of the departments who remained in association with him until the close of that administration."

And yet Seward writes:

"Immediately after Mr. Stanton took office he put himself into direct communication with me at my house, employing Mr. Watson for that purpose. Every day thereafter until the inauguration passed, I conferred either in the morning or in the evening or both with Mr. Stanton through the same agency, and the question what either of us could or ought to do at the time for the public welfare was discussed and settled. Mr. Watson often brought with him suggestions in writing from Mr. Stanton and returned to Mr. Stanton with mine. . . . One day as I was riding through F Street from the Capitol, I met Mr. Stanton on foot. We recognized each other and a hurried explanation concerning our relations . . . took place. We separated quickly, from the motive on my part, and I suppose on his, of avoiding public observation. This was the only occasion as I remember, on which I met Mr. Stanton until after the expiration of Mr. Buchanan's presidential term."

Sumner, also, writes that in the month of January, 1861, relying on the remembrance of their former friendship, he called on the Attorney-General at his office for information and counsel.

"He was in an inner room, where he received me kindly, seeming glad to see me. Looking about and seeing somebody in the room, he whispered that we must be alone, and then passed into the anteroom, where there was also somebody, and then into the next room and then into the next, when, finding somebody in each room, he opened the door into the corridor, where he began an earnest conversation, saying that he must see me alone, that this was impossible at his office, that he was watched by the traitors of the South, that my visit would be made known to them at once, and he concluded by proposing to call at my lodgings at one o'clock that night, when he would tell me of the fearful condition of affairs as he saw them." "He came at one o'clock that night, and was alone with me for an hour"; describing "the plan" of "the Southern leaders" "to obtain possession of the national capital and the national archives so that they might substitute themselves for the existing government."

Stanton, however, never disclosed to the President or to any of his fellow-members of the Cabinet, that he was in daily communication with the incoming Secretary of State, or the "plan of the Southern leaders" which he confided to one of the leading enemies of the administration, of which he was a part, in the dead hour of the night.

According to Henry Wilson, "he put himself in communication with the Republicans in Congress, and kept them well informed of what was going on in the councils of the administration." "So anxious" was he "to baffle the conspirators, that he made an arrangement with" William A. Howard and Henry L. Dawes, the radical members of a special committee appointed "to investigate treasonable machinations and conspiracies" by which they "were informed of whatever occurred tending to endanger the country and which he desired should be thwarted by the friends of the incoming administration." "He believed that Mr. Toucey, Secretary of the Navy, was false to his country, and that he ought to be arrested." A committee of vigilance was organized by the radicals, of which Wilson and Colfax were members, and at that time Wilson became acquainted with Stanton "and consulted with him, and received from him warnings and suggestions. He was in almost daily consultations, too, with members of both Houses." According to Howard, it was Stanton who wrote the resolutions providing for the committee introduced by him on the ninth of January, 1861 (the committee being appointed the next day), which in terms were directed against Cabinet ministers; and, according to Dawes, it was Stanton who inspired the resolution of censure on Toucey. Howard testifies:

"I do not think that I saw Mr. Stanton any time between the 1st of January and the 4th of March, 1861; but I think I heard from him more times than there were days in those two months. . . . We were put upon this inquiry'' (as to the acceptance of resignations of naval officers by the Secretary of the Navy and antedating them, for which he was eventually censured by the House) ''by information brought to us by a 'bird' which flew directly from some Cabinet minister to the Committee room.'' ''We were more than once told that it would probably be necessary to arrest a certain member of the Cabinet for treason. Once we were told it would probably have to be within an hour, but to wait until we could hear a second time. Word came to hold on. Those messages certainly came from some member of the Cabinet.''

According to Dawes:

''Some of the most important and secret plans of the conspirators became known and were thwarted by means of communication from Mr. Stanton to the Committee.'' ''Once a member of that committee read by the light of the street lamp these words: 'Secretary —— is a traitor, depend upon it. He declared in Cabinet to-day that he did not want to deliver this government intact into the hands of the black Republicans. Arrest him instantly or all will be lost.' The paper went back to its hiding place but the Secretary, though he walked the streets unmolested, was watched from that hour.''

Remembering the composition of the Cabinet after the resignation of Thomas on the eleventh of January, the suspected officer could have been no other than Toucey.*

* My authorities for the foregoing statements and extracts concerning Stanton, except where otherwise indicated, are: 1. Henry Wilson's papers in the *Atlantic Monthly* for February and October, 1870. 2.

In the light of these statements and counter-statements of such astonishing discrepancy, the reader will fully appreciate a few of the utterances of Stanton himself. After the close of Buchanan's administration, every member of his Cabinet who continued with him to the last, kept up a friendly and confidential correspondence with the ex-President. Stanton continued to reside in Washington, and, on the tenth of March, wrote to his late chief, at Wheatland, to give him "as full information as I possess of the state of public affairs at Washington." He states:

"At the depot, on the afternoon of your departure, I parted with Mr. Holt and Mr. Toucey and I have not seen them since." Mentioning that before his successor had qualified, he had drawn up, at the request of Mr. Seward, a nomination of Crittenden for "Judge of the United States Court," he states that "the general understanding is that it *will not be*" sent in. "The rumor is that the *red blacks* oppose it, and also many Democrats, and that Mr. Holt will be nominated. He appears now to be the chief favorite with the Republicans." Mr. Seward gave him "some comments of General Scott's on the report of Mr. Holt in relation to Major Anderson and Fort Sumter," "the remarkable character" of which induced him to obtain permission to show them to General Dix and to procure a copy if possible, for his correspondent. He then proceeds to point out "errors" in them; among the rest that Mr. Toucey was unwilling to send the Brooklyn to Charleston, whereas he says: "My understanding is that

Black's two letters in reply, first printed in the *Galaxy* for June, 1870, and February, 1871, and republished in 'Black's Speeches and Essays.'
3. Trial of Sickles (pamphlet).

Mr. Toucey wanted to send the Brooklyn,'' ''but that General Scott and Mr. Holt preferred'' sending the Star of the West, ''and overruled Mr. Toucey''; also, rebutting the charge that ''Mr. Toucey made such difficulty about furnishing the ships, that the relief of Major Anderson was abandoned.'' He writes further: ''Mr. Seward mentioned to me that Mr. Lincoln and his Cabinet, when this subject came up'' (*i. e.,* Scott's views) ''would desire me to be present, and also Mr. Holt. I told him that if *all of the late Cabinet* were requested to be present, I would have no objections, but I did not think it proper *unless all* were present. He said of course an invitation would be extended *to all.*'' Taking up another topic he writes: ''I am perfectly satisfied that Major Anderson *will be withdrawn.* . . . I am also convinced by the general tone prevailing here that there is not the least design to attempt any coercive measures. A continuation of your policy to *avoid collision* will be the course of the present administration.''

Under the date of the twelfth he writes:

''It is now the universal impression in this city, that Sumter and Pickens will both be surrendered. . . . It would not surprise me to see Virginia out in less than ninety days and Maryland will be close at her heels. Lincoln and the family at the White House are represented as greatly elated at Douglas joining in the defence of the new administration.''

Under the date of the fourteenth he writes from the Supreme Court room:

''If the Court ever reassembles there will be a considerable change in its organization. . . . Lincoln will probably (if his administration continues four years) make a change that will affect the constitutional doctrines of the Court."

Under the date of the sixteenth:

"Every day affords proof of the absence of any settled policy or harmonious concert of action in the administration. Seward, Bates and Cameron form one wing; Chase, Welles, Blair the opposite wing; Smith is on both sides, and Lincoln sometimes on one and sometimes on the other. There has been agreement in nothing. . . . I do not believe there will be much further effort to assail you. . . . The embarrassments which surrounded you they now feel; and whatever may be said against you must recoil as an argument against them. And in giving reasons for their action, they must exhibit facts that controlled you in respect to Sumter."

In another letter of the same date he writes:

"I do not think there will be any serious effort to assail your administration in respect to Fort Sumter. That would imply a coercive policy on their part and hostility to your pacific measures. The tendency of General Scott's remarks were rather to impute blame to Mr. Toucey than to any one else. And as Mr. Holt and the General concurred in everything done or written, their concurrence will defend you."

"I shall write to you often and apprise you of what is going on."

April 3 he writes:

"Mr. Toucey left here last week." "There has been a rumor for the last two or three days, that, notwithstanding all that has been said, there will be an effort to reinforce Fort Sumter; but I do not believe a word of it. . . . The first month of the administration seems to have furnished an ample vindication of your policy, and to have rendered all occasion of other defence needless."

On the tenth:

"I send you a copy of General Scott's views, etc." "Doctor Gwin has just returned from Mississippi. He speaks with great confidence of the stability and power of the Confederacy, and evidently sympathizes strongly with them."

"Apprehensions are entertained of a hostile attack upon Washington. But I think that apprehension is as groundless as the rumor that hurried Lincoln from Harrisburg to Washington."

P. S. 12 o'clock: "It is certain that the administration is panic stricken from some cause. . . . It is now reported . . . that the *batteries have opened on Sumter.* Soldiers are being placed in the departments."

On the eleventh:

"There is great 'soldiering' in town the last two days. . . . The feeling of loyalty to the Government has greatly diminished in this city. Many persons who would have supported the Government under your administration refuse to be enrolled. Many who were enrolled have withdrawn, and refuse to take the oath. The administration has not acquired the confidence and respect of the people here. Not one of the Cabinet or principal officers has taken a house or brought his family here. Seward rented a house 'while he should continue in the Cabinet' but has not opened it, nor has his family come. They all act as though they meant to be ready 'to cut and run' at a minute's notice—their tenure is like that of a Bedouin on the sands of the desert. . . . And, besides, a strong feeling of distrust in the candor and sincerity of Lincoln personally, and of his Cabinet has sprung up. If they had been merely silent and secret, there might have been no ground of complaint. But assurances are said to have been given and declarations made in conflict with the facts now transpiring in the South, so that no one speaks of Lincoln or any member of his Cabinet with respect or regard."

The next day:

"We have the war upon us. . . . The impression here is held by many: 1st, that the effort to reinforce will be a failure; 2nd, that in less than twenty four hours from this time, Anderson will have surrendered; 3rd, that in less than thirty days Davis will be in possession of Washington."

On May sixteenth, he writes:

"The fling of Mr. F. W. Seward about 'negotiations' " (a remark "that the days for such things had passed away since the 4th of March") "would merit a retort if there were an independent press and the state of the times admitted discussion of such matters. The negotiations carried on by Mr. Seward with the Confederate Commissioners through Judge Campbell and Judge Nelson will, some day, perhaps, be brought to light, and if they were as has been represented to me, Mr. Seward and the Lincoln administration will not be in a position to make sneering observations respecting any negotiations during your administration."

. . . "No description could convey to you the panic that prevailed here for several days after the Baltimore riot, and before communications were reopened. This was increased by the reports of the trepidation of Lincoln that were circulated through the streets. . . . In the present state of affairs I do not like to leave home, or I would pay you a visit."

On the eighth of June he writes:

"No sooner had the appearance of imminent danger passed away, and the administration recovered from its panic, than a determination became manifest to give a strict party direction, as far as possible, to the great national movement. After a few Democratic appointments, such as Butler and Dix, everything else has been exclusively devoted to Black Republican interests. . . . General Dix informs me that he has been so badly treated by Cameron, and so disgusted by the general course of the Administration, that he intends immediately to resign. . . . Indeed, the course of things for the last four weeks has been such as to excite distrust in every Department of the Government."

On July 16, with reference to a "historical sketch" of the close of his administration, which Buchanan had written and sent to members of his Cabinet, Stanton writes:

"Last evening Judge Black and General Dix met at my house, and we consulted together with regard to it. We concur in opinion that a publication at present would accomplish no good. The public mind is too much excited," etc. "The narrative appears to me to be a clear and accurate statement of the events of the period to which it relates with one exception of no national consequence. . . ."

"So far, however, as your administration is concerned, its policy in reference to both Sumter and Pickens is fully vindicated by the course of the present Administration for forty days after the inauguration of Lincoln.

"I think the public will be disposed to do full justice to your efforts to avert the calamity of civil war. . . . General Dix is still here. He has been shamefully treated by the Administration."

His comments on Bull Run, under date of July 26, may close the correspondence:

"The dreadful disaster of Sunday can scarcely be mentioned. The imbecility of this Administration culminated in that catastrophe; an irretrievable misfortune and national disgrace never to be forgotten are to be added to the ruin of all peaceful pursuits and national bankruptcy, as the result of Lincoln's 'running the machine' for five months. . . . It is not unlikely that some change in the War and Navy departments may take place, but none beyond those two Departments until Jeff. Davis turns out the whole concern. The capture of Washington seems now inevitable. . . . While Lincoln, Scott and the Cabinet are disputing who are to blame, the city is unguarded and the enemy at hand. Gen. McClellan reached here last evening. But if he had the ability of Cæsar, Alexander or Napoleon, what can he accomplish? Will not Scott's jealousy, Cabinet intrigues, and Republican interference thwart him at every step?"*

After reading the foregoing extracts, it will be easier to credit the statements of Judge Black:

* The foregoing extracts are taken from Chap. XXVII of Vol. 2 of Curtis' Life of Buchanan.

> "His (Stanton's) democracy did not cease when the War opened. In the summer of 1861 when the 'anti-constitutional principles'" (of the Republican party) "began to be practically carried out by the kidnapping of innocent citizens, by the suppression of free speech, and by the enslavement of the press, he imprecated the vengeance of God and the law upon the guilty authors of those crimes with as much energy as any Democrat in the nation. Only a short time before his appointment as Secretary of War his love of liberty and legal justice impelled him to curse Mr. Lincoln himself with bitter curses. He called him contemptuous names, and with simian, if not with 'swinish phrase, soiled his addition.'"*

The next moment we catch sight of this duplex figure is on the eve of the meeting of Congress in December, 1861, when we find him "cordially indorsing" an "important passage" in Secretary Cameron's annual report "recommending the freeing and arming of the slaves," which that Cabinet officer, deeming it "a delicate matter"—too far advanced as yet—submitted in confidence to "several of his friends," all of whom "disapproved of the policy" except Stanton who, so intimate were the two men according to Cameron, "taking his pen, modified one or two sentences, remarking that he would fix it so that the lawyers will not carp at it." The "important passage," we are informed, "did not meet the views of Mr. Lincoln, and he required its suppression." And so it happened in the following January when Cameron was gently pressed out of the Cabinet, the whilom Attorney-General of Buchanan's Administra-

* June *Galaxy*, 1870.

tion was made Secretary of War of Lincoln's at the suggestion of his predecessor in that department, whose radicalism, though too strong as yet for the President, he so heartily shared. While the appointment was yet in abeyance, Cameron gave a breakfast in honour of his contemplated successor to which senators Chandler and Wade were invited. Chandler had "never met" the coming favourite before, while Wade had enjoyed a "long acquaintance"; but both were "much pleased with the suggestion" of the appointment which, it appears, if offered, their modest guest "reluctantly gave" them "to understand he would accept." President Lincoln, according to Cameron, also "hesitated; but after listening to me (him) for a time, he yielded." When the nomination of Edwin M. Stanton was announced in the Senate, Sumner rose at once and declared "within my knowledge he is one of us."*

It is unnecessary for our purpose to dwell on his official career during the years of actual conflict. That he discharged the onerous duties of his department with great ability, energy and promptitude will not be questioned. But to call him a great War-minister like the elder Pitt is a manifest exaggeration. His position had nothing in common with that of a great statesman moulding and carrying out a national policy in the conduct of a great war. Nor does he rise to the same grade as the French "organizer of victory" who won that title more by strategic combinations with different armies, than by the manipulation of regiments and the prompt supply of the sinews of war. Stanton's labours were

* Wilson in *Atlantic Monthly* for October, 1870.

confined to the routine work appertaining to his department, which he drove along with a rampant energy, oftentimes, in his relations with subordinates or with persons unfortunate enough to come into collision with him, degenerating into downright brutality.

General Grant, in his Memoirs, comparing Lincoln with Stanton, says:

> "They were the very opposite of each other in almost every particular, except that each possessed great ability. Mr. Lincoln gained influence over men by making them feel that it was a pleasure to serve them. . . . It distressed him to disappoint others. In matters of public duty, however, he had what he wished, but in the least offensive way. Mr. Stanton never questioned his own authority to command unless resisted. He cared nothing for the feelings of others. In fact it seemed to be pleasanter to him to disappoint than to gratify. He felt no hesitation in assuming the functions of the Executive, or in acting without advising him. If his act was not sustained he would change it—if he saw the matter would be followed up until he did so." And further: "The Secretary was very timid, and it was impossible for him to avoid interfering with the armies covering the capital when it was sought to defend it by an offensive movement against the army guarding the Confederate capital. He could see our weakness but he could not see that the enemy was in danger. The enemy would not have been in danger if Mr. Stanton had been in the field."*

Although Stanton appears to have been very often a thorn in the flesh to his great chief, still, during the three years and over of his service, he kept himself safe

* Personal Memoirs of U. S. Grant, Vol. 2, pp. 536–7.

within the circle of the President's widening popularity. He did not follow Chase, his early friend and now his colleague, into open disaffection. Indeed, at the time of the creation of the Freedmen's Bureau, there appears to have been going on a certain rivalry between the departments of the Treasury and of War; Sumner favouring the giving over of the freedmen to the care of Chase, while Wilson still clung to the "intense and abounding patriotism" of the man who, when a boy, sat upon the knee of Lundy, and, when a young man, surrendered to the arguments of Weld. Whether he secretly assured Wade and Henry Winter Davis of his sympathy with their revolt in 1864, we have as yet no private correspondence or memoirs to show, but, so far as his public actions are concerned, he stood firmly by Lincoln's plan of reconstruction. We know that he still kept up the secret alliance which dated so long back; for, on the Sunday night succeeding Lincoln's death, as we have seen, he was holding a conclave with Sumner, Dawes, Colfax, Covode and several others, reading "Cabinet papers not as yet matured" relating to reconstruction, and allowing Sumner and Colfax to interpolate into the executive order Stanton had prepared for submission to the Cabinet "a paragraph on the subject of suffrage" satisfactory to them.*

Such was the protean personage who, through all the vicissitudes of the bitter conflict between the Congress and the President and the consequent open schism in the party, had hitherto managed to keep his place at the head of the department of War. There is no evidence

* *Supra*, Section I, p. 15.

that he opposed a single step taken by the President in the reconstruction of the Southern states or in the reconciliation of the Southern people. Every measure that provoked the angry censure of the radicals and, at length, threats of impeachment, was apparently supported by him or acquiesced in without opposition. Even after the breach became open on account of the President's speech on the twenty-second of February, 1866, there is nothing to show that he did not take his stand on the side of his chief. He enshrouded himself as much as possible in the official secrecy of the Cabinet, but a serenade by a Johnson Club in May of the same year forced him with other members of the Cabinet to declare himself to some extent. The speech he made was carefully prepared—written out and read, in fact. At first, he said, he was inclined to the view that some sort of coloured suffrage should be incorporated in the reconstruction measures, but he had yielded and given a "cordial acquiescence" to the plan of the President. He could not approve of the fourteenth amendment of the joint committee because of the third section (at that particular date disfranchising classes of southern whites until 1870). He advised approval of the Freedmen's Bureau bill; but it was now dead by the veto and, therefore, had ceased to be a subject of dispute. The civil rights bill, on the contrary, was now a law and, therefore, of course not subject to debate. Though he could not approve the plan of the joint committee he acknowledged that Congress was the ultimate judge.* His tes-

* Speech in Washington Newspapers. See *Globe,* 1st Sess. 39th Cong., p. 2960.

timony before the Impeachment committee revealed the same state of affairs during the previous two years, viz., the absence of all opposition on his part to the course of the administration. It is clear that whatever may have been his real feelings he must have effectually suppressed all serious persistent objections, else he would long ago have been removed from his place by the President who, up to the passage of the Tenure-of-office act, possessed the unquestioned right to dispense with the society of a Cabinet officer who thwarted his policy. Johnson, as it appears, never liked him, for a long time distrusted him, and may have suspected him of having underhand dealings with his adversaries. But he was loth to disturb any member of the Cabinet of Lincoln, or to turn out of office a single incumbent appointed by his predecessor who stopped short of publicly denouncing his policy or reviling his person. In the summer of 1866, Dennison and Speed and Harlan found their want of agreement with their official chief an insuperable objection to their remaining any longer, and they, one after another, voluntarily retired. But Stanton staid on. Even down to a period as late as the passage of the Tenure-of-office bill, he must have still maintained his attitude of acquiescence, at least, in the course of the administration, and of friendliness to the President, as he was requested to write the message to accompany the veto of that bill, on account of the clearness with which he demonstrated its unconstitutionality. Yet, notwithstanding all this, from the very beginning of his term he appears to have enjoyed the confidence of the very men who were assailing his chief with the bitterest epithets. The radicals regarded him as their trusty outpost in the camp of the enemy. His ostensible agreement with the 'Apostate' seems to have troubled them not at all. They implored him to stay. They deprecated his resignation. They were in daily fear of his dismissal. They must have counseled him to simulate acquiescence in the policy they detested in order to remain where he was. Seward continued on, and Welles, and McCulloch, of the old Cabinet of Lincoln; but none of them left room for doubt of his fidelity to his chief, and each of them was the mark of radical abuse. Stanton, alone, sitting alongside of them at the council-table of the President and voting with them, continued to be the object of the tenderest regard to the most implacable opponents of the administration. His secret allies devised the proviso in the first section of the Tenure bill to force the President to keep their spy in the midst of his official household; and, as soon as that bill became a law, his attitude of masterly passivity underwent a change. The mask he had worn for two years was gradually withdrawn. He let it be known to the President and his associates that he could not go with them in approving the veto of the main reconstruction act, some of the most stinging paragraphs of which his early friend and benefactor, Judge Black, had written. After the first supplementary act was passed, he waxed louder in his opposition. The surer he felt of his position the more defiant in his disagreement he became and the more offensive in his manner. In the Cabinet meeting on the twenty-first of June, which endorsed the Attorney-General, settled the course of the administration and brought the members of Congress hurrying across the country to the July session, he stood out the one uncompromising dissentient. When the Congress sent to the President the second supplementary act, he regarded the complete prostration of the South under the heel of the military as an endorsement of his revolt. The harmony of the Cabinet was at an end. The President began to throw out hints that the proper place of an opponent of his policy was outside the inner circle of the administration, that the confidential servant of the radicals could not consistently with his own honour play the role of confidential adviser of the President. But he soon ascertained that hints, which in such a delicate relation had heretofore been effectual, in this instance and upon this officer were thrown away. The unpleasant discovery gradually dawned upon his mind that the one of his confidential advisers in whom he had lost all confidence intended with undreamt-of hardihood to repudiate his own well-known opinion of the Tenure-of-office act and, taking refuge behind its provisions, to thrust his offensive presence and antagonistic principles upon the council-table of the administration. When their relations had come to such a pass there could be but one issue with such a man as Johnson. In his subsequent communication to the Senate he quietly says: "I had come to the conclusion that the time had arrived when it was proper Mr. Stanton should retire from my Cabinet. The mutual confidence and accord which should exist in such a relation had ceased." Sheridan's course, too, continued to run counter to the President's instructions, and on the thirtieth of July by an imperial edict that commander decapitated Throckmorton, the governor elected by the people of the reconstructed state of Texas, and appointed Pease, the defeated candidate for that office, in his place. On the first day of August, 1867, in a personal interview, the President told General Grant that he could no longer tolerate Stanton in his Cabinet and was contemplating the removal of Sheridan. Grant endeavoured to dissuade him, especially on behalf of his favourite subordinate; and, after the interview and on the same day, in a private letter addressed to the President protested against "the removal of the very able commander of the fifth military district" and expressed his disapproval of the removal of Stanton in these words: "His removal cannot be effected against his will without the consent of the Senate. . . . It certainly was the intention of the legislative branch of the Government to place cabinet ministers beyond the power of Executive removal and it is pretty well understood that" the act "was intended specially to protect the Secretary of War."* This letter, clothed in such positive terms and signed by the most renowned name in the country, could not have been without effect, and the President paused, perplexed in the extreme. The first day of August—the date of the letter—was Thursday. On Monday, the fifth, something happened.

The trial of John H. Surratt for the murder of Abra-

* See letter in McPh. Recon., p. 307 *n.* And yet Gen. Schofield states that at the date of this letter Gen. Grant, in Richmond, Va., "in the most emphatic terms announced his intention to demand, on his return to Washington, that the President either remove Stanton or accept his (General Grant's) resignation." Art. "Controversies in the War Department," *Century Magazine* for August, 1897.

ham Lincoln began in the city of Washington on Monday the tenth day of June, 1867, and the testimony closed on Saturday the twenty-sixth day of July. On the first day of August, Mr. Merrick, one of the counsel for the prisoner, was addressing the jury. Ever since the execution of Mrs. Surratt, a rumour that five members of the military commission that tried her had signed a petition to the President recommending a commutation of the death-sentence had been flying about. No such document had ever been published, although an authorized report of the trial, including the several verdicts, sentences and the President's approval, was printed with the certificate of the proper officer to its accuracy; but still the rumour lived on. In allusion to this story and to a promise made by the prosecution at the opening of the case to set this question at rest, Mr. Merrick, in the course of his speech, pressed the query: "Where is your record? Why didn't you bring it in? Did you find at the end . . . a recommendation to mercy . . . that the President never saw?" Stirred by this taunt Edwards Pierrepont, the leading counsel for the United States, immediately sent to Joseph Holt, the Judge-Advocate-General, for the original record; and it was brought to him in the court-room by Holt himself who related to Pierrepont in the presence of "three gentlemen" its history. The next day, Mr. Bradley, the senior counsel, in summing up for the prisoner, recurred to the failure of the government to produce the mysterious paper. So that when, on Saturday (the third), Pierrepont rose to make the closing argument, he felt himself bound, and not only bound but able, to give a conclusive answer to the sneers of his adversaries. Holding in his hand the record, he made this explicit statement:

> "President Johnson, when the record was presented to him, laid it before his Cabinet, and every single member voted to confirm the sentence and the President with his own hand wrote his confirmation of it, and with his own hand signed the warrant. No other one touched this paper, and when it was suggested by some members of the commission that in consequence of the age and sex of Mrs. Surratt it might possibly be well to change her sentence to imprisonment for life, he signed the warrant for her death with the paper right before his eyes—and there it is."

That same afternoon Judge Holt came back to the court-room to reclaim the paper and repeated its history as he had told it before and which Pierrepont had just rehearsed to the jury.*

The Sunday morning papers carried this declaration to the White House; and, in consequence, on the morning of Monday, the fifth, the President sent to the Secretary of War for "the findings and sentence of the conspiracy trial." When the message came General Grant happened to be at the War Office, and Stanton in his presence sent for the officer in charge of the Bureau of Military Justice (Judge Holt being temporarily absent) and ordered him to take the record to the President. On its arrival at the White House it was subjected to a "careful scrutiny" and the President discovered that, underneath the signature of the presiding officer of the

*Trial of John H. Surratt (official), Vol. 1, p. 27; Vol. 2, pp. 1207, 1237, 1249.

commission formally countersigning the record, Judge Holt had written on the death-warrant in such a place that, when handed to the President for signature, any paper coming after it would be likely to escape his observation; and that, there hanging as a superfluous leaf to the record proper, was, in very truth, a petition signed by five members of the commission praying the President, in consideration of the sex and age of Mary E. Surratt, "if he can find it consistent with his sense of duty to the country," to commute the sentence of death to imprisonment in the penitentiary for life. That flying leaf, the President instantly declared he had never seen or heard of before. He was convinced that it was not with the record when submitted for his approval. Judge Holt, he remembered, had brought the record to him in a private interview, had written out the warrant in his presence, presented to him for signature and carried the record away; so that Holt, surely, must have been a party to the imposition. And, if the Judge-Advocate was guilty, the Secretary of War must have either contrived, or connived at, the suppression; for who can believe a subordinate would dare to perpetrate so deadly a fraud without the knowledge of the head of the Department? The President had been hood-winked into signing the death-warrant of a woman whose life he might otherwise have spared. As he well knew, no such paper was ever laid before, much less considered by, his Cabinet of that date, and a summons to Seward, Welles and McCulloch (the only remaining members beside Stanton) would demonstrate the falsehood of that part of Holt's story. But, as it happened, the testimony of these officers was rendered unnecessary by Pierrepont himself. Continuing his address all day Monday without recurring to his statement of Saturday, on Tuesday (the sixth), as though in the meantime he had been warned of his error, he went out of his way to repeat that statement as if word for word, and yet, in repeating it, he omitted all mention of the Cabinet and of the presence of the paper before the Cabinet officers.*

At so critical a juncture as this, what stand Stanton took, whether he threw his shield over his hard-pressed subordinate, resolved to support him in his asseverations that the "identical paper" was "right before the eyes" of the President, we do not positively know: But this much we do know. The request for the record was made by the President to Stanton as Secretary of War; Stanton as Secretary of War transmitted the record to the President on the morning of the fifth; and on the same day Stanton received the following missive:

> "Sir: Public considerations of a high character constrain me to say that your resignation as Secretary of War will be accepted.
>
> "Andrew Johnson
>
> President of the United States."

* See original record in Judge-Advocate's office. Letter of Chief Clerk Wright to Holt contained in Holt's "Refutation" printed in the Washington *Chronicle* of December 1, 1873, and republished in pamphlet. Also Holt's "Vindication" printed in same newspaper, August 25, 1873, and republished in same pamphlet. Also Andrew Johnson's reply in same newspaper of November 12, 1873. Trial of John H. Surratt, Vol. 2, p. 1321.

To which he instantly replied:

"Sir: Your note this day has been received, stating that public considerations of a high character constrain you to say that my resignation as Secretary of War will be accepted.

"In reply, I have the honor to say that public considerations of a high character, which alone have induced me to continue at the head of this department, constrain me not to resign the office of Secretary of War before the next meeting of Congress.

"Edwin M. Stanton, Secretary of War."*

Is it not a likely presumption that the discovery of so detestable a deception concocted in the Department of War was the "last straw" banishing all hesitation from the President's mind and driving him to immediate action? It would be a most extraordinary coincidence that two such events should take place on the same day without being related to each other to some extent as cause and effect. One serious objection there is, it is true, to the adoption of this view. In communicating the reasons for Stanton's suspension to the Senate, the following December, the President failed to assign the suppression of the petition, although he did mention the suppression of General Baird's telegram sent just before the New Orleans riot. But, it should be remembered; that the suppression of the telegram was the act of Stanton, acknowledged to be so by himself,† whereas the sup-

* Given in President's Message to Senate on suspension. Trial of Andrew Johnson, Vol. 1, pp. 148, 149.

† Imp. Inv., p. 398.

pression of the petition, so far as the proof goes, was the act, not of Stanton, but of Holt. The record to which hung the incriminatory paper was not returned to the Judge-Advocate's office until the following December,* but, though the President kept it by him four months, he took no steps to punish the offender. When he did not suspend the Judge-Advocate he could hardly assign the Judge-Advocate's offence as a reason for the suspension of his superior officer. On the whole, it is probable that the President omitted to mention the suppression of the petition for the same reason that he did not court-martial Holt, viz: an instinctive revulsion, natural to a man in his situation, from entering upon a personal controversy over so tender a subject as the measure of severity dealt out to the convicted assassins of the martyr in whose seat he was sitting.

On this eventful fifth day of August, another startling revelation was made, touching the Judge-Advocate, if not the Secretary of War, just as close. John M. Binckley, acting Attorney-General in the absence of Stanbery, laid his report respecting the pardon of Charles A. Dunham, *alias* Sanford Conover, before the President. This document consisted of a recital of the contents of two parcels left at the executive office and referred to the Attorney-General. The first—left on the twenty-seventh of July, it is not stated by whom—was composed of four, or rather three, papers: 1. A letter from A. G. Riddle—one of the counsel for the United States in the preparation of the case against Surratt—to the President, dated the twentieth of July, eulogizing the services

* Wright's letter, *ut supra*.

which Dunham, although in jail, had been able to render before and during the trial of Surratt, in "giving much valuable information both as to the facts and witnesses for the United States," and, also, "the history of and facts concerning witnesses called for the defence," and in "communicating important facts and suggestions," for which, the writer states, "the Government are under great obligations to him" and should mark its appreciation of them in a way not to be mistaken. 2. On a leaf of the same sheet, a communication from Judge Holt, dated the twenty-fourth but unaddressed, in which, after signifying his concurrence in "the estimate of the value and importance of the services of Charles A. Dunham" made by Mr. Riddle, he, likewise, recommends his pardon. 3. A note from Ashley, dated July twenty-second, to Holt and Riddle suggesting that a petition for the pardon of "Mr. Dunham"—a draft of which was to have been forwarded with the note but was wanting—should be prepared and signed by them; Ashley adding: "I think he (Dunham) is clearly entitled to it, and I hope you will aid him all you can." 4. The last paper was a petition addressed to His Excellency, Andrew Johnson, President of the United States, dated July twenty-sixth and signed "Chas. A. Dunham," praying for a pardon.

It appears from the records of the court that, at this last-mentioned date, Dunham's final motion to suspend sentence further was denied, and he was taken at last to the Albany penitentiary. Abandoning all hope of aid from his present friends, he suddenly resolved to treat them to a dose of their own poison. The second parcel, left on the thirtieth of July by Mrs. Dunham, was composed of: (1) A long letter from Dunham dated the twenty-ninth, and addressed to the President, in which he denounced "the diabolical designs" of Ashley and the other "traitors and conspirators"; the "nefarious conspiracy" of "Ashley and Co.," by which, in consideration of the pardon they were to obtain for him, he should procure testimony connecting Andrew Johnson with Booth. His charges were most explicit. Ashley, he said, "thought it would be very plausible to prove" four circumstances, viz: 1. That Booth paid Johnson several visits at the Kirkwood House. 2. That Johnson corresponded with Booth. 3. That the placing of Atzerodt with weapons at the Kirkwood was a sham to make it appear that the Vice President was intended as a victim and thus divert suspicion of Johnson's connivance at Lincoln's murder. 4. That Booth stated just after the fourth of March to intimate friends at New York that he was acting with the knowledge of the Vice President; that it was arranged to kill Lincoln on the day of the inauguration, which accounted for Johnson's strange conduct on that occasion. Dunham confessed without hesitation that he assured Ashley he "should have no difficulty in finding persons of good standing and moral character to prove these matters, and it was agreed that" he "should do so as soon as released." "As an earnest" of what he could do in this line, Dunham tells that, at the desire of Ashley and Butler, he forwarded memoranda of the subject-matter of the testimony they were in need of to a "trusty friend" with "instructions for him to procure two other friends to commit to memory the statements enclosed to him, and, when sent for, to come here (to Washington) and repeat them." And these two persons, he stated, actually did come, "were inspected by Ashley and Butler, and were found to possess the requisite qualifications as to intelligence and personal appearance"; were "passed" and "introduced to several Radical members of the House." "Butler desired to have taken the depositions of these men at the time," but Dunham "would not consent to its being done" before his release. Accompanying this letter were (2) a specimen of the memoranda used to coach the false witnesses (which will be given hereafter at the date it was produced before the Impeachment committee), (3) four notes of Ashley on the business in hand, and (4) one of the Rev. Mr. Matchett. The last note of Ashley bears date July 8, 1867, and in it he writes: "If you can put the *originals* (*i. e.*, letters of A. J. to Davis and Booth) in my hands, I will say that no one shall take or destroy them without your express order in writing except you are released."

The foregoing report appeared in the public press on the morning of the tenth of August;* on the afternoon of which last-mentioned day, it may be stated in passing, the jury in the Surratt case, after three days' and three nights' deliberation, was discharged because of inability to agree.†

But (to return from this digression) be the undisclosed reasons for the suspension of Stanton, if any

* See Washington newspapers of that date. Dunham was pardoned, in February, 1869, by the President on the ground of ill-health.

† Surratt's Trial, Vol. 2, p. 1379.

undisclosed reasons there were, what they may, the defiant response of the Secretary to the President's request for his resignation was of itself a sufficient reason without seeking farther. As Johnson states: "One thing is certain, whatever cogency in such considerations, . . . it was official misconduct, to say the least of it, to parade them before his superior officer. . . . Necessarily it must end our most important official relations, for I cannot imagine a degree of effrontery which would embolden the head of a Department to take his seat at the council table in the Executive Mansion after such an act. Nor can I imagine a President so forgetful of the proper respect and dignity belonging to his office as to submit to such an intrusion."* In fact, even Stanton's phenomenal sense of official duty did not go so far as to force him to pose any longer as one of the constitutional advisers of the President. He clung to his office in the War department, but his chair at the Cabinet-table stood significantly empty. For his part, the President delayed the complete ejectment of this self-confessed ally of his enemies only long enough to determine upon the *modus operandi* and to find a successor. Aware that, according to the construction put upon the proviso of the first section of the Tenure act by its authors and now apparently accepted by the Republican party at large, the summary removal of Stanton would be denounced as an impeachable offence, he sought to avoid such an accusation by availing himself of the power of suspension granted to him by the Tenure act with a restriction; but which, he believed, being included under the power of

* Message *ut supra*.

removal vested in him by the Constitution, the Congress had no right to restrict. Moreover, he was greatly embarrassed to find a successor able and willing to displace the renowned War-minister with the Republican party at his back; and he seems to have thought it indispensable to secure the cooperation of Grant. In frequent interviews with the General, he strove to persuade him to take the place, assuring him that in any event Stanton should remain no longer. Grant finally consented, provided the displacement took the form of the suspension of the incumbent and a letter of authority to himself to discharge the duties of the office *ad interim*. An understanding having thus been effected, on the twelfth of August the President issued an order addressed to Edwin M. Stanton, Secretary of War, suspending him from office "by virtue of the power and authority invested" in the President "by the Constitution and laws of the United States"; and a letter addressed to Ulysses S. Grant authorizing him to act as Secretary of War *ad interim*. On the same day, Grant notified Stanton of his acceptance, softening the blow by expressing his "appreciation of the zeal, patriotism, firmness and ability" with which the officer he superseded had "ever discharged the duties of Secretary of War." On receipt of these two notes, Stanton penned a communication to the President as follows:

"Under a sense of public duty I am compelled to deny your right, under the Constitution and laws of the United States, without the advice and consent of the Senate, and without legal cause, to suspend me from office as Secretary of War. . . . But inasmuch as the General commanding the armies of the United States has been appointed *ad interim*, and has notified me that he has accepted the appointment, I have no alternative but to submit to superior force."*

Stanton was out at last but, although the General of the army was in, he was in only *ad interim*. The Tenure act provided in cases of suspension under it, that if the Senate refused to concur the suspended officer forthwith resumed the functions of his office. Now, if there was any one thing on which Johnson was resolved, it was that the man whom he had suspended in this case should never reenter his Cabinet or recommence his counter-mining in the department of War. To make himself sure that he held full control of the situation, a few days after the change was made he stepped over to the War-Office for an interchange of views with the new secretary concerning the course to be pursued in the too probable event of the non-concurrence of the Senate. Over certain particulars of this interview the President and General Grant subsequently fell out, but upon the more important features they substantially agree. Johnson first made clear his determination to prevent at all hazards the resumption of office by Stanton; and, then, he inquired whether Grant intended to stand by him in case the Senate voted to restore his enemy. Would he hold on to the office and drive Stanton to the courts, or, preferring to avoid the unpleasantness of legal controversy, resign in time for the President to fill the office with a person who would be troubled with no such reluctance? Grant replied, according to

* See letters in McPh. Recon., p. 261.

his own statement, that "in case the Senate should not concur in his suspension," Mr. Stanton, "to obtain possession of his office," "would have to appeal to the courts to reinstate him"; adding, however, that this was a "general principle," and, if on further examination of the Tenure-of-office act, he should "change his mind in this particular case, he would inform the President of the fact."*

Owing to the habit of strict military obedience to which Grant was enured, the constitutional commander-in-chief, for the next three months, held once more unchecked control over the department of War. One week after the new secretary seated himself in the seat of Stanton, the President sent him an order assigning General Thomas to the command of the fifth military district in the place of General Sheridan, who was transferred to the department of the Missouri, and directing him to give the necessary instructions to carry the order into effect. He condescended, however, so far as to send along with the order a note inviting any "suggestions" the secretary might "deem necessary respecting these assignments." Grant embraced the opportunity thus afforded him to "urge in the name of a patriotic people" that "the order be not insisted on," that "the expressed wish of the country is that General Sheridan should not be removed," and "the will of the people is the law of the land." "His removal will only be regarded as an effort to defeat the laws of Congress." "It will be interpreted by the unreconstructed element in the South . . . as a triumph. It will embolden them

* See Grant's letter, McPh. Recon., p. 283.

to renewed opposition to the loyal masses believing that they have the Executive with them." General Thomas, too, had always protested against being assigned to any of these military districts. This plain-spoken remonstrance produced no effect. The secretary might have the benefit of his "suggestions" if he only obeyed orders. There was a delay of a few days; the ill-health of General Thomas rendering necessary a modification of the original assignment. But, on the twenty-sixth of August, an order assigning General Winfield S. Hancock to the command of the fifth district and transferring General Sheridan to the department of the Missouri was issued by the President and promulgated by Secretary Grant. On the receipt of this order Sheridan turned over his command to his next in rank and departed. On the same day, a similar order was issued relieving General Sickles from the command of the second district and assigning General Canby to his place; the latter officer assuming command on the fifth of September. The remaining changes in the military commanders were not made until the twenty-eighth of December, when Meade relieved Pope in the third, and McDowell, Ord, in the fourth district.*

Hancock was summoned to Washington on his way to his new department and was made a lion of by the administration, its supporters and the Democrats. When, on assuming command he issued his first general order declaring as an unalterable principle the supremacy of the civil over the military power, a shout went up from the conservative portion of the people as though

* McPh. Recon., pp. 306–7–8, 345–6.

the republic had been reborn; and the glory of this single act in civil affairs surpassed, for a time, the glory of all his achievements in the field.*

* Order of November 29, 1867, McPh. Recon., p. 324.

CHAPTER IV

THE DEFEAT OF THE FIRST IMPEACHMENT, AND THE REINSTATEMENT OF STANTON

THE elections in the Northern states in the fall of 1867 indicated that the tide of popular opinion was running strongly against the reconstruction policy of the dominant party. In September, Maine at the extreme east reduced the Republican majority of 28,000 of the year before to 1,100; California at the extreme west elected (in the spring, however) a Democratic governor and two out of the three representatives in Congress. In October, Pennsylvania was carried by the opposition, and Ohio, though the Republican candidate for governor was successful by a narrow majority, elected a Democratic legislature which, the following year, revoked the ratification of the fourteenth amendment and elected a Democrat to succeed Wade. What was still more significant, the voters rejected a proposed amendment to the state constitution granting suffrage to the comparatively few negroes within her borders by a constitutional majority of fifty thousand. In November, New York went over to the Democrats by a majority nearly as large. New Jersey went the same way, electing a legislature which revoked the ratification of the fourteenth amendment and sent back to the Senate the ejected Stockton. The people of Kansas and Minnesota—sure Republican states—cast a verdict against negro suffrage on a direct submission to them of that issue. Though it was an odd year in politics and the result could have no effect upon the composition of the Congress, in every state where elections were held, even in Massachusetts, the trend was in the same direction. All idea of selecting as a candidate for President a true expositor of the policy of the party was abandoned, and every eye was turned to the soldier who, though a member of the administration, bore the charmed title of the Conqueror of the Rebellion.* On the other hand, the President regarded the result as but another justification of his habitual confidence in the people, to which he alluded in a speech which he read to a crowd that gathered before the White House on the night of the thirteenth of November to congratulate him on the recent victories. "The remedy for the present unhappy condition of the country must come from the people themselves," he said.

> "At the present time they cannot, according to the forms of the Constitution, repeal obnoxious laws; they cannot remove or control this military despotism. The remedy is nevertheless in their hands, and is a sure one, if not controlled by fraud, overawed by arbitrary power, or from apathy on their part too long delayed. With abiding confidence in their patriotism, wisdom and integrity, I am still hopeful that in the end the rod of despotism will be broken, the armed heel of power lifted from the necks of the people, and the principles of a violated Constitution preserved."†

* For the elections, see McPh. Recon., pp. 372, 353–4.

† Speech, Imp. Inv., p. 1175.

To the advocates of impeachment on the judiciary committee which met two days after, the speech was but another high misdemeanour, and a printed copy was put in evidence. "The echo of his last speech," they say in their report, "is still lingering in our ears"; and on the twentieth the committee once more came to a vote. It will be remembered that last June they decided against impeachment by a vote of five to four. Notwithstanding the fact that, after the investigation was reopened at the solicitation of the minority, no testimony of any importance was taken except General Grant's which was not unfavourable to the President, the committee now reversed its decision; one of the Republicans, who had voted in the majority before, joining his radical colleagues. The convert was John C. Churchill from Oswego, New York, who never publicly accounted for his change of mind. The adjourned session of Congress opening the next day, the committee was given time until the next Monday to make a report; and during the two working days intervening, a fitting close was put to the investigation by the reexamination of Baker and the examination of Ashley. The fugitive witness having returned of his own accord was called on to disclose the whereabouts of his mysterious Mrs. Harris. He had seen her, he swore, but he could name no person who had seen her in his company, or who had seen her enter the hotels where he professed to have met her, or who had seen her while there. He had pointed her out to Matchett who subpœnaed her to come before the committee, but she would not come without money, he said. "How much was wanted?" inquired a member of the committee. "$25,000," answered Baker. "Who made that proposition?" "This woman made it"; and with this prompt reply Baker was dismissed.* Ashley was the last witness, called seemingly by the Democratic members of the committee. He admitted that from the beginning of the impeachment movement he entertained the belief that Andrew Johnson was implicated in the assassination of Abraham Lincoln; that he had stated to members of the House of Representatives that he had evidence which satisfied him of that fact; that he believed that letters were in existence from Andrew Johnson to Jefferson Davis and to Booth establishing that fact; that he had been engaged ever since the investigation began in an effort to unearth these letters and to obtain legal evidence to bring before the committee; that he had employed Matchett; that he had held repeated interviews with Conover-Dunham in jail by day and by night; that after the conviction he had importuned the judges to stay the execution of the sentence until an application might be made for pardon; that he backed the convict's application to President Johnson for a pardon so that the convict might be used as a witness to accuse the man who pardoned him of complicity in the murder of his predecessor. The memorandum enclosed by Dunham in his petition of last July and which appeared in the report of the acting Attorney-General was produced and put in evidence.† It begins:

* Imp. Inv., p. 1193.

† See Ch. III, p. 281, *supra*.

"Shortly before the inauguration of Lincoln and Johnson, the latter, through or in connection with Booth, sent several letters to the Confederacy, one of which was intended for Jefferson Davis." These letters, it goes on, were taken to Richmond by one Allen who returned "bearing several letters from J. P. Benjamin" "enclosed to Booth." Allen delivered the package to Booth who taking one letter out "addressed to 'Andrew Johnson, Vice-President elect of the United States'" asked Allen to deliver it which he did in company with a friend whom Allen took along; both Allen and friend can be produced. There were two ex-rebel soldiers, one named Dawson, who would testify that they met Booth the second day before his death "near Garrett's" and he told them he had "killed Lincoln and thereby made a good southern man President." Dawson replied that on the contrary "if he meant that he had made Andy Johnson President, he had done the worse possible thing for the South, as he was more extreme in his views and a greater enemy to the South than Lincoln." "Booth replied that it was a mistake; that Johnson as a candidate and office-seeker had to say a great many things, but that as President he could do as he pleased; that he was bound to be a friend of the South; and that if he went back on him (Booth) he would have him hung higher than Haman."

Ashley explained what he called his "theory about this matter":

"I have always believed that President Harrison and President Taylor and President Buchanan were poisoned, and were poisoned for the express purpose of putting the Vice Presidents in the presidential office. In the first two instances it was successful. It was attempted with Mr. Buchanan and failed. It succeeded with Mr. Taylor and

Mr. Harrison. Then Mr. Lincoln was assassinated, and from my stand-point I could come to a conclusion which impartial men, holding different views, could not come. It would not amount to legal evidence.

"Q. Do you mean to say that you formed an opinion and expressed it to members of Congress that there was evidence to implicate Mr. Johnson which was not legal evidence?

"A. Yes, sir; it satisfied me.

"Q. State to the committee any evidence or fact that you know, tending in any degree to fasten the assassination on Mr. Johnson.

"A. I never withheld anything from the committee which I regarded as evidence.

"Q. Then you state now, as you did before, that you know of no other evidence tending to show that fact?

"A. I know none at present which I could bring to the knowledge of the committee, or I should bring it."*

On Monday, the voluminous farrago of testimony the committee had raked together was laid before the House accompanied by three reports. There was a majority report recommending the passage of a resolution that Andrew Johnson, President of the United States, be impeached of high crimes and misdemeanours. There was a report of the two Republicans in the minority recommending the passage of a resolution that the committee be discharged from the further consideration of the impeachment and that the subject be laid upon the table. There was a report of the Democratic members concurring with their associates of the minority respecting the law and the facts but dissenting from the censure of the political conduct of the President which the Re-

* Imp. Inv., pp. 1204, 1194 *et seq.;* 1198–9.

publican minority saw fit to pronounce.* As to the thoroughness of the investigation there was no dispute. The majority report says: the committee "have spared no pains to make their investigations as complete as possible, not only in the exploration of the public archives, but in following every indication that seemed to promise any additional light upon the great subjects of inquiry." The report of the Democrats in the minority declares:

> "A drag-net has been put out to catch every malicious whisper throughout the land, and all the vile vermin who had gossip or slander to detail, hearsay or otherwise, have been permitted to appear and place it upon record for the delectation of mankind. Spies have been sent all over the land to find something that might blacken the name and character of the Chief Magistrate of our country. Unwhipped knaves have given information of fabulous letters and documents. . . . That most notorious character, General L. C. Baker, chief of the detective police, even had the effrontery to insult the American people by placing spies within the very walls of the Executive Mansion; the privacy of the President's home, his private life and habits and most secret thoughts have not been deemed sacred or exempt from invasion; the members of his household have been examined; and the chief prosecutor has not hesitated to dive into loathsome dungeons and consort with convicted felons, for the purpose of accomplishing his object of arraigning the President on a charge of infamous crimes."

There were ninety-nine witnesses sworn on a variety of topics. But, as the report of the two Republicans in

* The reports are prefixed to the testimony in Imp. Inv.

the minority states: "a great deal of the matter . . . is of no value whatever. Much of it is mere hearsay, opinions of witnesses, and no little amount of it is utterly irrelevant to the case. Comparatively a small amount of it could be used on a trial of this case before the Senate."

On the law of the case there was a wide difference of opinion between the Republicans in the majority and the Republicans in the minority. The leading proposition of law upheld by the majority was that, under the section of the Constitution of the United States providing that "the President . . . shall be removed from office on impeachment for, and conviction of, treason, bribery and other high crimes and misdemeanors," a course of maladministration "involving usurpation of power and repeated violations of law" was impeachable although no offence indictable under the statutes of the United States was committed. The leading proposition of law maintained by the Republicans in the minority was that no offence, except the two specified in the Constitution itself, was impeachable unless at the same time indictable as a crime or misdemeanour, not merely at common law but under some existing statute of the United States. This latter proposition, after the flood of light thrown upon the subject on the trial of the President, will now be considered as altogether too narrow. At the time the words in question were used, the United States statute-maker not having yet come into being, there was no United States statute against treason or bribery and none, of course, defining any other crime or misdemeanour. Nevertheless, the framers of the

Constitution presupposed treason to be a high crime, and bribery, if not originally a high crime, a high misdemeanour; and they did so because of their familiarity with the common law and the statutes of the several states. So, also, when they used the phrase "high crimes and misdemeanors" it was not with any prophetic vision of what might be made high crimes and misdemeanours by some federal statute to come, but with the knowledge of what at that very moment were high crimes and misdemeanours by reason of the common law and the statutes of the several states. Besides, this position of the minority leads necessarily to a most dangerous conclusion. Mr. Boutwell, in the speech he made in defence of the majority report, pointed this out in words memorable for what was to come:

> "Assume that it is not possible to impeach the President or any civil officer for any offense of which he may be guilty, unless such offense shall have been declared previously by a law of the United States to be an indictable high crime or misdemeanor. But will it be assumed further on the one hand that Congress may by law declare an act to be a misdemeanor which, according to the principles of the common law, contains no one element or quality of a crime, and upon the doing of the thing inhibited proceed to impeach and remove the President of the United States from his office?"*

But, while the legal proposition of the minority is too narrow, the legal proposition of the majority, emasculating, as it does, the words "high crimes and misde-

* Appendix to *Globe,* 2d Sess. 40th Cong., p. 57.

meanors'' of all precise and definitive meaning, making offences impeachable that are not indictable at all, either by common law or statute, is a world too wide. The same line of argument they followed to refute the extreme conclusion of their opponents applies with equal force to their own. The history of the words in the convention that framed the Constitution, as narrated by Madison, seems decisive of the controversy. The original proposition submitted was to make the President removable on impeachment and conviction ''for mal or corrupt conduct,'' or ''for malpractice or neglect of duty.'' Afterwards, the clause was modified so as to read ''for treason, bribery, or corruption,'' and finally confined to ''treason and bribery'' alone. When, after being so amended, it was taken up once more for consideration, Colonel Mason moved to add ''mal-administration.'' Madison objecting that so vague a term would be equivalent to a tenure during the pleasure of the Senate, Mason withdrew the word and substituted ''other high crimes and misdemeanors against the state,'' which was agreed to, and on the general revision the last three words were deleted as superfluous.* So that, if any construction of a constitutional provision by resorting to its origin and gestation was ever valid, the phrase ''other high crimes and misdemeanors'' used in the Constitution must be held to mean only such malfeasance in office as constituted at common law a high crime or a high misdemeanour of a kindred grade, respectively, with treason or bribery.

* See Supplement to Elliot's Debates (1876, Lippincott), pp. 340, 507, 528. *Cf.* Groesbeck's argument, Trial, Vol. 2, p. 190.

Enough, at present, on the question of law. Coming to the facts, "the great salient point of accusation," according to the majority report (written by Williams) was "usurpation of power" with "the one great overshadowing purpose of reconstructing the shattered governments of the rebel states in accordance with his (the President's) own will, in the interests of the great criminals who carried them into rebellion, . . . by pardoning their offences, restoring their lands and hurrying them back—their hearts unrepentant, and their hands yet red with the blood of our people—into a condition where they could once more embarrass and defy, if not absolutely rule the Government which they had vainly endeavored to destroy. It is around this point and as auxiliary to this central idea that all the special acts of mal-administration . . . will be found to gravitate." Then follow the specifications: First, the President surrendered to the rebels the "system of railroads" "with their costly apparatus," existing in their states, and restored to the rebels large amounts of captured and abandoned property; in violation of the confiscation acts. Second, the President abused the pardoning power; instancing (1) telegrams of the President and Secretary of State promising pardons to delegates of the constitutional conventions, held in obedience to the President's proclamation, so as to qualify them to sit, and (2) the case of the West Virginia deserters, reference to which has already been made.* Third, the failure of the President to execute the laws by bringing the rebels to punishment. "In regard to the case of the leader of the

* *Supra,* Chap. II, p. 222.

rebellion himself the Committee are not agreed upon the propriety or necessity of indulging in any special commentary." But the pardon of Clement C. Clay, charged equally with Davis with the crime of complicity in the assassination, is mentioned with disapprobation. Fourth, the President abused the appointing power and with it the power of removal from office. How such an "abuse" which, the report admits, had been practiced "for the last thirty years of our history" could on a sudden become an impeachable misdemeanour, it is attempted to explain by the circumstance, that the "present incumbent without a party to represent his opinions, except it may be in the rebel States, . . . has felt no hesitation in declaring in a public speech: 'If you will stand by me I will kick them (the friends of the Congress in office) out as fast as I can,'" and has been doing it ever since. He also has refused to send nominations to the Senate for vacancies filled during recess, and has reappointed persons rejected by the Senate, on its adjournment. And he violated an act of Congress in permitting his provisional governors and revenue officers in the South to discharge their duties without taking the test oath. Fifth, the President abused the veto power. The exercise of a power expressly granted the President is transmuted into a high crime or misdemeanour by the allegation: "This power has been systematically employed to defeat the will of the people, and accomplish the criminal designs of the Executive." The negotiations with the Colorado senators-elect are cited as evidence.* Sixth, the President corruptly interfered

* *Supra*, p. 91.

in elections. Under this head are specified the efforts of office-holders at the Philadelphia convention and elsewhere, to uphold the policy of the President and "defeat the will of Congress"; the speeches of the President from that of the twenty-second of February, 1866, down to the speech of the thirteenth of November just past; his dissuasions of the Southern people from adopting the fourteenth amendment; and the riots at Memphis and New Orleans for which, without a single circumstance of proof, it is alleged the President is responsible.

In reviewing the facts as marshalled in the report, it is only necessary to remark that the main offence charged and all the subsidiary offences on which the greatest stress was laid—restoration of property, wholesale pardons, dispensations with the test oath—were committed before the meeting of the thirty-ninth Congress in December, 1865, and a year before the impeachment movement was begun, nay, before there was any open breach between the President and the Congress. Very little stress was laid on the speeches made during the famous tour, though these were the actual exciting cause of the present prosecution. And not a word was said of any failure to execute the Freedmen's Bureau or Civil Rights acts, and not a specific accusation made that in any one instance the reconstruction acts were not carried out. The President was to be punished, not for what he had done in the midst of the fight, but for what he had done before the fight began. There was even an aspect of the case in which the entire movement became ludicrous—an aspect to which the Democratic minority on the committee called attention. "The President is gravely arraigned,'' they said, ''for arraying himself against the loyal people of the country'' by pursuing a reconstruction policy which Congress antagonizes, ''when Congress itself for pursuing a reconstructing policy which the President antagonizes has just received the most withering and indignant condemnation and rebuke of the entire people from Maine to California.'' Indeed, one of the ''particular offences'' which haunted the mind of Mr. Boutwell was committed before Johnson was even Vice President. As he described it: ''Jefferson Davis was still at Richmond. The armies of Lee menaced the capital of his country. Andrew Johnson was approaching that capital for the purpose of taking the oath of office. That capital was merely a fortified garrison. He then declares that the country cannot be saved except by the old Democratic party.'' ''That casual expression discloses his mysterious course from that day to this.'' Even before he was President and when he had no reason to believe he would ever be President unless he had already foreseen the assassination of his predecessor, he had conceived the deep-laid scheme of turning the country over to the rebels and ''the old Democratic party''!* Mr. Boutwell never forgot it. Nearly twenty years after he quotes it as the key to the whole of Johnson's subsequent career.† Wilson, in his reply to Mr. Boutwell, reduced the incident to its true proportions when he said, that, so far from the remark being a crime in Johnson, it showed that ''we committed

* App. *Globe, ut supra*, p. 60.

† *North Amer. Rev.*, December, 1885.

a terrible blunder . . . when we selected Andrew Johnson as our candidate for the Vice Presidential office."*

No confutation could be more complete than was wrought by the report of the Republicans in the minority (written by James F. Wilson) of the charges presented by the majority. Concerning the animus displayed by the latter it states:

"The report of the majority resolves all presumptions against the President, closes the door against all doubts, affirms facts as established by the testimony in support of which there is not a particle of evidence before us which would be received by any court in the land. We dissent from all this, and from the temper and spirit of the report."

Again:

"All the testimony relating to the failure to try, and admission to bail of, Jefferson Davis, the assassination of President Lincoln, the diary of J. Wilkes Booth, his place of burial, the practice of pardon brokerage, the alleged correspondence of the President with Jefferson Davis, may be interesting to a reader, but is not of the slightest importance so far as a determination of this case is concerned. Still, much of this irrelevant matter has been interwoven into the report of the majority, and has served to heighten its color and deepen its tone."

Coming to the central charge, Wilson sweeps it away by as complete a *reductio ad absurdum* as was ever achieved. By simply incorporating in his report copious citations from the testimony of Stanton, Seward, and Grant, he demonstrates that in the inception of the recon-

* Wilson's Speech, *Globe*, 2d Sess. 40th Cong., App. p. 64.

struction policy of the administration, in the putting it in operation without calling together the Congress, the executive department acted as a unit; that in the so-called usurpation, every member of the Cabinet as well as the general of the army was a voluntary participant, and, if the President was guilty of a high crime or misdemeanour in this matter, they were all as guilty as he. This strong point, Mr. Boutwell, to whose imagination Andrew Johnson was a monster of depravity, endeavoured to meet in his speech in the House, by describing Johnson as also a monster in ability; pleading that his Cabinet officers "in the beginning did not understand the President's character, capacity and purposes"; further, that the President's "capacity has not been comprehended by the country. Violent sometimes in language, indiscreet in manner, impulsive in action, unwise often in declamation, he is still animated by a persistency of purpose which never yields under any circumstances, but seeks by means covert and tortuous as well as open and direct the accomplishment of the purpose of his life."* But this plea, Wilson had already anticipated by as complete an estoppel. He cites the report of the joint committee on reconstruction, of which Mr. Boutwell was himself a member, made long after the rupture between the President and the Congress and when the high crime of "usurpation" had been consummated, where the twelve Republican members do not "fail to consider the peculiar circumstances under which he acted," and, speaking of the authority of the people to frame a form of government, say: "Ordinarily this

* *Globe*, App., p. 60.

authority emanates from Congress; but, under the peculiar circumstances, your Committee is not disposed to criticise the President's action in assuming the power exercised by him in this regard." "While we do not for a moment impute to the President any such design" (*i. e.*, the very same design the majority report endeavours to fasten on him), "but cheerfully concede to him the most patriotic motives, we cannot but look with alarm upon a precedent so fraught with danger to the Republic." He then shows that, as a remedy, impeachment was not even thought of; but that the plan of the joint committee presupposed the validity of the states reconstructed under the policy now pronounced a usurpation, and "proposed to use the identical governments organized . . . in pursuance of the President's policy, as a means to insure its own success." Moreover, Congress, down to the present moment, has not set aside these governments, but the "affairs of those States are now administered through the machinery of the provisional governments, under the supervision of the military" by the sufferance of Congress. In short, even now the impeaching body is in some sort an accomplice of the President in his "colossal usurpation."

The central charge being annihilated, the subsidiary charges necessarily fell with it. "If the greater be not a crime," as the report states, "the less cannot rise to that importance." But the industrious chairman, nevertheless, took the pains to go over them and one by one give them their quietus. The first—restoration of property to the rebels—was disposed of on these grounds: 1. If there was any crime about the matter, the Secretary of War and the Quartermaster-General who, according to the testimony of Stanton himself, were the principal actors, were the criminals and not the President who, as far as appears, "did not give his personal attention to the subject to any considerable extent, except as relates to the railroads of Tennessee." 2. According to the opinion of Attorney-General Speed, a corporation cannot be guilty of treason and its property is not, therefore, subject to the confiscation acts. 3. The confiscation acts were war measures, and both Attorney-Generals Speed and Stanbery advised the President that the war being over it was not proper to continue them in force. 4. The Amnesty Proclamation carried with it a restoration of property to the pardoned offender; and this proclamation was issued in pursuance of an act of Congress. The second charge, viz: the abuse of the pardoning power, being very feebly sustained, is easily overthrown. "That the President has used the pardoning power in a vast number of cases is a fact of public notoriety. But this fact proves but one thing, namely, that a great many persons in the United States had committed crimes." The case of the West Virginia soldiers is detailed at length; it appearing that their desertion amounted to this—having got lost in the mountains they were absent from roll-call, but returned to their regiments as soon as it was possible, and served thereafter throughout the war. In order to show how a bulky charge may shrivel up into nothing beneath the breath of investigation, it may not be considered a digression to dwell for a moment on the pardon of one George W. Gayle. In December, 1864, there appeared in the *Selma*

20

Despatch, a newspaper published in Alabama, an anonymous advertisement headed: "A million dollars wanted to have peace by the first of March"; in which it was offered for a million dollars furnished by the Southern Confederacy "to cause the lives of Abraham Lincoln, William H. Seward and Andrew Johnson to be taken" by that day; $50,000 to be paid in advance, $1,000 whereof the advertiser promised to contribute. Before the assassination of President Lincoln, no attention was paid to this ridiculous card, but on the happening of that tragic event it suddenly assumed a terrible significance. The bloody offer figured largely before the military commission that tried the accused assassins as one of the connecting links between Booth and the leaders of the South. It being speedily discovered that Gayle was the guilty author, he was put under arrest and indicted for conspiracy. When the impeachment investigators lit upon the fact that this "miscreant" had been pardoned by one of the men he had proposed to assassinate, hands were raised in speechless horror and the crazy suspicion that Andrew Johnson might have connived at his own assassination flamed up afresh. The cold facts, however, put a rude extinguisher upon these lurid imaginings. In September, 1866, Gayle petitioned for his pardon; the only reason why he was excluded from the general amnesty being that he was in military custody at the time that the proclamation was issued. It appeared that he was by profession a lawyer, that he was old and feeble, with a wife and three daughters dependent on him for support; that he had sympathized with and aided the rebellion but not in the field; that he was a harmless and inoffensive man utterly incapable of doing a personal injury to anybody, and at the time of the advertisement he could not possibly have raised one hundred dollars for the purpose indicated or for any other; that the advertisement was a "mere canard," inserted for amusement, and Gayle was under the influence of liquor when he wrote it. His pardon was recommended by the officers and soldiers, late of the federal army, stationed in Dallas county, Alabama; by the Hartwill Chapter of Free Masons at Cahaba, Alabama; by the governor and every member of the Senate and House of Representatives of the state; and by the judges and principal members of the bar of Alabama; was approved by Stanbery on these papers, and granted by the President on the twenty-seventh day of April, 1867. So complete was the justification, that the pardon is not even alluded to in the majority report; yet this foolish piece of drunken bravado is still, sometimes, gravely cited even at this day as a portentous proof of the wide extent of the assassination plot.*

The third charge—the non-execution of the laws for the punishment of rebels—the minority report does not deign to notice. The fourth—appointments and removals for political reasons—is answered by an appeal to the practice of former administrations. "Did not the Republican party continue the practice? and is it now first discovered to be a crime?" As to the neglect to send in nominations to the Senate, the minority say: "the evidence does not support the charge." As to the

* Imp. Inv., pp. 564 *et seq.* "The Assassination of Lincoln," by Gen. T. M. Harris, a member of the commission, pp. 149, 150.

appointment of persons in the South who could not take the test oath, the testimony of the Secretary of the Treasury shows that none was appointed who had instigated or been active in the rebellion, or who could be considered in any way responsible for, or favourable to, it. Failing to find competent persons who could take the oath literally, the administration availed itself of those persons who had been substantially loyal; trusting to Congress for indemnification. Fifth—as to the charge of abusing the veto power, the chairman contents himself with a review of the Colorado case, pointing out that that veto had not yet been overridden, and in that sense may be considered approved by the Congress itself. Whether the President offered to approve the bill if the senators-elect would promise to support his administration or not is immaterial, as the bargain, even if it could be called corrupt, was not made. The sixth and last charge, viz: interference in elections, he remarks, is comprehended under some one or more of the foregoing and needs no further notice. The Republican minority only broke the force of their conclusion by swerving aside to aver that, while "the case fails upon the law and the testimony, from a political stand-point it is a success" and to subjoin a censure upon the President for "betraying the confidence" of "those who placed him in power" and joining "hands with their enemies."

The discussion of the several reports having been postponed until the third day of the regular session, the two Houses had nothing important to do; but, still, they would not adjourn without day for fear of a "recess"—a term which was understood to signify the interval between the end of one regular session and the beginning of another, during which the President might fill vacancies with persons whose commissions need not expire until the end of the next session; and, accordingly, they adjourned to the day and hour the regular session commenced—Monday, the second day of December, at twelve, noon. The annual message of the President plainly showed that the pending impeachment had no terrors for him. No former one breathed so glowing an ardour for battle and so fixed a determination to persevere in the contest. In tone and manner dignified and respectful, in argument it took the exasperating form of an exhortation to the Congress, in view of the disastrous effects of its course hitherto, to hasten to retrace its steps. "It is a source of profound regret," the President remarks, "that in complying with the obligation imposed upon him by the Constitution 'to give to Congress from time to time information of the state of the Union,'" he "is unable to communicate any definite adjustment, satisfactory to the American people." "On the contrary, candor compels me to declare that at this time there is no Union, as our Fathers understood the term and as they meant it to be understood by us." He coolly recommends "the repeal of the acts of Congress which place ten of the Southern States under the domination of military masters." He affects to hope that the majority may by "calm reflection" become satisfied that those acts are in direct violation of the Constitution, in which event he "does not doubt" but that they "will immediately strike them from the statute books." The President then warns Congress of the tremendous scale of expenditure these measures necessitate:

"It will require a strong standing army, and probably more than two hundred million dollars per annum to maintain the supremacy of negro governments after they are established. The sum thus thrown away would, if properly used, form a sinking fund large enough to pay the whole national debt in less than fifteen years. It is vain to hope that negroes will maintain their ascendency themselves. Without military power they are wholly incapable of holding in subjection the white people of the South."

For the first time he broaches a question fraught with peril:

"How far the duty of the President 'to preserve, protect, and defend the Constitution' requires him to go in opposing an unconstitutional act of Congress is a very serious and important question. . . . Where an act has been passed according to the forms of the Constitution by the supreme legislative authority, . . . executive resistance to it, especially in times of high party excitement, would be likely to produce violent collision between the respective adherents of the two branches of the Government. This would be simply civil war; and civil war must be resorted to as the last remedy for the worst of evils."

"It is true that cases may occur in which the Executive would be compelled to stand on his rights, and maintain them, regardless of all consequences. If Congress should pass an act which is not only in palpable conflict with the Constitution, but will certainly, if carried out, produce immediate and irreparable injury to the organic structure of the Government, and if there be neither judicial remedy for the wrong it inflicts nor power in the people to protect themselves without the official aid of their elected defender; if, for instance, the legislative department should pass an act even through all the forms of law to abolish a coordinate department of the Government; in such a case the President must take the high responsibilities of his office, and save the life of the nation at all hazards.''*

Such pungent utterances were too much for the temper of the Senate. Drake proposed a joint resolution of censure in which the rule was prescribed ''that when any act had been passed by two-thirds of both Houses over the President's objections, any subsequent official denouncement of it by him as unconstitutional, in the absence of any adjudication to that effect by the supreme judiciary of the nation, is a departure from official propriety, and a breach of official obligation, justifying and calling for the distinct reprehension on the part of the Senate and the House of Representatives''; and made a speech upon it wherein he showed his own notion of the courtesy due from one coördinate branch of the government to another by calling the President ''the nightmare that crouches upon the heaving breast of this nation,'' in one breath, and comparing him to a ''double-skinned rhinoceros,'' in the next. Howard denounced the message as ''a singular and most wanton libel upon Congress and upon every member of that body who, by vote or word, favoured the reconstruction acts.'' Sumner, likewise, denounced it as a libel and more: ''It is an incendiary document, calculated to stimulate the rebellion once more and to provoke civil war. . . . It is evi-

* Message in App. to *Globe,* 2d Sess. 40th Cong., p. 1.

dence of a direct coalition between the President and the former rebels." And both senators opposed the customary motion to print.*

In the House, the message stirred the moribund impeachment into some semblance of life. If only its defiant tone would screw up the courage of the conservatives to the sticking point, all might yet be well! When the matter came up in the House, Mr. Boutwell in an able speech exhorted his fellow-members to adopt the only expedient which he believed could make the party secure. He warned them: "We have not seen the end of this contest," and, referring to the message, prophecied "civil war" and "fratricidal strife" if the arch-apostate were not removed. But it was of no avail. Since the selection of Wade as the heir-apparent, the movement had flagged; the adverse vote of the committee in June and the differing reports of its Republican members proclaimed its failure; the elections gave it its death-blow; and Wilson, in his reply to Mr. Boutwell, simply announced its demise. He dismissed the latter's gloomy vaticinations in the following words:

"Are we to impeach the President for what he may do in the future? Do our fears constitute in the President high crimes and misdemeanors? Are we to wander beyond the record of this case and found our judgment of it on the possibility of the future? This would lead us even beyond the conscience of the House.

"Sir," he concluded, "we must be guided by some rule in this grim proceeding—something more certain than an impossibility to arraign the President for a specific crime.

* *Globe*, 2d Sess. 40th Cong., App., pp. 101–2, 20.

If we cannot arraign him for a specific crime, for what are we to proceed against him? For the bundle of generalities such as we have in the volume of testimony reported by the committee to the House? If we cannot state upon paper a specific crime, how are we to carry this case to the Senate for trial?''

At the close of his speech, Wilson moved to lay the whole matter on the table and he had the House with him. But, after filibusterng for parts of two days, the impeachers compelled the majority to consent that the vote be taken directly upon the question to impeach or not to impeach so as to expose backsliders; whereupon the resolution of the majority report was rejected by yeas 57, nays 108, the majority against it being fifty-one. Those voting yea were, of course, all Republicans. Of those voting nay, forty-one were Democrats and sixty-seven were Republicans, among whom were some of the ablest men in the House—Banks, Bingham, Blaine, Garfield, Dawes, Spalding, Washburne and Wilson.*

The primary and efficient cause of this failure, however, as was shown by the success of the final effort, was not the indefiniteness of the accusation; not the flimsiness of the testimony; not any lingering sense of justice or of judicial impartiality; but simply a well-founded apprehension that, if the revolutionary remedy were tried, it was doomed to disaster in the Senate. Garfield, a few weeks later, disclosed the motive that governed half, at least, of the Republican members who voted in the negative, in confessing his own:

* *Globe*, 2d Sess. 40th Cong., p. 68.

"When the proposition for the impeachment of the President was before the House . . . I voted against it not because I did not believe that his conduct deserved the severest condemnation but because I did not believe the attempt was likely to be successful. . . . It seemed to me it would be manifestly an interminable contest; that the President would pass out of office by expiration of term before it would be possible to conclude such a trial. And unwilling, therefore, to divert the attention of Congress from its legislative duties into a struggle of that sort, only to be foiled at last, I thought it best to vote against them and I did so."*

This state of mind of the neutrals was well-known to the sturdy phalanx of Impeachers who, consequently, notwithstanding their defeat, did not relinquish hope. They haunted the vicinity of Stanton who sulked apart in his enforced retirement. They counted it certain that, should a sudden access of pugnacity overmaster the President's wariness and furnish the technical occasion, the timid would no longer hold back. "Give us a specific offence!" they cried: "no matter about its criminality, only let it be specific!"

Five days after the impeachment was voted down in the House, the President sent to the Senate his reasons for the suspension of the Secretary of War. The paper was a strong presentation of the case on his part, especially keen and cutting in its analysis of Stanton's two insolent notes. The communication was referred to the committee on Military Affairs composed of six radicals

* *Globe*, 2d Sess. 40th Cong., p. 1560.

and but one friend of the President (Doolittle); and to Howard, one of the most uncompromising of the six, was assigned the task of refuting the President's "reasons" and vindicating the loyalty of the suspended officer. The President, in the meantime, could not refrain from indulging in a pleasure which he must have known would exasperate his judges on the committee. In July last, the House had passed votes of thanks to Sheridan, Sickles and Pope—the military commanders most inimical to the President. Now, the President sends in an official copy of General Hancock's celebrated order, and, after stating that "the distinguished honor belongs to him of being the first officer in high command south of the Potomac since the close of the civil war who has given utterance to these noble sentiments in the form of a military order," "respectfully suggests to Congress that some public recognition of General Hancock's patriotic conduct is due, if not to him, to the friends of law and justice throughout the country. Of such an act as his, at such a time, it is but fit that the dignity should be vindicated and the virtue proclaimed, so that its value as an example may not be lost to the nation."* But resolutions of thanks to Hancock could get no hearing; and the Houses took the usual holiday recess in the midst of the agitation caused by the call of the Republican national convention to meet on the twentieth of May next to nominate candidates for President and Vice President. Grant was evidently the coming man; and those radicals who were still disgruntled over his apparent closeness to the administration were driven to muttering among themselves the dubious name of Chase.

* *Globe*, 2d Sess. 40th Cong., p. 256.

For some reason—it may be the alarming conduct of Hancock during the recess, or the McCardle case involving the question of the constitutionality of the reconstruction acts, over which the Supreme Court had just affirmed its jurisdiction—the majority reassembled in a sullen mood. The distinction between conservative and radical seemed to have been obliterated. Many members openly regretted their votes against impeachment and were ready to welcome any occasion to repair their mistake. The House at once directed an inquiry into the expediency of depriving the President of the power to detail the military commanders and transferring it to the General of the army, or of comprising the five districts into one and subjecting the entire region to the command of the General alone. A joint resolution of thanks to Hancock being offered, Washburne—the early friend and now thought to be the mouth-piece of Grant—who all along opposed, and who voted against, impeachment, disclosed his change of mind by offering as a substitute a resolution "utterly condemning the conduct of Andrew Johnson acting President of the United States" in removing Sheridan, and thanking General Grant for his letter of remonstrance against the removal and also against the contemplated removal of Stanton; the House laid the one on the table and adopted the other in its stead without delay.*

On Friday, the tenth day of January, 1868, the committee on Military Affairs (having adopted the report on the suspension of the Secretary of War as written by Howard) laid it before the Senate. On every point it

* *Globe*, 2d Sess. 40th Cong., pp. 331–332.

was favourable to the displaced official and adverse to his chief. It inculcated the doctrine, in effect, that a Cabinet officer was no more the confidential servant of the President than the confidential servant of the Congress; that the President ought not to be allowed the privilege of suspending an officer so close to his person as the Secretary of War merely because friendly relations or even personal intercourse were no longer possible between them; that insolence on the part of a subordinate to his superior officer was not official misconduct; that harmony in the councils of an executive who betrayed his party was not at all desirable and that a loyal ally in the official household of a traitorous President was an ever-present help to a patriotic Congress. It defended the Secretary in detail from the specific charge of suppressing the New Orleans telegram on the eve of the riot. On the other hand it expressly admitted that, at the time of the veto of the Tenure-of-office bill, Stanton "thought the act unconstitutional," at the same time coupling the admission with words of praise that the Secretary thought, also, it should be no less obeyed; and there was no express denial of the President's statement that Stanton united with the other members of the Cabinet appointed by Lincoln in the presupposition that they were not within the law. In fact, the report ignores the point altogether, taking it for granted that the President made no question upon it as if there was but one construction possible. The Senate forewent the usual adjournment until Monday so as to consider the subject on the morrow. Rumours that, in case of an adverse decision, the President would throw the whole question into the courts were in circulation, and his adversaries were anxious to balk him in any such purpose. His whole plan of action, it should be remembered, depended upon the understanding between him and Grant entered into in the summer shortly after the suspension; and at this critical moment, he was, no doubt, relying with implicit confidence on the fulfilment of Grant's alternative promise—a promise which had been reiterated several times since it was made and the fulfilment of which, one way or the other, would leave him still master of the situation. General Grant, on the other hand, having in the meanwhile subjected the Tenure-of-office act to a closer reading, at length reached the conclusion, as he himself states, that he "could not without violation of law, refuse to vacate the office of Secretary of War the moment Mr. Stanton was reinstated by the Senate": a conclusion which, if he had reached it at any time before, he had not communicated to the President. As he says:

> "Learning on Saturday, the 11th instant that the Senate had taken up the subject of Mr. Stanton's suspension, . . . I went to the President for the sole purpose of making this decision known and did so make it known. . . . The President, however, . . . contended that he had suspended Mr. Stanton under the authority given by the Constitution, and that the same authority did not preclude him from reporting, as an act of courtesy, his reasons for the suspension to the Senate. That having appointed me under the authority given by the Constitution, and not under any act of Congress, I could not be governed by the act. I stated that the law was binding upon me, constitutional or not, until set aside by the proper tribunal. An hour or

more was consumed, each reiterating his views on this subject, until, getting late, the President said he would see me again."

Having thus informed the President that he had "changed his mind," and that he could not conscientiously participate in the plan to test the question in the courts, Grant did not follow the other branch of the alternative understanding and surrender his office into the hands of the President. He insists there was, in fact, no such alternative but, having informed the President that he would not hold out against Stanton in aid of the President, that he had fulfilled the whole extent of his part of the understanding, even though the result left him acting against the President and in aid of Stanton. He denies that he "promised to resign if he did not resist the reinstatement"; but he admits, "to soften the contradiction," that "the President might have understood" him, in their first conversation, to have made such a promise. That the President so understood is perfectly plain, because, otherwise, he gained nothing towards the accomplishment of his purpose by the conditional understanding with his appointee, but was left entirely at the mercy of that person's future caprices. Even in this very interview, as appears in the version of Grant himself, the President confined himself to combating the scruples of his subordinate at fulfilling one part of the understanding, not doubting, apparently, that in the event of his not succeeding in this direction, his conscientious appointee by discharging the other part of the understanding would enable him to find a more pliant instrument.

A very different and, it must be owned, a much more logical aspect is given to this interview by the President. He states that after a free discussion of the provisions of the Tenure-of-office act;—among other things the General expressing his aversion to subjecting himself to the penalties of fine and imprisonment, and the President replying that the act being clearly unconstitutional its penalties were not to be feared and that he would cheerfully assume them himself;—Grant, as before in their first conference, agreed that he "would either return the office to the President's possession in time to enable him to appoint a successor before final action by the Senate upon Mr. Stanton's suspension, or would remain as its head, awaiting a decision of the question by judicial proceeding"; and the interview ended with the understanding that there was to be a further conference on Monday when Grant was to decide which course he would take. Even from Grant's own statement, it is fairly inferable that the interview was indecisive, at least, of any mutual conclusion, and that both parties contemplated another meeting; although the General denies that he specifically agreed to see the President again on Monday.*

While this conversation was going on, the report of the committee on the suspension was being considered by the Senate in executive session. The Republican senators, as if resolved to end the matter that day, sat silent and left the discussion to the other side. But Dixon's physical weakness, evident while addressing his

* For Grant's letter see McPh. Recon., p. 283. For the President's, see *id.*, p. 284.

associates, forced them to consent at last to carry the debate over until Monday. An ominous resolution introduced on that day (the thirteenth) by Edmunds, before going into secret session, to inquire concerning rules of procedure in cases of impeachment and the suspension of the officer impeached, showed that rumours were abroad that the President meant to disregard an adverse decision of the Senate, and suggests also the probability that from some authoritative source the salient particulars of the Saturday interview between Grant and the President had been communicated to the Republican senators over Sunday. After adopting Edmunds' resolution, the Senate hurried into executive session to finish the pending business. Six hours more were spent in discussion, the majority, to a certain extent, abandoning their policy of silence so far as to break forth into eulogies of Stanton, in which it was noted Fessenden was profuse. Then came the vote of non-concurrence—thirty-five yeas, all Republicans, including Fessenden, Fowler and Trumbull of the seven who subsequently voted "Not Guilty"; six nays, all Democrats or administration men. There being one vacancy out of fifty-four senators (Thomas, of Maryland, kept out) there were twelve votes lacking; five of the opposition and seven of the majority. Of these seven, two (Henderson and Van Winkle) were paired with two opposition senators in favour of non-concurrence; three (Grimes, Sprague and Yates) were absent; and one (Ross) did not vote. The one remaining was Sherman; and his predicament must have been distressing.* The precise case he put

* Vote in McPherson Recon., p. 262 (error as to Vickers).

during the debate on the Tenure-of-office bill—the case when a Cabinet officer attempts "to hold office a moment beyond the time when he retains the entire confidence of the President," when "the personal relations of a Cabinet officer and the President become unpleasant so that they can have no social intercourse"; the very case, he said he could not "imagine," in which case, he declared, he "would not vote to retain him," "would as soon think of imposing upon the President a private secretary," that "any gentleman fit to be a Cabinet minister who receives an intimation from his chief that his longer continuance in that office was unpleasant to him would necessarily resign" and "if he didn't would show that he was unfit to be there"—this very case with unthought-of aggravation was now before him. In the face of his own printed words, he could not for very shame vote to disapprove the suspension and thus force Stanton back upon his unwilling master; but still, it seems, he could not muster up the boldness affirmatively to sustain the President and, therefore, kept silent.*

On the day this vote was taken (Monday), General Grant, whether he promised to or not, did not call on the President to continue the unfinished conversation of Saturday; but in his stead sent General Sherman, who had been engaged on Saturday evening with Reverdy Johnson in devising some such adjustment of the complication, to urge on the President the nomination of Governor Cox of Ohio, as Secretary of War, "and thus save all embarrassment." That night at about nine o'clock, the official notification of the action of the Senate

* Ch. II, *supra*, pp. 194–5

reached Stanton, Grant and the President. Tuesday morning early (fourteenth) the Secretary of War *ad interim* went to the War Office building, entered his room, "bolted one door on the inside, locked the other on the outside, delivered the key to the Adjutant General" and walked over to his old quarters on the opposite side of the street. Stanton must have been in the building already, for the acting Adjutant-General "then went up-stairs" and handed him the key, and he forthwith marched into the vacant apartments, and sent a curt message to the General of the Army that "he wanted to see him."* Neither of these subordinates showed the slightest regard for what might be the will of their superior officer in this affair, or the slightest consciousness that the President had any jurisdiction in the premises. Stanton never ventured to attend a meeting of the Cabinet, to enter the White House, or to show his face to his offended chief. He did not think it necessary even to notify the President that his assiduous counsellor was at his service once more. Grant was more scrupulous, and on the same morning sent to the President a written notification that, on the receipt of the official action of the Senate, his "functions as Secretary of War *ad interim* ceased."† The messenger who carried the note returned with the verbal reply that the President wanted to see his Secretary of War *ad interim* at the regular Cabinet meeting to take place that day at noon.

* 1. Grant's letter, McPh. Recon., p. 283; *cf.* Johnson's, p. 285. 2. Letter of O. H. Browning, Sec. Int., *id.*, pp. 289–290; *cf.* Gen Sherman's Mem. (4th ed., two vols. in one), Vol. 2, pp. 420–2, with Gorham's Life of Stanton, Vol. 2, p. 428.

† McPh. Recon., p. 262.

All were present except Stanbery when Grant entered and took his accustomed seat. Andrew Johnson sat at the head of the table. Beginning with the Secretary of State, he proceeded with the customary call upon the heads of the Departments in their order, and, reaching the Department of War, inquired of Secretary Grant if he had anything to present. Grant protested that he was not in attendance as a Cabinet minister but in obedience to the President's request; relating what he had done in consequence of the Senate's action. The President thereupon plied the General with the following questions: First, "Did you not agree shortly after your appointment as Secretary of War *ad interim* either to remain at the head of the War Department and abide any judicial proceeding that might follow the non-concurrence by the Senate in Mr. Stanton's suspension, or, should you wish not to become involved in such a controversy, to put me in the same position in respect to the office as I occupied previous to your appointment, by returning it to me in time to anticipate such action by the Senate?" This Grant admitted. Second, "At our conference on Saturday, when to avoid misunderstanding I requested you to state what you intended to do, did you not refer to our former conversations, saying that from them I understood your position and that your action would be consistent with the understanding which had been reached?" To this question Grant replied in the affirmative. Third, "At the conclusion of our interview on Saturday was it not understood that we were to have another conference on Monday before final action by the Senate?" To this question General Grant replied that such was the understanding but that he did not suppose the Senate would act so soon, and that on Monday he had been engaged in a conference with General Sherman and many little matters and expected General Sherman to call on the President with regard to the affair of the War Department, asking whether General Sherman had not called that day.* The colloquy was "respectful and courteous on both sides,"† and the meeting seems to have ended without altercation or ill-blood, the substance of what was said appearing in print the next day. On that day—Wednesday, the fifteenth—General Grant, in company with General Sherman, had an interview with the President during which Grant complained of the report in the newspaper as doing him much injustice. He, also, stated, either, as he himself says, that he thought Stanton would resign, or, as the President says, that he would urge Stanton to do so. On Saturday, the eighteenth, General Sherman addressed a letter to the President stating:

"At a conversation with the General (Grant) after our interview, (of the 15th) wherein I offered to go with him on Monday morning to Mr. Stanton and say that it was our joint opinion he should resign, it was found impossible, by reason of his going to Richmond and my going to Annapolis. The General proposed this course. He will call on you to-morrow and offer to go to Mr. Stanton to say that for the good of the service of the country he ought to resign—this on Sunday. On Monday I will call on you and if you think it necessary I will do the same—call on

* Grant-Johnson cor., McPh. Recon., pp. 285–6.

† Seward's letter, *id.*, p. 291.

Mr. Stanton and tell him he should resign. If he will not, there will be time to contrive ulterior measures. In the meantime it also happens that no necessity exists for precipitating matters.''

On Sunday (nineteenth), accordingly, Grant did call on the President and made the offer General Sherman describes, and the President took this occasion to give him verbal instructions to obey no order from Stanton as Secretary of War unless he had information it was issued by the President's directions. Grant then went to Stanton to advise him he ought to resign but found that ''any advice to him of that kind would be useless''; and on the next day he departed for Richmond. Up to this date, there appears to have been no interruption of the courteous relations subsisting between the President and the General, notwithstanding the trickery of which the President believed himself the victim, on the one hand, or the ''injustice'' which the General complained had been done him by the published colloquy in the Cabinet, on the other;—an account which the President, finding ''substantially correct,'' submitted to four of the five Cabinet ministers present who ''concurred in its general accuracy.'' Indeed, according to the recollection of General Schofield, then in command of the Virginia District, Grant, at the very time of this visit, said to him that the conduct of Stanton had become intolerable and declared in emphatic terms his intention to demand either the removal of Stanton or the acceptance of his own resignation.*

* For interview of fifteenth, Johnson's letter in McPh. Recon., at p. 286. Gen. Sherman's Mem. (ed. *ut supra*), Vol. 2, p. 423. For Gen.

Be this as it may, almost immediately after his return from Richmond, he made the first unmistakably hostile move against the President and that, too, manifestly in concert with Stanton and Stanton's allies. On Friday (twenty-fourth), he sent a letter, dated at Washington, to the President requesting to have in writing the verbal instructions to disregard the orders of Stanton, which he had received the previous Sunday without objection on that score; and, on the following Monday (twenty-seventh), Spalding, a strong opponent of the recent impeachment, was put forward in the House to offer a resolution directing the committee on reconstruction to inquire "what combinations have been made or attempted to be made to obstruct the due execution of the laws"—a resolution in effect, as subsequently recognized, "renewing the prosecution of the President with particular reference to his controversy with General Grant"—which was hurriedly passed under a suspension of the rules.* On Tuesday (twenty-eighth) Grant addressed a letter to the President that, for the first time in their official intercourse, betrays an intention to affront. Renewing his request for written instructions and announcing his purpose "till they are received" "to suspend action" on the "verbal ones," he added:

Sherman's letter see *id.*, pp. 423–4 (wrong date); *cf.* letter in *Globe*, speech of Morgan of Ohio, p. 1555. For interview of nineteenth, see Grant's request of January 24, 1868, McPh., *id.*, p. 283, and his letter in McPh. at p. 286. See Schofield's Forty-six Years in Army, p. 413. See note to p. 272 *supra*.

* *Globe*, 2d Sess. 40th Cong., p. 784. Phelps of Md. speech in App., p. 245.

"I am compelled to ask these instructions in writing, in consequence of the many and gross misrepresentations affecting my personal honor, circulated through the press for the last fortnight purporting to come from the President, of conversations which have occurred either with the President privately in his office, or in Cabinet meeting. What is written admits of no misunderstanding."

He then gives his version of the facts of the case as he claims them to be, the differences between which and the President's version we have already sufficiently indicated. Respecting the Cabinet meeting on Tuesday (the fourteenth), he says, that "after hearing the President through I stated our conversation substantially as given in this letter. . . . I nowise admitted the correctness of the President's statement of our conversations." Of this letter, the only notice the President took at the moment was to return, next day, Grant's note of the twenty-fourth with the instructions called for in writing indorsed in due official form on its back. In his acknowledgement of its receipt (on the thirtieth), the General bluntly declares:

"I am informed by the Secretary of War that he has not received from the Executive any order or instructions limiting or impairing his authority to issue orders to the Army," and "while such authority is not countermanded it will be satisfactory evidence to me that any orders issued from the War Department are authorized by the Executive."*

On the receipt of this notice, the President seems to have given up all hope of retaining the General of the

* McPh., p. 284.

army any longer by his side. On Friday, the thirty-first, he wrote out his version of the facts in reply to Grant's of the Wednesday before, and sent it to that officer.

In epistolary controversy Johnson was able to unite his dexterity in debate with his mastery of the pen, and the combination was irresistible. The two letters which constitute his share of the correspondence furnish a perfect example of the refutation of an adversary by an adroit yet strictly fair exposition of his own admissions. In his first, the President makes a succinct and careful statement of his own questions and Grant's answers at the Cabinet meeting, which we have repeated substantially in our account of that incident, and adds that the statement had been read by the Cabinet ministers present at the interview and "they without exception agreed to its accuracy." On the following Monday (February 3) the General sent in an angry rejoinder in which he tells the President that his letter is "but a reiteration of the many and gross misrepresentations" contained in the newspapers, and reasserts the correctness of his own version, "anything in yours in reply to the contrary notwithstanding." In his indignation he betrayed what he had come to believe was the real motive of his acceptance of office in the summer, which, if true, gave the whole transaction the character of a conspiracy by Stanton and himself to deceive the President.

"From our conversations, and my written protest of August 1, 1867, against the removal of Mr. Stanton, you must have known that my greatest objection to his removal or suspension was the fear that some one would be appointed in his stead who would, by opposition to the laws relating to the restoration of the Southern States to their proper relations to the government, embarrass the army in the performance of duties especially imposed upon it by these laws; and it was to prevent such an appointment that I accepted the office of Secretary of War *ad interim,* and not for the purpose of enabling you to get rid of Mr. Stanton by withholding it from him in opposition to the law, or not doing so myself, surrendering it to one who would, as the statement and assumptions in your communication plainly indicate was sought."

The close of the letter would indicate, on the contrary, that the writer considered that he was the one imposed upon.

"And now, Mr. President, when my honor as a soldier and my integrity as a man have been so violently assailed, pardon me for saying that I can but regard this whole matter, from the beginning to the end, as an attempt to involve me in the resistance of law, for which you hesitated to assume the responsibility in orders, and thus to destroy my character before the country."

That this letter was the subject of consultation with Stanton and with Grant's more intimate political disciples is shown by what took place in the House while it was on its way to the President. A resolution was adopted requesting the Secretary of War to transmit copies (1st) of all correspondence between him and the Executive limiting his authority to issue orders; (2d) of all correspondence between him and the General-in-Chief on the same subject; and (3d) of all correspondence which may have been furnished him between the General-in-Chief and the President relating to the disobeying by the General of any order of the War Department; and the next day Stanton sent to the House the correspondence between the General and the President from and including Grant's note of the twenty-fourth to and including the letter, extracts from which have just been given, with the information that the copies transmitted had been furnished him by General Grant; and, concerning the other correspondence called for, stating:

> "I have had no correspondence with the President since the 12th of August last. After the action of the Senate on his alleged reasons for my suspension from the office of Secretary of War, I resumed the duties of that office as required by the act of Congress, and have continued to discharge them without any personal or written communication with the President. No orders have been issued from this Department in the name of the President, with my knowledge, and I have received no orders from him";

and the papers were forthwith sent to the committee on reconstruction.*

In this correspondence was there not to be found a specific offence expressly declared to be a high misdemeanour? Did it not prove a violation of the Tenure act? Did it not establish the existence of a conspiracy to prevent the reinstatement of Stanton? And, surely, there was the Conspiracy act of 1861 which made it a high crime for two or more persons to conspire to obstruct the execution of any law! Over these questions, the reconstruction committee held high debate, and on Saturday (eighth) appointed a sub-committee to take the testi-

* *Globe*, 2d Sess. 40th Cong., pp. 936, 977.

mony of General Grant and the newspaper reporters. On Monday (tenth) Stevens applied to the House for an order to have the testimony taken on the late impeachment investigation handed over to his own committee, so that some of the former charges might be woven into the present proceeding. Brooks, one of the two Democrats on the latter committee, apparently aware that another letter from the President had gone to its destination that morning, prevailed on the House to add a call on the President "for any further correspondence he may have had with General U. S. Grant";* and the next day the President sent to the House a copy of his last epistle, which, it may as well be conceded, settled the matter in controversy. The entire letter should be read,† but we have room for that portion only which reviews the disclosure of the hidden motive for accepting the post of Secretary of War *ad interim* which Grant had allowed to escape him.

"First of all, you here admit that from the very beginning of what you term 'the whole history' of your connection with Mr. Stanton's suspension, you intended to circumvent the President. This was in your mind at the time of your acceptance. It was not, then, in obedience to your superior, as has heretofore been supposed, that you assumed the duties of the office. You knew it was the President's purpose to prevent Mr. Stanton from resuming the office of Secretary of War, and you intended to defeat that purpose. You accepted the office, not in the interest of the President, but of Mr. Stanton. If this purpose, so enter-

* *Globe*, 2d Sess. 40th Cong., p. 1087.

† See McPh. Recon., pp. 287, 288.

tained by you, had been confined to yourself—if, when accepting the office you had done so with a mental reservation to frustrate the President—it would have been a tacit deception. In the ethics of some persons such a course is allowable. But you cannot stand even upon that questionable ground. The 'history' of your connection with this transaction, as written by yourself, places you in a different predicament, and shows that you not only concealed your design from the President, but induced him to suppose that you would carry out his purpose to keep Mr. Stanton out of office, by retaining it yourself after an attempted restoration by the Senate, so as to require Mr. Stanton to establish his right by judicial decision."

Quoting the passage of Grant's letter of the twenty-eighth ult. where he admits he stated "Mr. Stanton would have to appeal to the courts to reinstate him," the President continues:

"Now, at that time, as you admit in your letter of the 3d instant, you held the office for the very object of defeating an appeal to the courts. In that letter you say that in accepting the office one motive was to prevent the President from appointing some other person who would retain possession, and thus make judicial proceedings necessary. You knew the President was unwilling to trust the office with anyone who would not, by holding it, compel Mr. Stanton to resort to the courts. You perfectly understood that in this interview 'sometime' after you accepted the office, the President, not content with your silence, desired an expression of your views, and you answered him that Mr. Stanton 'would have to appeal to the courts.' If the President had reposed confidence *before* he knew your views, and that confidence had been violated, it might have been said he made a mistake; but a violation of confidence after that conversation was no mistake of his, nor of yours. It is the fact only that needs to be stated, that at the date of this conversation you did not intend to hold the office for the purpose of forcing Mr. Stanton into court, but did hold it then, and had accepted it, to prevent that course from being carried out. In other words you said to the President, 'that is the proper course'; and you said to yourself, 'I have accepted this office, and now hold it, to defeat that course.' The excuse you make in a subsequent paragraph of that letter of the 26th ultimo, that afterwards you changed your views as to what would be the proper course, has nothing to do with the point now under consideration. The point is, that *before* you changed your views you had secretly determined to do the very thing which at last you did—surrender the office to Mr. Stanton. You may have changed your views as to the law, but you certainly did not change your views as to the course you had marked out for yourself from the beginning."

Enclosed with this letter were letters of the five Cabinet ministers present during the interrogation of General Grant by the President at the Cabinet meeting of January fourteenth. Welles, McCulloch, Randall and Browning were direct and explicit in their confirmation of the accuracy of the President's version. Seward, in his anxiety to do no injustice to the illustrious soldier, allowed the inference that General Grant's answers may have been only "indirect and circumstantial though not evasive," but the general effect of his letter was the same.* In Grant's rejoinder, sent to the House later on the same day, he makes no attempt to meet the damaging inferences the President draws from his own admission but puts in a technical defence against the charge of disobedience of instructions, which bears clear traces of Stanton's hand.† In truth, it was his colloguing with Stanton, whose traits of person and character he did not like, whose pertinacity in holding on to office he in reality despised, and whose tone of official condescension filled him with disgust, that landed the unsophisticated soldier in his present predicament.

These two letters followed the others to the reconstruction committee and put that body into something of a quandary. Stevens, its chairman, Boutwell, Farnsworth and Paine were among the fifty-seven who voted for impeachment before and, therefore, might be expected to support impeachment now. Farnsworth afterwards told the House: "In my opinion then and in my opinion now there was enough in that (correspondence) to justify the impeachment of the President."‡ Mr. Boutwell, also, said: "Upon the record, the correspondence between the President and General Grant, it is conclusively shown . . . that he intended by a contrivance, by a fraud, by a conspiracy, by a usurpation, in defiance of law, to oust Mr. Stanton from office."§ Stevens was known to be ready at any and all times to impeach Andrew Johnson on general principles of party policy.

* See Letters in McPh. Recon., pp. 289–91.

† *Id.*, p. 292.

‡ *Globe*, 2d Sess. 40th Cong., p. 1344.

§ *Globe*, App., pp. 161.

The three other Republican members, judging from their subsequent utterances, must have been of the same opinion. Bingham, in his argument before the Senate on the trial, insisted that Johnson's letter of February the tenth was positive proof of guilt of having contrived to defeat and prevent the execution of the law.* Beaman told the House: The President "attempts to draw General Grant into a conspiracy to violate the law."† Hulburd called it "no less than a mean attempt to inveigle into violation of law an honest and unsophisticated soldier."‡ Yet, notwithstanding this unanimity of opinion among the majority, the committee on Thursday (February 13), on motion of Bingham himself, laid the resolution to impeach on the table by a vote of six (including the two Democrats) to three. The truth is that Johnson's last letter killed this second impeachment project. How could they impeach him of conspiracy without implicating his co-conspirator? How would the testimony of the five Cabinet ministers sound before the High Court of Impeachment? Stevens stormed at such time-serving cowardice. The old veteran who, in truth, did not relish the coming nomination of 'Andy's' Secretary of War *ad interim,* rather rejoiced at the plight in which the correspondence placed Grant.

"A daring and bold conspiracy," he told the House afterwards, "was attempted" by the President "to induce the General of the Army to aid him in defeating

* Trial, Vol. 2, p. 462.

† *Globe*, 2d Sess. 40th Cong., App., p. 177.

‡ *Id.*, p. 266.

the operation of this law; . . . and he says that the general did enter into such conspiracy to aid him in obstructing the return of the rejected secretary notwithstanding the Senate might decide in his favour. This is denied by the General, and a question of veracity, rather angrily discussed, has arisen between them. Those gentlemen seem to consider that that question is one of importance to the public. In this they are mistaken."

"Which is the man of truth and which the man of falsehood is of no more public importance than if it arose between two obscure individuals. If Andrew Johnson tells the truth then he is guilty of a high official misdemeanor, for he avows his effort to prevent the execution of the law. If the General commanding tells the truth then the President is guilty of a high misdemeanor, for he declares the same thing of the President, denying only his own complicity. No argument can make this point plainer than the statement of the culprit. If he and the General told the truth then he committed willful perjury by refusing to take care that the laws should be duly executed."*

But his stormings were of no avail. The politicians were victorious, and the second project of impeachment followed the first into the limbo of the still-born.

Before leaving the Johnson-Grant correspondence we ought to observe that a perusal of these letters will satisfy any candid person that the claim of the President's accusers, that, in the suspension of Stanton and the submission of the reasons to the Senate, the President was acting from the beginning under the Tenure-of-office

* *Globe*, 2d Sess. 40th Cong., p. 1399.

act and was therefore estopped from questioning either its validity or the fact that the Secretary of War was within its terms, is without foundation. As early as the seventh of February, senator Buckalew speaking of the correspondence said:

> "I understand from it that the President asserts that he had power to suspend Mr. Stanton independent entirely of the act of Congress commonly called the tenure of office law, and that in exercising his power of suspension he did not necessarily proceed under the provisions of that law; that, although this act was done by him under his general constitutional power, there was no impropriety in submitting his reasons for the act to the Senate of the United States for their consideration."*

* *Globe*, 2d Sess. 40th Cong., p. 1035.

CHAPTER V

THE IMPEACHMENT OF THE PRESIDENT

IN the meanwhile, the President was making preparations to drive the intruder out of the War-Office. It may be that he would have resented the clandestine reentry by instant forcible dispossession, had he not been dissuaded from "precipitating matters" (to quote from the letter of General Sherman already given*), by the assurances of that officer and General Grant that they would tell Stanton he ought to resign. It did not take long, however, to convince him that there was no hope in that direction, and, further, that Grant, so far from standing by him, was in league with the clinging official who disregarded the advice given him as though it was a part of the game. From that moment he delayed no longer. He knew that the House of Representatives was watching for some misstep on his part to impeach him. He knew that a large majority of the senators were eager to condemn him, and that the General was ready with the army at his back to carry the judgment into execution. But his mind was made up that there was no longer room in one administration for Andrew Johnson, President, and Edwin M. Stanton, Secretary of War.

Treading among many pitfalls, he recognized the necessity of the utmost circumspection. The customary

* Page 325, *supra*.

method of removing a Cabinet officer while the Senate was in session consisted in sending a nomination to that body, the confirmation of which *ipso facto* worked the removal. But, in the present imbroglio, this method was impracticable because the Senate would consent to no appointment to displace Stanton. The President, therefore, fell back upon the exclusive power of removal which he believed was vested in him by the Constitution and to which the circumstance of the Senate being in session, though a restraint on the power of appointment, had no relevancy. He would remove Stanton, and the vacancy thus made he would fill under the act of Congress of February, 1795, by a letter of authority to some person to perform the duties of the office until a regular appointment could be made. Having settled upon the *modus,* he cast about for an army officer with independence of spirit enough to disregard the example of Grant and courage enough to beard the leonine War-Minister in his den. On Saturday afternoon, the twenty-fifth day of January, he sent for General Sherman and tendered him the place. The General made no final answer at the interview itself, but on the following Monday sent a letter inclosing one from Thomas Ewing, whom he promised the President to consult, advising him "to keep clear of political complications." On the thirtieth (Thursday) the President sent for Sherman again and told him that the relations between himself and Stanton and between Stanton and the other members of the Cabinet were such that he could not execute the office of President of the United States without making provision *ad interim* for the War-Office; that he had that right under the law, and his purpose was to have the office administered in the interest of the army and the country; and he offered it to Sherman with that view. Sherman asked him why the lawyers could not make a case; expressing his aversion to being brought into any legal controversy. The President replied that it was found impossible—a case could not be made up—adding quickly: "If we could bring the case into the court it would not stand half an hour." The General hesitated: If Stanton would simply retire, although it was against his interests and his wishes, personal and official, he might be willing to administer the office *ad interim*. The President thought him about to yield; but Sherman pressed the point: "Suppose Mr. Stanton does not yield?" "Oh," said Johnson, "there is no need to consider that question; you present the order and he will simply go away"; Sherman still doubting, the President added, "I know him better than you do. He is cowardly." Sherman begged for time to reflect upon the subject; the next day (Friday, the thirty-first) he, by letter, finally declined the office for reasons "mostly personal in their nature"; and, on the fourth of February, in the midst of the *furore* raised by the Johnson-Grant correspondence, went West to his department.*

The brother of senator Sherman evidently was not the man to take the post Grant had deserted, and fly in the face of the Republican party by dispossessing the reinstated Stanton. Still the President did not even yet relinquish the hope of securing the services of so power-

* Gen. Sherman's Mem. (4th ed.), Vol. 2, pp. 425–6. Testimony on Trial, Vol. 1, pp. 483–5, 521, 529.

ful an ally, if not to force Stanton out, practically to supersede both him and Grant by elevating the Lieutenant-General to a position on a level in authority with theirs. On the twelfth day of February, in compliance with the request of the President, a general order was issued by command of the General of the Army "creating a military division to be called the military division of the Atlantic to be composed of the departments of the Lakes, of the East and of Washington, and to be commanded by Lieutenant-General William T. Sherman, with his headquarters at Washington"; and, on the succeeding day, the President sent to the Senate a nomination of the officer designated to command the new division to be brevet general. Sherman telegraphed to his brother in the Senate to oppose confirmation and threatened to resign if forced to come to Washington. The telegram made confirmation impossible and the threat resulted in an order relieving him of the command of the new division. The President, then, turned to General Thomas; again astonishing the Senate by nominating that officer first as brevet lieutenant-general and then as brevet general. But the hero of Nashville battle shrank with unconquerable aversion from political controversies, and, in a telegram to the President of the Senate, earnestly requested that body not to confirm. The only vantage-ground the President gained by these maneuvres, beside the state of alarm in which they threw his adversaries, was the new military division which still remained, though without a commander, and which eventually (on March 28) he filled up by putting Hancock at its head; that officer's differences with Grant having made it necessary to relieve him from the command of the fifth military district.*

Despairing of help from Sherman, the President at length hit upon Lorenzo Thomas, the titular Adjutant-General. The selection was unfortunate in some respects, but, on the whole, in the prevailing dearth of fit instruments for the President's purpose, the best that could have been made. A native of Delaware, sixty-three years of age, a veteran of forty years' service, Thomas, it might be said by his critics, lagged superfluous on the stage. A gentleman of the old school, scrupulously polite, convivial in his habits and somewhat garrulous in conversation, he was, nevertheless, by nature and training, the embodiment of honour and the pink of chivalry. Having been appointed Adjutant-General in 1861, in March, 1863, he was sent to the Mississippi river on inspection duty and to organize the negroes into regiments. After the close of the war, he was employed on inspection duty throughout the country; the work of the office devolving upon the senior assistant Adjutant-General, whom Stanton preferred to have near him. In fact, Grant, if not Stanton himself, had recommended his displacement, but the President refused to set him aside. Since the beginning of this year, he had been sauntering about the capital, finishing, betweenwhiles, his inspection report of the national cemeteries, and anxious to resume his office duties. On Thursday, the thirteenth day of February, the President sent for him and gave him a note addressed to Grant requiring his restoration which, accordingly, took place

* McPh. Recon., p. 346. Sherman's Mem., *id.*, p. 432.

the next day; and he signalized his reentrance into his old office by summoning before him the heads of the different bureaus with their clerks, room by room, and delivering a formal address to each group, telling them that the rules governing attendance and office hours, which, it appears, during the interregnum had been too inflexible, should now be so far relaxed as to be tolerable to persons of gentlemanly habits. On the eighteenth (Tuesday), the President disturbed him in the midst of such congenial occupation by sending for him to say that he was thinking of making him Secretary of War. Obedience to orders being the first article in the old soldier's creed, he signified his readiness to accept, although, perhaps, somewhat astounded by the prospect of so unlooked-for a promotion.

On Friday, the twenty-first day of February, at about noon, the President summoned his restored Adjutant-General to the White House and on his arrival handed him two papers which he had already prepared—one, a letter addressed to Thomas himself authorizing him to discharge the duties of Secretary of War *ad interim*; the other, an order addressed to Edwin M. Stanton removing him from office and directing him to deliver the records, papers and property to Lorenzo Thomas appointed Secretary *ad interim*—telling Thomas to go and deliver the latter to the person addressed. Thomas undertook the embarrassing mission, not only without demur, but with a sprightliness indicative of an expectation of enjoyment in the coming encounter. The President expressing his determination to uphold the Constitution and the laws and requiring his subordinate to do the same, Lorenzo Thomas was the last man to say him nay. Taking the two papers he walked over to the War Department building, mounted the stairs, taking one of the assistant adjutant-generals with him, strode into the office where Stanton was embayed and handed him the order of removal. The War-Minister was evidently taken unawares. Reading the President's order he was perceptibly flurried, his first impulse being to gain time. With unwonted meekness he inquired: "Do you wish me to vacate the office at once, or will you give me time to remove my private property?" "At your pleasure," was the reply. General Grant coming in, the letter of authority was shown him and Stanton asked to be furnished with a copy. Eager to oblige, Thomas goes out and down to his late office, has a copy made, certifies to it as Secretary of War *ad interim*—his first act in that capacity—goes back upstairs and hands it to Stanton, who by this time has so far recovered his self-possession as to say: "I don't know whether I will obey your instructions or whether I will resist them"; and Thomas leaves him to his meditations.

Walking back to the White House he informs the President of what had passed, who jumped to the conclusion from what he heard that Stanton would make no fight and that Thomas was virtually in. The only remark he made was: "Very well, go and take charge of the office."* The regular Friday Cabinet meeting being just about breaking up, he congratulates his ministers on having at last got rid of their too adhesive colleague,

* Thomas' testimony on Trial, Vol. 1, p. 415 *et seq.;* Cross., 432–3; Clerks, 215.

and he sent a message immediately to the Senate informing that body of the removal and the filling of the vacancy. The likelihood of his impeachment was before his eyes, but only because he believed that the removal was an actuality and not a mere removal on paper. As it turned out, however, as soon as Thomas got out of the building, Stanton, with no thought of yielding, started to his feet and hoisted the signal for succour. As quickly as he could write and despatch them messages were on the way to the President *pro tem.* of the Senate and to the Speaker of the House stating that General Thomas had just delivered to him a copy of the enclosed order which they were requested to communicate to their respective Houses. The alarmed secretary sent the news, also, to senators Fessenden, Howe and Conness.

The momentous tidings threw the House into a twitter. Members gathered in knots here and there or ran singly to and fro. The committee of the whole made an effort to continue the business in hand, but could not keep it up. It rose, the House resumed, the committee sat again and then rose again. The strain was too great. Butler broke the spell by moving to rescind the order devoting to-morrow's session—Washington's birthday—to debate only, on the ground that sterner business was likely to be necessary. Covode followed with a resolution impeaching Andrew Johnson for high crimes and misdemeanours, which was referred to the committee on reconstruction whither Stanton's message had already been sent, and, within two hours of the reception of the startling tidings, the House, having initiated the counter-movement, adjourned;—many of its members streaming up the avenue to solace the martyr of their party clinging to his post of duty.*

In the Senate the same excitement reigned. The message of the President reached there about the same hour as Stanton's call for help. An important debate on the reconstruction measures was interrupted, the senators hurried into executive session, and seven hours elapsed before they emerged from under the veil of secrecy.† The more radical senators—and they constituted a majority of the Republicans—were fully as prone to precipitate action as the majority of the House. They even went so far that very afternoon as to send an informal committee to wait upon Stanton and advise him to stand firm. Others sent letters or telegrams imploring him to hold fast until they could come to his rescue. Sumner despatched a paper to him inscribed with the single word "Stick."‡ A few Republican senators, by reason of their recorded opinions at the time of the passage of the Tenure-of-office act, found themselves in an awkward predicament. The question presented by the removal wore a very different aspect from the question presented by the suspension. The suspension was made as if under the Tenure act and the reasons of the President were submitted to the Senate for its action. A vote to disapprove committed a senator to the opinion that Stanton was within the act no further than the submission of the reasons for the suspension to the Senate committed the President. A removal, on the other hand, was either

* *Globe*, 2d Sess. 40th Cong., pp. 1326–8, 1330.

† *Id.*, p. 1316.

‡ *Id.*, p. 1610, Hubbard's Speech.

outside the act or a violation of it, and brought the alternative directly before the members. Of the few senators on the record Sherman was in the most hopeless case. Publicly, upon the floor of the Senate, speaking as one of the conference committee appointed on the disagreeing votes of the two houses upon this subject, he had declared with emphasis again and again that the Tenure-of-office act was not intended to include and did not include the Secretary of War. The majority found it necessary, therefore, to accommodate the steps to be taken to the feelings of their indiscreet or over-scrupulous brethren; for it was considered imperative that to prove an effective bracer to the House the condemnation of the President's rash deed must receive the two-thirds vote required to convict in cases of impeachment. The first move in executive session was made by Edmunds, who offered a resolution simply disapproving the action of the President. Chandler moved to add the words "as a violation of the rights of the Senate and unauthorized by law." But this was disagreed to. Yates proposed to go farther yet and roundly declare the act of the President "simple resistance to law and revolutionary in character" and "advise" Stanton "not to surrender the office to any person whomsoever"; but this proposal, too, was voted down. Still, the majority could not rest satisfied with an expression of disapproval merely. Such a half-way measure brought no stimulus to the House, no encouragement to the besieged War-Minister. Wilson, accordingly, moved a resolution which, if we may credit the statement of senator Fowler made in a speech to the

Senate,* was drafted by a distinguished member of the House, afterwards one of the managers on the trial of the President, and so drafted as to meet every difficulty. It declared "that under the Constitution and laws of the United States, the President has no power to remove the Secretary of War and designate any other person to perform the duties of that office *ad interim.*" To such a declaration, senators committed to the opinion that Stanton was not within the act could subscribe on the ground either that the removal was in contravention of the Constitution because made during the session and not by means of a regular appointment, or that the designation of a secretary *ad interim* while the Senate was in session was without authority of law. In fact, Trumbull, as he afterwards owned, voted for it on the latter ground believing at the time that the act of 1795 under which the President claimed to have acted was repealed.† The resolution received twenty-eight affirmative votes including Ross, Trumbull and Van Winkle who voted "not guilty" on the trial. The nays were six, including Edmunds, who must have voted in the negative solely on account of a formal preference for his own resolution. There were eighteen senators recorded as not voting; among them Fessenden, who opposed the resolution in the debate on the ground that Stanton was not within the act, Howe and Grimes, who were of the same opinion, Sherman, the most deeply committed of them all, and Henderson and Fowler, who afterwards voted for acquittal. Seven majority and five minority senators were

* *Globe,* 2d Sess. 40th Cong., p. 4509.

† Opinion, Vol. 3 of Trial, p. 326.

absent. The real strength, therefore, of the majority on this question was twenty-eight plus the seven radicals absent and Edmunds, making thirty-six in all—one more than two-thirds.*

At half-past nine o'clock at night the doors of the Senate Chamber were reopened and messengers sped in hot haste to the White House and to the residence of the new Secretary *ad interim* to serve copies of the resolution. The President was easily found, but the lively veteran was not caught until a late hour, when, after an agitating search, he was found at a masquerade ball. In the meantime his facile tongue had been making mischief. In the afternoon he unbosomed himself to a newspaper man, telling him that on Monday (Saturday being a holiday) he would demand possession of the War Department and, if the demand was refused or resisted, he would apply to the General-in-Chief for a force sufficient for the purpose. That evening he reiterated his purpose to the same reporter, only changing the day from Monday to the next morning. To the delegate in Congress from Dakota territory, who called on him in the evening to find out what he meant to do, he also imparted the information that he intended to take possession the next morning at ten o'clock, inviting his visitor to call and see him in his new office. "Suppose Stanton resists?" queries the delegate. "I expect to meet force by force." "Suppose he bars the doors?" pursues this seeker after

* McPh. Recon., pp. 262–3. (McCreery and Vickers not yet seated.) Senators Sumner and Williams in their respective opinions give the vote 27 to 6, Trial, Vol. 3, pp. 261, 350. Senator Yates in his opinion, 29 to 6, *id.*, p. 107. *N. Y. Times* of 22d, 29 to 6. See Speech of Rep. Golladay in App. to *Globe* on p. 197.

evidence. "I will break them down," was the hardy response. These idle threats were instantly carried to Stanton's headquarters where they raised a most disproportionate commotion. Stanton himself, since his interview with Thomas, had not ventured to leave his rooms, but kept up communication with the outside world by means of messengers. To him there hurried his cronies of the House and Senate and around him they remained, ministering to the wants of their sentinel in the enemy's camp during the silent watches of the night. Rumours of the blood-thirsty purpose of the over-valiant Thomas pouring in fast upon them, at midnight the garrison resolve to invoke the protection of the law. They send for Judge Cartter of the Supreme Court of the District; Stanton makes affidavit that he is Secretary of War; that Andrew Johnson has issued an order to remove him from office and to appoint Lorenzo Thomas in his place; that such order is illegal and void and contrary to the provisions of the Tenure-of-office act; that Lorenzo Thomas delivered the order to the deponent, is now exercising the duties of the office and "gives out and threatens that he will forcibly remove your deponent from the building and apartments of the Secretary of War" and "forcibly take possession"; and the affiant alleges that the said Thomas, by accepting said appointment is guilty of a "high misdemeanor" under the fifth section of the act. The judge signs a warrant for Thomas' arrest returnable before him at chambers "forthwith," and armed with this document, William A. Pile, at present a representative in Congress from

Missouri—once a preacher, a chaplain in the army and then some sort of a general—sets out for the house of the clerk of the court, "between two and three o'clock in the morning" routs him up, takes him to his office, has him attest and seal the warrant, and then proceeds to put it into the hands of the marshal, whom, however, he does not venture to disturb until seven o'clock. The marshal, taking two assistants, instantly starts in pursuit of his man, whom he finds at home waiting for a breakfast the unsuspecting criminal is destined never to eat. Having returned rather late from the masquerade ball, his purpose wholly unaffected by the senatorial admonition, the aged warrior takes his arrest with the utmost coolness, requesting only permission to stop on the way to see the President. To this the officer assents, premising, however, that he "must not lose sight of his prisoner for a moment"; and he does not lose sight of him, following Thomas into the very presence of the President. The President hearing of the arrest remarks: "Very well—that is the place I want it in—the courts"; and directs Thomas to go to the Attorney-General. To the quarters of the Attorney-General the prisoner and the marshal go, and thence, after taking the advice of that officer, to the judge's chambers where they arrive at nine o'clock. There Thomas is held to bail in $5,000 for his appearance on Wednesday, and, as soon as he is released from custody, returns to the White House. Hearing what was done, the President says: "Very well; we want it in the courts. Now go and take charge." Without another word the obedient appointee, intent only upon the performance of his nearest duty, sets out to execute the order of the day before.*

In the meantime, at about ten o'clock, the night-watchers at the War Office were relieved from duty by the arrival of a delegation of representatives in Congress. There came Van Horn, Van Wyck and Clarke of New York, Moorhead and Kelley of Pennsylvania, Dodge of Iowa, Ferry of Michigan, and Delano of Ohio —the last an ex-member. They came to witness the onset of Thomas, if peradventure the terrors of impending imprisonment did not deter the veteran. Every one of his movements had been followed with absorbing interest. It was known that, after seeing the President, he had been taken before the judge, and that he had returned to the White House, where even now he was closeted with his high-placed accomplice. All eyes were fixed on the front of that mansion. When the white-headed old soldier emerged upon the lawn and turned his steps towards the War building, "There he comes!" they exclaimed, and, putting themselves in position to cover their chief, they drew out their pencils and arranged their pads. Thomas, for his part, as calm as if on parade, with no thought of danger or trouble, his dominant emotion, probably, gratified vanity because of the high duty he was about to discharge, proceeded on his way. The offices of the War Department were closed on account of the holiday, and he found his own (as Adjutant-General) locked. He then climbed the stairs

* See Testimony on Trial, Vol. 1, pp. 158–9, for service of notice; threats, pp. 210, 221, *id.;* affidavit of Stanton, *id.*, p. 515. Proceedings, pp. 509, 516; Thomas' testimony, *id.*, pp. 427–8.

to Mr. Stanton's room, where he found the group, according to his own description, "all sitting in a semi-ellipsis, the Secretary of War at the apex."* Three of the members of Congress present were careful to take notes—Van Horn, Moorhead and Ferry—and we will let one of them tell the story.

At twenty five minutes past twelve m., General Thomas, Adjutant General, came into the Secretary of War's office, saying "Good morning," the Secretary replying, "Good morning, sir." Thomas looked around and said, "I do not wish to disturb these gentlemen, and will wait." Stanton said, "Nothing private here; what do you want, sir?"

Thomas demanded of Secretary Stanton the surrender of the Secretary of War office. Stanton denied it to him, and ordered him back to his own office as Adjutant General. Thomas refused to go. "I claim the office of Secretary of War, and demand it by order of the President."

Stanton. "I deny your authority to act and order you back to your own office."

Thomas. "I will stand here. I want no unpleasantness in the presence of these gentlemen."

Stanton. "You can stand there if you please, but you cannot act as Secretary of War. I am Secretary of War. I order you out of this office and to your own."

Thomas. "I refuse to go, and will stand here."

Stanton. "How are you to get possession; do you mean to use force?"

Thomas. "I do not care to use force, but my mind is made up as to what I shall do. I want no unpleasantness, though. I shall stay here and act as Secretary of War."

Stanton. "You shall not, and I order you, as your superior, back to your own office."

* Trial, Vol. I, p. 428.

Thomas. "I will not obey you, but will stand here and remain here."

Stanton. "You can stand there as you please. I order you out of this office to your own. I am Secretary of War, and your superior."

Thomas then went into the opposite room across hall (General Schriver's) and commenced ordering General Schriver and General E. D. Townsend. Stanton entered, followed by Moorhead and Ferry, and ordered those Generals not to obey or pay attention to General Thomas' orders; that he denied his assumed authority as Secretary of War *ad interim,* and forbade their obedience of his directions. "I am Secretary of War, and I now order you, General Thomas, out of this office to your own quarters."

Thomas. "I will not go. I shall discharge the functions of Secretary of War."

Stanton. "You will not."

Thomas. "I shall require the mails of the War Department to be delivered to me, and shall transact the business of the office."

Stanton. "You shall not have them, and I order you to your own office."

At this point the Congressmen left the scene, their presence being required at the House. What followed their departure, it was left to Thomas to relate. Stanton handed him a note, dated the day before, forbidding him from acting as Secretary of War *ad interim;* and then the conversation continued as follows:

I said, "The next time you have me arrested, please do not do it before I get something to eat." I said I had had nothing to eat or drink that day. He put his hand around my neck, as he sometimes does, and ran his hand through my hair, and turned to General Schriver and said, "Schriver, you have got a bottle here; bring it out."

Schriver unlocked his case and brought out a small vial, containing I suppose about a spoonful of whiskey, and stated at the same time that he occasionally took a little for dyspepsia. Mr. Stanton took that and poured it into a tumbler and divided it equally and we drank it together.

A fair division, because he held up the glasses to the light and saw that they each had about the same, and we each drank. Presently a messenger came in with a bottle of whiskey, a full bottle; the cork was drawn, and he and I took a drink together. "Now," said he, "this at least is neutral ground."

Thomas departed and Stanton barricaded himself in his apartments. No serious attempt was made to molest him further. On Monday and again on Tuesday Thomas called, renewed his formal demand and, receiving the stereotyped answer, withdrew. He continued to attend meetings of the Cabinet, however, and was recognized by the President as Secretary of War *ad interim*, but he did no official act in that capacity. As late as March 10th he advised the President to write a note to General Grant, directing that officer to issue an order to the different bureaus to send all communications to him as Secretary of War; but the President remarked that the matter better lie over until after the impeachment trial.*

While this curious encounter was going on in the War Office the President, on his part, did two things. First, he sent to the Senate the nomination of Thomas Ewing, an aged statesman of wide experience, the father-in-law of General Sherman, for Secretary of the Department of

* See testimony of Ferry, Trial, Vol. I, pp. 232–3; of Thomas, pp. 429, 444–6.

War; but, the Senate having met only to adjourn on account of the holiday, the nomination came back. Second, he sent for General Emory, who was in the command of the Department of Washington, to ascertain whether there had been any recent movements of troops to or around the capital, rumours of which the President had heard but of which he had no official knowledge. Emory informed him that no movements had been made, and, incidentally, referred to a general order embodying that section of the army appropriation bill fixing the headquarters of the General at Washington and making it obligatory that all orders of the President or Secretary of War should be issued through the General of the army—a section which, as the President informed the House by message last March, was a gross invasion of his rightful prerogative but which he was compelled to appear to approve rather than veto the whole bill. The President seems to have forgotten the section, for, when Emory called his attention to it, he exclaimed: "This is not in conformity to the Constitution of the United States which makes me Commander-in-Chief, or with the terms of your commission. Am I to understand that the President of the United States cannot give an order except through General Grant?" That was General Emory's impression, he said—the lawyers had so advised—Robert J. Walker and Reverdy Johnson. The officers were "bound by the order constitutional or unconstitutional." The President let fall the remark: "The object of the law is evident." And with this harmless observation the interview terminated.*

* Ewing's nomination, Trial, Vol. I, pp. 555–6; Emory, pp. 235–6; section, Ch. II, *supra*, p. 201–2.

The House met at noon, seething with excitement such as had not been witnessed since the first days of secession. Wild rumours were afloat relating to the employment of troops. Thousands of armed men from Maryland, it was whispered, were on the march to protect the President. The galleries were filled to overflowing with a "vast, excited and expectant throng"; the lobbies jammed with persons striving to enter the chamber, and the floor itself, including the seats of members, the aisles and spaces outside the circle of seats and in front of the clerk's desk, uncomfortably crowded. The committee on reconstruction was busy preparing its report. Bingham, Farnsworth and Boutwell had been appointed a sub-committee to take what little testimony might be necessary and to formulate the foregone conclusion. But they needed no testimony and took none. The order of removal was before them; they procured a copy of the letter of authority and with that they considered the case against the President complete. The House was impatient to begin the business of which all foresaw the inevitable end. Some routine business was done. Pile—the midnight bearer of the warrant against Thomas—for one bright moment distinguished himself by asking leave to introduce a bill to abolish the office of adjutant-general. The crowd on the floor and in the galleries grew more and more restless. Senators, one by one, came wedging themselves in to watch the gestation of the proceeding they were expected to crown with judgment; Wade, whom the result was expected to make President of the United States, being provided with a seat near the Speaker. News of the President's interview with General Emory began flying about the crowded corridors outside, penetrated thence into the committee room and into the House itself;—a panic-distorted version filling the hearts of the timid with apprehensions of bloodshed and haunting the minds of all with the uneasy conjecture, 'Johnson means fight then?' At length, at twenty minutes after two o'clock, the committee winds itself in—Stevens, feebler than usual, tottering at its head. He presents the report signed by every Republican on the committee, a unit at last. After a reference to the resolution of the twenty-seventh day of January directing an inquiry whether there existed any combination to obstruct the law, came the order of the President removing Stanton and the letter authorizing Thomas to act *ad interim,* and then the resolution: "That Andrew Johnson, President of the United States, be impeached of high crimes and misdemeanors"—with the recommendation of its adoption. Stevens was for taking a vote immediately, but, so many of the majority desiring to speak, it was found impracticable to close the discussion with the day; and an agreement was entered into that the debate should continue during the evening, the session be carried over until Monday, and the debate continue on that day until five o'clock, when the vote should be taken.

In the beginning of the debate the majority wore an air of unbounded confidence. The very offence they so carefully described as a high misdemeanour with the express view to his impeachment—that very offence the President had committed. Said Spalding, who so strongly opposed the first impeachment: "We are not called upon to ascertain . . . whether the President has in fact committed a high misdemeanor, because Congress has, already, upon the face of its enactment, declared the alleged act of removal to be such.'' ''Here in two letters of Andrew Johnson,'' said Farnsworth, '' . . . we have a complete and perfect case. We need swear no witnesses; we need take no further testimony. Read the letters—read the constitution, and read the law, and the case is all there as clear and plain as if he confessed the crime'' Ingersoll prophesied: ''I shall for one be grievously disappointed if, within ten days from this time, honest old Ben Wade is not President of the United States. . . . Not more than ten days ought to be consumed in the trial of this case; for there is but a single crime and the President has been considerate enough to furnish the evidence of his guilt.'' Said another: ''It is of no use to argue the question. We have before us the law and upon the Speaker's desk the President's admission that he has violated the law.''

Beside this clear case for impeachment by the House, the Senate also was pledged to convict. ''Consider,'' said Bingham, ''the solemn judgment of the Senate pronounced but yesterday upon this act of removal. Neither the Supreme Court nor any other court can question or review this judgment of the Senate.'' ''There is no question,'' Mr. Boutwell exulted, ''as to what the judgment of the House is to be here and now, or that that judgment is to be finally sustained by the judgment of the Senate.'' Still, as the debate ran along, there began to be perceptible an uneasy consciousness of the exceeding slenderness of the single charge to which they had confined the case, and a lack of conviction that the act which was the basis of their proceeding partook of any criminality whatever. They read and reread the penal section of their statute but the words "high misdemeanor," "imprisonment," "fine" sounded like empty words after all. This troubled state of mind betrayed itself in various forms. Although the leaders congratulated themselves that the charge was all in a nutshell, they could not keep within the record. Almost every speaker on the majority side deserted the case at hand and harked back to the past misdeeds of the President for which they were not trying him. It was in vain that the Democrats reminded them of the two previous attempts at impeachment and the "unwilling verdict" wrung from this hostile Congress that "up to the last few days at least the President had so conducted himself" that no ground for impeachment could be found. They would not be bound by their own self-imposed limits. They fought shy of the compact little charge they had so carefully formulated, to soar and expatiate over the field of Andrew Johnson's numberless enormities which they had officially condoned. Kelley said: "The committee's arraignment is too circumscribed for me. It presents, however, a single point all sufficient for the purpose. But, sir, I hold and assert, that however concise may be the official arraignment we are about to bring to trial the great criminal of our age and country." Ashley confessed: "I regard this as the smallest of the many offences of which this man has been guilty. If Mr. Johnson had been guilty of no impeachable offence until his removal of Mr. Stanton, no one believes that a majority of this House could be induced to vote for his impeachment now." Julian spoke to the same effect: "It is true the removal of the Secretary of War is a relatively small matter, and I believe it would be regarded as scarcely a sufficient ground for this proceeding, if not considered in the light of greater previous offences." Butler "mournfully remembers the act by which the President was inducted into his high office," "his change of purpose in the summer of 1865," his every act of usurpation and violation of law since down to "his attempt to draw into a conspiracy with himself the general officer of the Armies of the United States." Mr. Boutwell pursues the same course:

"Now sir, what is the history of this man . . .? Is he not the man who, in the Senate Chamber on the ever-to-be lamented 4th of March, 1865, humiliated the nation and all the people, dishonored us in the presence of the civilized world, disgraced the office he held, while Booth was wending his criminal way through the crowds in the areas of the Capitol for the purpose of assassinating the President of the nation who within forty days thereafter was destined to fall by the hand of the assassin? Is he not the man who, in violation of his oath of office, appointed men to places of trust and power throughout the ten States of the South who could not take the oath of office prescribed by the law of the country?"

He concludes by indicating "the plot in which the President is engaged."

"He desired first to get control of the War Department . . . for the purpose of enabling him to succeed in his aspirations for the Presidency. He knew that if he could corrupt the leader of the Army . . . these ten States were in his control, and that he could send to the Democratic party convention . . . men who would sustain his claim for the Presidency. . . . He could secure the electoral votes of these ten States by excluding the negroes whom we have enfranchised from all participation in the election.

"If, by fortune, as was his hope, he could receive a sufficient number of votes in the North to make a majority, then, with the support of the Army which he had corrupted, he had determined to be inaugurated President of the United States at the hazard of civil war. To-day, sir, we escape from these evils and dangers."

The essential insincerity of the present proceeding was made plainer still by the floods of irrelevant abuse the speakers showered upon the President. Farnsworth called him: "This ungrateful, despicable, besotted, traitorous man"; "this accidental President made so by the assassin's pistol." Logan exhausted his vocabulary in an effort to enumerate the offences of the President:

"He has not only insulted the nation by his conduct as President of the Senate, but he has disgraced that high office in which he was placed by the death of his illustrious predecessor; he has dragged, as a demagogue, the robes of his high official position in the purlieus and filth of treason. . . . He has done every act a man can conceive, not only calculated to degrade himself, but to destroy the rights of the American people."

One member compared the President to Nero who "poisoned his brother" and "assassinated his wife and mother." Washburne—the silent but stern contemner of the first attempt at impeachment—outdid them all in the fierceness of his invective:

> "His whole official career as President has been marked by a wicked disregard of all the obligations of public duty and by a degree of perfidy and treachery and turpitude unheard of in the history of the rulers of a free people; his personal and official character has made him the opprobrium of both hemispheres, and brought ineffable disgrace on the American name."

A member just opened his lips to say: "I am in favor of the official death of Andrew Johnson without debate. I am not surprised that one who began his presidential career in drunkenness should end it in crime." Indeed, the longer the debate lasted the more manifest it became that the majority, while painting the President as the blackest criminal of the age, were proposing to impeach him for a harmless peccadillo.

The speakers of the minority, on their side, stuck the more closely to the actual case the farther the majority flew away from it. The two specific statutory offences were described in the sixth section of the Tenure-of-office act and, with an eye to some future proceeding such as this, declared to be "high misdemeanors" punishable by a fine of $10,000 and imprisonment for five years. They were: (1) "Every removal, appointment or employment made . . . contrary to the provisions of this act," and (2) "the issue of any letter of authority for or in respect to any such appointment or employment." The case must stand or fall, therefore, on the question whether the two acts of the President, as evidenced by the two letters, were "contrary to the provisions of the act." Viewed from this central stand-point, it soon became apparent that the case against the President rested entirely upon an error in the construction of the statute. The arguments by which this error was demonstrated were marshalled in full force by the Democratic leaders in this extemporized discussion; but, as they were repeated with greater elaboration and finish on a grander stage, we need not review them with any particularity here. One or two, however, it may be desirable to dwell upon for a moment so as to gather a clear idea of the gist of the matter from the start. Holman of Indiana, then in his youth, puzzled the impeachers by pointing out a state of affairs they could not very well controvert:

> "You propose to impeach the President upon a mere question of opinion, when, in fact, no crime or misdemeanor has been committed, nor, indeed, any material step taken toward the commission of any offence under any interpretation of the law. It can only be said that the President of the United States has assigned a military officer to a given duty, to the same duty to which he recently assigned the General of the Army, and that officer has sought to enter upon the discharge of that duty, but has failed to do so, and the incumbent remains in his office. It cannot be said, no matter what interpretation you place on the Tenure of office law, that an offence has been in fact committed; for, if Edwin M. Stanton was Secretary of War he is still Secretary of War; he is still in fact as he was in possession of his office; for the Senate has declined to confirm a successor."

How then could the President be said to have "made a removal" at all? The answer was made that there was no distinction between an attempt to remove and an actual removal. "It is a removal in the eye of the law." "The President would be liable to impeachment if he should attempt to violate a law he has sworn to execute." But the sixth section does not mention attempts, dealing only with consummated acts. This was, in fact, conceded by Lawrence: "The attempt of the President to remove the Secretary of War is not an indictable offence under the Tenure-of-office law. . . . I have examined the act of Congress critically, and no lawyer will controvert what I say. The signing of a letter of appointment is indictable but not the issuing of an order of removal."

But it was upon their main contention, viz: Stanton was not protected by the Tenure-of-office act, that the opponents of Impeachment won their most conspicuous triumph. The argument to establish this conclusion was stated in the clearest manner by George C. Woodward of Pennsylvania—formerly the chief justice of his state—a jurist of profound learning, a terse and logical speaker, and a Democrat of the most fearless and uncompromising type. He said:

"Mr. Speaker, this is the third attempt to impeach the President. The first, founded on his alleged usurpation of powers which the Constitution had delegated to the legislative department, was crushed to death by the ponderous volume of testimony of more than twelve hundred pages which was brought in with the impeaching resolution. The second attempt, founded on the Johnson-Grant correspondence, was strangled in the birth, and the issue of fact raised between those distinguished correspondents was left to be decided by each man for himself upon evidence that was altogether favorable to the President.

"Now comes for the third time during our present session, another resolution of impeachment, founded on the President's removal of E. M. Stanton from the War Department . . . ; this resolution is founded in a mistake, and any impeachment of the President on the idea that Secretary Stanton is within the protection of the tenure of office bill is what Fouche, the Chief of the French police, would have called worse than a crime—a blunder. . . .

"It is the removal of Mr. Stanton that is complained of, but the removal which the sixth section condemns is every removal 'contrary to the provisions of this act.' If Mr. Stanton is not within the act then the removal of him is not contrary to it."

Reading the first section he continues:

"Such is the tenure of Cabinet officers. A month after the expiration of the term of the President by whom they were appointed their tenure expires, and they become tenants at sufferance. Until that time they are removable by advice of the Senate; after that time they have no title and their possession can be ousted at the pleasure of the President. . . .

"Thus, then, it stands: the sixth section punishes removals contrary to the act; but Cabinet ministers can only be removed contrary to the act by the President who appointed them. Mr. Stanton was appointed by President Lincoln, and his title to office expired a month after Lincoln's death; from that time he retained his portfolio at the pleasure and will of him upon whom all the powers and duties of the office had devolved; he was a mere *locum tenens;* and when Mr. Johnson removed him he acted within the strictest bounds of the Constitution, and offended not against the statute; he went not 'contrary' to it, and so incurred not the penalties of the sixth section."

Mr. Boutwell, alone of the speakers of the majority, attempted an answer by claiming that the Constitution having defined the term of the President as a "term of four years" and, in case of death, devolving "not the office, not the term but the powers and duties of the office" upon the Vice President; "Johnson himself has no term" and it was in Lincoln's term that Stanton was removed. But Woodward exploded this verbal fallacy by anticipation:

"It was Mr. Lincoln's power and duty to hold his office for the term of four years, and at his death this power and duty, as far as they were unperformed, devolved upon the Vice-President by the very words of the Constitution. The term became Mr. Johnson's term for its unfinished period, as much so as the right to possession of the White House, the right to the salary, or to any of the perquisites and functions of the office. It would be as unreasonable to call Mr. Johnson's possession of these Mr. Lincoln's possession, or Mr. Johnson's Administration Mr. Lincoln's Administration, as to call Mr. Johnson's term of office Mr. Lincoln's term. Neither in popular language nor in constitutional phrase can such a misnomer be found. It would be as absurd as to confound their names, or the identity of their persons."

James F. Wilson, who was one of the members of the conference committee when the Tenure-of-office bill was passed, in his speech in this debate did not allude to this question, and Schenck and Williams, the other members, did not speak. Bingham made no attempt to show by the act itself that Stanton was within it, but, referring to the suspension of that officer and the Senate's action on it, declared that the President "recognized that act as embracing the Secretary of War," submitted that question to the judgment of the Senate, and "by its judgment the President and every other person is concluded."

But the majority were the less solicitous to maintain the validity of their case under the Tenure act, because they jumped to another conclusion, viz: that Stanton's removal in the circumstances under which it was made was without authority, independently of that act. From Stevens, who advanced the proposition in the few words he spoke when presenting the report of his committee, down to the last speech in the debate, every speaker on the side of the majority assumed as a matter of course that, in the case of an officer whose appointment was required to be made "by and with the advice and consent of the Senate," his removal without the consent of the Senate while that body was in session was a clear violation of the Constitution. "Nobody ever pretended that I ever heard of that the President during the session of the Senate could remove an officer," said one member. "I hold that his offence is complete, even if there had been no Tenure-of-office law in existence, for under the Constitution the President has no authority whatever, while the Senate is in session, to remove a Cabinet officer," said another. "It has never been contended that the Executive had the power of removal during the session of the Senate. The only course which he can pursue is to send a nomination to the Senate, which, if confirmed, displaces the person in office,'' said another.

But this second assumption, like the first, was founded in error and a lack of accurate information. As Woodward stated the case:

> ''An idea has got possession of gentlemen's minds, inspired, no doubt, by the Tenure of office law, that the peculiar enormity of the President's act consisted in removing Stanton while the Senate was in session. The Constitution does not forbid him to do so, but leaves him free at all times to rid himself of an unacceptable Cabinet minister. It is better done when the Senate is in session than when it is in recess, because the new nomination can be immediately considered without prejudice to the public interests from delay of a confirmation; and such has been the practice of the Government from its foundation. Indeed, the Senate is always in session when a new Administration comes in and substitutes new Cabinet officers for the old ones.''

When the vote came to be taken at five o'clock on Monday afternoon (the twenty-fourth), though the arguments of their adversaries may have made them uneasy over the unforeseen weakness of a case they at first thought invulnerable, there was no break in the serried ranks of the majority and but little abatement of enthusiasm. On the contrary, some injudicious warnings of a menacing character uttered by the Democrats served but to heighten their ardour. Brooks' prediction, that the trial, with all its cumbrous forms and ceremonial, would necessarily outlast the term of the President, only stimulated them to further haste; but his threat of resistance by the people to any departure from constitutional methods, such as suspension during trial, was greeted with derisive laughter. Woodward denied their "right to impeach anybody and the present Senate's right to try any impeachment."

"Says the Constitution: 'The House of Representatives shall have the sole power of impeachment,' and the House of Representatives shall be composed of members chosen every second year by the people of the several States. This House of Representatives is not so composed; but, on the contrary, the representatives chosen from ten of the 'several States' have been and are excluded from these Halls. . . .

"The Constitution says: 'The Senate shall have the sole power to try all impeachments,' and that the Senate shall be composed of two senators from each State. The ten excluded States are entitled to twenty senators upon that floor, and until they are admitted and incorporated into that body I deny that it is the Senate to whom the Constitution commits the power to try impeachments. What criminal was ever before arraigned before a court from which twenty of his legal triers had been excluded? . . .

"The flippant reply to this grave question is that we pass laws, and therefore we are a House and Senate to impeach. But the answer is, your legislative powers have not been questioned, your impeaching powers are;"

but when he ended his speech with the following menace he only concentrated the wrath and solidified the resolve of the majority:

"Mr. Speaker, so sure am I that the American people will respect this objection that I will say, if I were the President's counsellor, which I am not, I would advise him, if you prefer articles of impeachment, to demur both to your jurisdiction and that of the Senate, and to issue a proclamation giving you and all the world notice that while he held himself impeachable for misdemeanors in office before the constitutional tribunal, he never would subject the office he holds in trust for the people to the irregular, unconstitutional, fragmentary bodies who propose to strip him of it. Such a proclamation, with the Army and Navy at hand to sustain it, would meet a popular response that would make an end of impeachment and impeachers."

Stevens closed the debate in a short and sententious speech which is characteristic of the man and still more of the debate itself. He alludes to the "high misdemeanor" of the statute with a kind of contemptuous indulgence and then dogmatically affirms that "an indictable offence or an act *malum in se*" is not necessary to sustain impeachment. "The question is wholly political." He points to the removal of Stanton as a violation of law, but he makes no attempt to answer the argument that Stanton was not within the law. He treats the offence only as one of many grosser usurpations and higher crimes. He proposes to try Andrew Johnson for "misprision of bribery" in offering General Grant, if he would unite with him in his lawless violence, "to assume in his stead the penalties" of the law. He proposes to try him for violation of his official oath—"a solemn and enduring obligation"; adding with grim humour, "nor can he plead exemption from it on account of his condition at the time it was administered to him." He proposes to prove his (the President's) obstruction of the reconstruction policy of Congress:

"In my judgment his conduct in regard to that transaction was a high-handed usurpation of power which ought long ago to have brought him to impeachment and trial and to have removed him from his position of great mischief. He has been lucky in thus far escaping through false logic and false law. But his then acts, which will on the trial be shown to be atrocious, are open evidence of his wicked determination to subvert the laws of his country.''

His last words, and the last words in the debate, were:

''As we deal with the first great political malefactor, so will be the result of our efforts to perpetuate the happiness and good government of the human race. . . . This is not to be the temporary triumph of a political party, but is to endure in its consequence until this whole continent shall be filled with a free and untrammeled people or shall be a nest of shrinking, cowardly slaves.''

The vote was then taken; one hundred and twenty-six in the affirmative—every man a Republican; forty-seven in the negative—every Democrat on the roll but one and he was paired. Of the sixteen Republicans not voting, all were unavoidably absent but the one paired with the Democrat; one had not attended the House on account of illness since the session began; two made haste to apologize for their absence and announced their agreement with the majority; nine were proclaimed by colleagues to be in favour of the resolution; leaving three not recorded, one of whom voted for the first impeachment. So that it may be stated with substantial truth, that the solid representation of the Republican party in the House, without a dissenting or deprecating voice—the Speaker even rushing forward gratuitously to pillory himself in the gaze of all coming generations—joined in a deed, of which at the present day no intelligent human being acquainted with the facts—scarcely even one of the surviving participants—will utter a word in justification. They hated the President and yearned to make away with him because of political offences for which they tried once and again and failed to impeach him. They seize upon a technical infraction of an unjust statute—a statute they made haste to repeal as soon as they had a President of their own—as a pretext to drag him before a court they believed had already prejudged his case. They discover on the threshold that he is not and, on account of a blunder of their own, cannot be guilty of the trivial offence they have made a stalking-horse for their revolutionary aim; and they go right on and impeach him nevertheless.

A committee of two (Stevens and Bingham) having been appointed to notify the Senate of the action of the House, and a committee of seven to prepare articles of impeachment, the House adjourned.*

On this same Monday the nomination of Thomas Ewing sr., for Secretary of War, in the place of Edwin M. Stanton removed, reached the Senate chamber again, and this time was not, as on Saturday, hindered by an unlooked-for adjournment. It was accompanied by a message from the President in the nature of an answer to, or a protest against, the Senate's resolution of Friday night. The senators being in no mood to displace Stanton, the nomination was shelved as a matter of course. But the message was calculated to make them reflect. In

* For this debate, see *Cong. Globe* of the dates indicated. For vote, see *id.*, p. 1400; committees, p. 1402.

it the President dwelt almost exclusively on the construction of the proviso of the Tenure-of-office act which excepted from that law those members of his Cabinet who, like Stanton, were not appointed by himself. He stated that his opinion of its unconstitutionality, sent to the Senate with his veto of the bill, remained unchanged; but that, the bill having become a law over his objections, he had striven to observe it in every particular; making no removals contrary to its provisions except in the alleged instance of Stanton, and in his case only after coming to the conclusion that he was not within the letter or spirit of the statute. "If upon such a question I have fallen into an erroneous construction, I submit whether it should be characterized as a violation of official duty or law." "I have endeavored to proceed with the greatest circumspection and have acted only in an extreme and exceptional case, carefully following the course that I have marked out for myself as a general rule, faithfully to execute all laws though passed over my objections on the score of constitutionality." The stubbornness of pose and fearlessness of nature characteristic of the man are revealed in the closing paragraph:

> "In the present instance I have appealed or sought to appeal to that final arbiter fixed by the Constitution for the determination of all such questions. To this course I have been impelled by the solemn obligations which rest upon me to sustain inviolate the powers of the high office committed to my hands. Whatever be the consequences personal to myself, I could not allow them to prevail against a public duty so clear to my own mind and so imperative. If what was possible had been certain, if I had been fully advised when I removed Mr. Stanton that, in thus defend-

ing the trust committed to my hands, my own removal was sure to follow, I could not have hesitated, actuated by public considerations of the highest character."

The next morning, the House committee of two appeared, and Stevens "in the name of the House of Representatives and of all the people of the United States" impeached "Andrew Johnson, President of the United States, of high crimes and misdemeanors in office," promised to exhibit articles in due time and demanded that the Senate "take order for the appearance of the said Andrew Johnson to answer said impeachment." The President *pro tempore* responded that the Senate would take order, the committee withdrew and a select committee of seven was appointed by the Senate to consider and report upon the necessary preliminaries.

Meantime, the midnight warrant against Thomas, after having failed in its object of scaring off the new secretary, was turning into something very like a boomerang in the hands of the prosecution. Thomas retained Richard T. Merrick and a consultation was held by him with the President as to how the arrest of his client might be taken advantage of to get the case into the Supreme Court. The President, also, employed Walter S. Cox, another Washington lawyer, to institute proceedings after consultation with the Attorney-General, to test Thomas' right to the office and put him in possession. These two counsel attended on Wednesday (twenty-sixth), the day to which the criminal proceeding had been adjourned before Judge Cartter, and formally surrendered the defendant to the custody of the marshal; at the same time presenting to the judge a petition for a writ of *habeas corpus* on behalf of the prisoner. The counsel for Stanton protested vehemently that the defendant was not in custody, that he could not put himself in custody, that they did not want him in custody. The judge echoed their protestations, ruling that the defendant was not in custody, could not put himself in custody, that the judge did not desire to put him in custody, that his bare word was sufficient. The defendant's counsel then moved his discharge, the counsel for the complainant made no objection, the judge discharged the culprit with as much alacrity as he had signed the order for his arrest, and that was the last of the celebrated case of Edwin M. Stanton *vs.* Lorenzo Thomas.*

The Senate committee on Rules and the House committee on Articles were hard at work during the week, and the former succeeded in reporting to the Senate, on Friday, twenty-five "rules of procedure and practice in the Senate when sitting as a High Court of Impeachment"; but, when they were taken up for discussion the next day, grave and embarrassing questions immediately arose. The objection that the Senate sitting as a senate could not adopt rules to govern the Senate sitting as a court raised the question whether the Senate sitting for the trial of an impeachment was a court or not—a question on which a serious division of opinion existed among the majority. Conkling succeeded, after one defeat, in striking out the word "court" which the committee had employed in the draft, and in substituting for

* Testimony of Cox and Merrick. Trial, Vol. 1, pp. 605, 607, 617, 618–622.

the title "High Court of Impeachment" the title "The Senate sitting for trial of an Impeachment"; leaving the question "as it is left by the Constitution." "Calling this a court," as he said, "does not make it a court; and failing to call it a court does not prevent its being a court, if in truth it is so." The debate was drawn out to an unexpected and unwelcome length, going over until Monday (March 2) and continuing far into the night before the rules as amended were finally adopted.

The committee of the House had a much harder task. The object in view in confining the charges to the issuing the order of removal and the letter of authority was to dispense with the necessity of sustaining them with other than documentary evidence and thus preclude the possibility of an insufferable prolongation of the trial. But the debate on the resolution of impeachment taught the House that there was such a thing as making the charges too narrow, and the committee on the articles, therefore, felt the need, in the first place, of supporting the two letters by the production of some evidence, at least, that there had ever been an effort to put them in force; in the words of Butler, they "wanted to clothe these naked bones and sinews with flesh and enliven them with blood." Accordingly, with the utmost care and caution not to widen the door for oral testimony farther than absolutely necessary, the committee on Wednesday (February 26) heard the testimony of Burleigh and Wilkeson relating to the loose threats of Thomas, and of Van Horn, one of the members of Congress who gathered round Stanton when Thomas made his advance upon the War Office. They also heard the testimony of General

Emory relating the circumstances of his interview with the President, the details of which had been so magnified by rumour. They summoned another army officer (Col. Wallace) who had a brief conversation with the President on Sunday, the twenty-third, of the same tenor. And they summoned Thomas, just escaped from the clutches of the law that morning, and plied him with question after question until his head was in a whirl. This comprised all the testimony they took. A letter of the President notifying the Secretary of the Treasury of the change in the War Department comprised all the additional documentary evidence. They then turned to the formulation of articles, their chief anxiety being to meet every phase of opinion in the majority of the Senate; and on Saturday (twenty-ninth) they reported them to the House.

The first article related exclusively to the "order of removal";—charging it as an attempt to remove in violation of the Tenure act and, also, of the Constitution, the Senate being in session. The second related exclusively to the letter of authority to Thomas; the letter being charged as constituting a regular appointment and contrary both to the act and to the Constitution. The third differed from the second only by making no reference to the Tenure act. The succeeding five—called "the Conspiracy Articles"—charged a conspiracy between the President and Thomas, "by intimidation and threats," to prevent Stanton from holding office, in violation of the Constitution and the conspiracy act of 1861 (fourth); "by force" to hinder the execution of the Tenure act by preventing Stanton from holding office (fifth); "by force to seize" the property of the United States in the War Department contrary to the act of 1861 and with intent to violate the Tenure act (sixth); "to prevent and hinder" the execution of the Tenure act by preventing Stanton from holding office (seventh); "to seize" the property of the War Department contrary to the Tenure act (eighth). The ninth was a repetition of the second and third, charged with the additional intent to obtain control of the moneys appropriated for the War Department. The tenth and last was founded upon the Emory interview, and charged, in effect, that the expression by the President to an officer of the army of his opinion that a section of an act of Congress "depriving him of his powers as Commander-in-Chief was unconstitutional" was a "high misdemeanor."

From the time of Johnson's accession, the more spiteful of his adversaries were addicted to the habit of denying he was President, asserting that he was still Vice President and, for the time being only "Acting President." And yet by the articles reported he was impeached as "President of the United States." Mr. Boutwell affected apprehension that the Senate might decide that Johnson was not President and in that case the whole proceeding would have to be gone over from the beginning. "A different court," he said, "must be organized for the trial of the Vice-President from that authorized by the Constitution to try the President." And the objection gave Bingham the opportunity to trample this offspring of petty malice out of existence.

"I desire to say that I was not aware when the report was read there was a member of that committee who had the slightest doubt that Andrew Johnson was the President of the United States. I desire to say he must be impeached if he be impeached at all, either distinctively as President . . . or as Vice-President. . . . Again, Andrew Johnson is estopped by record in five hundred instances from denying that he is President of the United States. The Senate is estopped; the House of Representatives is estopped. Your Constitution declares that no bill shall be a law until it be presented to the President for his approval or disapproval. If he be not President, if the people have no President, then you can pass no law. If he be President, then let him be called President on your records."

From the very nature of things, his enemies were forced to place the crown on Johnson's head before they could indulge themselves in the pleasure of taking it off.

The discussion of the articles was for the most part but a repetition of the debate on the resolution; but the speech of Stevens, in which he exposed the duplicity of the whole proceeding in his most satirical vein, cannot be passed over without notice. "Never," said he, "was a great malefactor so gently treated as Andrew Johnson." The "monstrous usurpation, worse than sedition and little short of treason," of the President, "fundamental offenses much more worthy of punishment, the committee have omitted because they determined to deal gently with the President." Their "tender mercies have rested solely on the most trifling crimes and misdemeanors which they could select from the official life of Andrew Johnson." He then produced an article of his own which, he stated, he had offered in committee and thought it had been put in, but which, he suspected, had been omitted through mistake. "I will therefore read it and call it one and a half, as, in my judgment, it is the gist and vital portion of this whole prosecution." Reciting the suspension of Stanton and the submission by the President of his reasons to the Senate, the article charged that, while the Senate was considering their sufficiency, the President formed a deliberate design to prevent Stanton from resuming the office if the Senate should decide in his favour; and, when defeated by the integrity and fidelity of the Secretary *ad interim*, sought to arrive at the same end by issuing a letter of authority to Thomas. "If there be shrewd lawyers," he added, "as I know there will be, and cavilling judges, and, without this article, they do not acquit him, they are greener than I was in any case I ever undertook before the court of quarter sessions. If it be inserted . . . how, then, can he or his counsel hope to escape even if there were no other charge—it is worth all of them put together—unless it be upon what I know they will rely on, the unconstitutionality of the Tenure-of-office act." On that question, he remarked, the Senate had voted four times in favour of the law, and, "Let me see," said he, "the recreant who will now dare tread back upon his steps and vote upon the other side."

On Monday at three o'clock P. M. the committee reported a revised version in which the changes were merely verbal or unimportant, with the exception that the seventh was dropped; reducing the number to nine. Jenckes of Rhode Island having prepared a voluminous article now moved to add it to the others. It charged the issuing of the letters of removal and authority as the outcome of a premeditated design to usurp the entire control of the army, unlimited by the acts of Congress regulating the same, and by means of the army to obstruct the execution of the reconstruction acts. But, apprehensive that its insertion would render the trial interminable, the House voted it down without ceremony. Butler now came to the front. From the beginning of the movement, before he was a member of Congress, he had made the study of Impeachment a specialty. He considered it the one remedy for all the ills of the party under whose banners he was enlisted for the time being. Far and wide over the country, in the fall of 1866, he advertised its curative qualities, addressing meetings in various states and even a legislature or two; and he was sent to the fortieth Congress to preside over its administration. The wreck of the first project on what he regarded as a miserable technicality of law filled up the measure of his disgust; and he was profoundly dissatisfied with the meagre charges now made against the President in deference to a doctrine which he denounced as "unsound in law, fallacious in reasoning and dangerous in principle." Being suspected of opposition to the nomination of Grant, he was left off the committee to draft the articles. But he was a man who could not be silenced. The speeches of the President, at Washington and on his tour West, in 1866, seemed to him to furnish most convenient material for impeachment and an excellent opportunity to expatiate on the atrocities of Andrew Johnson. Finding a precedent in the case of Justice Samuel Chase where the charge of making an intemperate and inflammatory harangue to a grand jury obtained the greatest number of votes, he, too, prepared an article based on certain violent utterances of the President. The substance of the charge was that Andrew Johnson, intending to bring ridicule, reproach and popular odium upon the Congress and the laws passed by it, made certain speeches against that august body; extracts of which were set forth in three specifications; the first taken from the speech of the eighteenth of August, 1866, at the Executive Mansion in reply to the address delivered by Reverdy Johnson when presenting a copy of the proceedings of the Philadelphia Convention, the most notorious sentence of which was: "We have seen hanging on the verge of the Government, as it were, a body called, or which assumes to be, the Congress of the United States, while in fact it is a Congress of only a part of the States"; the second taken from the Cleveland speech in which Congress is said to be "trying to break up the Government"; the third from the St. Louis speech charging "the Radical Congress" with being the source of the New Orleans riot and containing Johnson's remarks about "Christ" and his "Judas." This article, he had pressed upon the committee in vain. Its subject-matter antedated the defeat of the first impeachment by more than a year, and a part of it had been included in the charges then made and passed adversely upon by the House. Besides, there, again, was the danger of prolonging the trial. Butler, not at all discouraged by its rejection by the committee, offered it to the full House, apologizing for the fact that not a particle of evidence had been adduced of the charges contained in it by saying that "the language cited was taken from perfectly reliable documents, and two of the three citations were proved before the judiciary committee" (*i. e.,* on the former investigation), "and there can be no doubt the speeches were delivered "; adding that he had "made no allegation of the truth or falsity of the utterances because it would not have been consistent with the dignity of the House." On the statement of Wilson that "it was agreed by the committee not to present an article based upon the subject-matter involved in this amendment," the House rejected the article by a vote by tellers of 48 yeas to 74 nays. At four o'clock, the nine articles, as agreed to in the committee of the whole, were reported to the House and adopted *seriatim.* The election of seven managers by ballot was next in order. The members selected in the caucus of the Saturday night before were put in nomination: Stevens, Butler, Bingham, Boutwell, Wilson, Williams and Logan. Bingham led the list with 114 votes out of 118 cast, and Stevens was at the foot with 105; the Democrats taking no part in the balloting. A message was sent to the Senate communicating the election of managers and the order that they exhibit the articles; and the House adjourned.*

The next day, when the message announcing that the Senate was ready to receive the managers reached the House, it found them in no condition to attend. Butler was engaged in pressing again upon the House his own article which the managers, in the meanwhile, reversing

* For debate on Rules in Senate and on Articles in House see *Globe* of dates indicated.

the course of action of the committee, had authorized him to report. To dispel the fear that it would protract the trial, to which he attributed its defeat the day before, he pointed out how quickly the speeches could be proved by the stenographers who took them down; "and besides," he said, "the managers have all this in their hands . . ." "If we find the article would cause unprofitable delay" we can withdraw it or any portion of it. He quieted Garfield, who expressed his anxiety on this point, saying: "I voted in the negative last evening, not because I was opposed to it but from fear it would increase the time"—with the information that "the reason why the person who drew the article drew it with three specifications . . . was that the managers could withdraw either specification . . . or offer proof under either." Finally Butler's article was adopted by a vote of but 87 yeas to 40 nays, and it became article X. Bingham, then, by the unanimous instruction of the board of managers, reported still another. Its authorship was attributed to Stevens and he openly fathered it, but it differed in almost every feature from the article offered by him the day before and which he commended to the House in such extraordinary terms. The gravamen of that article was the premeditated design of the President to prevent the reinstatement of Stanton after the Senate had non-concurred in that officer's suspension, as shown by the Grant-Johnson correspondence. The article now reported was a mosaic of fragments of those already adopted, of the Jenckes article rejected and of the original Stevens article; and the object of its concoction seems to have been to catch the votes of doubtful senators. Only one overt act was charged, viz: an attempt on the twenty-first of February to prevent the execution of the Tenure-of-office act; but this one act was buried under such a mass of indirect allegations by way of inducement to commit it and of means whereby it was committed, that it was almost impossible to disinter it. I. The declaration of the President in his speech of August 18, 1866, that the Thirty-ninth Congress was only a Congress of a part of the States (taken from the Butler article) is averred to be a denial that the legislation of that Congress was valid or obligatory upon Andrew Johnson except so far as he saw fit to approve it, and a denial of the power of that Congress to propose amendments to the Constitution (a new averment); and then it is alleged that the attempt was committed in pursuance of this declaration. II. The attempt itself, it charges, was committed (1) by devising means to prevent the reinstatement of Stanton (this is from the original Stevens article); (2) by devising means to prevent the execution of the army appropriation act (this is taken from the Emory article); and, also, (3) by devising means to prevent the execution of the reconstruction act (this is taken from the rejected Jenckes article). So elaborate a structure furnished common standing-ground for the advocates of impeachment on account of the President's course since the commencement of his administration—the movement defeated by the House; for the advocates of impeachment founded on the Johnson-Grant quarrel—the movement stifled in committee; and for the advocates of impeachment on account of specific offences made high misdemeanours by the sixth section of the Tenure-of-office act,—the movement now on foot. It is best described in the words of senator Buckalew:

"As an article on which to convict, its strength consists in its weakness—in the obscurity of its charges and the intricacy of its form. . . .

"Considered in parts it is nothing—the propositions into which it is divisible cannot stand separately as charges of criminal conduct or intention; and considered as a whole it eludes the understanding and baffles conjecture. . . .

"The matter of this article, so far as substance can be detected in it, is drawn mostly from the other articles; but that matter is arranged, manipulated, and combined together in a manner to vex the student and confound the judge; and the new particulars of charge or aggravation (whichever they may be) contained in the article are hinted at rather than expressed, and we vainly explore the context to discover distinctly their antecedents or the conclusions to which they lead."*

This Omnibus article, as it was fitly called, was accepted by a vote of 108 yeas to 32 nays, and numbered article XI.

The list being complete, the next thing to be done was to present the articles to the Senate. On Wednesday, the fourth day of March, the House resolved itself into a committee of the whole and followed the managers to the Senate chamber. The Senate had just listened to the reading of an opinion, sent in by the Chief Justice, to the effect that when the Senate sits for the trial of an impeachment it sits as a court; that, therefore, the

* Opinion, Trial, Vol. 3, p. 228.

organization of the Senate as a court should precede the actual announcement of the impeachment on the part of the House; that articles should only be presented to a court of impeachment; and that rules for the government of such a court should be framed only by the court itself. This opinion from so high an authority, the Senate disregarded entirely by proceeding immediately to listen to the managers read the articles in the presence of the House, the Speaker being provided with a seat at the right of the President *pro tem.* This ceremony over and the managers with their retinue gone, the Senate resolved that at one o'clock the next afternoon it would proceed with the Impeachment; notice to be sent to the House and a committee of three to wait upon the Chief Justice to conduct him to the chair. That evening, Chase held a reception at his residence. At about midnight the doors are thrown open, "the President of the United States" is announced, and Andrew Johnson, the Great Impeached, walks in. The ordinary exchange of courtesies between the distinguished host and his distinguished guest takes place, and the incident is at an end. But the report in the newspapers next morning sent a flurry through the ranks of the advocates of impeachment and, following as it did the opinion of the Chief Justice, convinced the radicals that the officer to preside at the trial was an enemy to their scheme.*

The next day—Thursday, the fifth—the Senate chamber is crowded by persons curious to witness the metamorphosis of a legislative body into a judicial tribunal. When the fine head of the Chief Justice comes into view

* Washington newspapers.

as he advances through the crowd of representatives flooding the back spaces and outer circles of desks, the lion-like countenance of Justice Nelson following, the senators all rise. Wade vacates the chair, and the Chief Justice, taking it, announces that he attends for the purpose of joining the senators "in forming a court of impeachment for the trial of the President of the United States," and is ready to take the oath. In prescribing a form of oath for its own members the Senate had ignored the Chief Justice as being merely a presiding officer and as such not required to be sworn. This theory, Justice Nelson demolishes by administering the senators' oath to the Chief Justice as being actually a member of the court; the senators looking on in silence. The roll is then called alphabetically, and the Chief Justice administers the oath to every senator, to "do impartial justice according to the Constitution and laws." The slow process is almost over when, in answer to the name of Benjamin F. Wade, that senator comes forward to be sworn. Hendricks protests that, in accordance with the spirit of the constitutional provision that when the President is impeached the Vice President cannot preside at the trial, the President *pro tem.*, being next in succession to the present Chief Magistrate, has no right to become a member of the court. Sherman comes to the defence of his colleague, pleading that Wade is a senator of Ohio, Ohio is entitled to two votes in the Senate, of which the state cannot be deprived; Wade is not Vice President and, therefore, the constitutional inhibition does not apply, and it is for him to say how far his interest in the event of the trial will suffer him to go.

Howard contends that there is no right of challenge in cases of impeachment and points to the fact that the son-in-law of the accused had already sworn in. Reverdy Johnson, on the other side, recalls the Stockton case, when Sumner championed "the honor of the American Senate." With his usual audacity in dealing with the facts of history, Sumner denies point-blank that the reason why the Vice President was incapacitated from presiding on the trial of the President was the one assigned by Hendricks, and states that "the reason for the introduction of the clause" (a reason heard of now for the first time) was "because the framers of the Constitution contemplated the possibility of the suspension of the President from the exercise of his powers, in which event the Vice President could not be in the chair of the Senate because he would be in the President's place." The discussion was carried over to the next day, when a senator impatient of the delay invoked the twenty-third rule as adopted by the Senate. The Chief Justice decided that the rule did not yet apply as the Senate was not yet organized for the trial of an impeachment—a decision which provoked the radicals to appeal and the chair was sustained by 24 to 20—the first significant vote in the proceeding. Hendricks finding some of his political associates of the opinion that the question under debate ought more properly to be raised when the court was fully organized, withdrew his objection, and "Bluff Ben" Wade, with unruffled countenance, took the oath.*

* A report of this debate is given at end of Vol. 3 of Trial.

It is not a subject of regret that the important legal question raised at this time, but never coming up again, was left undecided. In the absence of an express inhibition, there can be little doubt that a senator does not lose his constitutional right to be a member of the senatorial court on the trial of the President by being elected to the chair of the Senate and thus, because of an act of Congress, put in the line of succession to the chief magistracy. But, while this is so, there can be no doubt whatever that a senator occupying that invidious position is morally disqualified and ought at least to forego his privilege. In truth, the reason for the exclusion of the President *pro tempore* of the Senate, when *ex officio* Vice President, is much stronger than the reason for the exclusion of the Vice President. The Vice President proper can vote on the trial, even on incidental questions, only in case of a tie, can in no event vote on the final judgment because it takes two-thirds to convict, and, consequently, cannot contribute to his own elevation; whereas an *ex officio* Vice President, like Wade, can vote on all questions arising during the progress of the trial and his one vote may be decisive of the final judgment; thus literally making him President of the United States. In Wade's case, moreover, the impropriety was particularly glaring. He was one of the bitterest adversaries of the President, had denounced Andrew Johnson far and wide over the country, loading the name with opprobrious epithets in the use of which he was a master. He was universally known as an outspoken advocate of the deposition of the President. He was the only senator who publicly gloried in seizing on every advantage sickness or death might give him in the struggle for the two-thirds majority in the Senate; he was prominently conspicuous in urging the admission of undeveloped territories into the Union for the purpose of adding to the number of judges in the court of impeachment favourable beforehand to conviction; he had been lately rejected by his own state and a gentleman of opposite politics selected to succeed him; there was never from the beginning the slightest uncertainty about his vote of "guilty," and his partisans were even now betting that in ten, twenty or at most thirty days "honest old Ben Wade" would be in the White House. It was fortunate, therefore, that a decision of the naked legal right, which must have been one of affirmance, was never pronounced:—leaving the breach of the most fundamental canon of judicial decency to stand forth in all its grossness, unrelieved by cloak, apology or mitigation.

The remaining senators present having taken the oath, the Chief Justice, again calling attention to his disregarded opinion and giving the senators no opportunity for reflection or interruption, put the question whether the rules adopted on the second of March should be considered the rules of this body. The senators responded orally in the affirmative, and the Chief Justice scored another victory. It was about three o'clock when the managers demanded process against Andrew Johnson. The Senate ordered that a summons issue returnable on Friday, the thirteenth of March, and the "Court" ("to use a brief expression," as Howard said) adjourned to that day.

During the week's interval not much legislative business was done. It was thought "incongruous and improper to be sending bills to the President for signature when he is being tried for high crimes and misdemeanors"; Sumner being exceedingly sensitive about holding any intercourse whatever with a President "arraigned at our bar in the name of the people of the United States," even protesting against the Senate going into executive session. But when (on the ninth) the credentials of George Vickers, elected by the legislature of Maryland to fill "the unexpired term of the Hon. Philip F. Thomas who was refused a seat," were presented, the senator from Massachusetts challenged the validity of the election on the ground that Maryland had not a republican form of government and moved to refer the credentials; the effect of which action would have been to deprive the President of a friendly judge on the coming trial. The motion, however, met with little favour and Vickers was sworn in, making the Senate, as at present constituted, full.

There was more business out of doors. The managers summoned Thomas before them and for a second time he was put upon the rack. Stanton got hold of a witness for them—one George Washington Karsner from Delaware—who, on Monday evening, the ninth, in the east room of the President's House, whither he had gone full of curiosity to see the distinguished citizen of his own state now standing by the President as his *ad interim* Secretary of War, succeeded in getting eyes on his hero whom he took the liberty to exhort to stand firm, telling him that "the eyes of Delaware were upon him," and eliciting the off-hand reply: "In two or three days' time I will kick that fellow out." Of this conversation, the Delawarian boasted to one of the clerks of the War Department who carried him before his intrenched chief and thence he was sent in hot haste before the managers, and this bit of testimony secured.

On Friday, the thirteenth of March, the Senate chamber for the first time assumed the appearance it retained throughout the trial. The senators, having resolved to retain their seats and not transfer themselves to a platform put up for the purpose on each side of the chair, as was done in Judge Humphrey's case, the last preceding trial, confined themselves as far as possible to the two inner rows of desks; surrendering the outer rows, as well as the surrounding back spaces filled with chairs by their order, to the members of the House. The managers on their entrance were conducted to a place assigned them on the left of the chair. The sergeant-at-arms in a loud voice called Andrew Johnson thrice; but Andrew Johnson did not answer. Instead of so notable an appearance, manager Butler came hurrying in and, as the crier's voice resounded through the chamber, halted in mid-aisle, seemingly at a loss to conceive why so offensive a name should be hurled at him in so obstreperous a manner. The merriment excited by this incident died away as from an adjoining room there entered the President's counsel—Henry Stanbery (just resigned as Attorney-General), Benjamin R. Curtis and Thomas A. R. Nelson—who were conducted to a position to the right of the chair corresponding to the place assigned to the managers on the left. The House of

Representatives was then announced and the members, headed by Elihu B. Washburne chairman of the committee of the whole, surged into the chamber and spread themselves over the space assigned them, taxing the utmost capacity of the floor.

Thereupon, Mr. Stanbery rose and read a communication addressed to the Chief Justice and signed Andrew Johnson, notifying the appearance of the President by counsel (in addition to the three present naming Jeremiah S. Black and William M. Evarts), and asking for forty days to prepare an answer. He also read a statement, signed by all five counsel, to the effect that the time asked for, "with the utmost diligence," was no more than "reasonable and necessary." The managers were prepared for some such application, for some dilatory movement, but for no such "huge cantle" as this. "Forty days!" Butler exclaimed, "as long as it took God to destroy the world by a flood!" Forty days to plead not guilty! In the discussion that ensued, it was curious to hear with what scrupulosity the managers on their side addressed the presiding officer as "Mr. President," and the counsel for the President on their side as "Mr. Chief Justice." Edmunds, at length, moved an order that the respondent file his answer on or before the first day of April, the managers their replication within three days thereafter, and the trial begin on the sixth; whereupon the Chief Justice and the senators retired to the reception room for consultation. The audience instantly relaxes its attention, the buzz of conversation rises, members go in and out, groups gather on the floor, and comparative disorder reigns in the galleries. After a tedious interval of two hours, the court returns; there is an instant hush; and the Chief Justice announces the order granting the President ten, instead of forty, days.

This matter having been settled, the managers moved that upon the filing of the replication the trial proceed forthwith; and their motion gave rise to the second significant vote of the senators. Twenty-five Republicans voted for the motion and fifteen voted with eleven opposition senators against it; the motion being lost by one vote. The struggle over the fixing of a day certain for the trial to commence resulted in the indefinite order that it proceed immediately after the replication shall be filed, "unless otherwise ordered for cause shown"; and the court adjourned until Monday, the twenty-third, amid the angry ejaculations of the extremists: "Another ten days thrown away!"

During the interval the President lost the services of the most eminent of his counsel. Black was the leading lawyer for an American firm who claimed the small island of Alta Vela, lying near St. Domingo, (or the guano on it), by the right of discovery and occupation, but whose settlement and works there the Dominican government had broken up, and then leased the island to another American firm, who were now contesting the validity of the claim of the former before the executive of the United States. Black urged the redress of his client's grievance by the summary method of sending a United States vessel to take possession of the island, arguing the case before the Attorney-General and bringing his personal influence as a political friend and adviser to bear upon the President. But Seward was strongly averse to interference by the government, and, it was said, his opposition alone stood in the way of the President's yielding to the force of his own opinion that the original occupiers had a right to the possession of the island. Other and less justifiable methods were resorted to. The summons of the Senate in the impeachment proceeding was served on the President on Saturday, the seventh of March, and Black must have been already retained as one of his counsel. On Monday (the ninth) Col. J. W. Shaffer, one of the junior counsel with Black and a former aid-de-camp to General Butler, went to that gentleman in the House of Representatives and secured the manager's opinion, in the shape of a letter dated that day and addressed to Shaffer, favourable to the validity of the claim of his clients, and stating that the writer had "never been able to understand why the Executive did not long since assert the rights of the Government and sustain the rightful claims of its citizens to the possession of the island *in the most forcible manner* consistent with the dignity and honor of the Nation." This letter Shaffer carried around to manager Logan who wrote under its signature, "I concur in the opinion above expressed by General Butler; John A. Logan": and, then, to representative Garfield, who wrote underneath, "and I, J. A. Garfield." The document was given by Shaffer to Chauncey F. Black, the son of Judge Black, and another counsel in the case, who sent or handed it to the President. On Friday, the thirteenth, the elder Black's name was signed to the appearance entered by the President before the

Court of Impeachment, although he was not personally present. On the following morning, the younger Black enclosed to the President a copy of Butler's letter with the addenda of Logan and Garfield (the original of which was already in the President's hands) to which had been added in the meantime another concurrence signed by W. H. Koontz (a representative), J. K. Moorhead (one of the Stanton body-guard on the twenty-second), Thaddeus Stevens (manager), J. G. Blaine, and John A. Bingham (chairman of the board of managers). Here were four out of the seven managers of the Impeachment and four prominent members of the impeaching body, one of them a prospective witness for the prosecution, backing the leading counsel retained to defend the President in a demand upon that officer to send forthwith an armed vessel and take forcible possession of an island claimed by another power with which the United States were at peace, for the benefit of private parties—the clients of that counsel. As might have been foreseen by any one who knew Andrew Johnson, such covert attempts at coercion only rendered him the more immovable; and on Thursday, the nineteenth, Judge Black, who, it is but justice to state, knew nothing of the maneuvre, declined to appear further on the trial of the President. As he said: "When I found that Seward's policy was stronger than legal duty, I was done." The sudden retirement of this redoubtable champion, the circumstances of which were not accurately known at the time, was trumpeted abroad by the detractors of the President, as a proof not only of the incorrigible quarrelsomeness of his nature, but also of the inherent weakness of his defence;—since so great a lawyer refused to undertake it. On the other hand, the defection was denounced by the friends of the President as the outcome of a plot of the managers to rob him of the services of the most invincible of his defenders. The absence of Judge Black from the trial is in truth to be deplored. His participation would have lent a pungency to the proceedings adding greatly to their interest, and a speech of Jeremiah S. Black in defence of Andrew Johnson against the Republican party would have been an ever-living treat to students of the pathology of party politics, and taken rank with the classic invectives of ancient and modern times. His argument before the Electoral Commission in 1877 may give us a faint idea of what we have lost.*

When the "Court" reassembled on Monday, the twenty-third, Black's place was supplied by William S. Groesbeck, and the President's counsel for the first time appeared in full force. In response to the inquiry of the Chief Justice, Stanbery arose and stated that they were ready to read and file the answer. This pleading was lengthy, minute and elaborate; particularly the defence to the first article of Impeachment, which was read by Mr. Curtis and was a history of the attempted removal of Stanton given from the stand-point of the President's position, opinions and motives. The defences to the succeeding articles down to and including the ninth,

* For Alta Vela matter see Nelson's Speech on Trial, *ut infra,* and Debate in House, *Globe,* pp. 2337–2348.

were read by Mr. Stanbery. The defences to the tenth and eleventh—the Butler and Stevens articles—were read by Mr. Evarts. The reader, having become acquainted with the main outlines of the President's position during the progress of our narrative, can dispense with any elaborate analysis of the formal plea. It was called "a masterpiece of forensic argument," and its straightforward explanation of the President's motives and course of action produced a favourable impression throughout the country.

The managers announcing their expectation to be able to file their formal replication by one o'clock to-morrow, Mr. Evarts applied for an allowance of thirty days thereafter to prepare for trial; fortifying the application with a written statement of the necessity for that amount of time, signed by himself and his four associates. The prospect of still further delay threw the managers into another fit of exasperation. "Mr. President" and "Mr. Chief Justice" alternated in the discussion with redoubled pertinacity. Manager Bingham gave the Senate the first specimen of the kind of eloquence for which he was famous. Quoting the words of the answer claiming the exclusive power of removal, he "ventured to say

> before the enlightened bar of public opinion in America, by these words incorporated in his answer, the President is as guilty of malfeasance and misdemeanor in office as ever man was guilty of malfeasance or misdemeanor in office since nations began to be upon the earth. What! That he will suspend all executive officers of this Govern-

26

ment at his pleasure, not by force of the Tenure of office act, to which he himself refers, and which he says is void and of no effect, but by force of the Constitution of the United States; and that, too, he adds, while the Senate of the United States is in session! What does he mean by it? Let the Senate answer when they come to vote on this proposition for an extension of time. . . .

"If it be the judgment of the Senate that he has power thus to lay hands upon the Constitution of the country and rend it in tatters in the presence of its custodians, the sooner that judgment is pronounced the better."

Pending a motion to allow ten days, the court adjourned. The following day (Tuesday, the twenty-fourth), the managers being prompt to the moment with their replication, Sumner moved as an amendment that the trial proceed from day to day; and the court retired for consultation. After an absence of two hours, the court returned and announced the next Monday (the thirtieth) as the day fixed upon for the commencement of the trial; to which date the court adjourned.*

The veto of the bill cutting off the right of appeal to the Supreme Court in the McCardle case (a case which involved the question of the constitutionality of the reconstruction acts) at the moment it was about to be decided by that court, was sent to the Senate the next day; and the majority in both Houses spent the most of the week imbedding into the record of their proceedings an imperishable testimonial to their want of confidence in the validity of their own legislation and their distrust

* For Preliminaries see Trial, Vol. 1, pp. 11–86.

of another of the three coördinate departments of the government, by enacting this iniquity into a law.*

* The history of this piece of legislation is as follows: McCardle having been arrested in Mississippi in the fall of 1867, obtained a writ of *habeas corpus* from the U. S. Circuit Court directed to the military commander of the district, who made return that the prisoner was held under the reconstruction act, and he was thereupon remanded. From this order McCardle appealed to the Supreme Court of the United States under an act of Congress approved February 5, 1867. A motion was made to that court in December to dismiss the appeal for lack of jurisdiction under that act and after argument the court affirmed its jurisdiction and denied the motion. (*Ex parte* McCardle, 6 Wall. 318.) The appeal was argued upon the merits by eminent counsel on the second, third, fourth and ninth of March, 1868, and the court took the case under advisement. (*Ex parte* McCardle, 7 Wall. 507.) On the twelfth Schenck of Ohio asked and obtained the unanimous consent of the House to take up a bill of one section granting appeals in revenue cases, which had passed the Senate the day before; and James F. Wilson, of Iowa, as he subsequently avowed on the floor of the House for the purpose of cutting off the right of appeal in the McCardle case, moved as an amendment an additional section repealing so much of the act of February, 1867, as authorized appeals in certain cases to the Supreme Court of the United States or the exercise of jurisdiction by that tribunal on appeals "which *have been* or may hereafter be taken." The amendment was adopted *sub silentio* and the bill was sent back to the Senate. (*Globe*, pp. 1859, 1860, 1881, 2059.) Senator Buckalew, detecting the trick, strove in vain to obtain either explanation or postponement, and on the same day the amendment was concurred in. (*Id.*, 1847.) On the twenty-fifth the bill was vetoed on the ground that the second section, so surreptitiously smuggled on it, was pointed at a particular case pending in the Supreme Court; but, although in the discussion that followed in both Houses the trick was thoroughly exposed, the bill was passed over the objections of the President. The court instantly on its attention being called to the act stayed its decision until argument could be heard on the effect of the repealing section; and, in December following, dismissed the appeal on the ground that that section deprived the court of its jurisdiction. (*Ex parte* McCardle, 7 Wall. 507.) See Evarts' allusion to the mutilation, in his argument, on the Trial, Vol. 2, p. 272.

CHAPTER VI

THE TRIAL OF THE PRESIDENT

NEVER before in the history of the world did forensic orator face a higher tribunal, in a cause between parties more exalted and before a more splendid audience, than did Benjamin F. Butler, when, on the thirtieth day of March, 1868, he rose to make the opening argument in the trial of Andrew Johnson. Fifty-four senators, representing half as many states, presided over by the Chief Justice of the Supreme Court of the Union, constituted the tribunal; the House of Representatives numbering one hundred and ninety members chosen by thirty million constituents was the accuser; the accused was the elective ruler over a republic of continental dimensions and forty millions of people; and the audience seemed an epitome of the beauty of the women and the chivalry of the men of the country, set off by the pomp of ministers from foreign courts. Still, because of its spectacular grandeur, the theatricality of the whole performance was all the more instinctively felt. In those rare historic trials when mighty peoples called their rulers to account, the issue was so transcendent as to dwarf into insignificance the paraphernalia of the process. When Charles I stood before the High Court of Justice, when Louis XVI stood before the French Convention, what made the occasion capital was not the dignity of the court nor the confrontation of the majesty of the king with the majesty of the people, but the weightiness of the cause. In the impeachment of Warren Hastings, it was not that brilliant assemblage, painted as it has been upon its historic back-ground by the pen of Macaulay, that signalizes the trial as an event worthy of the notice of history, but the enormity of the charges against the defendant. Precisely the reverse were the circumstances of the present trial. Here was the High Court. Here were the exalted parties. Here the fit audience. But there was no case. The tribunal of Chief Justice and senators, the representatives accusing, the President defending, the amphitheatre of beauty and chivalry in which they were set;—without some supreme emergency summoning them upon the stage, what were they but "forms, modes, shows"—"actions that a man might play"? The ponderous two-handed engine of impeachment, designed to be kept in cryptic darkness until some crisis of the nation's life cried out for its interposition, was being dragged into open day to crush a too formidable political antagonist a few months before the appointed time when the people might get rid of him altogether. The *nodus* was lamentably unworthy the intervention of the god. And this sub-conscious impression did not arise from any widespread misgiving as to the result. On the contrary, the prevalent assumption that the judgment of the court was a foregone conclusion, if it did not originate, contributed materially to strengthen the feeling that the august performance was but a solemn farce. In full view of the audience sat the fifty-four senators, every senator in the attitude of an impartial judge; yet every onlooker was conscious that all but twelve belonged to the same political party as the one hundred and twenty-six members of the House who voted the accused guilty of high crimes and misdemeanours; that before the vote was cast twenty-eight of these judges had already passed condemnation upon the overt acts of the President which formed the basis of the charge; that a clear majority of the court were party partisans, as eager to contribute their vote to the removal of the 'Incubus' (as they did not scruple to style him) as the hottest fanatic ever was to add his fagot to the burning pile of the unbeliever.

Another conspicuous circumstance there was which enhanced the air of unreality hovering over the trial. This was the absence of the defendant. The presence of Charles I and Louis XVI, visibly contending for their lives before their judges, adds immeasurably to our impression of the dead-earnestness of the struggle and the tremendous interests at stake; and the iron countenance of Hastings softening only for a moment beneath the unrivalled eloquence of Burke, the imperturbability and skill with which he lent assistance to his counsel, and the lofty bearing with which he confronted his judges, are the features which convert the long trial into a living thing. But Andrew Johnson in person never entered the court room, never stood face to face with his accusers, never appeared before the court and the audience in the attitude of a culprit. The House was there; the Senate; the Chief Justice;—all visible in the flesh; but the defendant came not. His place was vacant. The Hamlet of the play was missing. And, from this point of view, so significant a gap in the programme suggested the idea that Andrew Johnson, having despatched his five counsel to play their part in the insubstantial pageant, had returned to the discharge of the multiplex duties of his exalted office, contemptuously indifferent to this make-believe game his enemies were playing with ancestral weapons much too big for their case.

To crown it all, the irony of events was seen playing round the hollow spectacle. Another trial had been set down for the coming month. Another President of another and a vanished republic was under prosecution. And, in his case, there was no need of pageantry to swell the proportions of the charge. Treason of no constructive character was the high crime; and the presence of the distinguished defendant was certain to be forthcoming. But, as it was shrewdly said, Jefferson Davis could hardly be tried for "insisting that the Southern States were out of the Union while Andrew Johnson was being tried for insisting they were in." The real trial was made to give place, therefore, to the sham trial; Chief Justice Chase protesting with much reasonableness that he could not act in both at the same time.

So that, all things considered, while manager Butler might be felicitated on the glorious theatre in which he was to play his part, the part assigned him—to raise a cause radically inadequate to the high plane of the imperial process—rendered him, rather, an object of commiseration. Moreover, it was singularly unfortunate that his own presence and participation served but to deepen the prevalent impression. Known as a keen and adroit lawyer, a ready and witty debater, a cunning and most versatile politician, his reputation for sincerity was not high; and his recent career as a volunteer warrior, whether deservedly or not, carried a histrionic air about it which sometimes suggested the comic. That General Butler was to open the cause of all the people of the United States against Andrew Johnson, the President thereof, arraigned for high crimes against the Union, was enough of itself to shake the gravity of the whole procedure. Nevertheless, Butler was, in truth, one of the sincerest among the leaders of the Impeachment. He may be said to have been the representative of its coarsest phase. But he knew exactly what he wanted and was not ashamed to own it. He wanted Andrew Johnson turned out of office as speedily as possible; and the validity of the pretext concerned him very little. Forms, it was unfortunately true, must be observed in order to capture the two-thirds vote of the Senate. But the two-thirds vote of the Senate once made sure of, forms might shift for themselves. Andrew Johnson once out, the means by which he was got out would never return to plague the inventors.

His opening argument illustrated the foregoing view of the trial and was characteristic of the man. It was carefully prepared and read from manuscript. There was but little straining after oratorical effect. It was a lawyer's plea tainted with a dash of the demagogue. No man knew better than Benjamin F. Butler that the President, in the two formal acts laid against him, had committed no offence deserving to be classed with treason and bribery. It was imperative, therefore, to concoct a definition of impeachable offences comprehensive enough to embrace any act, whether violative of common law or statute or not, and no matter how empty of criminality, which a majority of the House of Representatives for the time being might see fit to brand a "high crime against the nation." With the help of William Lawrence of the House, who compiled for him a brief of all the precedents and authorities on the subject both in England and in this country, he was able to evolve a definition which it was judged would pass muster.

> "We define, therefore, an impeachable crime or misdemeanor to be one in its nature or consequences subversive of some fundamental or essential principle of government, or highly prejudicial to the public interest, and this may consist of a violation of the Constitution, of law, of an official oath, or of duty, by an act committed or omitted, or, without violating a positive law, by the abuse of discretionary powers from improper motives, or for any improper purpose."

After defining every offence as impeachable the House chose to impeach, the manager proceeds to divest the proceeding before the Senate of every restraint incident to a trial by reducing it to a simple inquest of office, and the tribunal before him of every attribute of a court by absolving it from every rule of law, precedent or evidence. "As a constitutional tribunal, solely," he told the listening Senate, "you are bound by no law, either statute or common, which may limit your constitutional prerogative. . . . You are a law unto yourselves, bound only by the natural principles of equity and justice, and that *salus populi suprema lex.*'' The ''determining quality,'' principally dwelt upon by Butler, that distinguished the tribunal he was addressing from a court, was the immunity of its members from challenge for bias; but, the larger number of English precedents he cited being the ordinary trials of peers before the tribunal established by law for that purpose—unmistakably a court in every sense of that term and in fact so designated by the manager himself—showed on the contrary that immunity from challenge was no essential attribute of a court of judicature.

With so elastic a definition of the character of the offence to be proved; with so convenient a mode of procedure to prove it; with so absolute a tribunal to pronounce it proved:—the manager might well advance with confidence to the exposition of the articles. There being little to be said upon the first eight affirmatively, the first part of the manager's argument was devoted to demolishing the defences interposed to them. To Butler as to Bingham, the claim set up in the answer that the Constitution vested exclusively in the President the power of removal from office seemed a greater outrage than any offence charged in the articles. Said the counsel, ''the momentous question, here and now, is raised whether *the Presidential office itself* (*if it bear the prerogatives and power claimed for it*) *ought, in fact, to exist as a part of the constitutional government of a free people.*'' ''Whoever, therefore, votes 'not guilty' on these articles votes to enchain our free institutions, and to prostrate them at the feet of any man who, being President, may choose to control them.''

Upon that part of the President's defence which seems to us the most conclusive, to wit: that Stanton was not within the act, Butler's direct attack is but a repetition of the play upon the word ''term'' practiced, as we have seen, in the House. ''Whose presidential term was he (Stanton) holding under when the bullet of Booth became the proximate cause of this trial?''—is his allusive way of putting the case. ''Whose presidential term is the respondent now serving out? His own or Mr. Lincoln's? If his own, he is entitled to four years up to the anniversary of the murder, because each presidential term is four years by the Constitution.'' Again he argues: ''If Mr. Stanton's commission was vacated in any way by the 'tenure-of-office act,' then it must have ceased one month after the fourth of March, 1865''—or, if the act ''had no retroactive effect, then his commission must have ceased, if it had the effect to vacate his commission at all, on the passage of the act, to wit, March 2d, 1867''; and in that case the President has been guilty of a high misdemeanour in ''employing'' him ''contrary to the act.'' His passing eulogium on Stanton for holding fast to the place ''against the wishes of his chief'' was eminently Butlerian. ''The respondent *did not* call Mr. Stanton into his council. The blow of the assassin *did* call the respondent to preside over a cabinet of which Mr. Stanton was then an honored member . . .; and if the respondent deserted the principles under which he was elected, betrayed his trust, and sought to return rebels . . . again to power, are not those reasons why Mr. Stanton"—should, in a word, 'stick'? "*To desert it now* would be to imitate the treachery of his accidental Chief." The less able to meet the question of statutory construction in front, the more strongly did the manager insist that the President was estopped by his submission of the reasons for the suspension to the Senate. And, at this point, "the shameless avowal" (as he calls it) in the answer, that the President never meant to be bound by the decision of the Senate if adverse to his own views—a mental reservation studiously concealed from the Senate—aroused Butler's deepest indignation. The want of "open and frank dealing," of "a manly straightforward bearing," the "keeping back his claims of power," "concealing his motives" are declared to be characteristic of the culprit as self-revealed in his answer; while, at the next moment, they are denounced as "the subterfuge and evasion and after-thought which a criminal brought to bay makes to escape the consequences of his act." "Senators! He asked you for time in which to make his answer. You gave him ten days, and this is the answer he makes. If he could do this in ten days, what should we have had if you had given him forty?"

Passing to the letter of authority to Thomas, Butler contended that the act of February, 1795, under which the President claimed to have acted, did not apply to the case of a "vacancy caused by removal," because of the presence of the clause, "whereby" the officer "cannot perform the duties of his office"; although that clause was a stereotyped form of words used in all similar statutes. He argued, also, that the act of 1863 repealed so much of the act of 1795 as permitted the President to select any person to perform the *ad interim* duties of the office, and restricted his choice to the head of another executive department:—although the act of 1863 on its face provides for vacancies in cases of death, resignation, absence, or sickness, only; and not for vacancies caused by removal or expiration of term. The way he dealt with the claim that a President, believing a law to be unconstitutional, has a right to violate it to bring the matter before the Supreme Court for adjudication, is much more effective. He takes the ground that the right of the President to judge of the unconstitutionality of an act of Congress is exhausted when he vetoes the bill. After its passage over his veto, "he and all other officers must execute the law, whether in fact constitutional or not." To do otherwise, "would in effect be for him to execute his veto and leave the law unexecuted." He may do it "at his peril; but that peril" is impeachment. In answer to the question, will you condemn the President for a crime because in good faith he removed Mr. Stanton for the purpose of testing the validity of the law—even though he may not have had the right to do so? Butler promises to show that the President never took a step to submit the question to the courts; on the contrary, that he complied with the law in every particular, causing the forms of commissions of officers to be changed so as to conform to the act; in the very case of Stanton he acted under the law and never instituted proceedings in the nature of a *quo warranto,* as he alone could do, to try Stanton's title. Had he informed the Senate on the twenty-first of February that he had removed the Secretary of War for so innocent a purpose, then the manager acknowledged "the representatives of the people might never have deemed it necessary to impeach the President."

The last three articles, according to Butler, raise the inquiry "whether Andrew Johnson had so conducted himself that he ought longer to hold any constitutional office whatever,"—a question, he declares, that "sinks into merited insignificance compared with the grandeur" of the question raised by the first eight, that concerns the very existence of the presidential office itself. Nevertheless, it is in the exposition of one of these three comparatively "insignificant" articles, that the manager redeems his opening argument from the dullness associated with reading of a dry legal dissertation. The ninth article founded on the Emory interview, even Butler's ingenuity could not make much of; he himself admitting that "if the transaction set forth . . . stood alone . . . doubts might arise as to the sufficiency of the proof." And article eleven he thought it unnecessary to discuss, because, if the other articles fail "so large a part of the intent and purpose with which the respondent is charged in this article would fail of proof" also, while, if the other articles are sustained, "we shall take judgment upon this by confession." But the tenth article was his own—originated by him to give flesh and blood to the dry bones of the other charges. Upon this one he feels himself at liberty to expatiate freely. The sleepy senators and weary auditors wake up when he begins to read parts of the St. Louis speech. In a carefully prepared address he rings the changes with the greatest gusto on the offences against good taste, dignity and propriety, committed by Andrew Johnson in an *ex tempore* speech, delivered at night, in the open air, to an excited and disorderly crowd, some persons in which were present designedly to provoke the President's well-known pugnacity. The manager achieved a cheap and temporary triumph. It is probable this was the only part of his task he thoroughly enjoyed. On behalf of the American people, he apologized to the sneering monarchists of the old world for having such a President by telling them "this man" "by murder most foul succeeded to the Presidency, and is the elect of an assassin to that high office, and not of the people"; "we are about to remove him from the office he has disgraced by the sure, safe and constitutional means of impeachment"—"while your king, Oh, Monarchist! if he becomes a buffoon, or a jester, or a tyrant, can only be displaced through revolution, blood-shed, and civil war." But he said nothing of the fact that these speeches were delivered nearly two years ago; that the thirty-ninth Congress, whose sovereign dignity they were charged to have assailed, passed out of existence without embodying its resentment in any act; that a committee of the House of the present Congress failed to find in them ground of impeachment, and that the House itself, which, at the last moment under the whip and spur of Butler himself, consented to add his article, a month or two before, with the speeches before it, virtually acquitted the President on the same accusation.

His peroration is open to the same criticism. He closes his three hours' speech by replying to a question he might well imagine "to have arisen in the mind of some senator":—"Why are these acts of the President only presented by the House when history informs us that others equally as dangerous to the liberties of the people, if not more so, and others of equal usurpation of power, if not greater, are passed by in silence?" The answer, lying on the surface of things, that the House of Representatives, in December last, despite his own efforts, decided that these other acts of which "history informs us," were not of a character to call for the exercise of the power of impeachment:—he does not make. The answer that he does make is that the acts charged are but "the culmination of a series of wrongs, malfeasance and usurpations" which, although the House once condoned them, the House nevertheless means upon the present trial to spread before the Senate to characterize the "scope and design" of the acts charged. "For the evidence," he says, "we rely upon common fame and current history as sufficient proof." And, in two long paragraphs, he recapitulates the real charges against Andrew Johnson, on which the Republican party was anxious to put him out of the way. "I speak, therefore, not the language of exaggeration," was Butler's closing sentence, "but the words of truth and soberness, that the future political welfare and liberties of all men hang trembling on the decision of the hour."

It fell to manager Wilson to introduce the evidence on the part of the House, which he proceeded to do in the shape of documentary proofs; and the first day of the trial terminated in the middle of the reading of the President's message submitting his reasons for Stanton's suspension to the Senate.

The next day the oral testimony began. Witnesses were called to prove the service on the President, on Thomas and on Stanton, of the Senate's resolutions of non-concurrence and of disapproval, and to show the change in the forms of commissions after the Tenure-of-office bill became a law; and, then, representatives Van Horn and Moorhead repeated from the notes they were so careful to make what took place on the twenty-second of February, prior to their departure to the House, between Stanton and Thomas at the War Office. Burleigh, the Dakota delegate, was called to testify to the belligerent sparks he managed to strike out of Thomas. Stanbery objected. The Chief Justice thought the testimony competent, whereupon, his right to decide questions of evidence in the first instance being challenged by Drake, the court, after hearing long arguments by Butler and Bingham adverse to the right, resolved to retire by the casting vote of the Chief Justice, and after three hours' absence returned with a decision favourable to the right. This consumed the day.

Wednesday was ushered in by a motion of Sumner to declare the casting vote given by the Chief Justice the day before "without authority under the Constitution." A vote was taken without discussion and the roll-call was followed with intense interest. Twenty-one voted in the affirmative and twenty-seven in the negative. The question of the admissibility of Burleigh's testimony was then argued at length by counsel on both sides. The Chief Justice submitted the question to the Senate and the testimony was admitted by a strict party vote. This decision may pass; but the next seems indefensible. Thomas's talk to his clerks, just after he was restored to the Adjutant-General's office, concerning the relaxation of the rules—words uttered some days before he was notified of his new appointment—it was offered to prove; and, after the incompetency of the testimony on this ground was clearly pointed out by the President's counsel, and the Chief Justice pronounced it inadmissible, the Senate let it in by a vote of 28 to 22. Wilkeson then testified to Thomas's threats, and Karsner convulsed the audience with laughter by his version of the scene in the East Room of the White House, when he told Thomas that "the eyes of Delaware were upon him."*

On the fourth day, after representative Ferry read his memorandum of the encounter in the War Office, General Emory was sworn; and his testimony, it was universally felt, gave a death-blow to the ninth article, casting the first cloud over the superabounding confidence of the impeachers. The letter of General Grant requesting the President to put into writing the verbal order to disregard the orders of Stanton unless known to emanate from the President himself, and the President's instructions to that effect, were then read; and were followed by the reading of the President's final

* See *supra*, Chap. V, p. 394.

letter of the Johnson-Grant correspondence. The counsel for the respondent insisted that the accompanying corroboratory letters of the Cabinet ministers should also be read as part of the same communication; but the court decided adversely by a vote of 29 to 20. Col. Wallace's testimony as to his casual conversation with the President on the night of the twenty-second in reference to the movement of troops about Washington was even more colourless than that of Emory; its utter inadequacy provoking an outburst of petulance from Butler. The telegrams interchanged between Parsons —the first provisional governor of Alabama—and the President on the subject of the ratification of the fourteenth amendment by the legislature then in session, the President in strong language dissuading any such action, were then admitted after argument.

Friday and Saturday—the fifth and sixth days—were devoted almost exclusively to proving the President's speeches;—at the Executive Mansion in August, and at Cleveland and St. Louis in September, 1866. There was a tedious dispute over the accuracy of the reports, and several versions were introduced. The Chief Justice decided one inadmissible on the ground that the reporter used the notes of another person beside his own; but the Senate overruled him. The republication of the speeches did no injury to the President. On the contrary, it may be said that the manner in which they were again brought before the public caused a revulsion of sentiment. It was no longer Andrew Johnson exhibiting himself voluntarily in undignified positions; it was the managers with premeditated design searching out again these verbal indiscretions and, after the President's long and stately silence, flaunting them before the eyes of the country. But what more than anything else neutralized the effect of their reproduction was the absence of even the slightest whisper, either of accusation or of proof, of a scandalous charge connected with them. During that unfortunate tour, it was widely reported, that the whole party, including the President, was on a wild spree, and that the incoherencies of speech and the breaches of good taste disfiguring the addresses were the consequences of over-indulgence in drink. Before the investigating committee on the first impeachment, it was proved that Johnson was not under the influence of liquor during this tour; but few obtained access to the testimony and it was little known. Now, however, the absence of any such allegation from Butler's article and from his opening speech where it was sure to appear if it had the least foundation, and the absence of any attempt to prove it on the trial—although the managers had examined the witnesses concerning every incident of the tour—at once opened the eyes of the country to the falsity of these reports and the wrong they inflicted. Many persons had been chary about alluding to the disagreeable subject because General Grant was more or less involved in it; but from the time of the Impeachment trial—there was no more serious talk among well-informed people about the intemperate habits of Andrew Johnson.

On Saturday afternoon, after the introduction of a schedule of removals of heads of departments made while the Senate was in session from the foundation of the government, containing but one name—Timothy Pickering removed May 13, 1800; and a schedule of appointments of heads of departments during the session of the Senate, containing numerous names; and the correspondence between President Adams and his recalcitrant Secretary (which seems now to make for the defence); the managers announced the close of their case. Mr. Curtis, thereupon, applied for an adjournment until the next Thursday (April 9) so as to give three working days to the counsel for arranging and preparing the testimony for the defence; and, after considerable opposition in which Sumner was the most aggressive, the request was granted.

The popular impression produced by the first week of the trial was that the presentation of the proofs had added nothing to the strength of the case against the President. The alleged conspiracy between the President and his newly-appointed Secretary *ad interim*, the threats of General Thomas, the assault upon the War Office with force and arms, the secret preparations of the President to precipitate an armed conflict in and around Washington, looked much more formidable spread out in the phraseology of an indictment than after the words of living witnesses demonstrated the openness and publicity of every act of the President, the harmlessness of the old Adjutant-General, the interchange of peaceful courtesies between the two contenders for the War Office, the quiet talk of the President with the commander of the city, and the isolation and powerlessness of the Executive in the face of a hostile

General of the Army and triumphant majorities in both Houses of Congress. It was felt that the Conspiracy articles—and the Emory article—in short, every article where the supporting documents needed to be supplemented by oral testimony—were much damaged.

There was a reflow of the throng into the Senate chamber on the day of the opening for the defence. The tall form of William T. Sherman, clad in the gorgeous uniform of the Lieutenant-General, was noticed in the audience, and, close by, the venerable Thomas Ewing, whose nomination as Secretary of War was still lying on the table of the Senate soon to be withdrawn for that of General Schofield. The case for the prosecution was reopened to allow the examination of two witnesses whose testimony was of no importance; and then the court prepared to listen to the counsel for the President.

The counsel who arose to make the opening argument for the defence presented a striking contrast to the counsel who had discharged the corresponding duty for the prosecution. Both citizens of the same state, both lawyers, and both Benjamins—they could hardly have been more different men. Butler—despite his bald head, the younger by just nine years—always carried a devil-may-care air about him. Curtis was the very personification of judicial dignity. Butler oftentimes dropped into loose and easy-going attitudes, gestures and modes of statement. Curtis with undeviating regularity was precision itself. In their common profession the same divergence was apparent. Butler was at home in the cut-and-thrust combats before juries.

Curtis sought the retirement of the counsel's office, the stately contests of the appellate courts and the repose of the bench. Butler looked the alert, wily, active politician all over, wherever he was. Curtis looked like a statesman of the Websterian school, unbendable to the tricks of party warfare. Butler was the free lance, riding, unincumbered, hither and thither, heedless of corselet and helm. Curtis was the man-at-arms, cumbrous with defensive weapons, stately in march, slow in movement, deadly with the battle-axe, yet, once overthrown, liable to be suffocated by the ponderosity of his armour. It was curious to note that Butler, though he read his address from manuscript, conveyed an impression of extemporaneous speech, while Curtis, though he spoke like an advocate at the bar, turned out his sentences as though they were written.

The President displayed excellent judgment in his choice of counsel; but in no instance so much as in the choice of Curtis. As one of the two dissenting judges in the Dred Scott case, Curtis achieved a fame which the civil war had almost canonized. His opinion in that case was everywhere quoted as one of the classic documents of the struggle with slavery. Just after this decision he voluntarily retired from that illustrious bench where Marshall and Story and Taney were content to spend their lives, and resumed the practice of his profession; and from that retirement he emerged for the first time at the summons of Andrew Johnson. The contrast between the two arguments was as great as that between the two men. Butler's was a laboured effort to hoist the case made for him up to the level of the process; except in the matter of his own article where he threw off his harness and roamed in comparative freedom. Curtis's was a steady, gradual, unrelenting pulverization of the case against his client; except in the matter of the Butler article which he demolished with one or two quick strokes. With the art of a skilful advocate, he put the one invulnerable position of the defence immediately in the front. Stanton was not within the act. By showing this to be the case he took the life out of every article but one. And he showed it, first, by the words of the law. The proviso reads that "the Secretaries" (including the Secretary of War) "shall hold their offices respectively for and during the term of the President by whom they may have been appointed and one month thereafter." Stanton was appointed during the first term of President Lincoln. Therefore, the words "during the term of the President" do not apply to Stanton's case, unless the expounder of the law had the right to add, "and any other term or terms for which he may hereafter be elected"—which, of course, nothing short of legislative power can do. Again: was Stanton holding during the term of the President by whom he was appointed, when he was removed? The counsel used but few words to overthrow the position of the managers that Johnson had no term, but was merely serving out Lincoln's term—by knocking away the sole support they put up for it: viz., that a presidential term must be four years and no less. "The limit of four years is not an absolute limit. Death is a limit. A 'conditional limitation,' as the lawyers call it, is imposed on his tenure of office.''

> "When the President dies, his term of four years for which he was elected, and during which he was to hold, provided he should so long live, terminates and the office devolves on the Vice President. For what period of time? For the remainder of the term for which the Vice President was elected."
>
> "The term assigned to Mr. Lincoln by the Constitution was conditionally assigned to him. It was to last four years if not sooner ended: but if sooner ended by death, then the office devolved on the Vice President, and the term of the Vice President to hold the office began."

Second: he showed it by pointing out the reason why the exception of Cabinet officers was inserted in the act. They were made by the Constitution the advisers of the President, not only respecting the affairs of their respective departments, but, also, according to the correct grammatical construction of the provision and its practical interpretation from the beginning, respecting the duties of the entire executive department. They were the assistants of the President—to speak and act for him, and he was responsible for them. Therefore it was, that the legislature refused to fasten these confidential servants upon the President who had not made them his choice. Third: he showed it by the exposition of the act at the time of its passage: bringing Schenck, in the House, and Sherman, in the Senate, to bear witness (Sherman explicitly) that the proviso was not intended to apply to the case of Stanton. Recurring to article first the counsel points out that it does not allege a removal but only an attempt to remove, an offence which is not prohibited by the penal section of the act; moreover, the offence must not only be a removal, but a "removal contrary to the provisions of the act," and the counsel clenches this branch of his argument by the simple remark that, if Stanton was not within the act, his removal, if effected, could not have been contrary thereto.

But, pursues the counsel, the President is charged not merely with a violation of the act but with an intentional violation. Now, senators may have different views of the construction of this act; but all must admit there is a fair question of construction "whether it was applicable to Mr. Stanton's case; a very honest and solid question which any man could entertain." The President was bound to construe the law when the case came before him. He did construe it; and he came to the conclusion, not merely by an examination of the law itself, but by resorting to the advice which the Constitution enabled him to call for to assist him in coming to a correct conclusion. "Having done so, are the Senate prepared to say that the conclusion must have been a wilful misconstruction? . . . How is it possible for this body to convict the President of the United States of a high misdemeanor for construing a law as those who made it construed it at the time when it was made?"

Coming to the charge that, independent of the Tenure-of-office act, the order of removal was a violation of the Constitution because issued while the Senate was in session, Mr. Curtis soon clears away the misapprehension which seems to have prevailed on this point. If Stanton held under the act of 1789 and under the terms of his commission, he was removable at the pleasure of the President. There is no restriction as to the time—whether in recess or in session. That distinction has reference only to the filling of vacancies, not to the making of them. The first Congress came to the conclusion that the power of removal was vested in the President independently of the Senate. That decision may be proper to be reversed and may have been reversed by the thirty-ninth Congress; but—as long as it remains—the fact that the Senate is in session has no effect on the exercise of the power. If the Senate is not in session and the President makes a removal, a vacancy is created which is filled by a commission until the end of the next session of the Senate. If the Senate is in session and the President makes a removal, a vacancy is created which is filled by a nomination to the Senate. With the act of removal the Senate never has anything to do.

Here the counsel might have stopped, for the bottom was out of the main part of the case. But, as he said, "there is a broader view of the matter" which, although "not essential to the vindication of the President from this charge," it is due to him, should he be brought before the court. And, then, the counsel unfolds his position on the right of the President negatively to decline to execute or affirmatively to violate an act of Congress which he believes to contravene the Constitution, for the express purpose of testing the case before the judiciary. If it be the duty of every citizen to obey every law passed through all the forms of legislation without question;—then "there never could be a judicial decision that a law is unconstitutional, inasmuch as it is only by disregarding a law that any question can be raised judicially under it." It is universally recognized that it may be a patriotic duty of a citizen to raise the question, as for example in the case of John Hampden. In the case of a trustee for a third person, it might be a sacred duty to raise it. Why not then in the case of the Executive who is the trustee for the people? The counsel, however, is very careful to restrict this right within the narrowest limits. As a general proposition the President is bound to execute laws without reference to his own judgment on their constitutional validity. "He is not to erect himself into a judicial court." That would be indeed to execute his veto and prevent a judicial decision. As long as a law requires nothing of him but "ministerial action," or affects the interests of third persons alone—it is his duty to execute it. But when "a particular law has cut off a power confided to him by the people, through the Constitution, and he alone can raise the question," and "after due deliberation, with the advice of those who are his proper advisers, he settles down firmly upon the opinion that such is the character of the law"—it cannot be "a violation of his duty when he takes the needful steps to raise that question and have it peacefully decided." It is admitted that there are extreme cases when he may undoubtedly invoke the aid of the courts; but where is the line to be drawn? When the President came to consider the question whether the

Tenure-of-office act was unconstitutional, he found that, if Stanton was within it, it took away from him a power which the first Congress decided the Constitution vested in the President beyond the reach of Congress. And this contemporaneous exposition of the fundamental law, the counsel pointed out, met every one of the tests laid down by the learned commentators: "In the first place the precise question was under discussion; secondly, there was a deep sense of its importance; next, the determination was thereby to fix a system for the future; and in the last place the men who participated in the work must be admitted to have been exceedingly well qualified for their work." The President, also, found that "from 1789 down to 1867 every President and every Congress participated in and acted under the construction given in 1789"; and not only so, but it was sufficiently discussed among the people to bring the question to their consideration, yet so far from expressing any disapprobation, all parties favoured and acted under this system. In the debate of 1789 there were three distinct theories held. One, that the Constitution lodged the power of removal with the President alone; another, that the Constitution lodged the power with the President acting with the Senate; a third, that the Constitution lodged it nowhere but left it to the legislative power to regulate. The first two received by far the greatest attention; the third had but few advocates and only recently has come into vogue. Yet the Tenure-of-office act is founded upon this last theory; and it is not at all strange that the President could see nothing in it. The President had, also, to consider the consequences if Mr. Stanton were within the law. As the counsel ingeniously argued, the Constitution undoubtedly has given the President alone the power of choice. "In the first place, he alone can nominate. When the Senate has advised and consented to the nomination, he is not bound to commission the officer. He has a second opportunity for consideration." As Chief Justice Marshall, in *Marbury vs. Madison,* holds, there go to complete an appointment three operations: 1. The nomination, the sole act of the President and completely voluntary. 2. The appointment—also the act of the President and also voluntary—though it can only be performed by and with the advice and consent of the Senate. 3. The commission. It is not until the signature of the President is placed to the commission that his choice is finally made. Then "the time for deliberation is passed. He has decided. The officer is appointed."

If this be an accurate view of the law, then, if Stanton is within the Tenure-of-office act, his is a "legislative appointment," his is "a legislative commission." "The President has had no voice in the matter." Nor the Senate as the adviser of the President. If then the President, in view of these weighty considerations coming to the conclusion that the Tenure act of Congress, in attempting to deprive him of this particular power, in this unusually delicate case, contravened the Constitution he was specially sworn "to preserve, protect and defend";—is he to be impeached for holding such opinion, to be impeached "for acting upon it to the extent of obtaining a judicial decision whether the executive department was right in its opinion or the legislative department was right in its opinion?" And, here, the counsel fastens upon the acknowledgement of Butler that if the President, instead of the message announcing the removal to the Senate (which Butler stigmatized as "defiant"), had sent a message, such as he outlined, announcing the removal only for the purpose of testing the law, the House might never have impeached. "Strangely enough," exclaims the counsel, "the honorable manager says: 'No, he is not to be impeached for that.' So that it seems after all that it is not the removal of Stanton but the manner in which the President communicated the fact of that removal to the Senate after it was made."

The counsel makes short work of the doctrine of estoppel, sought to be applied in a trial for crime to a "President asserting a great public right confided to his office by the people"—the people who "if anybody is estopped, would be estopped themselves." First. There was nothing inconsistent in the President's acting, as far as possible without surrendering his right, on the line of a law he considered did not affect Stanton, or, if it did, was unconstitutional; and, second, he expressly stated the two questions involved under the law and the determination of himself and his Cabinet (including Stanton) thereon, in his message to the Senate. Besides, the counsel adds as he closes the first day of his masterly argument:

"The law may be a constitutional law; it may not only be a law under which the President has acted in this instance, but under which he is bound to act, and willing to act, if you please, in every instance; still, if Stanton is not within the law, the case remains as it was originally presented, and that case is, that not being within the law, the first article is entirely without foundation.''

In truth, this was the pivot of the entire impeachment. Stanton was out of the act—the eleven articles fell to pieces.

The following day the counsel attacked the second article, showing, first, that, whether Stanton was removable at the pleasure of the President or not, the issue of the letter of authority to Thomas was not a violation of the Tenure-of-office act which prohibited only appointments or employments to offices which, by reason of nominations not being sent to the Senate or because of rejections of nominations actually sent in, were to remain in abeyance. The claim that, even if Stanton was not within the act, the letter of authority to Thomas was without warrant of any law whatever, he answered by quoting the act of 1795 which met the case precisely, and by the argument that the act of 1863, not being repugnant and dealing partly with a different subject-matter, did not repeal the older statute. ''But whether it did or not,'' asked the counsel, ''is it not a fair question? Is it a crime to be on one side of that question and not on the other? Is it a high misdemeanor to believe that a certain view taken of the repeal of this earlier law by the later one is a sound view?'' So stringent a rule even the honourable managers do not contend for; ''their article alleges as matter of fact a wilful intention on the part of the President to issue this letter to General Thomas without authority of law;

not on mistaken judgment, not on an opinion which after due consideration lawyers might differ about; but by wilful intention to act without authority—and that, from the nature of the case, cannot be made out." Nor was this letter a violation of the Constitution because issued when the Senate was in session. The Constitution provides "two modes of filling offices. The one is by temporary commissions during the recess of the Senate; the other is by appointment by and with the advice and consent of the Senate. But cases occur to which neither of these modes would be applicable, cases of absence, sickness, resignation or removal when there is not time to make a regular appointment or issue a commission." And Congress, by the three acts of 1792, 1795 and 1863, endeavoured to supply the deficiency. They provided for the designation of a person to discharge the duties of the vacant office temporarily—*ad interim*—until the regular appointment be made. "It is entirely evident that these temporary vacancies are just as liable to occur during the session of the Senate as during the recess." And this has been the practical construction ever since 1792, as counsel showed by precedents—among others the designation of Postmaster-General Holt to discharge the duties of the War Department *ad interim* on the hasty resignation of Floyd, the Senate being in session: in which case, the Senate calling for the authority of the President, the President sent in a message with a long list of similar designations. The counsel, in this connection, takes up the eighth article, which he states differs from the second only in the particular that it charges an attempt to control the moneys in the Treasury appropriated for military service—on which particular there had been no proof.

The third article, he said, is founded on the erroneous supposition that the authorization of Thomas to perform the duties of the War Department was an appointment. It was in no sense an appointment. Even a commission issued in recess is not an appointment. The office is not filled. The President never had any idea of appointing Thomas Secretary of War. And, therefore, he did not apply to the Senate for its advice and consent in the case of Thomas as he did, in fact, in the case of Ewing. The averment that there was no vacancy at the time is simply begging the question whether Stanton was within the act or not. If he was not, there was a vacancy caused by the removal made at the same time with the issue of the letter of authority. "It is impossible for the honorable managers to construct a case of an intention on the part of the President to violate the Constitution out of anything he did in reference to the appointment of General Thomas, provided the order to Mr. Stanton was a lawful order and Mr. Stanton was bound to obey it."

It is unnecessary to follow the counsel in his remarks on the so-called Conspiracy articles. Incidentally, he points out that the Conspiracy act of 1861 on which two of them (the fourth and sixth) are founded has no application to the District of Columbia; and the other two (fifth and seventh) are founded on no law at all. The ninth article the counsel says is not only unproved but disproved by the testimony.

The Butler article is then taken up and most cruelly handled. The counsel, in asking what are impeachable offences under our Constitution, refuses to follow the manager back "to the times of the Plantagenets, the Tudors and the Stuarts" in search of precedents. He confines himself to the Constitution itself. "Treason, bribery and other high crimes and misdemeanors," according to Curtis, mean only "high criminal offences against the United States made so by some law of the United States." He contends that by the Constitution this tribunal is a court, this is a trial of a crime; there must be a judgment of conviction or acquittal; and there may be a punishment inflicted. How then are you "bound by no law"? If that be so what becomes of the prohibitions against bills of attainder and *ex post facto* laws? If you are bound by no law, then, by this proceeding, although "as Congress you cannot create a law to punish these acts if no law existed at the time they were done," yet, "while the case is on trial, you may individually each one of you create a law by himself to govern the case." The oath which the Constitution provides shall be taken by senators on the trial of an impeachment does not mean that they will observe the Constitution and the laws, but that they shall follow their own individual wills! In bills of attainder "the Parliament make the law for the facts they find. Each legislator is a 'law unto himself.' . . . According to the doctrine now advanced bills of attainder are not prohibited by the Constitution; they are only slightly modified. It is only necessary for the House by a majority to vote an impeachment and . . . two-thirds of this body vote in favor of conviction, and there is an attainder: and it is done by the same process and depends on identically the same principles as a bill of attainder in the English Parliament. The individual wills of the legislators, instead of the conscientious discharge of the duty of the judges, settle the result."

The tenth article, the counsel pressed on, "depends upon no law." "So far as regards the preceding articles, the gist of the charge is that the President broke a law. You must find that the law existed, you must construe and apply it to the case; you must find his criminal intent wilfully to break the law, before the article can be supported." But, in regard to the tenth, you need not be troubled with any law. "The complaint is that the President made speeches against the Congress." Really, not against the Congress proper, because "he undoubtedly did not mean the entire constitutional body; he meant the dominant majority in Congress. Everybody so understood it, everybody must so understand it. . . . Well, who are the grand jury in this case? One of the parties spoken against. And who are the triers? The other party spoken against. One would think there was some incongruity in this; some reason for giving pause before taking any very great stride in that direction."

"The House of Representatives has erected itself into a school of manners, selecting from its ranks those gentlemen whom it deems most proper by precept and example to teach decorum of speech; and they desire the judgment of this body whether the President has not been guilty of indecorum, whether he has spoken properly, to use the phrase of the honorable manager.''

The question whether the speeches are true or false is to be no test, it seems. For, the manager who opened the case proclaims that it is not within the power of any man to slander the Congress of the United States. ''That is a pretty lofty claim.'' The Plantagenet Parliaments did not venture to make it because, under their statutes, their ''prelates, dukes, earls and barons'' were protected only ''from horrible and false lies''; and, under our own odious sedition act making penal written libels against Congress, it was expressly provided that the truth could be given in evidence in defence. ''The prohibition of the Constitution against any legislation by Congress in restraint of the freedom of speech,'' as the counsel showed by reading some weighty words from Madison, ''is necessarily an absolute prohibition; and therefore this is a case not only where there is no law made prior to the act to punish the act, but a case where Congress is expressly prohibited from making any law to operate even on subsequent acts.'' ''What is the law to be? . . . that you may require the speaker to speak properly. Who are to be the judges whether he speaks properly? The Senate?'' or in effect each individual senator? And ''that is supposed to be the freedom of speech secured by this absolute prohibition of the Constitution!''

With a brief contemptuous reference to the eleventh article as a mere farrago of the others:—''Here are the speeches, we will have something about them,'' here is "the old matter of the removal of Stanton," we will say something on that and so on—the counsel ended with a sentence which, for its precise characterization of the occasion, deserves quotation alongside the rhetorical exaggeration of the corresponding sentence of Butler:

> "This" trial "is and will be the most conspicuous instance which has ever been or can ever be expected to be found of American justice or American injustice, of that justice which Mr. Burke says is the standing policy of all civilized states, or of that injustice which is sure to be discovered and which makes even the wise man mad, and which, in the fixed and immutable order of God's providence, is certain to return to plague its inventors."

After a recess of a few minutes, General Thomas was sworn and detailed the particulars of his appointment *ad interim,* of his interview with Stanton, and of his interviews with the President. When the witness came to describe the scene between Stanton and himself, which occurred after the body-guard of Congressmen had departed for the House and concerning which there had been no testimony before; when, with inimitable simplicity, he told of the caresses the great War-Minister lavished upon him, of the interchange of jokes between them, of the bottle from which the assailed succoured his famished assailant and drank with him the "equal" drink; the impression that hostilities between the rival claimants threatened a small civil war evaporated in a burst of laughter. When the witness was allowed, over the objection of the managers, to reply to the question whether the President at any time authorized or directed him to use force or threats to get possession of the War Office and swore that the President did not, there was an end, as it seemed to the audience, of the conspiracy articles. Butler's cross-examination of the guileless veteran was not a pleasing exhibition. The lynx-like attorney displayed his skill in bemuddling an honest but mentally confused witness, but the substance of his testimony (except in the confounding of the incidents of the two interviews of the twenty-first and twenty-second—which he was recalled to clear up) remained unshaken, and, though visibly under torture, he maintained a soldierly bearing and impressed all who heard him that, although unequal to cope with the wiles of the lawyer, he meant to be truthful in speech and was right at heart.

On Saturday (eleventh) a veteran of another sort took the witness-stand; one whom Butler would be much more chary how he handled. Lieutenant-General Sherman testified to the interviews he had with the President concerning the case of Stanton after the latter's reinstatement. But when he was asked what conversation took place between them on the first of them (January 15), strenuous objection was made by the managers and a long argument ensued, during which manager Wilson made the pregnant suggestion that, should such testimony be admitted, then, by introducing "conversations between the President, his Cabinet and General Grant," the defendant's counsel might precipitate upon the Senate "a question of veracity between the General of the Army and the President of the United States"—"in order that the preponderance of testimony (considered numerically at least) may weigh down the General of the Army." The Senate, overruling the Chief Justice, excluded the testimony by a vote of 28 to 23. The witness was then permitted to tell of the President's tender to him of the office of Secretary of War *ad interim* on the twenty-fifth of January and again on the thirtieth, and that he finally replied in writing; but what was said on these two occasions, generally or particularly, was rigorously excluded. This struggle consumed the day; and the second week of the trial was over.

On Monday, the efforts of counsel to get this testimony before the Senate were renewed and after several failures were finally successful. Reverdy Johnson put the following question: When the President tendered to you the office of Secretary of War *ad interim*, on the twenty-fifth and thirtieth of January, did he, at the very time of making each tender, state to you what his purpose in doing so was? To the surprise and mortification of the managers, the Senate admitted the question by a vote of 26 to 22, and General Sherman was permitted to give his testimony, the substance of which we have already detailed.

On Tuesday, the severe illness of Stanbery compelled an adjournment; and, on Wednesday, the remaining counsel for the President proceeded in his absence, confining themselves to the introduction of documentary proof.

On Thursday, Sumner enlivened the proceedings by one of his peculiar moves. He sent to the Chair "a declaration of opinion," as he called it, "to be adopted by the Senate in answer to the constantly recurring questions on the inadmissibility of testimony." The paper proposed, "considering" the irresponsible character of the tribunal "to hasten the despatch of business" by admitting "all evidence offered on either side not trivial or obviously irrelevant." Sumner, for his part, was so thoroughly convinced of the guilt of the President, he needed no testimony to sustain his prejudgment, and no evidence, whatever its weight, could have shaken his conviction in the slightest particular. He was impatient to reach a result he considered certain, and regarded these bickerings over questions of evidence with much disfavour. Hitherto he had acted on this idea and voted to admit every bit of testimony offered. His proposition got eleven votes and was laid on the table. Counsellors Cox and Merrick were then examined concerning the criminal prosecution of Thomas and its termination in his discharge—a matter already narrated. Several attempts to keep out so much of the evidence of these witnesses as tended to prove the intent of the President to get the question into the courts were made by the managers, but without success. Butler was much irritated and could not forbear from lashing out. Towards the end of the dispute he rose and said: "Mr. President, I wish it simply understood, that I may clear my skirts of this matter, that this all goes in under our objection and under the ruling of the presiding officer." To this insolent insinuation the Chief Justice quietly rejoined: "It goes in under the direction of the Senate of the United States." Edwin O. Perrin, who called on the President in company with a member of Congress on the afternoon of the twenty-first of February, was sworn for the purpose of showing that at the time of the interview the President supposed that Stanton had virtually retired and Thomas was already in office; but, after considerable discussion, although the Chief Justice thought the testimony admissible within the other rulings of the Senate, it was excluded by a large majority. At this point, Evarts intimating that, on account of Stanbery's illness, it would be more convenient for the defence to produce no more testimony that day, Butler's ill-suppressed dissatisfaction with the recent rulings of the court burst forth in a most extraordinary appeal. "The whole legislation of this country is stopping"; he cried. "While we are waiting for the Attorney General to get well, and you are asked to delay this trial for that reason, numbers of our fellow citizens are being murdered day by day. There is not a man here who does not know that the moment justice is done on this great criminal, these murders will cease." Waving aside the protests the President's counsel here interposed, he persisted in dragging before the court matters foreign to the issue, of which there was no proof, nor could properly be any: the Ku-Klux-Klan outrages; the flight of Spencer, register in bankruptcy; sales of gold by the Treasury at enormous sacrifices (a tabular statement of which he swung aloft in his hand); fraudulent purchases of U. S. bonds.

"Now, I say," he wildly implored, "for the safety of the finances of the people, for the progress of the legislation of the people, for the safety of the true and loyal men, black and white, in the South who have perilled their lives for four years; yea, five years; yea, six years; yea, seven years, in your behalf; for the good of the country, for all that is dear to any man and patriot, I pray let this trial proceed; let us come to a determination of this issue."

"Threats of assassination" are made, he said, "every hour and upon every occasion, even when objection to testimony is made by the managers." "We have not the slightest fear of these cowardly menaces; but all these threats, these unseemly libels on our form of government, will go away when this man goes out of the White House." Evarts, naturally, was shocked at such impropriety.

"I have never heard such a harangue before in a court of justice. . . . All these delays and the ill consequences seem to press upon the honorable managers except at the precise point of time when some of their mouths are open occupying your attention with their long harangues . . . and now twenty minutes by the watch with this harangue of the honorable manager about the Ku-Klux-Klan. I have said what I have said to the Senate."

And thereupon the Senate adjourned.

The greater part of the fourteenth day of the trial was consumed in taking the testimony of persons—reporters and others—who heard the speeches of the President and gave of them smoother versions. But towards the close of the session, a genuine sensation was raised by the calling of Secretary Welles. The first fresh fact he disclosed was that the Emory interview was occasioned by a rumour of the clandestine movements of troops which the Secretary himself carried to the President. The witness then detailed the conversation at the close of the Cabinet meeting of the twenty-first of February, showing that the President supposed Thomas was in possession and Stanton had yielded; requiring only time to remove his papers. Incidentally it was brought out that the nomination of Ewing was already written out. The examination reverting to the Cabinet consultation over the Tenure-of-office bill at the time of its passage, a formal offer was made to prove that the members of the Cabinet advised the President that the bill was unconstitutional, and that the task of preparing a message to that effect was devolved on Mr. Seward and Mr. Stanton. The managers at once perceived that this matter was vital. Butler "opened the debate" as he called it, by stating the question to be "whether after a law has been passed . . . the President can show what his opinions were, and the opinions of his Cabinet, before it was passed, as a justification for refusing to obey it and execute it"; and, at the close of a reply by Evarts, the Senate adjourned.

The next morning the managers came in anticipation of a field-day. They had assigned to Wilson the task of impugning the relevancy of this important testimony; and that manager had passed the night in the preparation of his argument which was, in truth, a dissertation adverse to the claim of the President to question in any way an act of Congress passed over his veto on the ground of its constitutional invalidity, and may be considered as the manager's contribution to the summing up of the cause, in which he did not participate. Mr. Curtis, who replied, declined to follow the manager into the large field he opened and contented himself with pushing the point that, the articles having charged the President with intending to violate the Constitution, the present offer was, certainly, material to rebut that charge—whatever might be its weight; the testimony was offered to establish what is necessarily the first step in the President's justification, namely: "that he honestly believed this law to be unconstitutional." The Chief Justice held the evidence admissible on the question of intent, and senator Howard promptly called for a vote. The question was considered a test one—decisive of one entire branch of the defence. The utmost interest was excited because it was known that Seward and McCulloch, Browning and Randall, stood ready to follow Welles, if his testimony in this particular was admitted; and also that Stanton might be forced to take the stand. The yeas were twenty, the nays twenty-nine.

Then followed another offer of proof more significant and vital still, viz: That at the Cabinet meetings at the time the Tenure-of-office bill was before the President for approval, Mr. Stanton being present, the question whether the Secretary of War and the other Secretaries appointed by Mr. Lincoln were within the restrictions imposed by the act was considered, and that the opinion was expressed that they were not. The Chief Justice held the testimony proper, but in deference to the previous ruling submitted it to the Senate, and it was excluded by a vote of 22 yeas and 26 nays. Two other offers were made; one to prove that the Cabinet considered that the public service made it desirable that upon a proper case a judicial determination of the constitutionality of the law should be obtained; the other to prove that in the deliberations of the Cabinet on the subject no suggestion of the use of force was ever made: —but with a like result. Welles was not allowed to speak and left the stand. The Secretaries of State, of the Treasury and of the Interior, in attendance ready to testify, were not sworn, and the Postmaster-General took the stand only to prove that Foster Blodgett—a witness for the prosecution, for whom its side of the case was reopened that he might testify that the reasons of his suspension were not communicated to the Senate —was, in fact, suspended because he had been indicted for perjury. Before Randall left the stand, senator Sherman submitted a question: "State if the question whether the Secretaries appointed by President Lincoln were included within the provisions of the Tenure act came before the Cabinet for discussion; and, if so, what opinion was given on the question by members of the Cabinet to the President?" Butler and Bingham objected that this was the same question just voted on and senator Howard challenged the right of a senator to repeat it. The Chief Justice promptly affirmed the right. Butler called for the reading of the recent offer; and then the Senate voted with the same result as before. Sumner's course on this important matter excited remark but, indeed, was characteristic of the man. He was the proposer of a rule to admit everything in evidence, not manifestly trivial, to avoid delay. And yet, on a crucial occasion coming almost immediately after his proposal, he sat silent in his seat and deliberately refused to vote.

There is reason to believe that these questionable decisions not only increased the popular reprehension of the Impeachment but actually contributed to the acquittal of the President; one, if not more, of the Republican senators who joined the Democrats in voting for the admission of the testimony, subsequently avowed that he could not vote for conviction after such material and important facts for the defence had been deliberately shut out by the court.*

The taking of testimony virtually ended with these votes; for, although the court adjourned until Monday, nothing of interest or importance took place on that day; and an adjournment was taken until Wednesday when the final arguments were to begin. From the opening speech of Butler to the close of the testimony (excluding intermissions), were sixteen days. Deducting the time consumed in incidental discussions, the taking of testimony consumed not more than four days on both sides; and what little oral testimony there was raised no serious conflict on a single question of fact. Yet the final arguments of both sides stretched from Wednesday, the twenty-second of April, to Wednesday, the sixth of May, of which period, deducting the two Sundays, the managers occupied six days and the counsel for the President seven. Wilson contented himself with his elaborate argument against the admissibility of the testimony of the Cabinet. Butler had already

* Henderson's Opinion, Vol. 3 of Trial, p. 304.

played his part in the opening address. Logan was forced to be satisfied with filing an argument of fifty pages of print. But the remaining four—Boutwell, Williams, Stevens and Bingham—were accorded the privilege of speaking as against four of the counsel for the President—Nelson, Groesbeck, Stanbery and Evarts.

The arguments *pro* and *con* of these eight lawyers on the question confronting them on the threshold of the cause and the determination of which in the President's favour would at once end the whole proceeding, followed the same line as the respective arguments of Butler and Curtis on the same subject; and it will be more profitable to extricate them from the bulk of the speeches and recapitulate them by themselves.

Mr. Boutwell insisted, as he did in the House, that Andrew Johnson had no term, that he was serving out Abraham Lincoln's term, and, therefore, Stanton came within the words of the proviso. He said nothing in answer to Curtis's argument that, Stanton having been appointed during Lincoln's first term, Lincoln, if living, would have been at liberty to remove him notwithstanding the Tenure-of-office act;—nor did he tell what had become of Andrew Johnson's term as Vice President. His whole argument upon this branch of the case occupies but three of his fifty-one printed pages. Groesbeck refuted him upon this point in a few words:

"The gentleman has said this is Mr. Lincoln's term. The dead have no ownership in office or estate of any kind. Mr. Johnson is the President of the United States with a term and this is his term. But it would make no difference if Mr. Lincoln were living to-day; if Mr. Lincoln were President to-day, he could remove Mr. Stanton. Mr. Lincoln would not have appointed him during this term. It was during the last term that Mr. Stanton received his appointment, and not this; and an appointment by a President during one term, by the operation of this law will not extend the appointee through another term because that same party may happen to be re-elected to the Presidency. Stanton, therefore, holds under his commission, and not under the law."

Bingham excelled himself in the vehement dogmatism with which he expounded the statute. The "term of the President by whom" these officers were appointed meant, he said, as many terms as any one President may be reelected to fill.

"That is the meaning of the law. That is all there is of it. The word 'term' determines it. Did that mean that a President re-elected for a term . . . should be relieved from his own appointees by operation of law, and that, too, without his consent, and, if you please, against his wish? It never entered the mind of a single member of the thirty-ninth Congress." "If Mr. Lincoln had lived . . . he could not have removed a single head of department appointed by himself at any time during his term: and I do not care how often his term was renewed it was still the term and answered to the statute." "They were to hold their offices . . . during the entire term, if it should be eight years, twelve years or sixteen years, of the President *by whom* they were appointed."

Williams, who, as one of the conferees on the part of the House when the Tenure act was passing, had

29

suggested this unlucky proviso "for the purpose," as he now admitted, "of obviating the objection . . . that the effect of the amendment would be to impose on an incoming President a cabinet that was not of his own choosing," was listened to with great attention when he touched upon this branch of the case. His solution was more novel than satisfactory. He stated that "if it was intended or expected that it (the proviso) should operate to create exceptions in favor of an officer whose notorious abuse of power was the proximate cause, if not the impelling motive, for the enactment of the law, I did not know it:" and in making this avowal he may well be believed. There cannot be much doubt that the majority of the House believed they had protected Stanton; and Williams, by his mode of meeting the point of the President's counsel, simply shows how he and the House with him happened to fall into this misunderstanding. "The argument of the defendant," he said, "rests upon the meaning of the word 'appointed.' "

> "That word has both a technical meaning and a popular one. In the former, which involves the idea of a nomination and confirmation in the constitutional way, there was no appointment certainly by Johnson. In the latter, which is the sense in which the people will read it, there unquestionably was. What, then, was meant by the employment of this word?
>
> "For the President of the United States to say, however, after having voluntarily retained Mr. Stanton for more than two years of his administration, that he was there only by sufferance, or as a mere movable, or heirloom, or

incumbrance that passed to him with the estate, and not by virtue of his own special appointment, if not 'paltering with the people in a double sense,' has very much the appearance of a not very respectable quibble. The unlearned man who reads the proviso—as they for whose perusal it is intended will read it—and who is not accustomed to handle the metaphysic scissors of the professional casuists who are able 'to divide a hair 'twixt west and northwest side,' while he admits the ingenuity of the advocate, will stand amazed, if he does not scorn the officer who would stoop to the use of such a subterfuge."

Mr. Boutwell revived the contention that, once shown to be out of the proviso, Stanton fell inevitably within the main body of the section. Stevens regarded this a "more conclusive answer" than the play upon the word "term." Williams, also said: "If Mr. Stanton was appointed by President Johnson within the meaning of the proviso, he holds, of course, until the expiration of his term. If not, he holds subject to removal like other officers under the enacting clause." Bingham was overwhelmingly emphatic on this point. "His (the President's) own counsel who opened the case . . . declares that there are no express words within the proviso that bring the Secretary of War, Edwin M. Stanton, within the proviso. That is his own position, and that being so, he must be within the body of the statute. There is no escape from it."

Evarts had no difficulty in escaping from it in the following complete fashion:

"The argument that if Stanton is not within the proviso then he is within the body of the section stumbles over this transparent and very obvious fallacy. . . . You have not made a law about Mr. Stanton by name. The question is whether the office of Secretary of War is within the section or within the proviso; and will any body doubt that? It is on the same footing as the other Secretaryships. The question whether the office of Mr. Stanton or the office of Mr. Browning is within one or the other alternatives of the section is not a question of construction of the law, but a question of whether the tenure or actual incumbency of the one or the other bring him within the proviso; his office being there, the fact that he is not in does not carry the office back into the first part because his office would be back there for the future as well as for the past and for the present. It is a statute made for permanent endurance and the office of Secretary of War, now and forever, as long as the statute remains upon the book, is disposed of one way or the other within the first part or within the proviso. . . . There is no doubt about the office being under the proviso. It says so:

" 'Provided, That the Secretaries of State, of the Treasury, of War, of the Navy, and of the Interior, the Postmaster General, and the Attorney General shall hold their offices respectively,' &c. That does not mean the men; it means the offices shall have that tenure."

It only remains to inquire whether the proviso covers Mr. Stanton's particular predicament:

"That is the question of fact in the construction of the proviso. He either stays in the proviso or he drops out of the proviso; and if he personally drops out of the proviso in his present incumbency he cannot get back into the operative clause, because he cannot get back there without carrying his office there, and his office never can get back."

And the counsel then throws in the following *reductio ad absurdum:*

> "How absurd a result that is, to give this poor President control of his cabinet, that those he appointed himself, if he should happen to be re-elected, he could get rid of in a month, and those that Mr. Lincoln appointed for him from the beginning, and before he had any choice in it, he must hold on to forever, till you consent that they shall go out."

In reply to the argument of Curtis that an erroneous construction by the President of an ambiguous statute could not be an impeachable offence, Mr. Boutwell freely admitted that in such a contingency the President "would be fully justified and upon no principle of right could he be held to answer as for a misdemeanor in office." "But," added the manager, "that is not this case." He could not and did not deny that the law was ambiguous, at least; but he claimed that the President from the first had no doubt about the intention of the Congress;—citing, in proof, the veto message where the President arraigns the bill as in conflict with the Constitution because it restricted the President's time-honoured power "to remove from their places any civil officer." Bingham in his turn avoided the same point in a similar manner. He even contended that the proviso was susceptible of but one meaning—was not ambiguous at all. "I have no doubt of its being the true construction of the law, neither had the accused"; and he stamped any other construction as "an afterthought."

With respect to the other of the two acts which constituted the proximate occasion of the Impeachment—the letter to Thomas—it would seem that the unlawfulness of this subsidiary exercise of authority was so wrapped up in the unlawfulness of the main act of removal that they must necessarily stand or fall together. Yet, for a reason which will become apparent when we come to consider the verdict, the managers were deeply solicitous to establish some semblance of criminality in the temporary designation of Thomas, even conceding the power to remove Stanton. To do this they were compelled to follow Butler in advancing arguments of such technical nicety as (1) that the act of 1795 did not apply to vacancies caused by removal, (2) that the six months' clause was violated for the reason that General Grant's term *ad interim* expiring on the 12th of February, no other *ad interim* supply was permissible; and (3) that the act of 1795 was repealed by the act of 1863; the first of which the President's counsel answered by appealing to the practice of the government; the second, by pointing out that suspension did not vacate an office at all, a vacancy being made only by a complete removal—in practice dating only from the date of removal; the third, by the argument that, there being no express repeal of the act of 1795 by the act of 1863 and the latter not covering cases of vacancies provided for by the former, there could be no total repeal by implication. But the most effectual refutation of this class of arguments when applied to such a cause lay in the absurdity, as Evarts expressed it, "that the removal of the President should depend upon the question whether an Adjutant General was a proper *locum tenens* or not, or whether, entangled between the horns of the repealed and unrepealed statutes, the President may have erred in that on which he hung his rightful authority.'' The same counsel, in another place, conceding for the sake of the argument this temporary appointment to be without any authority whatever, asks what it would amount to?

> ''It would simply be that the President in the confusion among the statutes, had appointed, or attempted to appoint, an *ad interim* discharge of the office without authority of law. You could not indict him very well for it, and I do not think you can impeach him for it.''

Or, as he remarks elsewhere:

> ''Truly, indeed, we are getting very nice in our measure and criticism of the absolute obligations and of the absolute acuteness and thoroughness of executive functions when we seek to apply the process of impeachment and removal to a question whether an act of Congress required him to name a head of a department to take the vacant place *ad interim* or an act of Congress not repealed permitted him to take a suitable person. You certainly do not, in the ordinary affairs of life, rig up a trip-hammer to crack a walnut.''

The managers hazarded the assertion that no *ad interim* appointment was warranted while the Senate was in session—that such an exercise of power was a virtual nullification of the right of the Senate to participate in the appointing power. The Constitution, they claimed, only recognized such *quasi* appointments during recess by providing that commissions might be issued to expire at the end of the next session of the Senate. But, here again, Evarts demonstrated that, respecting these temporary designations, the discrimination between session and recess could have no foundation. "*Ad interim* appointments do not rest upon the Constitution at all." They are "not a filling of the office which remains just as vacant . . . as if the temporary appointment had not been made."

> "When the final appointment is made it dates as from and to supply the place of the person whose vacancy led to the *ad interim* appointment. That in the very nature of things there should be no difference in this capacity between recess and session sufficiently appears, and the acts of Congress draw no distinction, and the practice of the Government makes not the least difference."

We have now given the substance of the arguments on the leading, it might properly be called the prerogative, issue in the cause; and it is evident that, had the summing up been confined to what Stanbery called "the head and front of the entire case,"—"Strike it out and all that remains is leather and prunella"—the orators must have exhausted the subject in two or three days at the longest. The kernel extracted, the several speeches may now be passed in review upon their main subject-matter, which, in the speeches of the managers at least, lay outside their treatment of the particular charges on which the Impeachment was founded. The managers were not troubled over the establishment of the validity of what was more or less consciously recognized as but a pretext for Impeachment, to such a degree as to waste six whole days and delay the result they regarded so certain for that length of time. Their chief concern was to find some public justification for this arraignment of the President of the United States as a criminal, and the dislocation of the whole administrative machinery of the government by his deposition. The inadequacy of the actual case to call forth this extreme remedy of state drove them to escape from its narrow limits, and, following in the wake of Butler, expend their powers of speech upon the transcendent magnitude of issues not before the court or not necessarily involved in the cause, and upon the countless enormities of Andrew Johnson for which the House of Representatives, nevertheless, had refused to impeach him. The counsel for the President, on their part, were forced to pursue their opponents along the circumference of the wide circle they cut, if for nothing else, to draw them back to the central nucleus of real matter, which seemed to work upon them with so centrifugal a force. It is for this reason that none of the speeches takes rank with the celebrated forensic efforts of history. The eloquence of a Sheridan or a Burke could have made nothing of the formal infraction of an ambiguous clause in a statute, that hurt nobody and loosened no cog in the machinery of government—nothing, of stale charges of treason, so vague, indefinite and intangible, that the accusatory body dared not make them the subject of a formal indictment.

In the final argument Mr. Boutwell led the way, as it was meet he should, because, if not the father, he was the nursing mother of the Impeachment. For the last two years he had worked early and late to bring this monstrous malefactor of his imagination to the bar, and now that his labours were crowned with success, he prepared himself to make the effort of his life to transfuse his own fervent conviction into the minds of the court and the country. Trusting nothing to the inspiration of the moment, he had written out his entire speech, and he read it from printed slips. It was a strong presentation of a case against the President, on which, however, he was *not* being tried. Starting with the admission common to all the managers that "the issues of record . . . are technical and limited,"—he makes haste to maintain that "the grave, national, historical, constitutional issue" is that raised, not by the articles of Impeachment, but by the claim made in the President's answer "of the power at any or all times of removing from office all executive officers for cause to be judged by the President alone." He proceeds to discuss the distribution of power between the respective departments of the government; and holds that the executive and judiciary, so far from being coordinate with the legislative, are in effect subordinate; Congress having, beside its coordinate sphere, a general supervisory and regulatory jurisdiction over the other two.

> "The legislative department has original power derived from the Constitution, by which it can set and keep itself in motion as a branch of the government, while the executive and judicial departments have no self-executing constitutional capacity, but are constantly dependent upon the legislative department. . . ."

> "In fine, the power to set the government in motion and to keep it in motion is lodged exclusively in Congress, under the provisions of the Constitution."

The conclusion he draws from this proposition is that "the people have vested discretionary power" in the Congress alone, "while they have denied to the executive and judicial departments all discretionary or implied power whatever." This is the reason why various enumerated powers are denied to Congress, to the United States and to the several states; but no power is specifically denied to the President except to pardon in cases of Impeachment. And therefore "the President . . . can exercise those powers only which are specifically conferred upon him and can take nothing by construction, by implication, or by what is sometimes termed the necessity of the case." Like the judge in a court of law, he must take the law as he finds it. When he has vetoed a bill his power is exhausted. If the bill is passed over his veto he has only to execute it without question or demur.

> "To the President in the performance of his executive duties all laws are alike. He can enter into no inquiry as to their expediency or constitutionality. All laws are presumed to be constitutional, and whether constitutional or not, it is the duty of the Executive so to regard them while they have the form of law. . . .
>
> "Hence it follows that the crime of the President is not, either in fact or as set forth in the articles of impeachment, that he has violated a constitutional law; but his crime is that he has violated a law, and in his defence no inquiry can be made whether the law is constitutional."

And the manager maintains that no senator on this trial has a right to inquire into the constitutionality of the law the President is alleged to have violated, nor to allow his opinion of its unconstitutionality to govern him in his verdict; and that the President, having no right even to question its constitutionality, could not possibly have violated it from any other than a bad motive. He sees in the President's alleged purpose to test the law in the courts nothing but a pretext to conceal his treasonable designs.

To minimize the force of the support of the President by his Cabinet, he heaps scorn upon the subserviency of such officers; revealing a singularly low conception of a position he himself, not long after, condescended to accept.

"Of what value can be the advice of men who, in the first instance, admit that they hold their offices by the will of the person who seeks their advice, and who understand most clearly that if the advice they give should be contrary to the wishes of their master, they would be at once, and in conformity with their own theory of the rights of the President, deprived of the offices they hold? . . .

"It was the advice of serfs to their lord, of servants to their master, of slaves to their owner. . . .

"The Cabinet responds to Mr. Johnson like old Polonius to Hamlet.

"The President is a man of strong will, of violent passions, of unlimited ambition, with a capacity to employ and use timid men, adhesive men, subservient men, and corrupt men, as the instruments of his designs. It is the truth of history that he has injured every person with whom he has had confidential relations, and many have escaped ruin only by withdrawing from his society altogether. He has one rule of life: he attempts to use every man of power, capacity, or influence within his reach. Succeeding in his attempts, they are in time, and usually in a short time, utterly ruined. If the considerate flee from him, if the brave and patriotic resist his schemes or expose his plans, he attacks them with all the enginery and patronage of his office, and pursues them with all the violence of his personal hatred. He attacks to destroy all who will not become his instruments, and all who become his instruments are destroyed in the use. He spares no one. Already this purpose of his life is illustrated in the treatment of a gentleman who was of counsel for the respondent, but who has never appeared in his behalf."

This blighting effect of the President's influence he illustrated by a reference to the position of the figures in Carpenter's Painting, "The signing of the Emancipation Proclamation":—

"It was natural and necessary that the artist should arrange the personages of the group on the right hand and on the left of the principal figure. Whether the particular assignment was by chance, by the taste of the artist, or by the influence of a mysterious Providence which works through human agency, we know not. But on the right of Lincoln are two statesmen and patriots who, in all the trials and vicissitudes of these eventful years, have remained steadfast to liberty, to justice, to the principles of constitutional government. . . .

"On the left of Lincoln are five figures representing the other members of his Cabinet. One of these is no longer among the living; he died before the evil days came, and we may indulge the hope that he would have escaped the fate of his associates. Of the other four, three have been active in counselling and supporting the President in his attempts to subvert the government. They are already ruined men.''

As a matter of fact, of the two figures on the right (Chase and Stanton) Chase was already falling away. Of the five on the left, two—the same number as on the right—Smith and Bates—''remained steadfast,'' and thus marred the symmetry of the orator's ''providential'' arrangement, while Blair, like Chase, was never in Johnson's Cabinet or under Johnson's influence.

Upon his doctrine of the sovereignty of the legislative department, the manager ingeniously constructs his theory concerning the power of removal. Not being mentioned in the Constitution except in cases of impeachment, that power in fact resides nowhere. The executive taking nothing by implication does not possess it. And it is not specifically granted the Congress. It is not an independent power, but only an incident of the power of appointment, and, so far as the Constitution deals with it, can only be exercised by making an appointment. It is nothing more than a power of supersession exercisable only while the Senate is in session. There being, then, no provision in the Constitution for the removal of incapable or dishonest officials during recess, Congress, under the grant of power to make all laws necessary or proper to carry into execution all the powers vested in any department of the government, can step in and supply the *casus omissus* by statute. Congress neglected its duty, in this respect, until it passed the Tenure-of-office act, and the practice that grew up during this long interval is of no account upon "a subject clearly within the jurisdiction" of the law-making power. The act of 1789, according to Mr. Boutwell, simply recognized "the power of removal during the recess of the Senate"; the practice under it "upon the opinions of Attorney Generals" having been tolerated by the country until 1867. The habit of ignoring inconvenient facts or reversing the conclusions of history, to which many fervid advocates are addicted, is exemplified by the manager's treatment of the great debate in the first Congress on this subject. He deliberately interjects the distinction between removal during session and removal during recess—a distinction of which there is no trace in the debate itself. He belittles "Madison's views" which he declares "were gradually and finally, successfully undermined." He dwells almost exclusively on the arguments of Roger Sherman and other members of the minority who insisted that, in the exercise of the power of removal as in the exercise of the power of appointment, the Senate was associated with the President; quoting the remarks of Sherman at great length and challenging Evarts "to overthrow the constitutional argument of his illustrious ancestor." This method of quotation is very much like the citation of a dissenting opinion to ascertain the principle of law decided in a given case. The exact reverse of the conclusions arrived at could not be more accurately stated than is done in what follows:

"The results reached by the Congress of 1789 are conclusive upon the following points: that the body was of opinion that the power of removal was not in the President absolutely, to be exercised at all times and under all circumstances; and, secondly, that during the sessions of the Senate the power of removal was vested in the President and Senate to be exercised by their concurrent action; while the debate and the votes indicate that the power of the President to remove from office, during the vacation of the Senate, was, at best, a doubtful power under the Constitution."

Mr. Boutwell closes this branch of his argument by holding that, without the Tenure-of-office act at all, the President was guilty of a violation of the Constitution, even under the act of 1789, because he removed Stanton during the session of the Senate.

We do not propose to follow the manager in his extremely technical argument to establish the conclusion that the *ad interim* appointment of Thomas was without authority of law; nor in his laboured exposition of the conspiracy articles and his inflammatory exaggeration of the Emory article—already recognized by almost everyone as doomed—but to hurry on to the close of his address where the real source of his zeal for the removal of the President discloses itself in the bitterness of his speech. He demands a conviction on the tenth article—not because the President slandered or libelled the Congress; this he could not do; but because the speeches show him "unfit for the office that he holds." In this connection he lays down a proposition of law, so vague and elastic that, if once incorporated into the fundamental law of the country, it would render impeachments as common as elections.

> "We claim that the common law of crimes, as understood and enforced by Parliament in cases of impeachment, is in substance this: that no person in office shall do any act contrary to the good morals of the office; and that, when any officer is guilty of an act contrary to the good morals of the office which he holds that act is a misdemeanor for the purpose of impeachment and removal from office."

The eleventh article it is that furnishes Mr. Boutwell the text from which he rises to the height of his invective. The President's most heinous offence is his resistance to the congressional plan of reconstruction. Confounding all distinction between accusations of the former impeachment and accusations incorporated into the articles, the manager goes back to the beginning of the administration of Andrew Johnson, and, because of the course of policy the President adopted on the subject of reconstruction, arraigns him as a tyrant, a usurper, an apostate and a traitor. "His entire scheme of criminal ambition," the manager cries out, "was no less than this":

> "To obtain command of the War Department and of the army, and by their combined power to control the elections of 1868 in the ten States not yet restored to the Union; . . . to inaugurate a policy throughout the ten States by which the former rebels, strengthened by the support of the Executive here, and by the military forces distributed over the South, would exclude from the polls every colored man, and to permit the exercise of the elective franchise by every white rebel; . . . to control the entire vote of the ten rebel States; . . . to secure the elec-

30

tion of delegates to the democratic national convention favorable to his own nomination to the presidency, . . . to secure first, the nomination of the democratic party in the national nominating convention, and, secondly, the electoral vote of these ten States. This being done, he had only to obtain enough votes from the States now represented in Congress to make a majority of electoral votes, and he would defy the House and Senate should they attempt to reject the votes of the ten States, and this whether those States had been previously restored to the Union or not; . . . and he would have been inaugurated on the 4th of March next president of the United States for four years."

The rapt orator continues:

"Never in the history of any free government has there been so base, so gross, so unjustifiable an attempt upon the part of the executive, whether Emperor, King or President, to destroy the just authority of another department of the government.

"The exhibition which he made in this chamber on the 4th of March, 1865, by which the nation was humiliated and republican institutions disgraced in the presence of the representatives of the civilized nations of the earth, is a truthful exhibition of his character."

He compares Andrew Johnson unfavourably with the most celebrated impeached culprits of history. The offence for which the Earl of Macclesfield was convicted was "a trivial crime compared with the open, wanton and defiant violation of law" of this Chief Magistrate. Warren Hastings, even "if the charges preferred against him had been fully sustained," "would be regarded as an unimportant criminal when compared with this respondent." Verres—"the great political criminal of history"—by reason of the small area of the country he scourged, was an insignificant malefactor beside him. Andrew Johnson, the manager declares, "takes the place of Charles I," and Stanton the place of John Hampden. Having thus pictured forth the monstrous figure inflaming his own imagination, he felt impelled to invent for it a punishment as fantastic as itself:

> "Travellers and astronomers inform us that in the southern heavens, near the southern cross, there is a vast space which the uneducated call the hole in the sky, where the eye of man, with the aid of the powers of the telescope, has been unable to discover nebulæ, or asteroid, or comet, or planet, or star, or sun. In that dreary, cold, dark region of space, which is only known to be less than infinite by the evidences of creation elsewhere, the Great Author of celestial mechanism has left the chaos which was in the beginning. If this earth were capable of the sentiments and emotions of justice and virtue, which in human mortal things are the evidences and the pledge of our Divine origin and immortal destiny, it would heave and throw, with the energy of the elemental forces of nature, and project this enemy of two races of men into that vast region, there forever to exist in a solitude eternal as life, or as the absence of life, emblematical of, if not really, that 'outer darkness' of which the Saviour of men spoke in warning to those who are the enemies of themselves, of their race, and of their God."

Thomas A. R. Nelson, who followed Mr. Boutwell, was the personal friend as well as counsel of the President. Born and brought up in the same section of Tennessee, although opposed to each other in the days first of the Whig and then of the American parties, they were united in their stand for the Union. A representative in the Congress that immediately preceded the outbreak of the civil war and an ardent opponent of the extreme measures of the majority of his colleagues from the South, Nelson witnessed the unequal fight the solitary senator from his state made against the banded forces of their common section; and, subsequently, in his retirement, he looked on while Andrew Johnson bore off the standard of Tennessee through the encompassing hosts of her rebellious sons. With such remembrances fresh in his mind, he was shocked by the wholesale denunciations and abusive epithets hurled at the President by Butler and Boutwell; and his speech is chiefly remarkable as an impulsive outburst of righteous indignation at what appeared to him such gross and almost inconceivable injustice.

> "Who is Andrew Johnson?" he cried. "When treason was rife in this capitol . . . where was Andrew Johnson then? Standing here, almost within ten feet of the place in which I stand now, solitary and alone, in this magnificent chamber, when 'Bloody treason flourished over us,' his voice was heard arousing the nation. Some of you heard it. I only heard its echoes as it rolled along from one end of the land to the other. . . . He who has periled his life in a thousand forms to put down treason—he now is stigmatized as a traitor himself. . . . Who is the President of the United States? A Democrat of the straightest, of the strict constructionists: an old Jacksonian, Jeffer-

sonian Democrat: a man who proclaimed his democracy in the very letter of acceptance which he wrote when nominated for the Vice-Presidency."

The resolution of July, 1861, of which he was the author, setting forth the real object of the war, "is the chart that has guided him in the discharge of his official duty; there is the platform on which he stood."

"Up to the assembling of the Congress of the United States in December, 1865, who was there in all this broad land, from one end of it to the other, that dared to point 'the slow, unmoving finger of scorn' at Andrew Johnson and say that he was a traitor to his party, or say that he had betrayed any trust reposed in him? He was faithfully carrying out what, I repeat, he believed to be the policy of Congress and of his predecessors. He was anxious that this Union should be restored. He was anxious to pour oil upon the troubled waters and heal the wounds of his distracted and divided country. If he erred in this, it was almost a divine error."

And yet, the counsel exclaims in sheer wonder:

"Never since the days of Warren Hastings, ay, never since the days of Sir Walter Raleigh, has any man been stigmatized with more severe reprobation than the President of the United States. All the powers of invective which the able and ingenious managers can command have been brought into requisition to fire your hearts and to prejudice your minds against him. A perfect storm has been raised around him."

"But," he adds with a pardonable pride,

"I have the pleasure to state to you, senators, to-day, and I hope that my voice will reach the whole country, that in the midst of it all he still stands firm, serene, unbent, unbroken, unsubdued, unawed, unterrified, hurling no words of threat or menace at the Senate of the United States, threatening no civil war to deluge his country with blood; but feeling a proud consciousness of his own integrity, appealing to heaven to witness the purity of his motives in his public administration, and calling upon you, senators, in the name of the living God, to whom you have made an appeal, . . . to pronounce him innocent of the offences which have been charged against him."

Mr. Boutwell's allusion to Black's abandonment of the defence provoked the counsel to give the Senate a narrative of the attempt to extort a favourable decision from the President in the Alta Vela matter, in doing which he stated the contents of Butler's letter and its date of March ninth;* and, in connection with this revelation, he mentions one trait of Andrew Johnson:

"He is a man of peculiar temperament and disposition. By careful management and proper manipulation he may, perhaps, be gently led; but it is a pretty difficult thing to do that. But with his temperament and his disposition, no man, no power under the heavens can compel him to go one inch beyond what he believes to be right; and although he knew that in rejecting this claim in the peculiar situation in which he was placed he might raise up enemies against him, although he was well aware that a powerful influence might be brought to bear against him in this trial, and that it would be trumpeted abroad from one end of the Union to the other that Judge Black had become disgusted with his cause and dissatisfied with it, and had deserted it and abandoned it on account of his full conviction of his

* See *supra*, Chap. V, p. 397.

guilt . . . he was determined not to employ the whole power of the United States in a war against a little power down here that had no capacity of resistance.''

William S. Groesbeck, who followed Nelson, was the least known of the President's counsel. Though born in the city of New York in the year 1815, he had spent the whole of his active life in the city of Cincinnati engaged in the practice of his profession. A Democratic representative in the thirty-fifth Congress (57–9); a member of the Peace Congress in 1861; and a senator in the Ohio legislature the following year:—this was the extent of his public service and, as he was by nature modest and unobstrusive, he made no noise in the world. He was a lawyer rather than a politician—and a lawyer who loved the still air of delightful studies more than the loud contentions of the forum. Substituted at the last moment for the distinguished Black, he sat through the trial without uttering a word; content, apparently, with the unpretentious function of private consultation and silent preparation; and, probably, he did not expect to speak at all until it was ascertained that four of the managers would participate in the final argument. When he arose to address the court he was labouring under severe physical indisposition so perceptibly that before he had proceeded far senator Fessenden proposed to relieve him by an adjournment. This kind offer he put aside with the remark—"I have apprehensions that I shall not be better if this matter is postponed"; and continued right on to the end of the day. His argument was plain, sententious, straightforward, without digression and without a flaw. Coming immediately after Nelson's incontinent declamation, it struck with double force. His terse and impressive exordium at once attracted the undivided attention of the court:

> "Since the organization of our government we have had five trials of impeachment—one of a senator and four of judges who held their office by appointment and for a tenure that lasted during their life or good behavior. It has not been the practice, nor is it the wise policy, of a republican or representative government to avail itself of the remedy of impeachment for the control and regulation of its elective officers. Impeachment was not invented for that purpose, but rather to lay hold of offices that were held by inheritance or for life. And the true policy of a republican government, according to my apprehension, is to leave these matters to the people. They are the great and supreme tribunal to try such questions, and they assemble statedly with the single object to decide whether an officer shall be continued or whether he shall be removed from office."

We cannot follow him in his neat demonstration that the tribunal he was addressing was a court, presupposed to be so by the words of the Constitution, designated by itself a court in every one of the five precedents of our history; and that, being a court, there could be no trial of any charge but those preferred in the articles before them, and they must be sustained, not by "common fame," or "newspaper rumor," or "views of party policy," but "upon the evidence offered here and nothing else." Nor is it necessary to give even a summary of his argument proving, first, the President's right to remove Stanton and, second, his right to issue the letter of authority to Thomas, two propositions on the establishment of which he says truly; "the first eight articles fell into ruins instantly," "there is nothing left of them":—the less so as we have already cited the passage which is its keystone. But we cannot refrain from glancing at the admirable manner in which he answers Mr. Boutwell's theory of the superiority of the legislative department over the others and the abject servitude of the executive under an act of Congress. "Our government is composed of three departments," Groesbeck quietly premises. "They are each independent of the other. No one is responsible to the other. They are responsible to the people or to the state. All this is carefully set down in the Constitution."

"Those who have charge of these various departments, by the theory and structure of the government, are enjoined each to take care of its own prerogative, if I may use such a word, and to protect itself against all possible encroachment from the others. This they do, each and every department, by observing with the utmost fidelity the provisions of the written Constitution." "At the head of one of these departments stands the President." "He is required, in addition to the oath covering his ordinary executive duties, to swear to the best of his ability to preserve, protect and defend the Constitution of the United States. That oath is administered to the President alone of all the officers of the government.

"It does seem to me that the terms of such an oath solemnly imposed upon him would impress him with the idea, or any of us with the idea, that it was the first paramount duty that he should ever, in all his executive conduct, keep his eye upon the Constitution of the United States; in all trial that he should look to it; in all doubt that he should lean toward it; in all difficulty that he should take shelter under it."

"The sum and substance" of Mr. Boutwell's eloquent argument, "was that the President is but the constable of the Congress; no more; that he is put into his place merely to execute the laws of Congress. Why, senators, this is not the right interpretation of the Constitution. He is the Chief Magistrate of the nation, having charge of one of its great departments; and he is faithless to his trust if he do not protect the powers conferred by the Constitution upon that department." What then? "Shall he disregard law? Never. He should never in mere wantonness disregard any law of Congress that may be passed." "Shall he execute all law?" as the manager insists.

"Let me tell the gentleman, in answer to his long argumentation upon this point, that he makes no distinction between law whatever, that if an act of Congress be unconstitutional it is no law; it never was a law; it never had a particle of validity, although it went through the forms of congressional enactment; from the beginning *ab initio* it was null and void, and to execute it is to violate that higher law, the Constitution of the United States, which declares that to be no law which is in conflict with its provision."

. . . .

"If a law be declared by the Supreme Court unconstitutional he should not execute it. If the law be upon its very face in flat contradiction to the plain express provisions of the Constitution, as if a law should forbid the President to grant a pardon in any case, or if a law should declare that he should not be Commander-in-chief, or if a law should declare that he should take no part in the making of a treaty, I say the President, without going to the Supreme Court of the United States, maintaining the integrity of his department, which for the time being is intrusted to him, is bound to execute no such legislation; and he is cowardly and untrue to the responsibilities of his position if he should execute it."

But "the difficulty is not here. The difficulty arises in doubtful cases."

"Suppose an act of Congress interpret the Constitution for the first time, shall the President execute it? I say yes. Suppose an act, instead of giving an interpretation for the first time in a doubtful case, contradicts a long accepted previous interpretation—in this supposition we are approaching the case before us—what is to be done? To follow the Constitution is the first and paramount duty of the President, and to maintain the integrity of his department is also a duty; and if an act of to-day is contrary to a long established interpretation of the Constitution upon a question of power, and a fit case presents itself when he is required to act, it is right and proper, in a peaceable way, with due regard for the public welfare, to test the accuracy of the new interpretation in the forum which is the highest and the final interpreter of such questions."

The counsel then goes on to show that the act of 1789 was "constitutional interpretation":

"Washington approved the bill, Adams's vote passed it, Jefferson maintained the same position, Madison drew the bill, Monroe and Jackson and the Presidents that followed them all maintained the same construction, and every President, including President Lincoln, through all our history of eighty years and twenty administrations maintained this construction upon the question of where the power of removal is lodged,'' and every subsequent Congress down to the Thirty-ninth.

On the other hand, the civil tenure act of 1867 is also "constitutional interpretation,'' and between the two the question arises, what is the duty of the President?

"All the Presidents, every revered name that ever filled the office, affirming this doctrine; the Supreme Court uttering itself upon this doctrine; thirty-eight Congresses affirming this doctrine; this on one side and one Congress on the other. May not human reason pause? May not human judgment doubt? . . . was it criminal, I say, that he, too, believed in that way, and thought that it was a proper case, it being simply a question of constitutional interpretation, to pass to that tribunal which has a higher right than the Executive and higher than Congress upon the subject of interpretation?''

"Now what was Mr. Johnson's condition? He had a cabinet officer who was unfriendly to him personally and politically.''

"He carried on the department without communication with the President; a sort of secondary executive. The unity of the Cabinet was gone. . . . That was the case, his own case, a case pressing upon him, not sought; and in executing the duty, as he conceived it to be, to effect that change he came in conflict with this law, and proposed to have its constitutional validity tested.

"But, say the gentlemen, he executed this law in other respects, he changed the forms of his commissions; he reported suspensions under this law. So he did; and, senators, it is one of the strongest facts in this case. He did not take up the law and tear it to pieces. That is lawlessness. He took it up to have it interpreted in the case that pressed upon him individually, and in all other respects he executed it without the surrender of his own convictions. . . .

"He tried to pluck a thorn out of his very heart. . . . You fastened it there and you are now asked to punish him for attempting to extract it. What more? He made an *ad interim* appointment to last for a single day. You could have terminated it whenever you saw fit. You had only to take up the nomination which he sent to you, which was a good nomination, and act upon it, and the *ad interim* appointment vanished like smoke."

Coming to the tenth article he threw that specimen of pleading into a shape that made its charges ridiculous.

"In 1798 some good people in the country seem to have been operated upon very much as the managers, or rather the House of Representatives, were in this instance, and they took it into their heads to get up what is called a sedition law, which is very like article ten."

Reading the law he remarked:

"It was the most offensive law that has ever been passed, since the government was organized. So offensive was it that the people would not rest under it although it was passed to last but three years. They started, as it were, the hue and cry against everybody who defended it or was concerned in it, and hunted them to political death. But it was a good law compared to article ten. It condemned the act of coolly and under no provocation or excitement preparing and publishing a libel against the government. . . . But so unpopular was it, that Congress has not ventured to pass a law upon the subject of libel against the government or any department from that day to this.

"It has been reserved for the House of Representatives, through its managers, to renew the practice in a more objectionable form. And I take it upon myself to suggest that before we are to be condemned in a court of impeachment we shall have some law upon the subject; and I have ventured to draw up . . . the draught of a bill which I have made on article ten of this impeachment."

The reading of the bill making penal the acts charged in the article was greeted by the spontaneous laughter of the court.

The peroration of the address ought to be given without mutilation; but we are compelled to excerpt:

"But, says the gentleman who last spoke on behalf of the managers, he tried to defeat pacification and restoration. I deny it in the sense in which he presented it—that is, as a criminal act. Here, too, he followed precedent and trod the path on which were the footprints of Lincoln, and which was bright with the radiance of his divine utterance, 'Charity for all, and malice toward none.' He was eager for pacification. He thought that the war was ended. It seemed so. The drums were all silent; the arsenals were all shut; the roar of the cannon had died away to the last reverberations; the army was disbanded; not a single enemy confronted us in the field. Ah, he was too eager, too forgiving, too kind. The hand of conciliation was stretched out to him and he took it. It may be he should have put it away, but was it a crime to take it? Kindness, forgivness a crime? Kindness a crime? Kindness is omnipotent for good, more powerful than gunpowder or cannon. Kindness is statesmanship. Kindness is the high statesmanship of heaven itself. The thunders of Sinai do but terrify and distract; alone they accomplish little; it is the kindness of Calvary that subdues and pacifies.

"What shall I say of this man? He is no theorist; he is no reformer. I have looked over his life. He has ever walked in beaten paths, and by the light of the Constitution. The mariner, tempest-tossed in mid-sea, does not more certainly turn to his star for guidance than does this man in trial and difficulty to the star of the Constitution. He loves the Constitution. It has been the study of his life. He is not learned and scholarly, like many of you; he is not a man of many ideas or of much speculation; but by a law of the mind he is only the truer to that he does know. He is a patriot, second to no one of you in the measure of his patriotism. He loves his country. He may be full of error; I will not canvass now his views; but he loves his country. He has the courage to defend it; and I believe to die for it if need be. His courage and his patriotism are not without illustration. . . . How his voice rang out in this hall in the hour of alarm for the good cause, and in denunciation of the rebellion. But he did not remain here; it was a pleasant, honorable, safe, easy position; but he was wanted for a more difficult and arduous and perilous service. He faltered not but entered upon it. That was a trial of his courage and patriotism of which some of you who now sit in judgment on more than his life know nothing. I have often thought that those who dwelt at the north, safely distant from the collision and strife of the war, knew but little of its actual and trying dangers. We who lived on the border know more. Our horizon was always red with its flames; and it sometimes burned so near us that we could feel the heat of it upon the out-stretched hand. But he was wanted for greater peril, and went into the very furnace of the war, and there served his country long and well. . . .

"And it seems hard, it seems cruel, senators, that he should be dragged here as a criminal, or that any one who served his country and bore himself well and bravely through that trying ordeal should be condemned upon miserable technicalities.

"If he has committed any gross crime, shocking alike and indiscriminately the entire public mind, then condemn him; but he has rendered service to the country which entitles him to kind and respectful consideration. He has precedents for everything he has done, and what excellent precedents! The voices of the great dead come to us from the grave sanctioning his course. All our past history approves it. How can you single out this man, in this condition of things, and brand him before the world, put your brand of infamy upon him because he made an *ad interim* appointment for a day, and possibly may have made a mistake in attempting to remove Stanton? I can at a glance put my eye upon senators here who would not endure the position which he occupied. You do not think it is right yourselves. You framed this civil tenure law to give each President his own cabinet, and yet his whole crime is that he wants peace and harmony in his."

As the unassuming orator, faint from the illness he so far had mastered, sank into his seat, a wave of admiration swept over the court and the audience, thence to roll on to the farthest borders of the republic and make the hitherto unknown name of Groesbeck familiar as a household word. Well might that stern old Cato—Stevens—say of him: "The gentleman in his peroration on Saturday implored the sympathy of the Senate with all the elegance and pathos of a Roman senator pleading for virtue; and it is to be feared that his grace and eloquence turned the attention of the Senate upon the orator rather than upon the accused."

Stevens, in fact, followed him, resolute to play his part in the drama to the end in spite of his pitiable state of physical infirmity. He stood a few minutes reading his address until he was forced to take a seat, and in this position continued to read for about a half-hour when, his voice becoming too weak to be heard, Butler concluded the reading. So indomitable a resolve we may be sure did not spring from the mere love of display—of which there was not a grain in his composition. Like an Indian warrior incapacitated by age for the war-path, he was not to be deprived of his share in the torturing of the captive. The ruler of the dominant faction of his party, he must do his best to keep weak-backed senators in line by the terrors of his scorn. Besides, he had an article he called his own to defend.

> "I shall discuss but a single article," he, therefore, opened, "the one that was finally adopted upon my earnest solicitation, and which, if proved, I considered then, and still consider, as quite sufficient for the ample conviction of the distinguished respondent and for his removal from office, which is the only legitimate object for which this impeachment could be instituted."

As there was to be "no personal punishment" "it is apparent that no crime containing malignant or indictable offences higher than misdemeanors was necessary either to be alleged or proved. If the respondent was shown to be abusing his official trust to the injury of the people . . . the true mode of dealing with him was to impeach him . . . and thus remove him from the office which he was abusing." "What does it matter, then, what the motive of the respondent might be?" "Mere mistake of intention, if persevered in after proper warning . . . is quite sufficient to warrant the removal of the officer." Nevertheless, he charged the President with "the foul offence" of "misprision of official perjury"—which at least sounds like a high crime. It consisted in the breaking of his official oath by obstructing the execution of the civil tenure act; and the peculiar felicity of the article was that it let in the letter of the President to General Grant which Stevens insisted established the offence.

> "Whichever of these gentlemen may have lost his memory, and found in lieu of the truth the vision which issues from the Ivory Gate—though who can hesitate to choose between the words of a gallant soldier and the pettifogging of a political trickster—is wholly immaterial, so far as the charge against the President is concerned. That charge is, that the President did attempt to prevent the due execution of the tenure of office law by entangling the General in the arrangement; and unless both the President and the General have lost their memory and mistaken the truth with regard to the promises with each other, then this charge is made out."

But it was the faintheartedness of certain senators that this one of the managers mainly feared, and for this reason he waved that resolution of their own, condemnatory of the President, *in terrorem* over their heads:

"And now this offspring of assassination turns upon the Senate, who have thus rebuked him in a constitutional manner, and bids them defiance. How can he escape the just vengeance of the law? Wretched man, standing at bay, surrounded by a cordon of living men, each with the axe of an executioner uplifted for his just punishment. Every senator now trying him, except such as had already adopted his policy, voted for this same resolution, pronouncing his solemn doom. Will any of them vote for his acquittal on the ground of its unconstitutionality? I know that senators would do any necessary act if indorsed by an honest conscience or an enlightened public opinion; but neither for the sake of the President nor any one else would one of them suffer himself to be tortured on the gibbet of everlasting obloquy. How long and dark would be the track of infamy which must mark his name, and that of his posterity! Nothing is therefore more certain than that it requires no gift of prophecy to predict the fate of this unhappy victim."

It is unnecessary to review the argument of manager Williams who followed Stevens, because, outside of his exposition of the Stanton proviso already given, it was but an expansion of the arguments of his speech explanatory of the Tenure bill which he introduced in the House, and a repetition of the charges made in the majority report on the first Impeachment, of which he was the author. Of all the addresses made on this trial, his was the most ornate in diction and metaphorical in style, and, in its description of the enormity of the defendant's guilt and its personal assaults upon Andrew Johnson, it was more hyperbolical and more bitter even than Mr. Boutwell's. Of all the managers, he was the only one who ventured to cast doubt upon the patriotic disinterestedness with which Andrew Johnson took his stand against secession. "I will not stop to inquire whether his resistance to the hegira of the southern senators was not merely a question, himself being the witness, as to the propriety and wisdom of such a step at that particular time." Against the Cabinet he seemed to cherish a special animosity—"the trusted counsellors" who "so largely comforted and encouraged" the President "through all his manifold usurpations." "These gentlemen," he sneered, "have not been allowed to prove their opinion and advice. It may be guessed, I suppose, without damage to our case, that if allowed, they would have proved it." He regretted that "the public curiosity has been balked by the denial of the high privilege of listening to the luminous expositions of these learned Thebans." He stigmatized the institution as "this illegitimate body, this excrescence, this mere fungus, born of decay"; and Johnson's Cabinet in particular as "a mere cabal which looked for all the world like some dark conclave of conspirators plotting against the liberties of the people"; "mere beds of justice" to register the decrees of "an imperious and selfwilled man like the present Executive." Judge of the condition of the brain of an orator who, under the actual circumstances of this case, could address to the High Court of Impeachment engaged in the trial of the Chief Magistrate of the republic, an exhortation like the following:

"If you acquit him, you affirm all his imperial pretensions and decide that no amount of usurpation will ever bring a Chief Magistrate to justice, because you will have laid down at his feet your own high dignity, along with your double function as legislators and advisers, which will be followed of course by that of your other, I will not say greater, office as judges. It will be a victory over you and us which will stir the heart of rebeldom with joy, while your dead soldiers will turn uneasily in their graves; a victory to be celebrated by the exultant ascent of Andrew Johnson to the Capitol, like the conqueror in a Roman triumph, dragging not captive kings but a captive Senate at his chariot wheels, and to be crowned by his reentry into the possession of that department of the government over which this great battle has been fought. It is shown in evidence that he has already intimated that he would wait on your action here for that purpose. But is this all? Hug not to your bosoms, I entreat you, the fond illusion that it is all to end there. It is but the beginning of the end. If his pretensions are sustained, the next head that will fall as a propitiatory offering to the conquered South, will be that of the great chief who humbled the pride of the chivalry by beating down its serried battalions in the field, and dragging its traitor standard in the dust; to be followed by the return of the rebel office-holders, and a general convulsion of the state which shall cast loose your reconstructed laws, and deliver over the whole theater of past disturbances to anarchy and ruin."

Williams closed about the time of the usual recess; and the expectation that Evarts would follow crowded the Senate chamber with an eager audience. They were compelled to wait, however, while Butler fell foul of Nelson on account of his statement of the Alta Vela matter, which he stigmatized as an "insinuating calumny," "injurious to some of the managers and other gentlemen, members of the House, who have no opportunity to be heard." He averred that "his opinion," as he called his letter, "must have been given in the early part of February"; certainly before the act was committed by Andrew Johnson which brought on his impeachment. Nelson rose, in great heat, to justify his introduction of a subject so foreign to the trial by pointing out the previous allusion to it by Mr. Boutwell: "It was for that reason and for no other that I spoke of it, not with any desire to make an assault upon the managers." And, then, hurried on by his wrath, he turned on Butler:

> "I treated the gentleman on the other side with courtesy and kindness. He has rewarded me with insult and with outrage in the presence of the American Senate. It will be for you, senators, to judge whose demeanor is most proper before you, that of the honorable gentleman who foully and falsely charges me with insinuating calumny, or my course in vindicating the President of the United States in the discharge of my professional duty here. So far as any question that the gentleman desires to make of a personal character with me is concerned, this is not the place to make it. Let him make it elsewhere, if he desires to do it."

Being promptly called to order, the counsel begged pardon of the Senate, proceeded with his explanation and, insisting that the date of the original Butler letter was March ninth, 1868, and promising to bring all the original letters into court, asked permission to lay them before the Senate. Manager Logan rose and stated that he "signed the letter long before there was anything thought of impeachment." This closed the incident for the day, but we may as well follow it to its end. The next morning, Sumner sent an order to the chair declaring that Mr. Nelson for using language "intended to provoke a duel" "justly deserved the disapprobation of the Senate"; which Sherman's objection carried over the day. Despite Sumner's strenuous protest, Nelson was allowed to produce and file the letters, among them Butler's, which, notwithstanding his and Logan's disclaimer, bore date as of the ninth of March. The next day, Sumner's resolution coming up, Reverdy Johnson moved to lay it on the table; and before taking the vote senator Anthony inquired of the counsel "if, in the remark" he had made, "it was his intention to challenge the manager to mortal combat?" Nelson replied:

> "I cannot say I had the idea of a duel particularly in my mind, as I am not a duelist by profession; but, nevertheless, my idea was that I would answer the gentleman in any way in which he chose to call upon me for it. I did not intend to claim any exemption on account of age or any exemption on account of other things that are apparent to the Senate. That was all that I meant to signify, and I hope the Senate will recollect the circumstances under which this thing was done."

So manly a frankness, while it only hardened Sumner who demanded that his resolution be read again, touched the hearts of the majority and the order was laid on the table by the vote of 35 to 10.

From this unpleasant episode we now turn to the address which it interrupted. William M. Evarts had come to Washington heralded as one of the greatest lawyers of the state of New York; and this high reputation he well sustained in the incidental discussions during the trial. Since the defeat of William H. Seward, his favourite for the presidential nomination in 1860, he had mingled but little in politics. The candidate of the Seward wing for United States senator in opposition to Horace Greeley when the contest resulted in the election of Ira Harris, he had made no nearer approach to federal affairs. All eyes were turned on his tall, slender figure as he arose to address the court. Something extraordinary in the way of argument and eloquence was expected from him, and, in certain respects, his auditors were not disappointed. Although tied to the ground by the essential pettiness of the cause he was engaged in, the speech of Evarts may be said at times to soar. It reaches almost, if it does not quite, the classic heights. One superficial but all-pervading fault it had—the inveterate proclivity of the speaker to entangle himself in the involutions of his long-drawn-out sentences. With this drawback, however, and although it was the longest of all the arguments—occupying three days in its delivery—the speech is entitled to be called a great oration. Evarts, it is true, was preeminently a lawyer. He undoubtedly belonged to that class of men whom Mr. Boutwell lunged at as "attorneys whose practice of the law had sharpened but not enlarged their intellects'';—a sneer which the counsel made him smart for. But if Evarts was a lawyer, he was a lawyer of the philosophic mind. His intellect was acutely penetrative, able to ferret through the most intervoluted complications of a case, traverse the sharpest edge of technical law and pierce the best-laid scheme of logic to its central fallacy. But, at the same time, it was comprehensive enough to grasp the fundamental principles which elucidate concrete complications, show subtlety sometimes to be wisdom, and illumine the narrowest cause by viewing it in the light cast by the massive forces with which it is environed. He was able on the present occasion, therefore, not only to wring the life out of the record prosecution to its minutest extremities; but to dissolve it into its essential nullity by re-immersing it into the heated political atmosphere whence it arose.

''All the political power of the United States is here''; with this stroke he began. The House of Representatives, the President, the Senate, the Chief Justice. But all at some disadvantage. The House and the Senate, owing to rebellion, deprived of the full attendance of members. The Executive, owing to assassination, ''in the last stage of its maintenance under mere constitutional authority.'' ''If the President be condemned . . . there will be no President of the United States,'' and ''the office sequestered will be discharged by a member of the body whose judgment sequestered it.'' ''The sober thoughtful people of this country,'' ''never fond of pageants, are thinking of far other things than these.'' They are thinking of their Supreme Court sent away with its jurisdiction cut off "by the sharp edge of a congressional enactment"; of their President elected by their voices, "accused by one branch of Congress, to be tried by the other, his office put in commission and an election ordered"; of his oath "to preserve, protect and defend the Constitution." "They are converts of no theories of congressional omnipotence. They understand none of the nonsense of the Constitution being superior to the law except that the law must be obeyed and the Constitution not." "When they hear that this tremendous enginery of impeachment . . . has been brought into play, that this power which has lain in the Constitution like a sword in its sheath, is now drawn, they wish to know what the crime is that the President is accused of."

> "They wish to know whether the President has betrayed our liberties or our possessions to a foreign state. They wish to know whether he has delivered up a fortress or surrendered a fleet. They wish to know whether he has made merchandise of the public trust and turned authority to private gain. And when informed that none of these things are charged, imputed, or even declaimed about, they yet seek further information and are told that he has removed a member of his cabinet."

They are very familiar with removal from office. Like the old lady who cried out that if you took away her "total depravity" you took away her religion, many of them might say if you take away removal from office you take away their politics. " 'How came this to be a crime?' they inquire." Why, Congress passed a law calling it a high misdemeanour. The President "has removed or undertaken to remove a member of his Cabinet and he is to be removed himself for that cause. He undertook to make an *ad interim* Secretary of War, and you are to have made for you an *ad interim* President in consequence." "'Was the Secretary of War removed then?' No; he was not removed, he is still Secretary, still in possession of the department. 'Was force used?' No; it was all on paper and all went no further" than making a case for the Supreme Court. But here Congress intercepts, again prevents the Supreme Court "from interposing its serene judgment" and declares that the case shall be determined by process of impeachment. The people do not see why this is not "a question between the omnipotence of Congress and the supremacy of the Constitution."

His treatment of the argument of Butler that the tribunal before him was not a court exhibits a still airier touch. "The intrepid manager" "knew that the only way he could prevent his cause from being turned out of court was to turn the court out of his cause." But he does "not tell us what this was, if it was not a court."

> "It is true he said it was a Senate, but that conveys no idea. It is not a Senate conducting legislative business; it is not a Senate acting upon executive business; it is not a Senate acting in caucus on political affairs; and the question remains, if it is not a court what is it?"

He answers his own question: "It is an altar of sacrifice if it is not an altar of justice"—an altar erected to "the savage demon" of "party hate and party rage."

> "If this is not a court it is a scaffold: and an honorable manager (Stevens) yesterday told you so, that each one of you brandished now a headsman's axe to execute vengeance, you having tried the offender on the night of the 21st of February already."

"Forensic discussion" it has hitherto been supposed is the true method of dealing with such issues as the present—"a method to penetrate the position and if successful to capture it"; not "the Chinese method of warfare which is the method of concussion and consists of a great braying of trumpets, sounding of gongs, shouts and shrieks in the neighborhood of the opposing force." Manager Butler "seems to have repeated the experiment he tried during the war."

> "The air was filled with epithets, the dome shook with invective. Wretchedness and misery and suffering and blood, not included within the record, were made the means of this explosive mixture. And here we are surviving the concussion, and after all reduced to the humble and homely method of discussion which belongs to 'attorneys whose intellects have been sharpened but not enlarged by the practice of law.'"

The chief aim of the counsel in this branch of his argument was to extricate the actual charge from the political elements which enveloped it, to show how intrinsically insignificant it was, and to demonstrate that "whatever else there is, attendant, appurtenant, or in the neighborhood," was "wholly political, and not the subject of jurisdiction in this court or in any court, but only in the great forum of the popular judgment."

1. "The formal contravention of a statute," he argues first, "could not be an impeachable offence merely because it was qualified by the word 'high' in the penal section of the act. You must look at the punishment. That could not be a 'high' crime which Congress allowed a judge in his discretion to punish by a six cents fine or one day's imprisonment." In the course of the discussion of this section at the time of the passage of the Tenure-of-office bill, Sumner "suggested that it would be well, at least, to have a moderate minimum of punishment that would secure something like substance necessarily in the penal infliction"--say "$1000 or $500 as the lower limit"; but Edmunds and Williams would have none of it; Williams remarking that "this is a mere offence created by statute"—"not involving moral turpitude, but rather a political offence."

2. He showed that "in act, purpose and in consequence the whole criminality we can attach to the imputed offence is a formal contravention of a statute."

> "Up to twelve o'clock on February the 21st, 1868, the President was innocent and unimpeachable, and at one o'clock on the same day he was guilty and impeachable of the string of offences that fill up all the articles except that devoted to the speeches" and the Emory article.
>
> "Nothing was done whatever except to issue a paper and have it delivered, which puts the posture of the thing in this condition and nothing else: the Constitution, we will suppose, says that the President has a right to remove

the Secretary of War; the act of Congress says that the President shall not remove the Secretary of War; the President says 'I will issue an official order which will raise the same question between my conduct and the statute that the statute raises between itself and the Constitution.' . . . He issues an order on paper which is but an assertion of the Constitution and a denial of the law, and that paper has legal validity if the Constitution sustains it, and it is invalid and ineffectual, a mere *imbelle telum,* if the law prohibits it and the law is conformed to the Constitution."

3. "All else is political." And here the counsel calls attention to the actual condition of the two contending departments of the government. The executive is not filled by one who has received the suffrage of the people for that office and on this account "discord, dislocation, deficiency, difficulty show themselves." And "this weakness of the Presidency is encountered in the present state of affairs by an extraordinary development of party strength in Congress"—a three-fourths majority in both Houses. The "three barriers against the will of Congress"—the requirement of a two-thirds vote to expel a member, to override a veto, to convict and remove the President—are broken down. The abnormal, unbalanced condition of these two great departments furnishes "ground to pause and consider";—will you precipitate the struggle to its fatal pitch—involving "the greater and higher question" "whether it is in the power of a written Constitution to draw lines of separation and put up buttresses of defence between the coordinate branches of this government?"

"And with that question settled . . . that one can devour, and having the power, will devour the other, then the balances of the American Constitution are lost and lost forever. Nobody can reinstate on paper what has once been struck down in fact. Mankind are governed by instances, not by resolutions."

It is "the political situation which forms the staple of the pressure on the part of the managers to make out a crime, a fault, a danger that should enlist the terrible machinery of impeachment and condemnation."

"If the honorable managers will go back to the source of their authority, if they will obtain what was once denied them, a general and open political charge, it may, for aught I know, be maintainable in law; it may be maintainable in fact; but then it would be brought here; it would be written down; its dimensions would be known and understood; its weight would be estimated; the answer could be made."

The counsel neatly turned the laugh on Mr. Boutwell's "astronomical" mode of punishment. Many professors, he gravely affirmed, are wholly ignorant of any such facts as the manager describes.

"But nevertheless, while some of his honorable colleagues were paying attention to an unoccupied and unappropriated island on the surface of the sea, Mr. Manager Boutwell, more ambitious, had discovered an untenanted and unappropriated region in the skies, reserved, he would have us think, in the final councils of the Almighty, as the place of punishment for convicted and deposed American Presidents.

"At first I thought that his mind had become so 'enlarged' that it was not 'sharp' enough to discover the Constitution had limited the punishment; but on reflection I saw that he was as legal and logical as he was ambitious and astronomical, for the Constitution has said 'removal from office,' and put no limit to the distance of the removal, so that it may be, without shedding a drop of his blood, or taking a penny of his property, or confining his limbs, instant removal from office and transportation to the skies."

But, as nobody knows where the space is but the manager himself, "he is the necessary deputy to execute the judgment of the court." And the counsel draws a picture of "the honorable and astronomical manager," "with the President fastened to his broad and strong shoulders," taking his flight from the top of the capitol, and the two Houses of Congress and all the people shouting *"Sic itur ad astra!"* As "he passes through the constellations," "what thinks Böotes as he drives his dogs up the zenith in their race of sidereal fire?" (*sic*).

Evarts' second full day was chiefly devoted to an exploration of the controversy over "the allocation" of the power of removal; and, in doing so, he opened up an entirely new vein, digging deeper than any of the speakers before him. The inroad upon the solid mass of executive power vested in the President, made by the association of the Senate in the power of appointment, he showed, was due, not, as had been taken for granted, to any jealousy of the executive, but to the memorable "contest in the body of the Convention" over "the balance between the weight of numbers in the people and the equality of the States." And here it was that those "opinions of Roger Sherman," which Mr. Boutwell had challenged his descendant to confute, ''had their origin.'' Sherman's ''firm maintenance of the equality of the States,'' it was, that impelled him to insist that participation in appointments should be accorded to the Senate; while his opponents thought this ''too great a subtraction from the sum of executive power.'' John Adams ''died in the conviction'' that this participation ''would be the point on which the Constitution would fall.'' ''When you add to that this change which gives to the Senate a voice in the removal from office . . . you change wholly the question of the Constitution.'' ''You break down at once the balance between the executive and legislative powers, . . . you break down the federal election of President at once and commit to the equality of States the partition and distribution of the executive power of the country.''

As a matter of fact, however, ''the power of removal is and always has been claimed and exercised by the Executive of this government separately and independently of the Senate''; says the counsel, once more unfolding a novel view of the subject. Until the Tenure act ''the actual power of removal by the Senate never has been claimed.'' Nor does this act even ''assume in terms to give the Senate a participation in the distinct and separate act—the removal from office.'' ''The scheme of the law is—to change the tenure of office, so that removability as a separate and independent act . . . is obliterated from the powers of this government.'' During recess a delinquent officer may be suspended, not removed. During the session of the Senate, a delinquent cannot even be suspended. The only way an officer can be removed, no matter under what ''stress of public necessity," is by a "complete appointment of a successor concurred in by the Senate and made operative by the new appointee going into and qualifying himself in the office."

> "The legislative construction of 1789, as worked into the bones of the government by the indurating process of practice and exercise,"—the counsel concludes,—"the doctrine that finally triumphed, was this: primarily the whole business of official subordinate executive action is a part of the executive function; that being attributed *in solido* to the President, we look to exceptions to serve the turn and precise measure of their own definition, and discard that falsest principle of reasoning in regard to laws or in regard to conduct, that exception is to breed exception or amplification of exception. The general mass is to lose what is subtracted from it by exception, and the general mass is to remain with its whole weight not thus separately and definitely reduced. When therefore these statesmen said you find the freedom of executive action and its solid authority reduced by an exception of advice and consent in appointment, you must understand that that is the limit of the exception, and the executive power in all other respects stands unimpaired."

The last consideration the counsel advanced in support of "the view that all here that possesses weight and dignity is political and not criminal or suitable for judicial cognizance," was, singularly enough, the very thing which the managers held up in the faces of the senators as a solemn pledge binding them to convict. If by passing the Tenure-of-office bill in the first instance, if by passing it over the veto of the President in the second instance, if, finally, by resolving that the President had no power to remove Stanton and to appoint Thomas, senators had already decided the matter in dispute between two of the departments of the government—what is the true conclusion? Surely, not that they have predetermined the President's guilt of "crimes involving turpitude and personal delinquency!" No principle of justice is more immutable than these: "that no man shall be a judge in his own cause, and that no man shall be a judge in a matter in which he has already given judgment." "You must have regarded it as a matter of political action"—"as a matter that could not possibly be brought before you in your judicial capacity." As was said "by the great and trusted statesman of the Whig party" when the Senate was debating the resolution condemnatory of President Jackson's removal of the deposits: "If there was in the atmosphere a whisper, if there was in the future a menace that impeachment was to come, debate must be silenced and the resolution suppressed." "The other principle is equally contravened." "You are to pass judgment" on "the partition of the offices of the government between the President and yourselves. The very matter of his fault is that he claims them; the very matter of his condemnation is that you have a right to them." You are a court, "and yet you are full of politics. Why? Because the question is political; and

the whole point of my reference is as an absolute demonstration that the Constitution of the United States never forces honorable men into a position where they are judges of their own cause, or where they have in the course of their previous duties expressed a judgment. . . . It is all political. All these thunder-clouds are political, and it is only this little petty pattering of rain and these infractions of statutes that are personal or criminal.''

We shall not follow the counsel in his examination of the articles *seriatim*. He takes them up in reverse order, beginning with the eleventh, on which he scarcely pauses, and ending with the first or main article, of his treatment of which we have already given a specimen. The Butler article he, like Groesbeck, laughs out of court. ''It is a novelty in this country to try anybody for making a speech.'' What is to be the standard of propriety? The rule ought to work both ways—in the legislative as well as in the executive branch. In the Senate, Sumner calls the President ''an enemy to his country.'' In the House, representatives Butler and Bingham—now brothers in the same cause—belabour each other over Jefferson Davis, Fort Fisher and Mrs. Surratt; and he adds:

> ''I am not entirely sure that when you make allowances for the difference between an *ex tempore* speech of the President to a mob, and a written, prepared, and printed speech to this court, by an honorable manager, but that there may be some little trace of the same impropriety in that figure of argument which presented Mr. Carpenter to your observation as an inspired painter, whose pencil was guided by the hand of Providence to the apportionment of Mr. Stanton to perpetual bliss, and of Governor Seward to eternal pains.''

We should like to linger over one or two delightful turns of argument, *e. g.*, where the counsel, observing that Stanton holds under his commission as well as under the act, points out that the President by revoking his commission—which was all in fact he did—ought to have the right to force him to fall back on his naked statutory title; but we forbear and hasten to the closing words of the orator respecting Andrew Johnson himself.

> "And I ask you to notice that, bred in a school of Tennessee democratic politics, he had always learned to believe that the Constitution must and should be preserved; and I ask you to recognize that when it was in peril, and all men south of a certain line took up arms against it, and all men north ought to have taken up arms in politics or war for it, he loved the country and the Constitution more than he loved his section and the glories that were promised by the evil spirits of the rebellion. . . .
>
> "He is no rhetorician and no theorist, no sophist and no philosopher. The Constitution is to him the only political book that he reads. The Constitution is to him the only great authority which he obeys. His mind may not expand; his views may not be so plastic as those of many of his countrymen; he may not think we have outlived the Constitution, and he may not be able to embrace the Declaration of Independence as superior and predominant to it. But to the Constitution he adheres. For it and under it he has served the State from boyhood up—labored for, loved it. For it he has stood in arms against the frowns of a Senate; for it he has stood in arms against the rebellious forces of the enemy; and to it he has bowed three times a day with a more than eastern devotion."

When the court reassembled after the recess that followed Evarts's speech, it was observed that Stanbery was present. Up to the eleventh day of the trial the ex-Attorney-General had borne the chief burden of the defence—he being not only the senior in years of his associates but, by reason of the office he had resigned to come amongst them, the closest to the President. On that day—more than a fortnight ago—he was stricken down by illness, and, although most anxious to be present, had not been well enough since; his share of duty devolving upon Evarts. There was no public expectation that he would be able to take part personally in the final argument, and, consequently, there was a buzz of astonishment when it was discovered that he had rallied sufficiently to drag his limbs to the Senate chamber. Stanbery was a remarkably handsome man of imposing presence. As a lawyer he stood in the front rank of his profession, and he carried his preeminence with dignity and grace. He possessed a persuasive manner, his voice was musical, and his elocution finished. To the Republican senators he was an object of special disfavour because of his official opinions; and his ambition to sit upon the bench of the Supreme Court, they had once taken pains to thwart. But, when with signs of weakness and distress he raised himself to speak on this occasion, a sympathetic stillness descended on Senate and audience; and every heart yielded a responsive throb as these sentences fell upon the ear:

"Mr. Chief Justice and Senators, it may seem an act of indiscretion almost amounting to temerity that in my present health I should attempt the great labor of this case. I feel that in my best estate I could hardly attain to the height of the great argument. Careful friends have advised me against it. My watchful physician has yielded a half-reluctant consent to my request, accompanied with many a caution that I fear I shall not observe. But, senators, an irresistible impulse hurries me forward. The flesh indeed is weak; the spirit is willing. Unseen and friendly hands seem to support me. Voices inaudible to all others I hear, or seem to hear. They whisper words of consolation, of hope, of confidence. They say, or seem to say to me: 'Feeble champion of the right, hold not back; remember that the race is not always to the swift nor the battle to the strong; remember that in a just cause a single pebble from the brook was enough in the sling of the young shepherd.' "

Despite his resolution, the counsel was soon compelled to beg the indulgence of the court, and an adjournment was taken until the morrow. The next morning, he proceeded for awhile until forced to ask permission that a young friend present might relieve him "by reading from his brief." His friend read for him during the main part of the session, but towards its close he resumed and concluded. The written argument, in which there is very little new, it is not necessary to go over; but we cannot refrain from giving the noble tribute to Andrew Johnson with which the orator closed. Its concluding paragraph touches a higher mark of eloquence than any other utterance on the trial.

"Now, listen for a moment to one who, perhaps, understands Andrew Johnson better than most of you; for his opportunities have been greater. When, nearly two years ago, he called me from the pursuits of professional life to take a chair in his cabinet I answered the call under a sense of public duty. I came here almost a stranger to him and to every member of his cabinet except Mr. Stanton. We had been friends for many years. Senators, need I tell you that all my tendencies are conservative? You, Mr. Chief Justice, who have known me for the third of a century, can bear me witness. Law, not arms, is my profession. From the moment that I was honored with a seat in the cabinet of Mr. Johnson not a step was taken that did not come under my observation, not a word was said that escaped my attention. I regarded him closely in cabinet, and in still more private and confidential conversation. I saw him often tempted with bad advice. I knew that evil counsellors were more than once around him. I observed him with the most intense anxiety. But never, in word, in deed, in thought, in action, did I discover in that man anything but loyalty to the Constitution and the laws. He stood firm as a rock against all temptation to abuse his own powers or to exercise those which were not conferred upon him. Steadfast and self-reliant in the midst of all difficulty, when dangers threatened, when temptations were strong, he looked only to the Constitution of his country and to the people.

"Yes, senators, I have seen that man tried as few have been tried. I have seen his confidence abused. I have seen him endure, day by day, provocations such as few men have ever been called upon to meet. No man could have met them with more sublime patience. Sooner or later, however, I knew the explosion must come. And when it did come my only wonder was that it had been so long delayed. Yes, senators, with all his faults, the President has been more sinned against than sinning. Fear not, then, to acquit him. The Constitution of the country is as safe in his hands from violence as it was in the hands of Washington. But if, senators, you condemn him, if you strip him of the robes of office, if you degrade him to the utmost stretch of your power, mark the prophecy: The strong arms of the people will be about him. They will find a way to raise him from any depths to which you may consign him, and we shall live to see him redeemed, and to hear the majestic voice of the people, 'well done, faithful servant; you shall have your reward!'

"But if, senators, as I cannot believe, but as has been boldly said with almost official sanction, your votes have been canvassed and the doom of the President is sealed, then let that judgment not be pronounced in this Senate Chamber; not here, where our Camillus in the hour of our greatest peril, single-handed, met and baffled the enemies of the republic; not here, where he stood faithful among the faithless; not here, where he fought the good fight for the Union and the Constitution; not in this chamber, whose walls echo with that clarion voice that, in the days of our greatest danger, carried hope and comfort to many a desponding heart, strong as an army with banners. No, not here. Seek out rather the darkest and gloomiest chamber in the subterranean recesses of this Capitol, where the cheerful light of day never enters. There erect the altar and immolate the victim."

On Monday, the fourth of May, there was a great rush to the capitol to hear the chief of the managers wind up the prosecution. Bingham was well known as a clever and forcible speaker, overflowing with rhetorical phrases, patriotic appeals and the still warm rallying cries of the war. Besides, he possessed a store of uproarious invective which he could turn on the momentary victim of his wrath with prodigious effect. The more ardent impeachers, therefore, packed the galleries to hear him demolish in Western style the too stately Curtis and trample over the too scholarly Evarts; but, especially, "to feast their ears on his excoriation of 'Andy.'" The task before him, however, was by no means easy, for not a single argument remained that had not been already threshed out backwards and forwards, three or four times. And he himself laboured under one heavy disadvantage which had not hampered his associates. Alone among the managers (except Wilson, who did not participate in the summing up) he had opposed the first impeachment movement, and the second, he had stifled in committee. Butler and Boutwell and Stevens and Williams scrupled not to sweep into the field of view the long series of charges which the adverse vote of the House had made obsolete; because they really believed the House had shirked its duty and that in these charges lay the real crimes of the President. But from Bingham, who had voted these charges either unproved, or undeserving the exercise of the impeaching power, any such license of expatiation was shut off. He, at least, from very shame, must confine himself to the law and the testimony, and not permit himself to wander among extraneous offences his own vote had condoned. Yet, notwithstanding these disadvantages, the manager proved equal to his task. In truth, he enjoyed two gifts from nature that probably made him unconscious of any difficulty. He could talk upon any subject for any length of time, and his self-sufficiency was so entire that the possibility of failure never entered his mind. It was not a necessary antecedent to the uninterrupted flow of his argument that he should believe in his case. A certain measure of sincerity, we may accord to Butler, Boutwell, Stevens and Williams, because, in one way or another, they believed that Andrew Johnson was guilty of a long series of offences for which he ought to be turned out of office. If they did not believe in the present case as made by the record, there could be no doubt of their belief in the case outside the record. Their speeches, consequently, in some parts at least, have the true ring. With Bingham it was not so. His vote on the first impeachment and his active opposition to the second demonstrate that, up to the twenty-first day of February, 1868, he believed the President guilty of no impeachable offence; and it was freely admitted by members more radical than Bingham, that, standing alone, the acts of the twenty-first of February were not such as to call forth the exercise of the impeaching power.

That this view is not too uncharitable, the speech of Bingham, taken as a whole, proves. The thought is constantly recurring to the reader's mind that the speaker does not, at heart, believe what he is saying. The speech is full of self-glorifying demolitions of positions the defendant had never taken up, of wholesale begging of the questions in dispute, of reiterations of propositions unaccompanied by proof and of refutations which do not refute, accompanied by vociferous assertions of there being no doubt whatever about the propositions and nothing whatever left of the defence. At the threshold of his address he protests that he comes to the argument "in no mere partisan spirit, in no spirit of resentment or prejudice"; and immediately proceeds to falsify this protest by dragging before the court "the disgraceful part which Andrew Johnson had played here upon the tribune of the Senate on the 4th day of March, 1865";—an incident, not relevant to the issue, not comprehended in the proof, and to which none but the bitterest partisan would have permitted himself to allude. To a certain extent he does respect the barrier raised by his previous votes, and takes no long flight into events antedating the twenty-first of February. Nevertheless, he will not be tied to that fatal date. He cannot go back; therefore he must go forward. Debarred from the past, he launches into the future. According to the manager, the crime the Senate is trying is not what the President did on the twenty-first nor what he did before that day, but the crime consists in the defence he sets up now.

"The fact is we are passing upon the question whether the President may not, at his pleasure, and without peril to his official position, set aside and annul both the Constitution and the laws of the United States, and in his great office inaugurate anarchy in the land. . . .

"No matter what demagogues may say of it outside this chamber, no matter what retained counsel may say of it inside this chamber, that is the issue; and the recording angel of history has already struck it into the adamant of the past, there to remain forever; and upon that issue, senators, you and the House of Representatives will stand or fall before the tribunal of the future. That is the issue. It is all there is of it. It is what is embraced in the articles of impeachment. It is all that is embraced in them. In spite of the technicalities, in spite of the lawyer's tricks, in spite of the futile pleas that have been interposed here in the President's defence, that is the issue. It is the head and front of Andrew Johnson's offending, that he has assumed to himself the executive prerogative of interpreting the Constitution and deciding upon the validity of the laws at his pleasure, and suspending them and dispensing with their execution. . . . The man who has heard this prolonged discussion running through days and weeks, who does not understand this to be the plain, simple proposition, made in the hearing of senators, insisted upon as the President's defence, is one of those unfortunates whom even a thrush might pity, to whom God in his providence has denied the usual measure of that intellectual faculty which we call reason."

This defence means, he claims, that the courts at the last have a supervising power over the power of impeachment vested in the House and over the power to try vested in the Senate. "On this proposition I am willing to stand, defying any man here or elsewhere to challenge it successfully. The position assumed by the accused means that or it means nothing." "Just nothing." All day long, the first day, he rings the changes on the enormity of this defence—"the monstrous plea interposed for the first time in our history"—striking the top of his compass in such a note as this:

"The Constitution itself, according to this assumption, is at his mercy, as well as the laws, and the people of the United States are to stand by and be mocked and derided in their own Capitol when, in accordance with the express provision of their Constitution, they bring him to the bar of the Senate to answer for such a crime than which none greater ever was committed since the day when the first crime was committed upon this planet as it sprung from the hand of the Creator; that crime which covered one manly brow with the ashy paleness and terrible beauty of death, and another with the damning blotch of fratricide!"

This monstrous claim "is the defence and the whole defence of the President." "It cannot be otherwise. It is written in his answer. It is written in the arguments of his counsel printed and laid upon your tables. No mortal man can evade it. It is all there is of it."

Bingham goes farther than any of his associates had ventured, in boldly denying that in any case, no matter how extreme, the President could be justified in protecting the Constitution against the laws;—for example, not even against "a law declaring he shall not be Commander-in-Chief of the Army, a law declaring that he shall not exercise the pardoning power in any case whatever." The President in no event is to interfere. That is for the people to do by repealing the law. The air of condescension with which John A. Bingham speaks of Thomas Jefferson, whose opinions on this subject happened to clash with his own, is characteristic:

"I am not disposed to cast reproach upon Mr. Jefferson. I know well that he was not one of the framers of the Constitution. I know well that he was not one of the builders of the fabric of American empire. While he contributed much to work out the emancipation of the American people from the control and domination of British rule and deserves well of his country, *one (!)** of the authors of the Declaration of Independence, yet I know well enough that his opinions on that subject are not accepted at this day by the great body of the American people and find no place in the authoritative and commanding writers upon the text of your Constitution."

We cannot follow the manager in his review of the articles and the evidence; nothing novel or noteworthy being developed. It was not, indeed, to hear expositions of articles or demonstrations of guilt, that his enthusiastic admirers in the galleries and on the floor exultingly followed him through three long days, and went about extolling the performance as "a splendid speech." The supremely confident bearing of the speaker, the swelling tones of his voice rising higher and higher as he piled one "I demand to know" on top of another, and the graceful sweep of his gestures carried along the thin thread of his reasoning in a kind of momentary triumph. But for the reader, alas! all these superficial adjuncts are absent, and the speech lies bare in all its intrinsic vapidity. To compare it with a piece of close-wrought logic such as the argument of Curtis, or with a plain terse specimen of forensic argumentation such as that of Groesbeck, or with a philosophic oration like that of Evarts, is impossible because it belongs to a different species of address. On the other hand, comparing it with the arguments of his associates, it falls below Mr. Boutwell's statesmanlike method of arranging his propositions; with all its affected bitterness it has not the genuine stinging power of Stevens; notwith-

* Italics and punctuation mine.

standing its frequent outbursts of patriotic fervour, it does not rise to the height of feeling we still detect beneath the ornate periods of Williams; with the hollow tone that runs through its most passionate invective, it lacks the downright vigour which Butler's earnestness lent to his blows.

Overlooking particular arguments and matters of detail, the central aim of the speech, as we have already pointed out, is directed against what the speaker brands as "the monstrous claim," put forward by the President, of the right to test the constitutionality of a law in the courts. With a fierce attack upon it he began; with a final desperate charge upon it he ended:

> "Is it not in vain, I ask you that the people have thus vindicated by battle the supremacy of their own Constitution and laws, if, after all, their President is permitted to suspend their laws and dispense with the execution thereof at pleasure, and defy the power of the people to bring him to trial and punishment before the only tribunal authorized by the Constitution to try him? That is the issue which is presented before the Senate for decision by these articles of impeachment."

It was the same defence, he continued,—this right to dispense with the laws—that Charles I and James II set up to justify their usurpation. The one lost his head, the other his throne. Surely such a defence "ought to cost Andrew Johnson his office."

> "May God forbid that the future historian shall record of this day's proceedings, that by reason of the failure of the legislative power of the people to triumph over the

usurpations of an apostate President through the defection of the Senate of the United States, the just and great fabric of American empire fell and perished from the earth! . . . Pardon me for saying it; I speak it in no offensive spirit; I speak if from a sense of duty; I utter but my own conviction, and desire to place it upon the record, that for the Senate to sustain any such plea, would, in my judgment, be a gross violation of the already violated Constitution and laws of a free people. . . . I put away the possibility that the Senate of the United States, equal in dignity to any tribunal in the world, is capable of recording any such decision even upon the petition and prayer of this accused and guilty President. . . . I ask you to consider that we stand this day pleading for the violated majesty of the law, by the graves of half a million of martyred hero-patriots who made death beautiful by the sacrifice of themselves for their country, the Constitution and the laws, and who, by their sublime example, have taught us that all must obey the law; that none are above the law, that no man lives for himself alone, but each for all; that some must die that the State may live; that the citizen is at best but for to-day, while the Commonwealth is for all time; and that position, however high, patronage, however powerful, cannot be permitted to shelter crime to the peril of the republic."

These final words, devoid as they are of any genuine spirit-stirring power, drove the crowded galleries frantic. To the grand perorations of Groesbeck and Stanbery they listened in silence. They now broke out into noisy and disorderly manifestations of approbation. Men and women rose to their feet cheering, clapping hands and waving handkerchiefs. The appeals of the Chief Justice for order were greeted with laughs of derision and hisses of hate. The galleries were ordered cleared, and the court sat silent and shamed, while the people, the innocent with the guilty—even the reporters of the press—were slowly driven out. Thus ended this celebrated trial. The case was now wholly withdrawn into the bosom of the court. The next day, behind closed doors, a rule was adopted fixing Monday, the eleventh, for deliberation on the articles and the day following for the final vote.

[The authority for the statements and extracts contained in this chapter being, of course, the official report of the trial, a more particular reference was considered unnecessary.]

CHAPTER VII

The Acquittal

To the New Hampshire Republican convention which met on the fourth of May to elect delegates to the national convention to nominate General Grant, Washburne sent a telegram: "Bingham is making a splendid speech. All looks well. The Constitution will be vindicated, and the recreant put out of the White House before the end of the week"; and Butler regaled the same body with similar tidings put into poetic form: "The removal of the great obstruction is certain. Wade and prosperity are sure to come with the apple-blossoms."* But the confidence of the majority of the leaders in the success of the movement was not so overweening. Butler himself was more than half convinced that his pet charge would have to go by the board. The Emory article, also, it was almost universally admitted, was demolished beyond reparation. Even the conspiracy articles depended for their life upon the rhetoric of Bingham, who, since his memorable achievement in the assassination "Conspiracy Trial," was looked up to as an expert in dealing with that species of crime. Before the arguments were over it was generally felt that the prosecution must rely for conviction on the charges of attempting to remove Stanton and of appointing Thomas, involved in the first three articles, or, in case

* See Prefatory note.

the unlucky proviso stood in the way, then upon the enigmatic eleventh which had been concocted at the last moment for just such an emergency.

Great was the uneasiness over particular senators. The test votes, taken while the court was being organized and during the trial, were carefully studied, and, at the close of the case for the prosecution, the Republican politicians were able to spell out twenty-nine senators sure to vote guilty on one or more articles, including Wade who thus far had abstained from voting. This left thirteen Republican senators whose votes were favourable to the President in a majority of instances, thus casting doubt over their attitude on the final question. At the close of the testimony, when the yeas and nays on the closest vote excluding the evidence of the members of the Cabinet were subjected to scrutiny, the twenty-six senators who voted in the negative, together with the five not voting (Conkling, Morton, Nye, Sumner and Wade) making thirty-one, were counted as solid for conviction. Only five more were necessary. Of the eleven Republican senators who voted in the affirmative, Fessenden, who opposed the resolution censuring the President, was almost despaired of; Grimes and Trumbull were impervious to outside influence; Anthony was an intimate friend of the Chief Justice, and Sprague was his son-in-law; Sherman was committed adversely on the Cabinet proviso; the two West Virginia senators were in the habit of taking opposite sides on momentous questions; Henderson, Fowler and Ross were silent and claimed by both the President's counsel and the managers; yet out of these the indispensable five must come.

From the outset, the Republican representatives never made any secret of their practice of bringing party influence to bear upon members of the court. Secret meetings of senators, representatives, office-holders, office-seekers, party bosses and party leaders were held, in which the result of the trial was canvassed with all the eagerness of a party conclave preliminary to a nominating convention. In truth, the entire impeachment trial was, in effect, as much a convention of the Republican party to put Andrew Johnson out, as the assembly to meet in Chicago was a convention of the Republican party to put General Grant in. Indeed, but few of the majority senators thought it obligatory to hold themselves aloof from discussing the merits of the case out of court. On the day the impeachment was voted, senators were seen on the floor of the House urging the representatives to do their duty; and during the trial senators kept lists on which the doubtful judges were noted in order to extort from them a declaration of opinion. When the case was closed and the court about to deliberate in secret, the suspense over members who, in spite of every importunity, persisted in maintaining silence, rose to such a pitch that the leaders threw off the last vestige of decorum, went into caucus and organized a far-reaching combination to coerce the suspected judges into submission to their party's decree. Detectives kept a secret eye on their residences and on the residence of the Chief Justice. Spies mingled in the social circles they frequented, to catch some unguarded word, and agents were employed to pester them with every species of importunity to disclose their real intentions. They were threatened in the party press; their constituents were stirred up to threaten them from home; letters were sent to them from all quarters filled with threats of political ostracism and even of assassination, in the event of their treason. Crowds of professional bettors flocked to Washington, and during the week before the eleventh much money was staked on the result—the odds being in favour of acquittal. On the eighth, Stevens reported a bill for the admission of Arkansas under her Africanized government, and when the minority protested against his attempt to put it on its passage before they had time to examine the constitution of the state, avowed: "There are reasons which I do not think it proper or necessary to mention now, why this bill should be considered, passed and sent to the Senate before next Monday"; as though it might be necessary in the last resort to add two more senators to the court.

On Monday (the eleventh) after the galleries were cleared and the doors were closed, the Chief Justice read the views he had prepared at the request of the Senate upon the mode of putting the question on the several articles of impeachment, in which, among other things, in answer to a suggestion that the eleventh article be divided into clauses and the vote taken clause by clause, he stated "that he found himself unable to divide the article" because the "several facts are so connected that they make but one allegation, and they are charged as constituting one misdemeanor." "The single substantive matter charged," according to the Chief

Justice, "is the attempt to prevent the execution of the Tenure-of-office act; and the other facts are alleged either as introductory and exhibiting the general purpose, or as showing the means contrived in furtherance of that attempt." This matter being disposed of, Sumner pressed forward a rule, offered by him some days before (April 25), providing, in case of conviction, that judgment of removal from office which necessarily followed should be pronounced forthwith, but that "any further judgment shall be on the order of the Senate." He had, also, offered an amendment to the rules that "any further judgment," the infliction of which was optional with the Senate, *i. e.,* disqualification from office, "shall be determined by a majority of the members present." In short, this judge of the High Court was already devising a way to deprive the convicted and deposed President of his last resource—an appeal to the people. The proposed order was debated until the hour fixed for the final deliberation on the verdict (eleven o'clock), when action upon it was necessarily suspended and the matter never came up again. From the hour mentioned until eleven o'clock at night, with the exception of twenty minutes recess at about two and of two hours recess at half-past five, the proceedings were shrouded in almost impenetrable secrecy, while the concentrated anxiety of the whole nation was symbolized by the crowds surging around the closed doors. Under the rules, every senator might speak on the articles, but no longer than fifteen minutes and but once; he might file, however, a written opinion within two days after the vote was taken. An effort had been made to secure the ultimate publicity of the discussion by allowing the official reporters to take down the speeches, but the senators would not consent; so that what individual senators took part and what any of them said can only be gathered from reports, more or less reliable, current at the time, and the few indications the opinions, afterwards filed, afford. During the two intervals of recess and after the session was over at midnight, the released senators were beset by groups of curious people imploring information. And the stalwarts, whose opinions were known and who were themselves active in electioneering their less forward associates, were not scrupulous in keeping the secrets of the tribunal. The first item of interesting news that leaked out was that the first article was in peril. Sherman had declared that in the face of his record he could not vote for it, and Howe followed him with a similar declaration. Then it was reported that Edmunds and Stewart had come out in support of it; but the effect of this report was immediately neutralized by the counter-report that Van Winkle and Willey agreed with Sherman and Howe. The President's stock rose. One of the many telegrams sent out described the situation as follows: "Hell going on in Senate now." Later on came the decisive information that Fessenden, Grimes and Trumbull had delivered opinions favourable to the President on all the articles. At the two hours recess for dinner, it was ascertained that Sherman and Howe, notwithstanding their falling away on the first, were for conviction on some of the other articles and it was rumoured that Willey would vote for the second; so that there was a momentary reaction; but it was soon authoritatively stated that Henderson had spoken against the first eight articles before he was cut off by the expiration of his time. As the senators flocked out to dinner Henderson was seen, in company with the Chief Justice, Reverdy Johnson and Sprague, to enter Sprague's carriage, and all were driven to the Chief Justice's residence where Henderson dined. The spirits of the Impeachers fell. "We are sold out," Butler came into the House exclaiming, and the majority exhibited premonitory symptoms of a panic. They were anxious to adjourn over the national convention (to meet on the twentieth), so as to enable members to attend, but in the dubious straits they were now in they knew not what to do. First, by the vote of the Speaker on a tie, they laid the resolution to adjourn over on the table. Then they took it up again and adopted it by a majority of one. Stevens reported from the reconstruction committee a bill for the admission of North Carolina, South Carolina, Louisiana, Georgia and Alabama; and it was made the special order for the next Wednesday, so that the prospect of ten more senators, as well as the two from Arkansas, might be before the eyes of the judges on the morrow. During the night session, it leaked out that Harlan, Conness, Pomeroy and Morton had spoken strongly for conviction on the principal articles; but this, being no more than was expected, did little to allay the prevailing disquietude; while, coupled with this report came another, that Fowler talked so unreliably as to be almost given over, and Ross kept up the same ominous silence he had persisted in all day. At midnight, the impeachers were assured that, despite the malign influence of Chase, Anthony and Sprague were sound on at least one of the articles, but even, with those senators, they were unable to make out a list of the indispensable thirty-six without including Willey and Ross. There was no sleep that night for the leaders of the impeachment, whether in the House or in the Senate. Howard, whose vote, as they now saw, they could not do without, had been absent from the secret session, and it was announced that he was too ill to be present on the morrow. An adjournment was therefore imperative; and in the meantime the heaviest pressure from all quarters was at once to be brought to bear upon every senator whom they had the slightest hope still to secure.

Before the court assembled on the twelfth, and when as yet postponement was formally undetermined, the Republican representatives in Congress from Missouri laid siege in due form to their backsliding senator. John B. Henderson—a Douglas Democrat in 1860—was sent to the Senate in 1862 to fill the vacancy caused by the expulsion of Trusten Polk—gone over to the secessionists; and, in the following year, was elected for a full term. He was one of the majority of Republican senators, who in the winter of 1864-5 sustained President Lincoln in his purpose of admitting Louisiana and other reconstructed states—a purpose frustrated by the tactics of Sumner. He had, consequently, preserved at least a remnant of his conservative tendencies during the succeeding period of white disfranchisement and negro enfranchisement in his state. A man of superior ability and unblemished character; anxious to preserve harmony between the administration and his party; never indulging in abuse of the President; planting himself from the first upon a policy, original with himself, that the states should be allowed to regulate the suffrage, subject only to a constitutional restriction that in prescribing the qualifications of the voter there should be no distinction on account of race or colour; his speeches in the Senate, while justly liable to no charge of infidelity to his party, presented in one aspect a refreshing contrast to those of his impetuous colleague and the reckless band of fiery radicals that the doctored constituencies of his state had sent to the House. And yet a studious observer of his career can discover that his conservatism halted upon one foot; that, when it came to the decisive point, the senator frequently supported by vote measures he deprecated in speech. He seemed hampered by the changed condition of affairs in his state. He said he did not believe in such legislation as the Freedmen's Bureau act, yet he voted for it. The fourteenth amendment ran counter to his favourite remedy concerning suffrage, yet he supported it. He recoiled from lending active aid to such an iniquity as the expulsion of Stockton; yet by voting against postponement he indirectly contributed to its success. And his trimming did him no good eventually with the zealots that swarmed in his state. His term was to expire in the ensuing spring, and he must have been aware that the legislature of his state would select a more daring radical than he could pretend to be. His course on the Impeachment was typical of the temper of mind which his embarrassing situation superinduced. He did not vote on the non-concurrence with the suspension of Stanton, but it was stated he was paired with Hendricks in its favour. On the resolution declaring that the President had no power to remove Stanton, he did not vote. During the trial, on the test votes for and against the admissibility of evidence, he was always with the conservatives. Since the close of the case he had expressed to one or more of the favourers of Impeachment his belief that the President ought to be convicted, and that, while he could not support the main articles, he was inclined to vote for the eleventh; and, the afternoon before in the secret session, as we have seen, he had consumed his fifteen minutes in delivering an opinion against the first eight articles; the ninth and tenth, it was to be presumed, would fare no better at his hands. The incident of his going to Chase's house for dinner had grown in bulk during the night, and it was believed in the morning that, following the carriage that took him there, was a hack hired by Chase, containing four more senators—Fessenden, Trumbull, Grimes and (as it was variously stated) Fowler or Van Winkle—who, also, alighted at the Chief Justice's and dined there; the guests being plied with wine and arguments against impeachment while consulting with their host concerning the organization of a third party.*

Such was the situation, when on the morning of the twelfth, five of the eight Republican members of the House from Missouri, together with a member of the Missouri legislature to whom Henderson had ex-

* New York *Sun* correspondence of May 11.

pressed the equivocal opinion mentioned above, invaded the rooms of their wavering senator. They told him that the position he had taken on the Impeachment question was against the almost unanimous wish of the "Union" party of their state, and that violence and bloodshed, they feared, would follow the President's acquittal. So peremptory were they in their language, that Henderson must have lost his self-possession, judging by the proposition he made in reply. After saying that he could not as a man of honour vote contrary to the opinion he had expressed in the Senate on the first eight articles, that he was no less decided in his judgment against the sufficiency of the ninth and tenth, and was in doubt only as to the last, he offered to telegraph his resignation to the governor who could without delay appoint his successor, so that by four o'clock that afternoon they would have a senator to their liking, whose credentials would be here in time for the vote on Saturday (the day to which it had been informally decided the court would adjourn). Inquiries were naturally made whether the new appointee, not having sat during the trial, would be allowed to vote on the judgment; and it appears that the senator assured the delegation that such a course was legal, and there would be no difficulty on that question. The representatives, however, were not satisfied on this point and protested that they did not want his resignation, what they wanted was his vote; on those articles on which he had expressed an opinion, he might withhold his vote, but on the eleventh and on any others he might favour he could vote in the affirmative. The senator requested his friends to retire, hold a consultation among themselves, and advise him what they thought proper to do under the circumstances. In compliance with this singular request, the visiting members withdrew, called to their aid their colleagues, and the following letter was sent the same morning:

Washington, May 12, 1868.

Sir:

On a consultation of the Republican members of the House of Representatives from Missouri, in view of your position on the Impeachment Articles, we ask you to withhold your vote on any article upon which you cannot vote affirmatively. This request is made because we believe the safety of the loyal people of the United States demands the immediate removal of Andrew Johnson from the office of President of the United States.

Respectfully,

George W. Anderson
William A. Pile
Benjamin F. Loan C. A. Newcomb
John J. Benjamin Joseph W. McClurg
Joseph J. Gravely.

Hon. John B. Henderson,
United States Senate.

The court convened at the usual hour, Henderson in his seat. Chandler announced that his colleague (Howard) had been delirious all day yesterday and was now so ill as to be unable to be present; and, as was anticipated, the court adjourned until Saturday. That evening, another interview took place between Henderson and his colleagues of the House (except Anderson). The senator told them that he could not comply with their request without a degree of humiliation and shame to which he was satisfied they would not wish to subject him. They agreed to reconsider their request, but still insisted that duty required the senator to cast a vote of guilty on one article, if that vote were found indispensable to secure a conviction. Henderson pointed out the difficulty attending this suggestion; senators were so reticent he could not ascertain their position, and they were liable to change their minds at any moment before the final vote was taken. He exhibited a list of thirty-six senators, beside himself and Wade, who, he thought, would vote for conviction on the eleventh article, and thereby the President might be removed without his vote. The delegation assured him that conviction was all they wanted, and that he need not resign unless his vote was absolutely indispensable and he could not bring himself to cast it for the eleventh article. He promised to ascertain the probable event on one or two articles; see senators Anthony, Sprague, Willey and Van Winkle, and, if they would agree to vote for the eleventh article, then the desire of his Missouri friends would be accomplished and he would retain his seat. He felt, so he said, inclined to vote for the single clause of the eleventh article which charged that the President attempted to prevent Stanton from resuming the office of Secretary of War, but the Senate had wrongly refused to permit a vote to be taken on the separate clauses, and a vote for the article entire would seem to endorse the Emory article which no one approved; he would give them his final conclusions by twelve o'clock to-morrow.

The next day he received the following telegram:

St. Louis, May 13, 1868.

Hon. John B. Henderson:

There is intense excitement here. Meeting called for tomorrow night. Can your friends hope that you will vote for the eleventh article? If so, all will be well.

E. W. Fox.

Samuel S. Cox, an old-time political comrade of Henderson's, at this time out of Congress and residing in the city of New York, who had been sent for on the idea that he might influence the senator in the President's favour, happened to call on him just after the receipt of the foregoing message. As Cox states: "His sense of justice had been affronted by this. In this mood the writer found him. He seemed to want advice and counsel. It was not long before the writer was requested to pen and send a telegram" in answer.

E. W. Fox, St. Louis, Mo.

Say to my friends that I am sworn to do impartial justice according to law and evidence, and I will try to do it like an honest man.

J. B. Henderson.

This act seems to have restored his usual sense of honour and propriety, and he wrote a letter to the representatives of his state, informing them that he could not ascertain the probable outcome of the trial; that he could not, consistently with the obligations of his oath, resign; and that he had resolved to remain at his post and to do his duty as it was given him to know it.

"If I resign and a successor should come, perhaps a proper sense of delicacy would prevent him from violating every precedent on this subject by casting a vote at all. . . . If he voted affirmatively and thus secured conviction, this manner of obtaining conviction would likely neutralize in the end every advantage to be derived from impeachment."*

Following the example of the Missouri delegation, the eleven Republican members of the House from Illinois held a meeting and discussed a proposition, supported, doubtless, by Logan, Farnsworth and Washburne, to unite in a letter to Trumbull "with a view to influence his vote for conviction, or of inducing him to withhold his vote if he could not vote for conviction." But, in this instance, so much opposition was made by five of the delegation that no letter was sent—a failure, to which the apprehension that such a missive would have met with a sterner reception than the one sent to Henderson, may have contributed.†

The method of coercing wavering senators by pressure from home was set on foot systematically by an organization of Republican members of Congress called "the Union Congressional Committee." Senators as well as representatives belonged to it, and senators as well as representatives showed no hesitation in undertaking work of this kind. Robert C. Schenck was chairman, and, on the twelfth, sent to every state having a

* *Globe,* 2d Sess. 40th Cong., p. 2471. Henderson's testimony before Com. of Investigation. S. S. Cox's Three Decades, p. 594. Howland's and Gravely's testimony before Com. of Investigation, quoted in Butler's report of managers, Cong. Doc., No. 75.

† As to Trumbull see *Globe, id.*, p. 2529.

senator whose position was not definitely ascertained the following circular telegram:

Washington, D. C. May 12, 1868.

Great danger to the peace of the country and the Republican cause if impeachment fails. Send to your senators public opinion by resolutions, letters and delegations.

Robert C. Schenck, Chairman.

And they came—from Maine, from Illinois, from Kansas, from Rhode Island, from West Virginia, from Tennessee—resolutions, letters, telegrams, delegations, all demanding the conviction of the President and denouncing the least hesitation on the part of his Republican triers. Even Holden, the first of Andrew Johnson's provisional governors—rewarded for his desertion with the governorship of his Africanized state—joined in hounding on the impeachment and flashed over the wire the words, "Strike the usurper from his seat." The general conference of the Methodist Episcopal Church being in session at Chicago on the fourteenth of May—composed of nine bishops and two hundred and forty-two delegates "representing," as was stated, "more than eleven hundred thousand members" —after referring in a preamble to "painful rumors in circulation that partly by unworthy jealousies and partly by corrupt influence, pecuniary and otherwise, most actively employed, efforts are being made to influence senators improperly and prevent them from performing their high duty," thought it no blasphemy unanimously to "appoint an hour of prayer from nine to ten A. M. to-morrow to invoke humbly and earnestly the mercy of God upon our nation and beseech Him to save our senators from error, and so influence them that their decision shall be in truth and righteousness." The action of this powerful ecclesiastical organization was telegraphed immediately to the seat of government, and on the same day its example was followed by the African M. E. Church in conference at Washington; the coloured brethren, however, employing no pious circumlocution but addressing their prayer for the conviction of the President, not to the Deity, but directly to the Senate.* The managers, also, in this stirring campaign of intimidation could not be idle. Their legitimate work being done, they organized themselves into an Inquisition. Certain newspaper correspondents were so positive about the opinion of certain senators and the consequent acquittal of the President as to arouse painful suspicions; the Chief Justice had given another dinner, and several senators were tracked coming away from the entertainment at a late hour; and a secret examination of reporters for the press was immediately begun. Stanton, of course, was at work day and night. Every rumour of defection focussed in the War Office; and, sitting there in seclusion, the secretary marked down each doubtful senator. A military officer, likely to be of influence because of previous intimacy with the suspected man, was summoned to headquarters and given his instructions. Generals, deprived of their command and sore against the President, were told that the friends of Andrew Johnson were engaged in tamper-

* See Prefatory note and *Globe*, 2d Sess. 40th Cong., speech of Doolittle, pp. 2521, 2525.

ing with some particular senator, and thereby induced to go and tamper with him in their turn. Grant, with habitual caution, kept silent in the background; but it was published abroad everywhere that the prospective candidate for President was "of the opinion that Andrew Johnson ought to be removed." All his old cronies in the army proclaimed it. Logan made no secret of it. Washburne was now among the fiercest of the fierce in pushing on the movement. The silent, undeviating course of Roscoe Conkling on every question arising during the trial is strong evidence of Grant's inveteracy against the President. From the very first day, Conkling displayed a stubborn hostility against the accused entirely foreign to his character as a statesman and a lawyer, and wholly unaccountable upon any other hypothesis than that he was disposed to comply with the wishes of the man whose devoted supporter he was and continued to be afterwards through every vicissitude of fortune. He said nothing. He delivered no opinion. He filed none. He voted guilty *sans phrase.* The one instance, in which he veered round to the conservatives on the question of the admission of the letters of the Cabinet officers corroboratory of the President's version of the colloquy between himself and General Grant, tells the same story; he would not have his hero appear to shrink from any testimony seemingly adverse to him on a question of veracity.

The inclinations of the General of the army once ascertained determined the direction of the efforts of a host of officers. Aides-de-camp, they rushed hither and thither as if upon the battle-field, delivering reports concerning the whereabouts and doings of certain senators, or directing their fire directly upon the men themselves, or laying down the lines of the siege to be made upon them. Never, perhaps, were men subjected to such an ordeal of pressure as were the four or five senators reported doubtful during the days that elapsed from the Monday when the Senate deliberated, to the Saturday when the Senate voted. Henderson having been given up, the West Virginia senators were allowed no peace. Willey, it was reported, was sure on the second article, but Van Winkle seemed wrapped up in impenetrable dubitation.* Both, it was said, were engaged in writing opinions without having reached any conclusion. It was suspected that, if both votes of the state were necessary to prevent conviction, both would be forthcoming; whereas, if one would suffice for acquittal, the other would go the other way. At length, it was announced that Van Winkle must have written himself into a state of mind favourable to the President, as he was consorting with Trumbull and dining with Chase. A determined effort was then made to rescue Willey who, it was discovered, had been able to write nothing, and showed symptoms of a teachable disposition. He was a prominent Methodist, and it was said that that Church had him prominently in her eye when she "unanimously" resorted to the Throne of Grace. He was kept under constant care, supervision

* Pomeroy testified before the managers that Van Winkle told him in the interval between Monday and Saturday that "his mind was to vote for conviction on the eleventh article and was preparing an opinion to sustain his vote." Butler's Report, p. 32.

and drill up to the last hour; and, after all, went to the testing a riddle to his trainers and a perplexity to the believer in the efficacy of prayer.

Senator Fowler was subjected to a somewhat different course of treatment. An early offspring of the Brownlow government, his vote had been considered from the first a fixed asset of the party. But it turned out that his electors had not been sufficiently circumspect. He was not a man very easy to rule. A professor in a Nashville college, a pious man, an unostentatious citizen, on the Union and slavery he had convictions of his own which at the outbreak of secession whirled him into unlooked-for prominence in the stormy atmosphere of his state. But, although after their going over to negro suffrage, he made himself agreeable to the Brownlowites by his advocacy of that measure, he still cherished an admiring remembrance of Andrew Johnson's career as a Unionist and Military Governor, and he could not shake off the conviction that it was impossible so heroic a patriot should have become the traitor the senator's party associates represented him to be. Great were the surprise and indignation of the radicals, in and out of his state, when, during the trial, he was found voting with the conservative senators on incidental questions, and, after the trial, either keeping a suspicious silence, or talking in a manner most exasperating by reason of its inconclusiveness. Him, therefore, the official manipulators of the senatorial laggards, wisely concluding that ordinary methods of persuasion would be thrown away, undertook to scare back into the ranks by a disinterment of his record. As long ago as the tenth of

January—at a meeting of the Union Congressional Committee—it was recalled that Fowler made certain remarks on the subject of impeachment. His words were not taken down at the time—the minutes disclosing only the bare fact that certain senators and representatives had spoken. To a copy of the minutes of this meeting, William D. Kelley of the House now appended a report of Fowler's remarks; certifying that it was his "recollection of their tenor and phraseology," and, further, that the senator had "frequently pressed the same views upon him and upon others in his presence." He makes Fowler advocate the impeachment and removal of Andrew Johnson as absolutely necessary to prevent bloodshed in the South, restore peace to the country, and the enforcement of the laws. The accuracy of his version is certified to by Robert C. Schenck and seven others who were present at the meeting. This document*—minutes, speech and certifying signatures—was printed; a copy sent to Fowler on the evening of the fifteenth, and the next morning—the day the vote was to be taken—it appeared in the radical organs in flaming colours. The implicated senator afterwards denounced the speech as a forgery; declaring in the Senate: "I did not utter one single sentence that Kelley has coined. He neither gives the spirit nor the connection nor the object of my remarks"; stating further that his allusion to impeachment was only for the purpose of stimulating the committee to more strenuous efforts to carry the

* The document will be found in the speech of the senator cited *infra* and in Butler's Report of Managers, printed as No. 75, pp. 28–9.

state of Alabama; that, since Congress had failed to impeach Andrew Johnson who was a·man of power and desired the success of his policy, it was the duty of the committee to combat him in the open field of the state; that if they failed to carry the state the fault would be their own. Whatever may be the truth on this particular matter in dispute, the underlying motive of the whole proceeding becomes manifest when we hear the balance of the senator's story:

> "A few hours after the forgery came to me, three persons visited my rooms to poll my vote. I detected their sinister motives by a false and contradictory statement of one of them, and the arrogance, insincerity and weak presumption of another. I shall not stop to speak of the ungentlemanly conduct of the chaplain of the company, who seemed thoroughly in the interest of the revolutionary leaders. Those men left disappointed. I met the reverend meddler the next morning in the Capitol, and he threatened the investigation of the inquisition, the exposure and expulsion from the Senate. I will only add that the same threat had been made by others."

They might badger the Tennessee senator; they could get no satisfaction out of him. Over him, to the last, they hovered between hope and fear. For, as he historically stated: "I expressed no opinion of any article involved in the trial of the President until the Chief Justice asked my decision."*

With Grimes, Fessenden and Trumbull outspoken for acquittal; with Henderson despaired of; with Van Winkle and Willey see-sawing between "Guilty" and

* Fowler's speech, *Globe,* 2d Sess. 40th Cong., pp. 4507, 4510.

"Not Guilty"; with Fowler stubbornly non-committal: the full brunt of the struggle turned at last on the one remaining doubtful senator—Edmund G. Ross. That a senator from Kansas should ever be a source of apprehension to the radicals seemed like a malignant stroke of fate. As Sumner testified before the managers: "It was a very clear case, especially for a Kansas man. . . . I did not think that a Kansas man could quibble against his country."* Just at the close of the first session of the thirty-ninth Congress (July 25, 1866), Ross took his seat in the Senate at the same time with Joseph H. Fowler. He was appointed by the governor to fill the place of James H. Lane, who died by his own hand on the eleventh of that month, and who enjoyed in life so curious an intimacy with Andrew Johnson; and he was subsequently elected by the legislature to fill out Lane's unexpired term. We have his own authority for stating that he was "baptized in politics in the old Abolition party in 1844," and "led a colony to Kansas in 1856." He entered the ranks of the Union army as a private soldier, and served with gallantry and well-earned promotion during the war. He was unknown to the country at the time of his entrance into the Senate (he had then reached his fortieth year), and, since his admission, he had contented himself, except at an early period when he read a declaration of his adherence to the radical policy, in giving a silent vote for all the political measures of the Republicans; simply following in this respect the example of his older and more experienced colleague. The possibility of defection on his

* Butler's Report *ut supra*, p. 30.

part in the fight with the administration never dawned upon the mind of the most nervous radical. Yet, somehow, from the beginning of the pending impeachment, his conduct had been eccentric. When the Senate resolved to non-concur in the suspension of Stanton by a vote of thirty-five, including Fessenden, Fowler, Trumbull and Van Winkle, the Kansas senator, though in his seat, did not vote; owing, it was said at the time, to a quarrel with the Secretary of War. On the other hand, when the more decisive action declaring the removal of the same officer unlawful was taken, he voted with the majority. During the trial, on incidental questions he was so often found with the conservatives as to excite curiosity, though not so invariably as to excite alarm. When the trial was about half over (so Sumner testified) he approached that senator for the first time in his life and volunteered the information that, notwithstanding these equivocal votes, he expected to vote with Sumner in the end.* After the trial was over, he himself confessed in open Senate, "to having entertained doubts on the eleventh and other articles until a few days before the vote was taken," and then, as he expressed it, he resolved the question in his own mind by giving his country the benefit of his doubts; that it was his intention to support a portion of the articles—an intention he communicated to "numbers of those who approached him on the subject," but, he emphatically added, "no man had from me a positive assurance that I would vote for conviction or acquittal" before Thursday, the fourteenth.† Nevertheless, he was claimed by

* Butler's Report, *ut supra*, p. 30.

† Speech in *Globe*, 2d Sess. 40th Cong., p. 2599.

both sides with almost equal positiveness; and he certainly succeeded up to the very last in keeping both sides in a fever of suspense. During this week, Washington was crowded with all sorts of people from all parts of the country—every one intent upon the impending result; and this hitherto undistinguished senator moved along among them, the target of every eye; his rooms beset by his radical constituents, associates and friends wild to gain some satisfactory inkling of his mind. His outgoings and incomings, his companions and his convivialities, his breakfast, his dinner, his lodgings, were marked and set down in note-books; his name speeding over the wires, back and forth, to and from all points of the compass, and ringing from every one's mouth in all quarters of the swarming, simmering, half-delirious capital. Wrapped in the solitude of his own impenetrability, he calmly watched the raging eddies of which he was the centre. His political pedigree and his domestic affiliations were probed from top to bottom. It was discovered that from the time of his election, and even before, he was mixed up in some unexplained manner with the business of the Indian Bureau out in Kansas; that Thomas Ewing, Jr., who was the attorney of certain contractors for Indian supplies, was friendly to him; that Perry Fuller, an enterprising Indian agent and for a long time his friend and supporter, was the son-in-law of the woman at whose house he lodged, and whose remaining daughter, living at home, was Vinnie Ream, the sculptress, now engaged in modeling the statue of Abraham Lincoln, under a contract with the government, in a room furnished her in the crypt of the capitol. Browning, the Secretary of the Interior, in whose department was the Indian Bureau; Taylor of Tennessee, the Commissioner of Indian affairs by appointment of the President; Fuller and Ewing:—were all known as supporters of the President and ready to do their utmost for his acquittal. Miss Ream—hardly more than a girl when, in July, 1866, she was awarded her valuable contract—proved herself then an adept in the practice of influencing congressmen; the award passing the House without any opposition and the Senate by a large majority, in the face of the active hostility of Sumner and Howard, both of whom impugned the capacity and skill of the artist. It was bruited about that the Kansas senator was in the habit of frequenting her studio and talking of the impeachment, and that she was using her influence in persuading him to vote for acquittal; and, on the faith of these rumours, George W. Julian was commissioned by several of his fellow members to warn her against such a course of conduct. It was stated and restated on the floor of the House that Julian "threatened her that if she did not use her influence for conviction, it would be the worse for her." The threat Julian denied; but he admitted that he talked to her on the matter and that she denied the report of her mission, telling him Ross was going to vote for conviction, as Ross himself told him on the following day.*

At length, the leading impeachers could stand this suspense no longer. They determined in caucus (senators as well as representatives attending) to force the

* *Globe*, 2d Sess. 40th Cong., pp. 2674–5.

delinquent to speak. That stout radical, Samuel C. Pomeroy, known to fame in 1864 as the author of the "Pomeroy Circular" and, after the Credit-Mobilier scandal, under the sobriquet of "Subsidy Pom"—he must tackle his rebellious younger brother and teach him to obey the curb. It was on Wednesday, the thirteenth, that Pomeroy made his first attack. Noticing that his colleague had gone into the room of the sergeant-at-arms in the dangerous company of senator Trumbull and following him there, he found the two in animated conversation on the subject of impeachment. Waiting until the interview was over and Trumbull gone, he took Ross into a corner of the room and proceeded to put him to the question. He had provided himself with the printed list of senators commonly in use for taking the yeas and nays, and upon it he had noted opposite the name of every senator counted on for conviction, including his own, the articles it was supposed he intended to vote for. He commenced operations by asking his partner plumply and without apology, how he was going to vote on the impeachment. Ross replied that he was uncertain, that he would probably vote for some of the articles and not for the others. Pomeroy said that he was canvassing the Senate, that he had got the names of thirty-five senators, pledged, every one of them in their own handwriting, for conviction, and that he wanted Ross's pledge to make conviction sure. Ross asking to see the list, the veteran canvasser produced it; when, among other names, Ross noticed his own set down for conviction on the first, second, third, eighth and eleventh articles. Upon his expressing surprise at this summary disposition of his vote, Pomeroy claimed that from previous conversations he supposed those were the articles his colleague would vote for. Perceiving that all the marks on the paper were in the same handwriting, and suspecting therefore that the whole thing was guess-work and a plan to entrap him into a written committal for conviction, Ross with some asperity repudiated his colleague's authority to put him down on the list at all either for or against conviction, and then explicitly defined his position as follows:

> "That I should probably vote for conviction on the first article, as that, in my judgment, contained all there was in the whole bill of indictment; that the eighth I should not support, and that as to all the others enumerated, I was undecided; that their fate depended very much on that of the first article. If that were carried I said to him, these would be very much strengthened thereby, but if that were lost, in my opinion all the others went with it."

Thereupon, Pomeroy, taking a pencil, drew a circle around the eighth to indicate that Ross would not support it, made a dot over the others, except the first, to indicate they were doubtful, and then hied himself away. As it had already been determined in caucus, because of the refusal of Sherman, Howe and others to vote for the first, to commence the vote with the last, Ross's equivocal promise did not meet the crisis. Votes for the eleventh article were what was wanted and Pomeroy went after his colleague once again. On the night of Thursday, the fourteenth, he found him in the rooms of senator Van Winkle with Trumbull, Henderson and Willey, and, unabashed by the company he was in, began a conversation on the result. In answer to doubts expressed by Henderson, he insisted that conviction was certain on the eleventh article, because he had conversed with a sufficient number of senators to know that it would be carried by one vote. Ross inquired if he was numbered among the thirty-six, and Pomeroy answered in the affirmative. The Kansas senator then repeated the conversation of the day before, and assured his colleague that he need not count on his vote for conviction under any circumstances. That same evening a member of the Kansas legislature called on Ross "to talk the matter over," and Ross told him that he was opposed to bringing on a vote at this time; that "the best thing was postponement, the next best conviction." The next day (Friday) a telegram arrived from Kansas addressed to both senators of that state, as follows:

> Leavenworth, May 14th. Kansas has heard the evidence, and demands the conviction of the President.
>
> D. R. Anthony, and 1000 others.

Ross called at the residence of his colleague in the evening to procure a copy of this dispatch and stayed to dinner. Pomeroy importuned him again, and he replied as before; admitting, however, that the eleventh was the strongest article and that he was freer to vote for that than the others. As late as half-past eleven that night, he was seen in a restaurant with Van Winkle and Henderson by a friend to whom, after the senators were gone, he said he thought it was dangerous to take a vote in the morning and was himself in favour of postponement until the first of July. Even at this late hour, the impeachers gave him no rest. General Sickles, urged on by Stanton, sought him at his lodgings and remained until four o'clock in the morning, determined to see him and "save him"; but was denied the opportunity by Miss Ream who told him, at last, with tears and wringing of hands, that Ross "would support the President."* Spies traced the pestered senator to his breakfast that morning at the residence of Perry Fuller, where Henderson was, also, a guest; and, ten minutes before the vote was taken, in the lobby of the Senate and in the presence of Thaddeus Stevens who looked grimly on, Pomeroy bearded his colleague for the last time, warning him that to vote otherwise than for conviction would be his political death, and threatening that a vote for acquittal would be investigated on a charge of bribery. That morning Ross had sent the following reply to the Anthony telegram:

Washington, May 16.

Gentlemen:

I do not recognize your right to demand that I shall vote either for or against conviction. I have taken an oath to do impartial justice . . . and I trust I shall have the courage and honesty to vote according to the dictates of my judgment and for the highest good of my country.

To D. R. Anthony and 1000 others. E. G. Ross.

* Correspondence from Topeka, Kan., October 20, 1896, to the Chicago *Record;* reprinted in N. Y. *Sun* of October 25, 1896.

And, before the day was over, he received the following spicy but not fragrant rejoinder:

Leavenworth, Kansas, May 16, 1868.

Hon. E. G. Ross, United States Senator, Washington, D. C.

Your telegram received. Your vote is dictated by Tom Ewing, not by your oath. Your motives are Indian contracts and greenbacks. Kansas repudiates you as she does all perjurers and skunks.

D. R. Anthony and Others.*

The most astonishing feature of this crusade against the doubtful senators was the apparent absence of any sense of its impropriety on the part of the actors. Such a course of conduct, undertaken in an ordinary prosecution before a common law court or jury, would have subjected the perpetrators to the reprobation of mankind as well as to an indictment for felony, and would have vitiated any verdict obtained by such disreputable means. And the parties engaging in any such enterprise would have carried on their operations under the cover of darkness and secrecy, conscious they were violating the fundamental principles of justice, as well as the commandment of the law. But, here, on this world-stage, before this high tribunal, in this historic state-trial, every thing that was done was done openly, publicly, as it were boastingly and defiantly, without shame and with a consciousness of impunity, if not of deserving well of the country. In the light of history and precedents, it may be true, that the utmost strict-

* Concerning Ross, see his speech in self-vindication, *Globe*, 2d Sess. 40th Cong., p. 4513. *Cf.* Pomeroy's testimony before managers, quoted in same speech.

ness of judicial propriety cannot be expected from a court such as is the Senate organized for the trial of impeachments; that senators must be allowed freer movements than ordinary judges; may act on testimony they have not heard and arguments they have not listened to; pass more than half the time of the trial outside of the tribunal, as one of the senators from Illinois notoriously did on this occasion, and reappear only at times when a vote against the accused is wanted. It may be true that senators, as Sumner contended, cannot divest themselves of their political capacity; have a right, therefore, to form and express their opinions on the guilt or innocence of the President before hearing the evidence; and may look upon the wearisome trial as a concession to constitutional forms necessary in order to reach a conclusion already predetermined; that the votes of the senators on impeachment differ in no respect from their votes on measures of legislation and that, therefore, the senators being equally responsible to the people must be answerable to popular influence and criticism in the one case as in the other. It may be true that from the very nature of the proceedings it is impossible to shut out political and personal influences which in ordinary courts would be reprobated as illegitimate and improper. For instance, it has been related by a writer who was at the capital during these days, on the authority of a warm friend of the President, that some of the doubtful senators expressing to Grimes their apprehensions that the President, if acquitted, might break loose in some high-handed attempt to put a stop to congressional reconstruction, Reverdy Johnson brought about a casual meeting at his house of the President and the senator without the foreknowledge of either, when the President was led to express sentiments negativing any such notion—sentiments subsequently conveyed by the senator to the waverers with the desired effect.* Again: according to a memorandum which General Schofield states he made at the time (May, 1868), he called upon Mr. Evarts, at the request of that counsel of the President, on the twenty-first of April, *i. e.* the day after the testimony on the trial was closed and the court had adjourned over to the twenty-second to hear the arguments. Evarts sounded the General upon the question of his acceptance, should the President send to the Senate his nomination as Secretary of War; representing that "a majority of the Republicans in both Houses of Congress now regret the commencement of the impeachment proceedings, since they find how slight is the evidence of guilty intent"; that "the removal of the President for political reasons would be ruinous to the party and cause the political death of every senator who voted for it"; that such was the view of "several among the most prominent Republican senators" from whom, in fact, "came the suggestion," which the counsel had made to the General "in order that the Senate might vote upon the President's case in the light of that nomination." And, understanding "this proposition as coming originally from the Republican side of the Senate and as being accepted by the President in the interest of peace and for the purpose of securing harmony between the legis-

* Cox's Three Decades, pp. 592–4.

lative and executive departments of the government, and a just and faithful administration of the laws,'' the General, the next day, ventured so far as to say he would ''deem it my (his) duty to say nothing on the subject of accepting or declining the appointment until the Senate acted upon it'';—and, on the twenty-fourth, the President sent the nomination to the Senate where, as everybody must have foreseen, it lay unacted upon until the result of the trial forced Stanton to 'relinquish' his post.* No one of the high parties engaged in these respective maneuvres, it may be admitted, even so much as dreamed they were violating the proprieties of a court of justice. And, as we are saying, such may be the correct view of trials of this peculiar character. But —granting all this for the sake of the argument, it not being necessary to insist on any rigid enforcement of the rules governing ordinary judges—there can be no doubt that under the Constitution the President was entitled to the actual judgment of the individual senators on the articles presented against him. If, after hearing the testimony and the arguments of counsel, a senator—however greatly influenced by party considerations or by personal bias—became convinced that the charges were not proved;—any and all attempts to induce or coerce him to declare otherwise because of party considerations or considerations of friendship must be classed in the same category of offences as tampering with an ordinary court or jury when deliberating on a decision or verdict. And this is just what the impeachers in this case did with reference to Henderson, Fowler

* Schofield's Forty-six Years in the Army, p. 413 *et seq.*

and Ross. They did not seek to influence their reason on the facts and the law. They cared nothing for the conclusion the senators had actually come to. They wanted these senators to vote 'Guilty' whether they thought the President guilty or not. And to this end they bent all their energies. To them, as party politicians, it was self-evident that Andrew Johnson ought to be removed from office. The mode of accomplishing this necessary end was immaterial. Whether Johnson was guilty or not as charged made no difference. He was guilty of rebellion against the party and of obstructing its policy. Republican senators ought not "to quibble with their country." This was the character and style of pressure brought to bear upon these judges, in a cause pending before them, and at times when they were out of court; and if such a course of conduct does not deserve the everlasting condemnation of all fair-minded men—then the process of impeaching and trying a President of the United States is but a mockery of forensic justice; the prostitution of a solemn judicial proceeding into a sort of by-election of a new President to take place whenever a majority of the House and two-thirds of the Senate become too restive under the incumbent for the time being to await the expiration of the constitutional term.

The dragooning of senators necessarily ceased, for a time at least, when, at noon, on Saturday, the sixteenth of May, Chief Justice Chase took the chair and called the High Court of Impeachment to order. Of the fifty-four senators, every man was in his seat except one. Howard was there, but Grimes, it was whispered, had been taken ill, and his seat was empty. All seven of the managers were in attendance. Of the President's counsel, Stanbery, Evarts, Nelson and Groesbeck appeared in their place. The House of Representatives was present in mass, and the galleries were packed. The prevailing excitement had reached a pitch of intensity that manifested itself by a stillness that is felt. A realizing sense that the deposition of an American President was something more than a politician's game seemed to have descended at last upon the entire assemblage; and that the destiny of the great modern Republic might be hanging on the decision of the hour. Williams of Oregon, the mouthpiece of the caucus which the majority of this senatorial court had deemed it decorous to hold, was the first to break the spell. He moved the adoption of an order that the Chief Justice, in directing the secretary to read the several articles, should direct him to read the last article first, upon which the question should be taken, and thereafter on the other ten successively as they stood. The motion was a critical one, the yeas and nays were demanded, and the order was agreed to by 34 yeas to 19 nays, absent 1. Wade had voted at last, but the required two-thirds were not quite there. Of the seven suspected senators, every one was in the negative except the absent Grimes, and his place was supplied by Willey.

Edmunds moves that the Senate proceed to judgment. The decisive hour has come. For an instant,

Fessenden staves it off by begging for time that Grimes may be present. But Reverdy Johnson announces in sentences broken by the strain of the moment: "The Senator is here. I have sent for him. He is downstairs. He will be in the Chamber in a moment. He is here." And Grimes, faint and pale, is borne through the press and fairly lifted into his seat. The High Court is full and there is to be no delay. The Chief Justice directs the secretary to read the eleventh article; and it is read to impatient and unheeding ears. A thousand hearts stand still as the Chief Justice rises, grasps the sides of the desk before him and utters the words: "Call the roll." "Mr. Anthony," the clerk calls; and the Rhode Island senator stands up in his place. The Chief Justice puts the question: "Mr. Senator Anthony, how say you? Is the respondent, Andrew Johnson, President of the United States, guilty or not guilty of a high misdemeanor as charged in this article?" And, looking into the eyes of his eminent friend, the senator dispels the last cloud of suspicion arising from their intimacy by responding 'Guilty.' Two Democrats follow with their anticipated answers, when Cameron provokes a momentary laugh by running right over the presiding officer with his eager 'Guilty' before the question is half out. Seven votes for conviction are heard in quick succession; then three for acquittal; then three for conviction; when at the name of Fessenden there is a breathless pause, and his 'Not Guilty,' high and clear, is followed by a sigh of relief. Fowler comes next. The tremendous nervous strain is too heavy for him and his faltering articulation is mistaken for the word 'Guilty'; there is a thrill of triumph or despair, when, on the demand of the presiding officer, the senator, repeating his actual answer, half stuns his hearers by the violence of the reaction.* When Grimes is called, his feebleness is so manifest that the Chief Justice suggests his voting in his seat; but the senator is bound to furnish no handle to an accusation of shamefacedness, and with the assistance of friends he staggers to his feet to declare his independence as a judge. Howard, likewise, declines the same privilege and conquers his physical weakness to record in the most conspicuous manner his belief in the guilt of the President. The eyes of the managers and of the Missouri representatives burn with a wicked light when Henderson is called. He has not resigned; will he withhold his vote? If a glimmer of hope still flickers in their breasts, his prompt response extinguishes it forever. Ten votes for conviction follow, interspersed with five for acquittal, when the clerk calls a fatal name. Twenty-four 'Guilties' have been pronounced and ten more are certain to come. Willey is almost sure and will make thirty-five. Thirty-six are needed, and with this one vote the grand consummation is attained, Johnson is out and Wade in his place. It is a singular fact that not one of the actors in that high scene was sure in his own mind how this one senator was going to vote, except, perhaps, himself. "Mr. Senator Ross, how say you?" the voice of the Chief Justice rings out over the solemn silence. "Is the respondent, Andrew Johnson, guilty or not guilty of a

* Julian's Political Recollections, p. 317.

high misdemeanor as charged in this article?'' The Chief Justice bends forward, intense anxiety furrowing his broad brow. The seated associates of the senator on his feet fix upon him their united gaze. The representatives of the people of the United States watch every movement of his features. The whole audience listens for the coming answer as it would have listened for the crack of doom. And the answer comes, full, distinct, definite, unhesitating and unmistakable. The words 'Not Guilty' sweep over the assembly, and, as one man, the hearers fling themselves back into their seats; the strain snaps; the contest ends; impeachment is blown into the air. The clerk drones on—Mr. Sherman, Mr. Sprague, Mr. Stewart, Mr. Sumner; but the voices of the respondents are unheeded. The two Nebraska senators fulfil the contract of their admission and duly "reinforce'' the majority, but they might as well be still knocking at the door. "Would that Colorado were in!'' Trumbull's vote has been discounted. At the call of Van Winkle there may have been a feeble afterglow of hope; but the senator votes 'Not Guilty' with no sign of compassion. Wade comes next; no glittering prize dangling before his eyes, his presidency *pro tem.* clattering like an empty clog at his heels; but he votes 'Guilty,' like the Duke of Orleans, "in his heart and conscience." Willey's vote is no longer a source of anxiety; he may keep to his conservatives now. But Willey, once his colleague has made acquittal sure, reverts irresistibly to the majority and to the Methodist Church. Williams, Wilson, Yates follow like the last drops of an exhausted vein, and the roll-call ends. "Andy" has escaped conviction by one vote. There are whisperings between senators; representatives rush hither and thither; and there is a bustling and a rustling in the galleries. The Chief Justice quietly directs the secretary to read the first article. A vote on the first article, with Sherman and Howe committed against it, cannot fail to prove still more disastrous than the vote just taken; and Williams, in the distraction of the moment, proposes a recess of fifteen minutes for consultation. Such a breach of judicial decorum finds, even at this high crisis, no favour, and the senator finally moves the adjournment of the Senate sitting as a court for ten days. Pending this motion, the announcement of the result on the eleventh article, hitherto overlooked in the excitement, is called for; and the Chief Justice proclaims that thirty-five senators have voted "Guilty" and nineteen "Not Guilty." "Two-thirds not having pronounced guilty, the President is, therefore, acquitted on this article." The question then recurs on the adjournment. The Chief Justice decides the motion out of order on the ground that the execution of an order already made by the Senate is pending. There is an appeal from the decision; and the Chief Justice is overruled. Henderson, then, moves to adjourn to the first of July—a proposition which receives the votes of the memorable nineteen and Willey's besides. McCreery's common sense amendment to adjourn without day gets but six votes. The Court then adjourns to the twenty-sixth.

Meanwhile, the audience has streamed forth from the capitol, and the tidings of the President's acquittal are sent careering through the country on the wings of the lightning. At all the commercial centres, the news is received with a feeling of relief. The business men, without distinction of party, had always deprecated the project as essentially revolutionary and as destructive of the material interests of the people. The champions of the President, we may be sure, did not leave him long in suspense. During the actual trial, his secretaries kept him informed of the incidents of every day; and, on the decisive occasion, every vote was telegraphed from the capitol to the White House. On the formal announcement of the result, Stanbery and Nelson escaped from the Senate chamber and hastened to congratulate their client; Nelson, especially, being beside himself with delight. The President received the news without visible emotion. Indeed, throughout the whole of this trying time, the demeanour, carriage and conversation of Andrew Johnson were enough of themselves to stamp him as an extraordinary man. Confronted by an overwhelming majority of both Houses of Congress, every one bent upon turning him out of office; outside of his Cabinet and a few prominent office-holders, with hardly a serviceable friend upon whom to rely—he appeared wholly undismayed, unflurried, serenely confident in his ultimate triumph. While every one else was going wild with excitement on his account, he alone was calm and cool. His prosecutors appeared over-heated and nervous at all times; when affairs were not to their mind they were peevish, irascible and abusive; when affairs were on the mounting hand they were reckless, domineering, coarsely incontinent. He, on the contrary, was always placid, cheerful, apparently indifferent. When the prospect was blackest, no word of despondency or petulance escaped his lips; when the horizon lightened, there was no burst of undignified hilarity, no fitful study of revenge, no arrogant boasting. Not that he had lost one jot of his native pugnacity. In fact, he was more than ever resolved to fight the multitude of his enemies, every day and at all times, as, in fact, he did to the end. An unwonted playfulness of humour was observed in him as the days of stress went by. "Well, what are the signs of the Zodiac to-day?" was his greeting to his secretary when that official came to make his evening report. We have said that he was *apparently* indifferent to the result. We might have said that in point of fact he *was* indifferent. At times, he seemed buoyed up by a belief in the impossibility that the Senate of the United States, of which he had been so long a member, could convict him of a crime; and, when he did break his habitual reticence on the subject, it was to express the conviction that among the Republican senators there would be found in the end enough high-minded men to emancipate themselves from party ties so far as to declare that the President had committed no offence deserving impeachment. But, on the other hand, there were moments when he must have looked an adverse judgment in the face. His counsel, his most confidential advisers, his most intimate friends, were troubled with grave misgivings and at times gave up hope. There were moments when he, too, seemed sunk in deep meditation, when he would sit stern and silent in his chair or pace up and down the rooms and halls of the White House in the still hours of the night. Yet, the resultant impression left on the minds of those nearest and dearest to him was, that he was not only careless about the result but that to him conviction would be welcome. That he contemplated forcible resistance is not likely. He believed, as was stated in open court by his intimate friend as well as counsel, that the Senate, with twenty of its members shut out, had no constitutional right to try him; but he did not plead to its jurisdiction, and, therefore, we may believe that he concluded to waive the point once for all. It is possible he may have counted up his resources, calculated the cost and meant, in the last extremity, calling upon General Hancock for assistance, to put his fate to the touch and win or lose it all; and, in such a contingency, we can understand why an adverse judgment might in a certain sense have been welcome. But, considering on the one hand the slenderness of his available forces and on the other the plenitude of the power of his adversaries, we may put aside any such supposition as out of the question. If, however, conviction had been secured by so gross an outrage as the introduction at the last moment of senators who had taken no part in the trial, we may rest assured that, rather than submit, he would have been hewn to pieces on the threshold of the White House. But, had conviction come under the regular constitutional forms, however illegal and unjust in substance it may have appeared to him to be, there is little doubt but that he had schooled himself to yield and, at once, appeal to the people. It may be objected to this view that the Senate would have precluded the possibility of a renewal of the contest by superadding to the removal the further penalty of disqualification from office; a penalty we have already seen Sumner laying his plans to impose by a majority vote. But, even if the senator from Massachusetts had succeeded in carrying out his vengeful purpose and thus shut out Johnson from contesting the Presidency, still, the additional punishment the Senate might constitutionally inflict extending no further than disqualification to hold office "under the United States," would not have debarred the unconquerable defendant from seeking public favour in his own state and coming back to the Senate.

Waiving these hypothetical considerations, what we have to record as matter of fact is that, after the acquittal on the eleventh article, which the public mind naturally assumed to be the final disposition of the whole proceeding, but little time elapsed before it began to look that, if the martyrdom of removal from office was what the President was itching for, he might still have his wish. For, what could be the meaning of this sudden breaking off in the process of giving judgment, leaving ten articles still undetermined, and adjourning the court for ten days and over the date of the meeting of the Republican national convention? The testimony was all in—in nearly a month ago; the arguments were closed—closed ten days before; the secret deliberation of the court was over—over five days before. Why, then, did the majority not go on and end the proceeding—a proceeding blocking all legislation, keeping every one concerned in it in a fever of unrest and vexing the heart of the nation? Why did they prolong the agony ten days more? There can be but one answer to these questions. In the depth of their disappointment they still clung to the hope that they might yet impale their enemy on some one of the other articles. They lacked but a single vote. Give them but time, and, with the superabundance of their resources, that vote surely might be captured. How they were to capture it, was the next topic on which conjecture became rife. Would they move to re-open the case for additional testimony? Would they prefer additional charges, as the House had expressly reserved the right to do? Would they throw aside all sense of fairness and decency and reinforce the court with the hybrid representatives of the Africanized South, now wandering about the streets of the capital, ready to jump at any chance, no matter how disreputable, to demonstrate the loyalty with which they were overflowing? Would they make a combined attack on one of the back-sliding senators and compel him to come in? Such queries as these gained increasing reasonableness and pertinency from what went on in the two Houses during the interval.

After the acquittal on the eleventh article, as soon as the Chief Justice left the chair and the representatives the chamber, the President *pro tem.* called the Senate to order and the senators plunged into a controversy over the resolution sent from the House to take a recess until the twenty-fifth instant, in order to enable members of Congress who so desired to attend the Chicago convention. Vigorous opposition was made on the ground, as stated by Wilson, that the bills to restore "Arkansas and five other Southern States," already passed by the House, should be passed by the Senate "within the next three or four days." Sumner, who, as he said, could not recall a single instance when he had voted for "adjournment or recess," now favoured the resolution in the following fashion:

"I have always felt from the first moment he (the President) was arraigned at our bar that it was unbecoming the Senate to transact business with him. I have felt as if it was the same as if the judge on the bench should continue to transact business with the criminal in the dock, or, if the Senate prefers that term, with the culprit in the dock. . . . Profoundly believing the President of the United States guilty of high crimes and misdemeanors—and I can have no hesitation in declaring it, for I have voted to-day on one important article—having that profound conviction, and knowing that there are other articles that still await the judgment of the Senate, how can I as a senator, consent to continue in communication with him on important public business?

"It may be that when these proceedings are brought to an end, that he may come forth with a nominal acquittal of one vote. Condemned by a majority of the Senate, as he has already been condemned in advance by two-thirds and more of the House of Representatives, and, as is unquestionable, condemned by the great body of the American people, it may be, I say, that he may go forth from this Chamber with a nominal acquittal; but he must go forth as a blasted public functionary. That is his inevitable destiny."

Nye, on the other hand, was in favour of putting the Arkansas bill "through all the forms" "before the sun goes down." "Let the President have another sweet morsel to roll under his tongue. Let him veto it and we will meet it. . . . The President, I think, will waive the peculiar circumstances which he is in and admit her. I have no doubt the message is written already." Yates came out still more plainly:

"I wish to send him (the President) such a bill as that. I wish to send it to him in the interim between now and the final vote on impeachment, . . . so that we might have for our Republican colleagues, our Republican friends, a new veto upon human rights and upon the best interests of our country. . . . I believe in some respects it would be as well for Congress to adjourn and for members to go home and breathe the breath of popular opinion among their constituents, and understand how a great people feel outraged and indignant at the verdict which has been pronounced here to-day on this most important trial."

He could not favour an adjournment because of the important business before the Senate, but he trusted that "in the meantime we shall be able to hear from the country and feel the effect of popular opinion." "I do not mean upon the votes of the members; but I mean that, if that opinion can in any way influence our decision, it will be for the best interests of the country." The Senate, at first, rejected the resolution and then reconsidered and adopted it; too late, however, because the House had also reconsidered and voted it down.

On a motion to take up the Arkansas bill, the question was raised whether the senators from the new state, provided they were admitted on the floor, can become members of the court of impeachment. "Of course they can be," said Sumner. Fessenden remarked:

> "I should not envy the condition of that member of the Senate who should propose to administer the oath as a member of the court of impeachment to either of those gentlemen if they should come here as senators from Arkansas. Still less should I envy the condition of any one who proposed to take the oath and to act as a member of the court under such circumstances."

But Dixon insisted:

> "There are Senators in this body, able and distinguished men and lawyers, who think that if the Arkansas gentlemen were admitted as Senators of the United States, there is no power here to refuse them the oath; and, moreover, there are some senators who believe they would be compelled to act."

He cited the New York *Tribune* and the Washington *Chronicle* as having "suggested the idea that these senators should be admitted, and that they should be sworn as members of the court of impeachment and act upon the case." In the case of Warren Hastings (as manager Butler pointed out in his opening speech), of the more than one hundred and seventy peers who commenced the trial but twenty-nine sat and pronounced the verdict at the close; and, during the trial, there had been by death, succession and creation, more than one hundred and eighty changes in the House. Doubtless, the swearing in of additional members after the court was in process of giving judgment, would be going a step farther than any precedent even of the most lawless periods of English history; but, notwithstanding this, there were more than a few senators and many representatives who argued that the impropriety of the act could not alter the right of the senator to make one of a court into which the Senate from time to time resolved itself. It was said that such an outrage was impossible, because the ten days allowed the President to veto a bill would preclude the admission of the senators until after the day fixed for the completion of the judgment; but a second adjournment would be as easy and not much more indecorous than the first. The Senate, however, disposed of the question by refusing to take up the Arkansas bill.*

The proceedings of the House were much more unequivocal. When the representatives, leaving the Senate, flocked across the capitol into their own chamber, the managers, snatching up their papers, departed to hold a secret session. It has been already noted that, during the week before the vote, they had been hearing witnesses detail the movements and sayings of senators and describe the guests and their doings at the dinners of the Chief Justice; and they imagined they had struck the track of a conspiracy to make Chase President. After a brief conference on this occasion, they filed into the House and, by the mouth of their chairman, presented a preamble reciting that "information has come to the managers which seems to them to

* *Globe*, 2d Sess. 40th Cong., pp. 2492–6, 2514–6.

furnish probable cause to believe that improper and corrupt means have been used to influence the determination of the Senate upon the articles of impeachment,'' and a resolution directing the managers ''for the further and more efficient prosecution of the impeachment of the President'' to summon witnesses, send for persons and papers, employ a stenographer and appoint subcommittees to take testimony. Bingham explained that, at the formal close of the testimony, he had notified the Senate and the counsel for the President ''that the House of Representatives did not surrender its right at any time before judgment to present additional testimony''; and, further, ''the Constitution having vested in the House 'the sole power of impeachment' has clothed this body with power unto the day of judgment to investigate all corruptions by any man or any men, with a view to prevent the decision of this case according to the law and the evidence.''

> ''I am not talking of impeaching senators. But, sir, at an early day in the history of the country nobody challenged the right to do it. The House proceeded to the bar of the Senate and demanded the sequestration of the seat of a senator and it was done. This House is clothed with full power to do this thing and no man can challenge it here or anywhere else successfully.''

An effort was made by the Democrats to have the investigation confided to a committee on which they might have at least one representative; but the majority would not yield an inch, and the preamble and resolution were adopted. Stevens, on Monday, offered a resolution requesting the Senate to transmit to the

House a certified copy of the proceedings of the last two days of the trial; in order, as he proceeded to explain, to have an official record of the votes of different senators. His remarks, of which the following is a specimen, for some reason were at times almost unintelligible:

> "There will undoubtedly be some further proceedings had in regard to this impeachment; what those proceedings will be I do not know. I suppose that we shall be able in some way or other to vote upon the articles which are still before the Senate. . . . I do not suppose that any one believes that the question which was passed upon on Saturday last is to remain a defunct question. I do not suppose that any one believes that that question is to be carried to the country in its present condition. . . .
>
> "I make no accusation; I charge nobody with anything. But to me it seems amazing that a body of that kind, having before it a body of men of the highest character, will give to themselves and to others the character which they have given, and which they feel disposed to stamp upon the country. . . . We are therefore asking that as these matters have been sent before the Senate for the purpose of being investigated, every opportunity shall be allowed for the purpose of ascertaining who have been willing to listen and who have refused to listen to the instructions of the accused. That there has been great, manifold, deep damnation, and that there is somewhere to be found the greatest of all mysteries, the mystery of this great prevalence of evil, no one can doubt. Let us therefore have the whole matter in such a shape that there may be every opportunity to investigate, so that all men may see who it is that is wrong, and who it is that is right."*

* *Globe,* 2d Sess. 40th Cong., pp. 2504–5, 2530.

The resolution was adopted without a division and sent immediately to the Senate, where it gave rise to a heated discussion as an encroachment upon the prerogatives of that body and an insult to some of its members. Sumner, however, did not see it in that light. He said:

> "We know from the evidence before us something of the character of the President of the United States; we know how utterly unprincipled and wicked he is; it is in evidence. We also know what some of his agents and representatives . . . have openly said."

And the senator read a communication from the New York *World* to the effect that there were fourteen radical senators whose terms of office expire in 1869 (Sumner himself being one of them), eight of whom might certainly be bought for a million apiece; read it as though it was an editorial and the suggestion a serious one, when it was apparent, as the newspaper hastened to explain, that it was an ironical exemplification of Sumner's own doctrine that the trial of impeachments was not so much a judicial as a political function, and the vote of a senator on impeachments should be governed by political considerations and his own interest as a member of his party. Sumner's motion to comply with the request of the House failed for lack of a quorum, and the managers procured the record in some indirect way.*

This band of seven disappointed partisans had inaugurated a reign of terror in certain quarters of the

* *Globe*, 2d Sess. 40th Cong., p. 2520.

capital. They hardly waited for the authority of the House before they descended upon the telegraph offices of Washington and Baltimore, seizing every despatch which had been sent to or from the city for four or five days preceding the fatal Saturday. They invaded the banks and forced the officers to disclose the accounts of senators and other suspected depositors. They could not wait for the seal of the Speaker or for the lapse of Sunday, but on that day issued a subpœna signed by their chairman, and caused it to be served on one Charles Woolley—a sporting gentleman who had been betting heavily on the President's side, talking loudly in favour of acquittal and telegraphing in cipher in various directions, mysteriously, about large sums of money. Woolley fooled them to the top of their bent; worrying Butler by suddenly disappearing in the direction of New York with the apparent intention of disregarding the process served on Sunday; as suddenly reappearing, just in the nick of time to escape arrest; and, when at last caught, answering all questions fully and freely up to a certain point when, all at once, he closed up his shell and became ominously silent. The recusant witness was finally ordered into confinement; and, there being no darker dungeon within reach than the cell in the crypt of the capitol where Miss Ream was at work on her statue of Lincoln, the House turned her out of it to make place for the prisoner, notwithstanding her personal protest that to move the model would be its ruin.*

* For Woolley, see *Globe*, 2d Sess. 40th Cong., pp. 2536–7, 2541, 2575–9. For Miss Ream, *id.*, pp. 2672, 2751.

Henderson became a special mark for the managers. They sent him an official letter requesting his presence before them to give his testimony; to which he replied that their inquisition was a direct insult to the Senate and of most dangerous tendency for the future; that "if a member of the court can now, before the rendition of the judgment, be withdrawn from consultation, and subjected to the inquisition of the prosecutors, that inquisition may reach all proceedings, and thus subvert the dignity and independence of the Senate." A committee having been appointed, in the meanwhile, at the request of the Democrats backed by the Missouri representatives to investigate the attempt of the latter to intimidate their senator, Henderson appeared before it (on the twentieth) and gave his version of the transaction, answering, as he said, in addition, "all questions propounded in reference to the conduct of Chief Justice Chase, the reported organization of a new party, the rumors of new Cabinet appointments, reported presidential pledges of protection to what is foolishly termed Conservative Senators, dinner-table talk with friends and even my own private opinions." And, then, on Thursday (the twenty-first) he laid the managers' letter, his reply and the foregoing information before the Senate for its direction, subjoining that, were he to appear before the managers, he could but repeat what he had already testified to, whereas, on the other hand, he objected to submit to an inquisition so insulting to the Senate and so derogatory to the personal honour of senators and their independence as judges. Sumner, however, "knowing," as he said, "from public report that it is among the possibilities that a further article of impeachment may be exhibited against the President," thought it "a work of superfluity at least," which he could not comprehend, that any senator should seek to throw in its way the dignity of the Senate. "Sir," exhorted this model judge, "let justice have a free course and take its way. The way of justice cannot be stopped. Technicalities are out of place; they do not belong to a case like this."* The Senate came to no conclusion upon this question; the final determination of the Impeachment depriving it of vitality.

The managers still kept on swearing witnesses, overhauling senators, following up false scents of bribery and corruption, and pursuing flying rumours of this or that judge being tampered with. As was inevitable in such a mad game, they did not fail to run across the professional false witness. Their "Conover" proved to be one Legate or Legget, a special Post-Office agent for Kansas and New Mexico appointed by the Postmaster-General the year before at the earnest solicitation of senator Pomeroy. This creature testified to some vague stuff concerning Ross and his friends, conclusive of nothing and contradicted point-blank wherever it could be brought to book; but, because of over-anxiety that he might not swear to enough, he went too far and, to the managers' mortification, implicated Pomeroy, and that too in the most explicit fashion. According to his testimony, Pomeroy, through his brother-in-law, had been hawking about his own

* *Globe*, 2d Sess. 40th Cong., pp. 2548–9.

vote and the votes of three or four of his colleagues, to be cast for acquittal at the aggregate price of forty thousand dollars. And a copy of a letter, dated April 16, 1867, purporting to have been written by Pomeroy to Legate just before the latter's appointment, and shown by Legate to the Postmaster-General—the original having been taken back but the copy retained and given to the President—was produced by the Postmaster-General himself; in which Pomeroy promises that, if the Postmaster-General or the President "get in trouble, even if it be impeachment, they can count on me to aid in getting them out, by word and vote." Pomeroy testified he never wrote such a letter; but Thurlow Weed, also a witness before the managers, stated in the public prints that "Senator Pomeroy either intended to dispose of three votes (his own, Nye's and Tipton's) or he was willing that his friends should use his name to make money; or, as some believe, there was a conspiracy between Butler and Pomeroy to implicate the President, thus obtaining new material for impeachment"; and the subsequent career of "Subsidy Pom" shows that he was none too pure to have been guilty of any one of these three iniquities.* This managerial investigation was kept on foot even after the final termination of the trial, but merely to wreak the spite of some of the Board on the men who had disappointed them, by collecting together every little circumstance, incident or saying connected with

* See Butler's report of managers, pp. 11, 12, ordered printed July 3, *Globe*, p. 3731. Henderson's speech on, *id.*, p. 4463 *et seq.* Butler in reply, App. p. 471.

the giving of their votes, which could be tortured into evidence of a change of mind at the last moment from weak or corrupt motives. It gradually degenerated into a farce. One by one the managers became ashamed of it and fell away, so that when Butler, the sole survivor, made a report in July, he could get no one of his colleagues to sign it and was obliged to take the responsibility himself. No action was taken on it —the report itself in fact neither proposing nor calling for any. An investigating committee appointed by the Senate held two meetings during the session, made no report, was continued at the next session, but did nothing; and at the close of the fortieth Congress, which ended with the administration of President Johnson (March 3, 1869), the chairman of the committee announced that there would be no formal report made; that "neither at the former session nor at the present one has any information been communicated to that committee upon the subject in regard to which they were appointed. From no quarter have we received any information which would even justify us in entering upon any regular investigation, and . . . nothing has appeared to justify any imputation upon any member of the Senate."*

In their desperate effort to capture the one vote they needed, the managers were aided by the national convention of their party; indeed, Bingham and Logan were on the spot. Although the platform adopted did not read the recusant senators out of the party, as was first proposed, it denounced Andrew Johnson as a crimi-

* *Globe*, 3d Sess. 40th Cong., p. 1865.

nal of the deepest dye, declared him to have been "justly impeached for high crimes and misdemeanors and properly pronounced guilty thereof by the votes of thirty-five senators." At meetings of several state delegations, speeches were made violently assailing the motives of the acquitting senators; the resolutions of the convention of soldiers and sailors, held at the same time and place, arraigned "any senator who has voted for acquittal as falling short of the proper discharge of his duty in this hour of the Nation's trial, and as unworthy of the confidence of a brave and loyal people"; and Logan publicly vouched for Grant as having "stood at the back of the managers in Congress during the whole course of the trial."

Whatever hope the authors of this system of intimidation may have had at the start of coercing others of the recusant senators, circumstances point unmistakably to the particular one they must have centered upon before the close of the week. Fessenden, Trumbull and Grimes were of course out of the question. They had written their opinions upon every article, read them to the Senate, and they were already on file. Of the remaining four, Van Winkle had never been doubtful on any article but the eleventh, on which he and his colleague, as the latter stated in the press, were driven in opposite directions by the construction given it by the Chief Justice.* Fowler, on the day he voted not guilty on the eleventh article, publicly responded to a telegram invoking blessings on his head: "I acted for my country

* Ross' speech at p. 2599 of *Globe*, 2d Sess. 40th Cong.

and posterity in obedience to the voice of God."* Henderson had delivered his opinion in the Senate against the first eight articles before his vote on the eleventh, and the ninth and tenth articles were hopeless in any event. He stated in open Senate, besides, that he expected to vote on all the articles as he had voted on the eleventh.† But Ross was not committed against any of the remaining articles. In fact, according to his own admission, he had expressed himself as favourable to the first article and as undecided as to the second and third. He was the one single senator who had so conducted himself as to have left open a loop-hole for retreat or recantation. As none could say before the vote was taken how he would vote on the eleventh article, so, now, none could say how he would vote on the remainder. He was, consequently, the main target at which the managers aimed. It is not probable that any of them held a personal conference with him, although it was rumoured that Butler and he had come together. His colleague, as we have seen, threatened him with an investigation on the charge of bribery. His intimate friends and his patrons at the capital were examined and cross-examined. His colleague, his constituents, his fellow-senators, swore to his previous statements favourable to conviction. His Indian office connection; his visits to the studio of Vinnie Ream; his lodging at her mother's; his association with advocates of the President;—were exploited: the menace that, unless he redeemed himself from his corrupt apostasy, a chain

* Butler's Report, p. 28.

† *Globe*, 2d Sess. 40th Cong., p. 2494.

of circumstantial evidence would be fastened about him and he himself pilloried before the nation, flashing like a drawn sword in the background. Those ten days must have been days of torture to him, at the mercy of the venal tongue of any professional witness who might find favour with the managers. He bore the ordeal with the fortitude of a stoic and the inscrutability of a sphinx.*

When the High Court re-assembled, there was still room, therefore, for speculation. Ten articles were yet to be voted on; thirty-five votes of 'Guilty' were certain on at least one of them; but one vote was needed to convict; and out of the nineteen who voted 'Not Guilty' on the eleventh, one senator's mind was not surely known. The Senate Chamber was crowded as before. The House of Representatives, headed by Washburne, who, with many of his fellow members, was fresh from making the next President, appeared, once more, to participate in an attempt to unmake the present President. The Chief Justice, the object of so much partisan objurgation, sat quietly in his chair. The holding of a caucus by the majority senators that morning to determine the order of voting on the remaining articles had given rise to the report that there was to be another postponement. But this expectation was speedily dispelled by Williams' offer of a resolution to rescind the previous order of reading and voting on the articles so far as it remained unexecuted. Every senator was in his place; Grimes, who had obtained an indefinite leave of absence on account of illness and it was hoped might not be able to be present, sitting implacably in his seat. The Chief

* Butler's report. Ross's speech in vindication, *Globe*, 2d Sess. 40th Cong., p. 4513.

Justice ruled the motion to rescind out of order, but he submitted the question to the Senate and the Senate overruled him by 29 to 25;—Ross, alone of the seven recusant senators, voting with the majority. Conkling then offered as a substitute an order that the voting do now proceed under the rules and the Senate rejected the substitute; Ross, alone of the seven, again voting with the majority. There was another vote on a point of order raised by Trumbull against the proposed change of rule; and, again, Ross was in the same company. A motion was made by Morrill of Maine to adjourn the court to the twenty-third day of June; and Ross moved as an amendment the date of the first of September, his amendment obtaining fifteen votes including those of the seven except Grimes. The motion to adjourn to the twenty-third of June was then voted down by a tie vote —27 to 27; every one of the seven senators voting in the negative, except Ross who voted in the affirmative. The motion to rescind was then adopted. The object of this motion was to get rid of the necessity of voting on the first article which everybody knew was certain to fail; and Ross's going with the majority to effect this significant evasion was looked upon by the impeachers as a harbinger of the return of the prodigal. Williams, still carrying out the decree of the caucus, now moved to proceed to vote on the second article. The second article was read, charging the *ad interim* appointment of Lorenzo Thomas. The call of the roll proceeded. When the name of Ross was reached there was a sudden accession of the almost insufferable strain of ten days ago. Again, the fate of the President, of the Republican party, of the nation, seemed to hang upon the lips of this one man. Again, the Chief Justice asks: "Mr. Senator Ross, how say you, is the respondent, Andrew Johnson, President of the United States, guilty or not guilty of a high misdemeanor as charged in this article of impeachment?" And, again, the Senator calmly lets fall the words 'Not Guilty.' The President is acquitted on the charge by the same vote as before—35 to 19. There is to be one more throw. Williams moves a vote on the third article. The third article is read. The roll-call passes with the same result; Ross still answering 'Not Guilty,' with the promptitude and relentlessness of an automaton. Again 35 to 19. Twice has 'Bluff Ben' Wade—Colfax, his successful competitor, smiling in his face—laid his already stricken honour on the altar of his party, knowing the sacrifice to be vain. The prosecutors dare go no further in the list of articles, lest a worse fate befall them. Williams moves an adjournment without day; every convicting senator votes for it but two who are absent; the High Court, foregoing the completion of its judgment, dissolves, leaving the first article on which the whole proceeding hung, the conspiracy articles elaborated with such care, the much-vaunted Emory article and Butler's masterpiece of pleading, to the unescapable judgment of posterity.

It was frequently boasted by its advocates, at the time, that the movement was substantially a success because the President was convicted by so large a majority of the Senate and escaped by only one vote. Sumner, as we have seen, found solace in dwelling upon this fact. "The acquittal was only by one vote''; he said, ''there is a familiar saying that a man is saved by the skin of his teeth; and so . . . the President was saved by the skin of his teeth. He was saved by one vote. I call it a nominal acquittal. There is . . . a moral judgment against him.'' But this is an altogether mistaken view. It were no great achievement, surely, to secure from the Senate, more than three-fourths of whose members were the political adversaries of the President, a majority to condemn him for his course in obstructing their party policy. Indeed, if a majority had been all that was required, he could have been deposed long before; for a majority, ready to convict on the general ground of political apostasy, was obtainable at any time after the rupture between the President and the Congress became irreparable. As a matter of fact, out of the thirty-five who voted guilty a sufficient number to make a large majority of the Senate rested their judgment upon no other consideration. What the Constitution required, however, and what the Impeachment advocates started out to obtain was a two-thirds majority on certain specific charges of crime or misdemeanour. And from this point of view, the Impeachment must be regarded as an ignominious failure. On the chief accusation, without the existence of the subject-matter of which there would have been no impeachment, the Senate never came to a vote at all. The House passed an act to keep Stanton in the Cabinet in spite of the President, and unwittingly so worded it as to leave Stanton standing defenceless outside of its provisions. The Senate, in a pliant hour, openly, in the face of all men, so construed it. The representatives, shutting their eyes to their own blunder, blindly drove on the prosecution. But certain senators happened to be too deeply committed. They could not bring themselves to perpetrate the unparalleled iniquity of convicting the President for construing a law as they had construed it themselves; and, therefore, the bottom fell out of the case. The eleventh article was essentially meaningless. It was concocted as a refuge for those senators who could not see their way clear on the specific charge, but hated Andrew Johnson with sufficient vigour to vote him out of office on general grounds. The second and third articles, cut off from the first, were ciphers shorn of their governing integer; and were hit upon to enable senators, too deeply committed against the Stanton article to vote for it, to keep in line with their party by taking advantage of what might be made to look like a statutory infraction, however harmless. The House of Representatives advanced to the Impeachment with pœans of anticipated triumph and like an army with banners. The Senate beckoned them on by pronouncing judgment of condemnation beforehand. The trial ensued with all the pomp and circumstance befitting so historic an occasion; and, at the end of the procedure, the High Court ran away from the completion of its judgment because a majority of its members were afraid of the central charge. And this humiliating *fiasco* was a most fortunate event for the Republic. Had this first impeachment eventuated in the removal of the Chief Magistrate, a precedent would have been established of the most fatal character—constituting a perpetual menace to the stability of our executive, a spreading blight upon our character and credit as a nation, a standing reproach to the republican form of government, and gradually leading to a national habit of capricious political convulsions to put one president in the place of another such as have disgraced some of the republics of Central and South America. To quote the weighty words of Senator Trumbull at the close of his opinion in this case:

> "Once set the example of impeaching the President, for what, when the excitement of the hour shall have subsided, will be regarded as insufficient causes, as several of those now alleged against the President were decided to be by the House of Representatives only a few months since, and no future President will be safe who happens to differ with a majority of the House and two-thirds of the Senate on any measure deemed by them important, particularly if of a political character. Blinded by partisan zeal, with such an example before them, they will not scruple to remove out of the way any obstacle to the accomplishment of their purposes, and what then becomes of the checks and balances of the Constitution, so carefully devised and so vital to its perpetuity? They are all gone."

As it turned out, however, the precedent was decisively the other way. Never will the practice of deposing presidents by political impeachment become domiciliated in this republic. Centuries will pass by before another President of the United States can be impeached, unless the offence of which he is accused is clearly non-political and amounts unmistakably to a high crime or misdemeanour.

Of the opinions written and filed by senators, something remains to be said. Of the twelve opposition senators, six filed opinions none of which calls for special remark. Of the seven recusant senators, all, except Ross, filed opinions discussing every article and concluding on every one with judgment of acquittal. Of the thirty-five senators voting guilty but eighteen filed opinions; so that of the judgments of seventeen on all the other articles, except the three voted on, we have no record. Of the eighteen, two pronounced the President 'Not Guilty' on the first article (Howe and Sherman); five pronounced him 'Not Guilty' on the fourth; three 'Not Guilty' on the fifth; five 'Not Guilty' on the sixth; two 'Not Guilty' on the seventh; one 'Not Guilty' on the eighth; eight 'Not Guilty' on the ninth; and five 'Not Guilty' on the tenth. Of the whole eighteen, but two found the President 'Guilty' specifically on every article. Cattel, Harlan, Morrill, of Maine, Stewart, Williams, Wilson and Yates pronounced him guilty generally, but those of them who descended to particulars discussed only the first article and the three actually voted on; Wilson confining himself, wholly, to generalities, and, alone of the senators, expressing his intention to vote, not only for conviction, but unhesitatingly for the disqualification of the removed President from thereafter holding any office under the United States. Tipton and Howard were for conviction on all but the ninth; even on the ninth Howard found the President censurable. But the proud distinction of sustaining, *seriatim,* each and every count in the indictment—the exploded Emory article and all—was enjoyed by Pomeroy and Sumner alone.

Sumner, in fact, confessed that he would vote, if he could: "Guilty on all and infinitely more." His opinion is a characteristic production. The longest one of all, filling thirty-four pages of print, carefully elaborated in the closet, regimented into sections, labelled with *ad captandum* headings, accompanied by a voluminous brief against the right of the Chief Justice to rule or vote; it is saturated with an animosity to the President so bitter and intense that its only natural source would seem to be a rancorous personal spite. This is the way the senator opens a judicial deliverance:

"This is one of the last great battles with slavery. Driven from these legislative chambers, driven from the field of war, this monstrous power has found a refuge in the Executive Mansion, where, in utter disregard of the Constitution and laws, it seeks to exercise its ancient, far-reaching sway. All this is very plain. Nobody can question it. Andrew Johnson is the impersonation of the tyrannical slave power. In him it lives again. He is the lineal descendant of John C. Calhoun and Jefferson Davis; and he gathers about him the same supporters. Original partisans of slavery north and south; habitual compromisers of great principles; maligners of the Declaration of Independence; politicians without heart; lawyers for whom a technicality is everything; and a promiscuous company who at every stage of the battle have set their faces against equal rights; these are his allies. It is the old troop of slavery, with a few recruits, ready as of old for violence—cunning in device and heartless in quibble. With the President at their head, they are now entrenched in the

Executive Mansion. . . . The enormity of his conduct is aggravated by his barefaced treachery. He once declared himself to be the Moses of the colored race. Behold him now the Pharaoh. With such treachery in such a cause there can be no parley. Every sentiment, every conviction, every vow against slavery must now be directed against him. Pharaoh is at the bar of the Senate for judgment."

In order to gain swinging room for his blows he sweeps away the flimsy barrier of the articles.

"It is very wrong to try this impeachment merely on the articles. It is unpardonable to higgle over words and phrases when for more than two years the tyrannical pretensions of this offender . . . have been manifest in their terrible heart-rending consequences."

Impeachment is a political, and not a judicial, proceeding, for the reason, according to this jurist, that the Constitution, having vested the judicial power in the courts, provided, nevertheless, that the Senate should have the sole power to try impeachments. Further, political offences are impeachable offences. "Show me an act of evil example or influence committed by a President and I show you an impeachable offence." This tribunal is not to be confined by the "rigid rules of the common law." It has "rules of its own, unknown to ordinary courts." "The precision of history is enough without the precision of an indictment." There can be no artificial rules of evidence to shut out the truth. "The ordinary rule of evidence," that the benefit of the doubt must be given to the accused, "is reversed." "If on any point you entertain doubts, the benefit of those doubts must be given to your country; and this is the supreme law." The President "must show that his longer continuance in office is not inconsistent with the public safety." As Blackstone said with reference to liberty, "we should 'catch at everything' to save the Republic." What is more, we can take cognizance without special proof on the trial of "whatever ought to be generally known within the limits of the jurisdiction, including the history of the country." "No gate can be closed."

As we read, we seem to hear Robespierre in the tribune of the French Convention advocating the condemnation of Louis XVI without proof and without trial.

Having thus laid down a mode of procedure lax enough for his purpose, he proceeds to its application. He makes the course of the President up to December, 1867, the main matter of his arraignment, without which the later acts charged in the article "would have remained unnoticed, impeachment would not have been ordered"; and, piling one abusive epithet upon another, branding the accused before the court, the country and the world, as the one "enormous criminal" of his age, he persists in demanding his condemnation for offences for which he not only was not on trial, but for which his constitutional accusers had formally declined to bring him to the bar. Let us listen once more to this upright judge, sworn "to do impartial justice":

"Applying this rule to the present proceeding, it will be seen at once how it brings before the Senate, without any further evidence, a long catalogue of crime, affecting the character of the President beyond all possibility of defence, and serving to explain the latter acts upon which the impeachment is founded. It was in this chamber, in the face of the Senate and the ministers of foreign powers, and surrounded by the gaze of thronged galleries, that Andrew Johnson exhibited himself in a state of beastly intoxication while he took his oath of office as Vice President; and all that he has done since is of record here. Much of it appears on our journals. The rest is in authentic documents published by the order of the Senate. Never was a record more complete.

"Here in the Senate we know officially how he has made himself the attorney of slavery—the usurper of legislative power—the violator of law—the patron of rebels—the helping hand of the rebellion—the kicker from office of good citizens—the open bung-hole of the treasury—the architect of the 'whiskey ring'—the stumbling block to all good laws by wanton vetoes and then by criminal hindrances; all these things are known here beyond question. . . .

"This is the transcendent crime of Andrew Johnson. For the sake of slavery . . . he has set at defiance the Constitution and the laws of the land and he has accompanied their unquestionable usurpation by brutalities and indecencies in office without precedent unless we go back to the Roman Emperor fiddling or the French monarch dancing among his minions. This usurpation with its brutalities and indecencies became manifest as long ago as the winter of 1866. . . .

"Plainly he ought to have been impeached and expelled at that early day. The case against him was complete. . . . So strong is my conviction of the fatal remissness of the House, that I think the Senate would do a duty . . . if it reprimanded the House of Representatives for this delay. . . . Meanwhile the President proceeded with his transgressions. There is nothing of usurpation that he has not attempted. . . . It is difficult to measure the vastness of this usurpation involving as it did a general nullification. Strafford was not bolder when . . . he boasted that 'the little finger of prerogative was heavier than the loins of the law.' . . . No monarch, no despot, no sultan, could claim more than an American President: for he claimed all."

The massacres in the South! It was Andrew Johnson "who animated the wicked crew." "He was at the head of the work." "Fire, Famine and Slaughter shriek forth—

'He let me loose, and cried Halloo!
To him alone the praise is due!'"

Referring to the President's speeches, this senator could write down and file for preservation in our national archives, such utterances as these: "From their brutalities and indecencies" they are "in the nature of a 'criminal exposure of his person,' indictable at common law, for which no judgment can be too severe." And

"They were the utterances of a drunken man; and yet it does not appear that he was drunk. ' Now it is according to the precedents of our history that a person disqualified by drunkenness shall be removed from office. This was the case of Pickering in 1804. But a sober man, whose conduct suggests drunkenness, is as bad at least as if he were drunk. Is he not worse? If without the explanation of drunkenness he made such harangues, it seems to me that his unfitness for office becomes more evident, inasmuch as his deplorable condition is natural and not abnormal. The drunken man has lucid intervals; but where is the assurance of a lucid interval for this perpetual offender? Derangement is with him the normal condition."

As on all questions where he took a side he was never troubled with a shadow of a doubt, so now he was absolutely certain of his cause. "To my vision the path is as clear as day. Never in history was there a great case more free from all doubt. If Andrew Johnson is not guilty, there never was a political offender guilty before; and, if his acquittal is taken as a precedent, never can a political offender be found guilty again. The proofs are mountainous."

Fessenden, in his opinion, says with great force and dignity:

"To the suggestion that popular opinion demands the conviction of the President . . . I reply that he is not on trial before the people, but before the Senate. . . . The people have not heard the evidence as we have heard it. The responsibility is not on them, but upon us. They have not taken an oath 'to do impartial justice according to the Constitution and the laws.' I have taken that oath. I cannot render judgment upon their conviction nor can they transfer to themselves my punishment if I violate my own."

Sumner, in the peroration he elaborated on the lines of the best models of vituperative oratory, takes a different view:

"Something also has been said of the people, now watching our proceedings with patriotic solicitude, and it has been proclaimed that they are wrong to intrude their judgment. I do not think so. This is a political proceeding, which the people at this moment are as competent to decide as the Senate. They are the multitudinous jury; for, on this impeachment, involving the public safety, the vicinage is the whole country. It is they who have sent us here as their representatives, and in their name to consult for the common weal. In nothing can we escape their judgment, least of all on a question like that now before us. It is a mistake to suppose that the Senate only has heard the evidence. The people have heard it also, day by day, as it was delivered, and have carefully considered the case on its merits, properly dismissing all apologetic subtleties. It will be for them to review what has been done. They are above the Senate and will 'rejudge its justice.' . . .

"The people cannot witness with indifference the abandonment of the great Secretary, who organized their armies against the rebellion and then organized victory. . . . Nor is it forgotten that the Senate, by two solemn votes of more than two-thirds, has twice instructed him to stay at the War Department, the President to the contrary notwithstanding. The people will not easily understand on what principle of Constitution, law, or morals, the Senate can twice instruct the Secretary to stay, and then, by another vote, deliberately surrender him a prey to Presidential tyranny. Talk of a somersault; talk of self-stultification; are not both here?"

The student of our history, who would gain a clear and adequate idea of the kind of man Charles Sumner really was, should not confine his glance to the haloed champion of the negro slave or to the unresisting victim of the blows of Brooks; he should turn aside from these high altitudes and spend a profitable hour in perusing the opinion of the senator sitting in judgment upon Andrew Johnson.

One more opinion claims a passing notice. John Sherman, the reader already knows, had put himself beyond the possibility of voting the President guilty of a crime in removing the Secretary of War, without an utter loss of self-respect; and, therefore, in the opinion filed he is only the more solemnly emphatic in saying so. Referring to the language of the proviso adopted by the conference of which he was a member, he writes: "To hold that the words inserted were intended to warn the President not to remove Stanton upon peril of being convicted of a high misdemeanor, is to punish the President as a criminal for the violation of a delphic oracle." He goes farther:

"I stated explicitly that the act as reported did not protect from removal the members of the Cabinet appointed by Mr. Lincoln, that President Johnson might remove them at pleasure; and I named the Secretary of War as one that might be removed. . . . I could not conceive a case where the Senate would require the President to perform his great executive office upon the advice and through the heads of departments personally obnoxious to him, and whom he had not appointed, and, therefore, no such case was provided for. . . . This construction of the law, made when these proceedings could not have been contemplated, . . . is binding upon no one but myself. But can I, who made it and declared it to you, and still believe it to be the true and legal interpretation of those words, can I pronounce the President guilty of crime, and by that vote aid to remove him from his high office for doing what I declared and still believe he had a legal right to do. God forbid.

"A Roman Emperor attained immortal infamy by posting his laws above the reach of the people and then punishing their violation as a crime. An American senator would excel this refinement of tyranny, if, when passing a law, he declared an act to be innocent, and then as a judge punished the same act as a crime. For this reason I could not vote for the resolution of the 21st of February, and cannot say 'guilty' to these articles."

He, therefore, acquits the President on the charge embodied in the first article; the corner-stone of the impeachment. And, yet, he convicts the President under the second and third that drew their whole validity from the first; for, if the President might lawfully vacate the War Office, his temporary appointment of Thomas, with or without statutory authority, could work no harm to the body-politic, carried no significance whatever and was utterly devoid of criminality. Even Sumner acknowledged that the removal of Stanton was "the pivot of the Impeachment; so much so that the whole case seems to revolve on this transaction." And Fessenden truly said of the *ad interim* appointment:

"To hold that an act of such a character, prohibited by no law, having the sanction of long practice, necessary for the transaction of business, and which the President might well be justified in believing authorized by existing law, was a high misdemeanor justifying the removal of the President would in my judgment be, in itself, a monstrous perversion of justice, if not of itself a violation of the Constitution."

Sherman struggles to show that the act of 1863 repealed the act of 1795; as if the technical want of authority in consequence made any difference whatever on the question of culpability in an *ad interim* appointment to fill a vacancy he himself acknowledges was lawfully made. He strives to believe that the President "had formed a fixed resolve . . . to fill the vacancy without the advice of the Senate"; and, in the face of the facts that the nomination of Thomas Ewing was sent to the Senate as quickly as possible and the nomination of General Schofield at the moment of his writing lay upon the table of the Senate, he claims that the President "might have secured a new Secretary of War by sending a proper nomination to the Senate."

The eleventh article, according to the construction put upon it by the Chief Justice, made but one substantive charge, viz: an attempt to prevent Stanton from resuming his office after the Senate disapproved his suspension; a charge of no validity to a senator who believed the President had a right to remove the suspended officer altogether. And, yet, the senator votes the President 'guilty' under it, assigning as a reason that the article "contains many allegations which I regard in the nature of inducement, but it includes within it the charge of wilful violation of law more specifically set out in the second, third and eighth articles; and I shall therefore vote for it." No mention is made of the *ad interim* appointment of Thomas in the eleventh article; and, according to the reasoning of his opinion, he found the President 'guilty' under it, because the matters, alleged in that article by way of inducement to the commission of an offence of which the senator felt obliged to acquit the President, led up to the commission of an offence, charged in the second article but not mentioned in the eleventh, for which the senator found himself able to convict. In short, the single act, for the doing of which Sherman found the President guilty of a misdemeanour deserving removal from office, consisted, wholly, in the issue of an unexecuted letter of authority to fill temporarily an office vacant, according to the senator's own opinion, *de jure,* but, owing to the unlawful and successful resistance of the actual incumbent, never for a moment vacant *de facto.*

The truth is that the course of Sherman was calculated and prepared beforehand. He was one of the most prominent senators in the caucuses which were held at every stage of the impeachment. At an early day he must have made known to his associates in the House and the Senate the perplexing predicament in which he stood; and there is very little doubt that the articles were manipulated into the shape they took, as it is certain the order of voting was changed, that he might find standing-room with his party in convicting the President without too ostentatiously convicting himself. The event proved otherwise, however. Andrew Johnson was acquitted. It was John Sherman who was convicted, and convicted by himself.

In the meantime, what had become of the great War Minister—the bone of this loud contention? Barricaded in the interior of the War Department; guarded by sentinels within and without; succoured, sustained and solaced by sympathizing senators, representatives and officers of the army; labouring incessantly through every available channel to compass the removal of the chief who had presumed to attempt his own—he bowed to the final vote of the Senate and, letting go his hold of the office to which he had so tenaciously clung, dropped from the surface of public affairs deeper than ever plummet sounded. He sent a letter to the President informing him, with quiet insolence, that the Senate, having failed to support its resolution condemnatory of the President's attempt to remove the Secretary of War by a sufficient majority to turn the President himself out of office, he "relinquished charge of the War Department"; and, then, he took himself off the scene. The President paid no attention to his letter. The Senate confirmed the nomination of Schofield as his successor. He received the thanks of both Houses of Congress. But it was everywhere felt that he was effaced. He continued to reside in Washington; but the high places of authority, which he so much coveted, knew him no more. We chance to hear of him in the fall orating for General Grant, notwithstanding the nominee seems to have turned a cold shoulder to him. At Cleveland and Philadelphia and other local centres, he is heard extolling the great soldier as eminently fitted for the high civil office to which he aspired. In a speech made at his native place, he told his former neighbours, among other warm words of praise, that General Grant's "capacity and integrity for civil administration were equally manifest in the vast territory in which he operated."

A year passes by; Grant has been elected and inaugurated; and, in December, 1869, Stanton is lying ill at his residence at Washington. On Friday, the seventeenth of the month, to senator Chandler who, in company with two friends, calls on him, the sick man "expresses the highest opinion of President Grant both as to his military and civil capacity." To Wade he also remarks: "The country knows General Grant to be a great warrior; I know he will prove a great civilian."* That same night the idea occurs to senator Carpenter of Wisconsin, "that something might be done to insure the appointment of Mr. Stanton as judge of the Supreme Court";—an appointment, talked about and expected, but that did not come. The President appeared to be unwilling. Carpenter draws up a letter to the President recommending Stanton for the office, and, taking it around the Chamber, in less than twenty minutes obtains thirty-seven signatures of Republican senators. The next morning, the senator rides to Mr. Stanton's house and shows him the letter; "and" (to use Carpenter's words) "as he glanced over it the tears started down his cheeks. He said not a word." The senator carries the letter to the White House, where Chandler by previous arrangement awaits him. The President seems "delighted to have the letter" which banishes as he says, the last lingering scruple that troubled him over the appointment, and he requests both senators to "go to Stanton's house and tell him his name would be sent in on Monday morning." On receiving this message Stanton exclaims: "The kindness of General Grant—it is perfectly characteristic of him—will do more to cure me than all the skill of the doctors." On Monday (the twentieth) the nomination of Edwin M.

* Chandler's speech, *Globe*, 2d Sess. 42d Cong., pp. 4282, 4283.

Stanton for Associate Justice of the Supreme Court of the United States, in the place of Justice Grier, is received by the Senate and instantly confirmed.*

Charles Sumner may now, again, take the floor. In an elaborate philippic against President Grant, delivered in the Senate May 31, 1872, he cites the "testimony of the late Edwin M. Stanton" as follows:

"On reaching Washington at the opening of Congress in 1869, I was pained to hear that Mr. Stanton, lately Secretary of War, was in failing health. Full of gratitude for his unsurpassed services, and with a sentiment of friendship quickened by common political sympathies, I lost no time in seeing him, and repeated my visits until his death, toward the close of the same month. My last visit was marked by a communication never to be forgotten. As I entered his bed-room where I found him reclining on a sofa, propped up by pillows, he reached out his hand, already clammy cold, and in reply to my inquiry 'How are you,' answered, 'Waiting for my furlough.' Then at once, with singular solemnity, he said, 'I have something to say to you.' When I was seated he proceeded without one word of introduction: 'I know General Grant better than any other person in the country can know him. It was my duty to study him, and I did so day and night, when I saw him and when I did not see him, and now I tell you what I know, *he cannot govern this country.'* The intensity of his manner and the positiveness of his judgment surprised me, for though I was aware that the late Secretary of War did not place the President very high in general capacity, I was not prepared for a judgment so strongly couched. At last, after some delay, oc-

* Carpenter's Speech, *Globe, id.*, App., p. 560.

cupied in meditating his remarkable words, I observed, 'What you say is very broad.' 'It is true it is very broad,' he replied promptly. I added, 'You are tardy; you tell this late; why did you not say it before his nomination?' He answered that he was not consulted about the nomination, and had no opportunity of expressing his opinion upon it, besides being much occupied at the time by his duties as Secretary of War and his contest with the President. I followed by saying, 'But you took part in the Presidential election, and made a succession of speeches for him in Ohio and Pennsylvania.' 'I spoke,' said he, 'but I never introduced the name of General Grant. I spoke for the Republican party and the Republican cause.' This was the last time I saw Mr. Stanton. A few days later I followed him to the grave where he now rests.*

What shall we say? Was there any real Stanton after all? Senator Carpenter asserted: "If Mr. Stanton made that declaration to the Senator from Massachusetts under the circumstances detailed by him, if there is a word of substantial truth in that whole paragraph, if it is not an infamous fabrication from first to last, then Mr. Stanton was the most double-faced and dishonest man that ever lived."† Judge Black, commenting on the eulogistic testimonials to Stanton's clandestine intercourse with the radicals while fawning on Buchanan—which Henry Wilson thrust upon the public with characteristic unconsciousness of their damning import—comes to the same hypothetical conclusion: "Surely if these things are true, he was the most marvellous impostor that ever lived or died."‡

* *Globe*, 2d Sess. 42d Cong., pp. 4112–3.

† His speech cited as above.

‡ Black to Wilson, *Galaxy*, June, 1870, February, 1871.

Four days after he attained the prize which, it is said, before his entrance into the War Office, had been the goal of his ambition—just after passing his fifty-fifth year—the news came that Stanton was dead. Despite his illness, his decease came upon his friends, as well as the country, with a shock of surprise. People were at a loss to account for it. Dark rumours, engendered by the mysterious secrecy enshrouding the last hours of the dying, and the obsequies of the dead, man, were soon everywhere afloat, and are not at rest even to this day. It would seem as if the Genius of Duplicity could not forsake so congenial a spirit even in the forecourt of the Undeceivable King.

[As a matter of fact, Stanton never was a justice of the Supreme Court. He was appointed in place of Judge Grier, whose resignation did not take effect until February the first, 1870. His commission, however, was issued to him, he was sworn in hurriedly in the article of death, and a sum equal to one year's salary of the office was appropriated by Congress to his widow and children. See Carpenter's speech *ut supra* and *Globe,* 2d Sess. 41st Cong., pp. 1799–1800, 2081.]

CONCLUSION

The Congress sat until the twenty-seventh day of July and, then, with an eye to the result of the campaign, adjourned only to the twenty-first of September, on which day, unless otherwise ordered, the two Houses were to further adjourn until the regular day of meeting. But, although the President still kept up the fight over reconstruction with undiminished ardour and with a confidence in the righteousness of his hopeless cause which the process of time proved to be not ill-founded;—vetoing the bills passed for the admission of those of the Southern states which the Congress decided to be sufficiently Africanized to vote on the 'loyal' side in the presidential election—no further effort was made to impeach him; the time drawing nigh when by the expiration of his term the majority would be rid of him, and the fiercest radical having had enough of so cumbrous and costly a remedy. Thaddeus Stevens, indeed, on the seventh day of July, exhibited five additional articles of impeachment, with no intent that they should be considered, but merely to serve as a vehicle for a valedictory tirade, of which the following extract may be fitly called the last words of this remarkable man.

"After mature reflection and thorough examination of ancient and modern history, I have come to the fixed conclusion that neither in Europe nor America will the Chief

Executive of a nation be again removed by peaceful means. If he retains the money and the patronage of the Government it will be found, as it has been found, stronger than the law and impenetrable to the spear of justice. If tyranny becomes intolerable, the only resource will be found in the dagger of Brutus. God grant that it may never be used.

"I can recollect but two men whom I deem absolutely impenetrable to temptation, he of Athens and he of Bethlehem. The counselor who gives the chief suggestions to our acquitted President did not deem the latter above corruption. He took him to the top of the highest mountain and offered him all the kingdoms of the earth to bow down and worship him. . . .

"My sands are nearly run and I can only see with the eye of faith. I am fast descending the downhill of life, at the foot of which stands an open grave. But you, sir, are promised length of days and a brilliant career. If you and your compeers can fling away ambition and realize that every human being, however lowly born or degraded by fortune, is your equal, that every inalienable right that belongs to you belongs also to him, truth and righteousness will spread over the land, and you will look down from the top of the Rocky mountains upon an empire of one hundred million of happy people.

"Still, we must remember not to place our trust in princes, for we have seen that in the richest heart, in the most cultivated mind, adorned with every literary grace, keen in argument as the Stagerite and fortified with an outward shield of bronzed austerity which seemed to forbid the approach of levity or corruption; this richest composition of human mold may be the abode of malignity, avarice, corroding lust, and uncontrollable ambition, as the owl, the prairie-dog, and rattlesnake nestle together in loving harmony in the richest soil of the prairie."*

He remained at his post to the end of the session but he was evidently struggling with death. Daily he was carried up the stairs leading to the House by coloured servants to whom, with that grim humour of his, he would say: "Boys, I wonder who will carry me when you are all dead!"† He died in Washington two weeks after the adjournment. In his will he directed his body to be buried at a spot chosen by himself in a private cemetery at Lancaster, and the following inscription, prepared by himself, placed upon his tomb:

"I repose in this quiet and secluded spot, not from any natural preference for solitude, but, finding other cemeteries limited by charter rules as to race, I have chosen it that I might be enabled to illustrate in my death the principles which I have advocated through a long life—the equality of man before his Creator."

While making no provision for the care of his own grave, he set apart an ample sum for the care of his mother's, ordering "that the sexton keep the grave in good order, and plant roses and other cheerful flowers at each of the four corners of the grave every spring"; and he left a legacy of one thousand dollars to the church of which his mother was a member, adding:

"I do this out of respect to the memory of my mother, to whom I owe whatever little of prosperity I have had on earth, which, small as it is, I desire emphatically to acknowledge."

* *Globe*, 2d Sess. 40th Cong., pp. 3790–1.

† Julian's Political Recollections, p. 313.

Sumner, for whom he bore an instinctive antipathy, closed the eulogy he pronounced upon him in the Senate with these eloquent words:

"I see him now, as I have so often seen him during life. His venerable form moves slowly and with uncertain steps; but the gathered strength of years is in his countenance and the light of victory on his path. Politician, calculator, time-server, stand aside! A hero-statesman passes to his reward."*

Here, this history, in accordance with its title, ought to end. But a sketch of the after-career of the man who was the only President of the United States ever impeached and who came within one vote of being convicted and removed from that high office, seems to us not an inappropriate appendix.

Before the Democratic national convention that met in the city of New York on the fourth day of July, 1868, Andrew Johnson, without doubt, was the logical candidate. He had been the protagonist of the opposition to the reconstruction acts. He had made the fight. He represented as no other man could one side of the real issue. But on the other hand he had no distinctive party behind him. His own section he had fought against. The party that had elected him Vice President now regarded him with universal hatred. The minority party looked coldly on him as a deserter from its ranks. And, what was most unjust of all, he was

* Stevens's obsequies, *Globe*, 3d Sess. 40th Cong., p. 129 *et seq.* Sumner's eulogy, p. 150–1.

considered out of the field because he happened to be a citizen of a Southern state. Johnson, himself, made no serious effort to obtain the nomination; at no time entertaining the faintest expectation of receiving it. Two days before the convention met, replying to a letter from ten eminent citizens of the city of New York inquiring whether he would allow his name to be presented to that body, he wrote:

> "I am not ambitious of further service—I may say, indeed, of further endurance in that elevated and responsible position, unless by a call so general and unequivocal that it would be an endorsement by the people of my endeavors to defend the Constitution and the reserved rights of the several commonwealths composing what was once in fact the Federal Union. Of such approval, in the present temper of parties, I can, perhaps, have no reasonable expectation.
>
> "All history proves that men who, in official position, oppose for any reason the cherished schemes devised by factions to acquire power, usually find more determined assailants than open and earnest defenders. Hence, in resisting measures which, although sustained by Congress, I honestly believed to be encroachments upon the Constitution, my task has been made arduous and seemingly ungracious by an opposition powerful, well-organized, and possessing a controlling influence in the halls of legislation unprecedented in the history of the country. . . .
>
> "In the midst of these embarrassments I have not been discouraged, when from the public prints, or from some unusually frank and outspoken friend, I have heard that I 'have no party.' The suggestion has only served to remind me of a memorable remark, uttered when faction

ruled high in Rome, that 'Cæsar had a party, and Pompey and Crassus each a party, but that the Commonwealth had none.' . . .

"Constrained, in occupying my position as the Federal Executive, to abide in silence wrongs and encroachments of the most insidious as well as desperate character, or sometimes, when incapable of arresting them, permitted only to employ futile protests; compelled, with only the privilege of remonstrance or the terrible alternative of counter-revolution, to resist revolutionary projects; obliged to stand in the attitude of a mere spectator, whilst the invaluable time of the nation has been wasted in causeless assaults upon myself and office for the benefit of a party, I cannot complain if the people, while witnessing the scene, have not been able to make my cause thoroughly their own—the defence of the Constitution and laws their own battle."

He received sixty-five votes on the first ballot, next in number to Pendleton who led with one hundred and five. The nomination was forced on Horatio Seymour whose chances of election were virtually destroyed by the advocacy of the "greenback" heresy in the platform and by an indiscreet letter written by General Blair before he was nominated for Vice President, recommending, in substance, armed resistance to congressional reconstruction, to be led by the President-elect. Still, when the Houses met, in September, the result was thought so doubtful that a sufficient number of members assembled to make a quorum and resorted to the extraordinary expedient of adjourning until the eleventh of October, the Friday succeeding the state elections in Pennsylvania, Ohio and Indiana—on that day, unless otherwise ordered, to further adjourn to the tenth day of November—one week after the presidential election—and on that day, unless otherwise ordered, to finally adjourn to the regular day of meeting. Had the three October states failed them, the majority were prepared, at the first adjourned session, to adopt some revolutionary measures to stem the rising tide of "disloyalty" in the North; and, had they been beaten in the general election, their November session would have been occupied in devising means for doing with Seymour what was done aftewards with Tilden. As it was, the October states were carried by the Republicans but by the narrowest majorities; and, this settling the result, the two adjourned meetings were merely formal.

When the Congress met for the regular session, the message of the President interrupted the jubilation of the majority over their triumph. Pleading his constitutional duty "from time to time" to "give to the Congress information of the state of the Union and recommend to their consideration such measures as he shall judge necessary and expedient," the President gravely informed the two Houses that their reconstruction acts "after a fair trial" had "substantially failed and proved pernicious in their results and there seems to be no good reason why they should remain longer on the statute-book"; that "the legislator or ruler who has the wisdom and magnanimity to retrace his steps, when convinced of error, will sooner or later be rewarded with the respect and gratitude of an intelligent and patriotic people"; that "legislation producing such baneful consequences should be abrogated''; that other acts, such as the ''Tenure-of-office bill'' and that section of the army appropriation act which interfered with the President's constitutional functions as commander-in-chief, had been ''passed under the influence of party passion and sectional prejudice'' and were ''unwarranted by the Constitution''; and that

> ''the repeal of all such laws would be accepted by the American people as at least a partial return to the fundamental principles of the Government, and an indication that hereafter the Constitution is to be made the nation's safe and unerring guide. They can be productive of no permanent benefit to the country, and should not be permitted to stand as so many monuments of the deficient wisdom which has characterized our recent legislation.''

To this language the Senate listened with visible impatience. But, when, in the course of an exposition of the financial condition of the government and the unprecedent amount of the public expenditures, the President declared that ''one hundred millions annually are expended for the military force, a large portion of which is employed in the execution of laws both unnecessary and unconstitutional''—the majority could bear it no longer. Conness started to his feet, interrupted the secretary and moved that the further reading of the ''offensive document'' be dispensed with. Howe thought the Senate not bound to listen to a ''lecture'' so disrespectful in language. Wilson thought it both disrespectful and untruthful, calling the President ''a disappointed, bad man''; to which characterization, Cameron subjoined: "he has disgraced the place he holds for nearly four years." It was not until they had slept upon the question that the senators came to the conclusion Morton expressed, that "the refusal to hear it will be regarded as a mere matter of spite, and will do the President less harm than it will do ourselves"; and the reading of the message was completed.

The method of treatment adopted by the House was more effective. The message was read through to unlistening ears and then the majority pounced upon an unlucky paragraph suggesting a plan for the extinguishment of the public debt:

> "Our national credit should be sacredly observed; but in making provision for our creditors we should not forget what is due to the masses of the people. It may be assumed that the holders of our securities have already received upon their bonds a larger amount than their original investment, measured by a gold standard. Upon this statement of facts it would seem but just and equitable that the six per cent. interest now paid by the Government should be applied to the reduction of the principal in semiannual installments, which in sixteen years and eight months would liquidate the entire national debt. Six per cent. in gold would at the present rates be equal to nine per cent. in currency, and equivalent to the payment of the debt one and a half times in a fraction less than seventeen years. This, in connection with all the other advantages derived from their investment, would afford to the public creditors a fair and liberal compensation for the use of their capital, and with this they should be satisfied. The lessons of the past admonish the lender that it is not well

to be over-anxious in exacting from the borrower rigid compliance with the letter of the bond."

This proposition Washburne considered "plain, undisguised repudiation," and denounced it "as a disgrace to the country and to the Chief Magistrate who has sent in this message." Schenck called it "a most gross, shameless and infamous proposition." Broomall offered a resolution declaring "all forms and degrees of repudiation of national indebtedness odious to the American people"—which was adopted on the succeeding Monday. The Senate, following in the wake of the House, "utterly disapproved and condemned" the proposition, but not until after a denunciatory discussion of some days. Several senators worked themselves into a towering rage over it. Nye shuddered at it; "it is a great crime to suggest it," he exclaimed with unwonted seriousness; "it is a crime to think of it; and a double crime for the Executive to send forth that alarming sentiment to the country." Warner—Ohio's precious gift to Alabama—who gloried, as he said, "in that progressive spirit which made him a carpetbagger," could not resist the promptings of his honest soul to offer a resolution distinctly stigmatizing it as "dishonest." Howard branded it as a "foul recommendation," "a recommendation of piracy and robbery."

The whole force of these heated epithets rests upon the assumption that the President meant to recommend the plan he outlined as a mode of liquidation compulsory upon the bondholders. And, read by itself, it must be acknowledged that the paragraph is susceptible of this construction. But, as was clearly pointed out by senators friendly to the President, when read in connection with the context, the plan suggested, so far from being compulsory, presupposed the consent of the bondholders, who, the President himself conjectures, may not "be averse to a settlement" "which would yield them a fair remuneration."*

At the close of the message, the President again recommends the proposal of a constitutional amendment to which he had in vain called the attention of the Congress by a special message in July. Its three main provisions, (1) the election of the President and Vice President directly by the people, (2) the election of senators in the same manner, (3) the limitation of the term of federal judges to a period of years, had been the subject of his advocacy even in ante-war days. The first two are still subjects of increasing popular agitation, but the third has never as yet met with much favour. To these was added a fourth, manifestly the fruit of the Impeachment. He recommends a distinct designation of the person to discharge the duties of President in case of vacancy of both presidency and vice presidency, and the person so designated not to be a member of the legislative department, as heretofore, for the reason, as appears by the special message, that "both are interested in producing a vacancy and . . . are members of the tribunal by whose decree a vacancy may me produced." On the contrary, the presidency should

* *Globe*, 3d Sess. 40th Cong., pp. 28–9, 44 in Senate, pp. 33–4 in House. Dixon's speech in App., p. 44.

devolve on the several members of the Cabinet in an order to be named, and thus the successorship be confined to the executive department where the vacancies belong. This desirable reform has since (1886) been effected, not by constitutional amendment, but by act of Congress.*

On Christmas of the year 1868—a season most appropriate for so beneficent a gift—the President issued his last amnesty proclamation. The three preceding proclamations—May, 1865, September, 1867, July, 1868—exhibited an ever-narrowing range of exceptions, the one of July excepting only those offenders actually under indictment. Now, even this last limit was swept away; and Andrew Johnson enjoyed the enviable privilege of proclaiming, "In the name of the sovereign people of the United States," "unconditionally and without reservation, to all and to every person who directly or indirectly participated in the late insurrection or rebellion, a full pardon and amnesty for the offence of treason against the United States, or of adhering to their enemies during the late civil war, with restoration of all rights, privileges and immunities under the Constitution and the laws." The Senate, not approving of this indiscriminate manner of dealing out relief—even to the unrepentant Jefferson Davis—called upon the President for his authority. The President replied that his authority was the Federal Constitution "understood to be and regarded" by him "as the supreme law of the land," the second section of the second article of which provided that the President

* For Message see McPh. Recon., p. 384.

"shall have power to grant reprieves and pardons"; and, also, "the precedent established by Washington in 1795, and followed by Presidents Adams in 1800, Madison in 1815, Lincoln in 1863," and himself in 1865. 1867, and 1868.*

The sole achievement of this session was the adoption of the fifteenth amendment to the Constitution, designed to guarantee manhood suffrage to the negroes throughout the land; over which it is not our purpose to linger. We cannot refrain, however, from giving a brief account of an attempt at legislation which, though unsuccessful for the time being, is memorable because of the light it reflects on the impeachment and trial of the President. On the eleventh day of January, 1869, not yet a year since the House impeached Andrew Johnson for its alleged violation, Washburne—the *fidus Achates* of the President-elect who, it was understood on all hands, desired the total repeal of the Tenure-of-office act—introduced a bill for that purpose. It was read a first and second time, the main question was ordered, and, with but a feeble murmur of remonstrance from a single member, the bill was instantly passed; Boutwell, Bingham, Butler and Wilson, who had lauded it as the palladium of the Republican officeholder and denounced its violation as a sacrilege of the most heinous kind, joining with the Democrats, who had always condemned it as unconstitutional and pernicious, in sweeping the measure from the statute book. In the Senate, however, although the majority were just as eager to effect the repeal, there lingered some sense of shame. The bill,

* For Proclamation, *id.*, p. 419.

on coming from the House, was referred to a committee, and the committee reported it back with an amendment in the form of a substitute amounting to repeal in a disguised form. The principal clause of the first section of the existing act prescribing the tenure of all civil offices (not inferior), was retained but the heart was taken out of it by converting the famous proviso into an unconditional exception of cabinet officers, and by giving the President arbitrary power to suspend any officer during the recess; thus of course dispensing with the necessity of stating his reasons in his report to the Senate. They left just enough of the old law to save the consistency of such senators as Edmunds and Howe, whose asseverations that the act was not legislation "for to-day, or to-morrow, or the next year, or the next four years, but for the country and the future," still echoed from the walls of the chamber. Even as it was, some senators with refreshing candour avowed their real desire. Said Morton: "I am in favor of the total repeal of the law. I believe it was a mistake from the beginning. I do not believe that the country or the Republican party ever derived any benefit from it. . . . This amendment is good so far as it goes in allowing the President to choose the members of his Cabinet . . . ; the idea of ever preventing a President from doing that was absurd, was contrary to the very nature of administration."*

The debate was postponed and the subject was not resumed at this session. But, as soon as the new Congress assembled, the perfunctory contest between the

* *Globe*, 3d Sess. 40th Cong., pp. 936–7 in Senate, pp. 282–3 in House.

twc Houses was recommenced. President Grant demands a free hand. The House again passes a bill of total repeal. The senators would fain accommodate the President, but some of them are still ashamed to stultify themselves so far. At last, the troublesome business is compromised by preserving for decency's sake two fragments of the famous law. One looks substantial—prohibiting, apparently, all removals except by the authority making the appointment; but, as is perceptible on a closer glance, confining its application to offices having a fixed term and therefore not including the heads of departments. The other makes what might have been so far substantial in the first nugatory by granting to the President an unlimited arbitrary power of suspension in respect to all civil offices during recess until the end of the next session of the Senate; nominations sent in to be followed in case of disapproval, not by the reinstatement of the displaced officer, but by—another nomination.*

Meanwhile, the bondsman and intended victim of the statute which its authors are now so diligent in clearing away from the path of his successor is quietly preparing for his exit. The "Plebeian Boy," as he styled himself in his inaugural address as Vice President, after having fought his way through every grade of office up to the highest, there to find no rest or respite but, on the contrary, the heaviest fighting of his life, is now putting off his well-worn armour. Beaten at every point, it was only by the merest chance that he has not been degraded and deposed. No administration was ever so utterly

* *Globe*, 1st Sess. 41st Cong., pp. 40, 394–5, 402–6.

thwarted in its substantial aims. No President ever laid down his office so bereft of a party. No lifelong public functionary ever retired from the stage of affairs whose lapse into oblivion looked so final. Amid the enthusiasm aroused by the inauguration of 'the Conquering Hero of the Civil War,' the whole world seemed to have turned its back upon him. His sun was not only setting and in clouds and darkness, but it appeared to have already set—gone down before its appointed time. In the gorgeous pageant with which the incoming President was ushered into his high place, there was no room for him. John Adams absconded from the capital rather than face his successful competitor; and Jefferson, in consequence, rode to his inauguration alone. Jackson shunned all personal intercourse with his predecessor whom he held responsible for the slanders heaped upon his wife in the recent campaign—slanders which he believed had hastened her death; and the second Adams was absent from the inauguration. With these two exceptions, from the foundation of the government, whenever there was an outgoing as well as an incoming President, the two chief figures sat side by side in the same carriage in the procession and stood side by side at the taking of the oath. But, on the present occasion, the figure of Andrew Johnson was conspicuous by its absence. Not because the outgoing President was not ready to discharge his share of the ceremony. Johnson had not a particle of that species of vanity which drives its possessor into foolishness through the chagrin of defeat; and he was of too magnanimous a nature to allow his personal disputes to interfere with the proper performance of a great public function. But the conqueror of Lee could not get over the question of veracity that had been so nakedly thrust upon him by the President with his Cabinet at his back, and he refused to ride in the same carriage or walk arm-in-arm with a civilian of so militant a disposition. So, with the booming of cannon, the beating of drums, the ringing of bells and the strains of martial music,—the Hero of the hour, sitting alone with his resentment, swept up the Avenue with the shouting multitude at his heels, leaving the despised Apostate behind.

And he? So far from being daunted or discouraged in the slightest degree, the despised Apostate acted as though he believed the real triumph was his own. Up to the last minute of the last hour of that term which his adversaries denied him in theory and of which they tried to deprive him in fact, he remained at his post; and then, as the clock struck noon on the fourth day of March, 1869, while his successor was taking the oath on the portico of the capitol, he stepped out of the front door of the White House, stepped down into the street and took up his place again in the ranks of the common people. Such a thing as final defeat he never for a moment acknowledged. The want of a party he did not feel. Obscurity was his birth-place and had no terrors for him. The unbroken isolation in which he found himself, so far from cowing his spirits, raised them to an unwonted height of self-glorification. At a moment when he seemed buried beneath a popular repudiation almost universal, he thought it no presumption to put himself on the same level with the most illustrious and the most masterful of his predecessors, and, like Washington and Jackson, speak to the people in the language of a father of his country. Side by side with the Inaugural Address of President Grant—of which all that is memorable now are the declaration that, while feeling "the responsibilities of the position," he, unlike Washington, "accepted them without fear," and the reflection cast upon the course of his immediate predecessor by the promise to execute all laws whether meeting his approval or not, and to have no policy to enforce against the will of the people—there sped across the country the Farewell Address of ex-President Andrew Johnson, vindicating the policy of his administration in terms of equal self-sufficiency, and rehearsing "the catalogue of crimes" of the majority in Congress in a style as direct and unsparing as that in which the writer of the Declaration of Independence denounces the usurpations of "Great George, Our King."* In short, after the four years battle, if the multitudinous hosts of the victors were at last taking exclusive possession of the field, it was no less true that the solitary vanquished was retreating with his face to the foe, his flag unlowered, his shield unbroken, proclaiming with a far-resounding voice his faith in the future triumph of his cause.

And, when viewed in the light of subsequent events, it must be admitted that is was not the self-assurance of Grant—regarded at the time by some of his worshippers as sublime—but the self-assurance of Johnson—regarded at the time as ridiculous when not disregarded

* **Published in pamphlet and in newspapers of the period.**

with contempt—that rested upon solid grounds. Wonderful as was the career of Andrew Johnson up to his accession to the Presidency, his exploits in the last six years of his life were more wonderful still. Hardly had he struck the bottom of the abyss into which his descent from the topmost pinnacle precipitated him, before he began to gather his scattered forces to begin the slow and toilsome reascent. Not a moment was wasted in supineness, in useless upbraidings of fortune, in unavailing lamentations; not even an hour spared for much needed rest. In fact, even before the close of his presidency he had signified to his friends in Tennessee his willingness to run for governor at the approaching election, with a view of being sent at once to the Senate of the United States. His own state was set all agog by the heralded return of her once favourite son, and his first footfall on her soil shook the hybrid tyranny that defiled her to its very base.

The Republican state convention of the twentieth of May, 1869, broke up in a fight between the faction that favoured the abandonment of a proscriptive policy against the whites and the faction that still kept up the cry of "No quarter to rebels!" and the result was two conventions and two tickets. Senter, the speaker of the Senate and, by virtue of that office, governor in the absence of Brownlow, was the candidate of the first faction; and, strange to say, he was favoured by Brownlow himself—the fiercest foe of Johnson—sitting now in the recent seat of Johnson's son-in-law in the Senate of the United States. Col. William B. Stokes was the candidate of the second. The opportunity afforded by this split the ex-President did not let slip. He advised his friends and the conservatives at large to throw their united force in favour of the candidate who would open the avenue which led to their normal supremacy. As for himself, the Senate of the United States was the goal on which he had fixed his eye; he longed for a return to that chamber which had witnessed his trial for high crimes and misdemeanours. Accordingly, his part in the ensuing canvass was to traverse the state, endeavour by speaking as of yore to the people to regain his former position and power, to help elect a conservative governor and, above all, to secure a legislature hostile to the radicals and friendly to his national policy and to the redemption of his fame. Before the campaign began, he was prostrated by an attack of a painful disease to which he was subject. During the campaign, he was summoned from a speaking tour by the untimely and sudden death of his son. But nothing could stay him—neither life nor death, principalities nor powers. He held right on to the end. The election took place in August, and the triumph of the whites was overwhelming. Senter was elected governor by fifty thousand majority, and the conservatives captured both houses of the legislature, reducing the ultra-radicals to a mere handful. As Tennessee was the first of the seceding states to undergo the yoke of carpet-bag Africanization, so Tennessee was the first to throw it off. The lower House rejected the fifteenth amendment by nays 57 to yeas 12, and the upper House did not deign to report it for action. And this sudden revolution was, to a great extent, due to the mere presence of Andrew Johnson within the borders of the state. Immediately after the election, it was taken for granted all over the country that the ex-President's return to the Senate was assured, and that, on the fourth of March, 1871, the defendant in the great Impeachment Trial, taking the seat of the much-abused Fowler, would beard the judges who condemned him in their own chamber.

But this exquisite piece of retributive justice was not to be accomplished yet. Johnson was not to remount the car that climbs the capitol by so speedy a process. As fortune was shaping events, his struggle for retrieval was but beginning. The peculiar and disheartening weakness of the ex-President's present position was the same that had pursued him during the whole course of his administration;—he did not, strictly, belong to either of the parties into which the country was divided. His lifelong connection with the Democratic party, he severed when its Southern wing went over into secession. His shortlived connection with the Republican party dissolved of itself when that party began to subordinate the restoration of the Union to the prolongation of its power. The consequence was that, for the time being, he hovered between the two. The Democrats turned a cold shoulder on him because of his alliance with the Republicans in a cardinal moment, while the Republicans banished him to what they considered the congenial company of his former friends. Neither could see that while it was they that moved, it was he that remained stationary. While he was doing battle for a Union such as he was brought up to believe the Constitution made perpetual, his state was overrun in the name of the Congress by enfranchised negroes led by a few whites; and this dominant faction, depending for its very existence upon the opponents of his policy in the nation, could cherish for him nothing less than the most deadly animosity. During the progress of the long fight, many of his adherents of former days were lured into the camp of the radicals by the potent consideration that the radicals were patronized by the party dominant in the United States. So that by the time he retired from the presidency, there were comparatively few Johnson Republicans in all wide Tennessee. This doleful prospect, the recent victory of conservative principles might have been expected to brighten. But that victory did not create a Johnson party; it accrued to the benefit of the Democratic party; and the Democratic party adopted the Johnson policy without altogether adopting Johnson. The leaders were ready to applaud him for his gallant stand while President on the question of reconstruction, but there were many who could not forget, even if they could forgive, his desertion of his section at the outbreak of the war or his iron rule as military governor over his prostrate state.

The newly elected legislature met in October; a majority of the members having been chosen to elect Johnson United States senator. But, because of the influences we have just indicated, that majority was somewhat heterogeneous and unreliable. Of the Democrats, many were lukewarm, to say the least, in the support of the old Unionist. Among the Republicans who shared in the Senter revolt, some yielded to the frantic expostulations of Brownlow who could brook the devil for a colleague rather than the "dead dog of the White House." According to the 'Parson's' own admission, money was freely used by himself and by the party of the administration to elect any other candidate. They made secret alliances with the more inveterate secessionists. They preferred a "red-handed rebel" to the indomitable "Andy." Notwithstanding these efforts of his adversaries, the genuine supporters of the ex-President would have maintained their majority, had it not been for an unexpected defection among their own number. It was the immemorial custom to choose the two senators alternately from different sections of the state, and the choice of Johnson as the successor of Fowler would throw both senators into the eastern quarter. Plying the wavering members with this argument, Brownlow, at last, offered to throw the votes of his followers to Henry Cooper who lived in the middle part of the state and was the brother of Edmund Cooper—for a time, private secretary of President Johnson, at this crisis a member of the legislature and one of the stanchest and most influential of Johnson's supporters. This maneuvre put an end to the contest; Edmund and his following being won over and Johnson defeated by one vote. The successful candidate, although elected by the help of Brownlow, after taking his seat in the Senate adhered without wavering to the opposition to President Grant's administration. The victory was won over Johnson in person but not over Johnson's policy.

Forced to be content with this one-sided triumph, Johnson retired from the field to await the next opportunity to achieve the object of his ambition. The senatorial term of the one man who had done so much to deprive him of the prize of the recent contest would expire in a few years, and he bent his eye upon the succession. During the years that must elapse he set to work organizing, solidifying and disciplining a party behind him. Standing midway between the ex-secessionists on the one hand and the reunited radicals on the other, he drew from the former those who could bring themselves to forget the wounds of the war in order to defeat the policy of the federal administration and swing the state into line with the steadfast Democracy of the North; and he drew from the latter the white men whom events day by day were convincing that prosperity would only return with the return of the intelligence, the industry and the honesty of the people to the government of the state. The gospel he preached was the necessity of securing the ascendency of the whites, and the folly of throwing the management of political affairs into the hands of the extreme Democrats; a course which could only result in the state being forced back into bondage by the federal authorities. The first term of Grant drew near its close; the condition of the reconstructed states under the treatment of his administration had already disgusted into open revolt many of the most high-minded members of his party in the North. Tennessee having been assigned another representative in Congress, because of the want of time to reapportion the state, the additional member was to be elected by the people at large in 1872. The Democrats nominated the ex-confederate general Cheatham, and the Republicans Horace Maynard, for the place. At the call of his friends, Johnson consented to anticipate the time he had set for his own rehabilitation, and for the sake of his middle party to shift his aim from the more striking triumph of a reentrance to the Senate to a seat in the House as the representative of the entire state. The campaign was bitterly fought. The three candidates appealed personally to the people; Johnson, the common mark of the other two on the right hand and on the left. Again, his course at the outbreak and during the war served to draw from his support the old-time Democrats, while its singular heroism was lost upon the radicals who applauded it so loudly at the time. "Traitor to his state and tyrant to his race" were the charges flung at him from one quarter—"Apostate from his party and ally of Jefferson Davis," from the other. Again, the Republican being elected, he suffered defeat, but only to fall back upon his original plan—the goal of which was the United States Senate.

From that time all his energies were strained to gain for himself a faithful majority in the legislature which was to elect the successor of Brownlow. The task seemed hopeless to every one but himself. The contest of 1872—both presidential and state—had resulted in throwing Tennessee back into the hands of the federal administration and reuniting the radicals for the sharing of the spoils. The Democratic opposition waxed more bitter; the heart-burnings of the war rekindled and to the more inveterate secessionists Johnson grew more and more distasteful. At the beginning of the campaign of 1874, however, a reaction had set in so powerful that the Republicans, despairing of electing a senator of their own party, were reduced to the expedient of making coalitions with the Johnson men in most of the counties and senatorial districts. The contest before the people, therefore, was narrowed down to one between Andrew Johnson, on the one hand, and the only other prominent avowed candidates—William B. Bate (the present U. S. senator) and John C. Brown, both democrats, on the other. When the legislature met in joint-meeting (January 20, 1875) Brownlow, who the day before in the House had but two votes, and Hawkins, who had but one—these two being the only Republican candidates—got none; so that the struggle continued before the legislature, as it had raged in the campaign, between Johnson and the Democrats proper. The first ballot stood Johnson 36, Bate 19, Brown 18, and others scattering—necessary to a choice 51. The balloting continued every day, until the twenty-sixth, with varying fortunes. The thirty-fourth ballot stood Johnson 34, Brown 32, Bate 10, when Brown was withdrawn; and, on the next ballot, the vote stood Johnson 33, Bate 24, Stephens 21, others scattering. On the last ballot taken on the twenty-fifth, the vote stood Bate 46, Johnson 44, Ewing 8, Sneed 1; when Brown was again put in nomination and Bate withdrawn. The next day, Brown having declined, the final and fifty-fifth ballot stood Johnson 52, Stephens

25, others scattering; and Johnson was declared elected.
A harder-won, better-deserved and more signal triumph does not adorn the annals of time. As was truly said on the floor of the Senate, after his death:

> "His last election to a seat on this floor as Senator was the work of his own hands, brought about by his own indomitable will and pluck, the reward of a long and terrible contest, continuing for seven years, unsuccessful for a time, and appearing to all the world beside himself as utterly hopeless; nevertheless, finally, he was triumphant. From what I have learned from those who are familiar with this, his last contest, he exhibited more openly his true and peculiar nature, than at any other period of his life—which was to fight with all his might and all his ability, asking no quarter and granting none; and although like bloody Richard now and then unhorsed, still to fight and never surrender, until victory perched upon his banner."*

On Thursday, the fourth day of March, 1875, just six years from the day when, as retiring President, he was conspicuous by his absence from the side of the President-elect:—Andrew Johnson reappeared on the floor of the Senate and was greeted by a spontaneous outburst of applause from the crowds assembled in gallery and corridor to do him honour. The next day, when the Senate organized in special session, at the call of his name, his sturdy figure, clad in old-fashioned black, marches down the aisle to take the oath. He stands before that desk where once was read the foul telegram of Brownlow, whom he has now pushed from his stool. He

* Speech of sen. Bogy at obsequies of Johnson. *Globe,* 1st Sess. 44th Cong., p. 340.

looks into the uneasy eye of Henry Wilson, who once pronounced him "a violator of the Constitution, a violator of the laws, and a violator of his oath," and expressed a desire to disqualify him from office forever; but who now as Vice President is constrained to tender him the book. Sumner—once so fond of calling him "a wicked man"; "an enemy to his country"; "the lineal successor of Jefferson Davis"—is gone. But Boutwell, who discovered the "hole in the sky" into which "to project this enemy of two races of men" sits there in the place of Wilson, meditating, perhaps, on that "mysterious Providence" which so fatefully arranged the figures in Carpenter's painting. As the new senator goes back to his desk which his admirers have covered with flowers, his colleagues flock around him with congratulations—even senators who had voted him guilty. Egotistic, as it was so often said he was, he wears his hard-won laurels with the utmost modesty. He seems to have harboured no grudges. Said Morton: "After I had voted for his impeachment, and met him accidentally, he wore the same kindly smile as in times before and offered me his hand. I thought that showed nobility of soul. There were not many men who could have done that!"* But, although all display of his emotions was suppressed, there can be no doubt but, as another senator said: "That was a grand occasion for him and his heart was glad." "This last triumph must have given him more sincere and deeply felt gratification than any other of his life." The first ex-President

* *Globe.*, 1st Sess. 44th Cong., p. 338.

of the United States who ever became a senator, Andrew Johnson is also the last.

But great as was his personal triumph, the triumph of his policy was still more significant. Six years of congressional reconstruction proved enough to bedim even the glory of the hero of Appomattox. The House of Representatives that once impeached Andrew Johnson by so overwhelming a majority is now in the hands of the Democrats. The two-thirds majority in the Senate, notwithstanding the reinforcements from ten dragooned states, has dwindled away. One by one, the Africanized rotten boroughs, despite the support of the federal administration and the United States army, have fallen or are falling. Soon no relic will remain of that hybrid empire, except South Carolina wallowing in the black mire of anarchy and corruption; Louisiana writhing in the forced embrace of a Kellogg; and a stray negro illustrating the equality of men by misrepresenting his state in the Senate or his district in the House; and these unhealthy survivals, even the colossal fraud of 1876 cannot keep alive. Everywhere throughout that region, the so-called "rebel element" is in the ascendent—and in the ascendent, too, by the connivance, if not by the invitation, of its original denouncers, themselves appalled by the intolerable miseries their own plan has entailed. Every measure forced through with all the violence of revolution to make sure the supremacy of the Republican party in the restored Union—the fourteenth amendment, the reconstruction acts with their martial law, their negro conventions, their negro elections and their negro constitutions—have proved worse than fruitless. To the much abused policy of Andrew Johnson, his adversaries are driven to come round at last. Nought remains of congressional reconstruction but unqualified negro suffrage, and that surviving achievement is more and more distinctly recognized as a curse to both races, as a stumbling block to good government and a deadly taint to the social order, which even the fifteenth amendment should be suffered no longer to perpetuate.

The special session was devoted to the consideration of the deplorable situation of public affairs in Louisiana and to the question of the admission, as one of her senators, of a mulatto rejoicing in the high-sounding name of Pinckney Benton Stewart Pinchback. On Monday, the twenty-second day of March, Andrew Johnson addressed the Senate. Great was the curiosity to hear the once-impeached President, before a tribunal many of whose members had pronounced him guilty of high crimes and misdemeanours, impeach, in his turn, the conduct of his successor. Once again, as in 1861, Andrew Johnson of Tennessee on the floor of the Senate was the hero of the hour. These were his opening words:

"Mr. President, notwithstanding I have been in the habit of speaking in public for a number of years, sometimes in deliberative bodies and sometimes before the people, I confess that I appear before the Senate this morning under great embarrassment. I fear that the fact of my having obtained the floor on Saturday night and notice having been given that I would address the Senate to-day may have created an expectation with some that cannot be realized, and especially so with those who are not acquainted with me. If any such expectation has been created in the minds of any of those here present, I trust and hope that they will let themselves down, for they will be greatly disappointed on this occasion.''

The same peculiarities of style and diction, the same traits of character, the same habit of keeping the people ever in his eye, that marked the first, mark this his last speech in the Senate. His personal self-sufficiency, his unbounded confidence in the rectitude of his public acts, the steady fire of his combativeness, and the determination to yield not an inch to opponents or betrayers—are all there. He handled the conduct of the Grant administration without gloves. Not without a suspicion of mischievous irony, he went so far as to maintain that the present President had the less excuse for his high-handed treatment of the Louisiana legislature because as general of the army under President Johnson he had before him a bright precedent in the refusal of that administration to aid governor Brownlow in dragooning the legislature of Tennessee. He struck directly at the two vulnerable spots in the President's armour;—his ambition for a third term and his frequent acceptance of gifts; in condemnation of the latter narrating in full the ignominious punishment Sir John Trevor, speaker of the House of Commons, was forced to inflict upon himself ''for receiving a gratuity of one thousand guineas from the City of London.'' He once again employed his favourite quotation: ''Upon what meat does our Cæsar feed that he has grown so great?'' He warned his countrymen against the advent of

"Stratocracy," a word, the etymology of which he characteristically is careful to give, and he wound up his speech by a studied exposition of the distinctive features of that form of government and the signs of its approach.*

On the next day but one, the Senate adjourned *sine die* and Andrew Johnson went home. If not with the northern section of his country nor altogether with his contemporaries in his own, with posterity he had vindicated his character both public and private. For him a new day seemed to have dawned. Before him a second senatorial career opened as glorious as the first. He was in the sixty-seventh year of his age, but, despite repeated attacks of a painful disorder which clung about him, time seemed to have dealt mercifully with him. His step was vigorous, his eye bright, his form erect, his spirits high. But all these symptoms were fallacious. In reality, his work was done. His return to the Senate, as it constituted the unique triumph of his career, was to be its last. He spent the spring and early summer at his home in Greenville in quiet. In the last days of July, he started on a visit to a daughter then living a few miles away, apparently in the best of health. There, on the twenty-ninth, he was stricken with paralysis, and after lingering in a state of semi-unconsciousness until the thirty-first, on that day he died. As befitted his character and career, his funeral was plain and unostentatious—without ecclesiastical ceremonial or the pageantry of woe; but, as was said by one of his fellow-senators, "the hills

* *Globe*, special session of Senate, March, 1875, p. 121.

and the valleys and the mountains and the rivers sent forth their thousands to testify to the general grief at the irreparable loss." From his modest brick dwelling standing flush with the street, his remains were first borne to the court house, where, wrapped in the flag of the Union, they lay two days in state; and thence to the summit of a conical hill just south of the village—the place selected by himself for his burial. A tall, graceful shaft of white granite, erected by the pious efforts of his most devoted daughter and visible for miles around, now marks the spot—on its top an eagle in act to swoop, near its base the inscription: "Andrew Johnson, seventeenth President of the United States. His faith in the people never wavered." In the distance, a grand outlying mountain-block, its hither side carved as it were in undulating folds of purple, keeps its everlasting watch. There, surrounded by his kindred dead, after his lifelong battle, rests, at last, the stubbornest fighter in civil affairs among the self-made champions of the modern democracy.

END.

INDEX